Partnerships for Livable Cities

"This volume will get a prominent place in my bookcase in the section 'nearly impossible but necessary'. Collaboration in multifaceted systems such as cities is difficult to accomplish but nevertheless necessary to make cities more livable. Cor van Montfort and Ank Michels have brought together an impressive number and multiplicity of contributions which distil down to some practical building blocks for successful partnerships towards more livable cities."
—Patrick Kenis, *Professor of Public Governance, School of Economics and Management, Tilburg University, The Netherlands*

"Given the number and diversity of case studies, the book has the potential to attract a global audience and remain relevant for the next decade."
—Antonio Tavares, *Adjunct Associate Professor at UNU-EGOV and Chair of the Department of International Relations and Public Administration, University of Minho, Braga, Portugal*

Cor van Montfort • Ank Michels
Editors

Partnerships for Livable Cities

Editors
Cor van Montfort
Tilburg Center for Regional Law and
Governance (TiREG)
Tilburg University
Tilburg, The Netherlands

Vrije Universiteit Amsterdam
Amsterdam, The Netherlands

Ank Michels
Utrecht University School of
Governance
Utrecht, The Netherlands

ISBN 978-3-030-40059-0   ISBN 978-3-030-40060-6   (eBook)
https://doi.org/10.1007/978-3-030-40060-6

This Palgrave Macmillan imprint is published by the registered company Springer Nature Switzerland AG.
The registered company address is: Gewerbestrasse 11, 6330 Cham, Switzerland

CONTENTS

Contributors

Roland Bal Erasmus School of Health Policy & Management, Erasmus University Rotterdam, Rotterdam, The Netherlands

Anna Berti Suman The Tilburg Institute for Law, Technology, and Society (TILT), Tilburg University, Tilburg, The Netherlands

Zilma Borges Fundação Getulio Vargas, Escola de Administração de Empresas de São Paulo, São Paulo, Brasil

Sanderijn Cels Harvard Kennedy School's Carr Center for Human Rights, Cambridge, MA, USA

Desiree Chew Peking University Post-Graduate, Singapore, Singapore

Carlo Maria Colombo Faculty of Law, Maastricht University, Maastricht, The Netherlands

Kate Dayana de Abreu Fundação Getulio Vargas, Escola de Administração de Empresas de São Paulo, São Paulo, Brasil

Jorrit de Jong Harvard Kennedy School, Cambridge, MA, USA

Martin de Jong Erasmus School of Law, Erasmus University Rotterdam, Rotterdam, The Netherlands
Rotterdam School of Management, Rotterdam, The Netherlands
Institute for Global Public Policy, Fudan University, Shanghai, China

Martijn Groenleer Tilburg Institute of Governance, Tilburg Center for Regional Law and Governance, Tilburg University, Tilburg, The Netherlands

Seung-Hun Hong Korea Institute of Public Administration, Seoul, South Korea

Niels Karsten Tilburg Law School, Tilburg University, Tilburg, The Netherlands

Femke Kaulingfreks Lectoraat Jeugd en Samenleving, Kenniscentrum De Gezonde Samenleving, Inholland University of Applied Sciences, Amsterdam, The Netherlands

Valesca Lima Maynooth University Social Sciences Institute, Kildare, Ireland

Zhi Liu Lincoln Institute of Land Policy, Beijing, China

Haiyan Lu Institute of Sinology, Free University of Berlin, Berlin, Germany College of Urban and Environmental Sciences, Peking University, Beijing, China

Ank Michels Utrecht University School of Governance, Utrecht, The Netherlands

Mary Muthoni Mwangi Kenyatta University Nairobi, Nairobi, Kenya

Giorgia Nesti Department of Political Science, Law, and International Studies, University of Padova, Padova, Italy

Lieke Oldenhof Erasmus School of Health Policy & Management, Erasmus University Rotterdam, Rotterdam, The Netherlands

Madeleine Pill Department of Government and International Relations, University of Sydney, Sydney, NSW, Australia

Lya Porto Fundação Getulio Vargas, Escola de Administração de Empresas de São Paulo, São Paulo, Brasil
Université de Montréal, École des Hautes Études Commerciales, Montréal, QC, Canada

Sabrina Rahmawan-Huizenga Erasmus School of Health Policy & Management, Erasmus University Rotterdam, Rotterdam, The Netherlands

Linze Schaap Northern Audit Office, Assen, The Netherlands

Peter Spink Fundação Getulio Vargas, Escola de Administração de Empresas de São Paulo, São Paulo, Brasil

Li Sun School of Sociology and Social Policy, University of Leeds, Leeds, UK

Hester van de Bovenkamp Erasmus School of Health Policy & Management, Erasmus University Rotterdam, Rotterdam, The Netherlands

Jeroen van der Heijden School of Government, Victoria University of Wellington, Wellington, New Zealand

Simone van de Wetering Tilburg Center for Regional Law and Governance (TiREG), Tilburg University, Tilburg, The Netherlands

Cor van Montfort Tilburg Center for Regional Law and Governance (TiREG), Tilburg University, Tilburg, The Netherlands
Vrije Universiteit Amsterdam, Amsterdam, The Netherlands

Carola van Eijk Institute of Public Administration, Leiden University, Leiden, The Netherlands

LIST OF FIGURES

LIST OF BOXES

LIST OF PHOTOS

LIST OF TABLES

CHAPTER 1

Introduction

Cor van Montfort and Ank Michels

1.1 INTRODUCTION

Urbanization is a global development. More than half of the entire population in the world now lives in cities, and this number will increase over the next decades. According to the UNDP, in 2018, 4.2 billion people, or 55 percent of the world's population, lived in cities. By 2050, the urban population is expected to reach 6.5 billion (UNDP 2015). People move to cities in a bid to find work, security and often a brighter future. However, the massive migration to the cities is also leading to new social, environmental and infrastructural problems. The world's cities are becoming increasingly congested and polluted, putting pressure on affordable housing and causing safety to become a major problem (Wolch et al. 2014). As a result, the livability of our cities is becoming a topic of increasing relevance and urgency. The relevance and urgency of this topic is also

C. van Montfort (✉)
Tilburg Center for Regional Law and Governance (TiREG), Tilburg University, Tilburg, The Netherlands

Vrije Universiteit Amsterdam, Amsterdam, The Netherlands
e-mail: c.j.vanmontfort@tilburguniversity.edu

A. Michels
Utrecht University School of Governance, Utrecht, The Netherlands
e-mail: a.m.b.michels@uu.nl

© The Author(s) 2020
C. van Montfort, A. Michels (eds.), *Partnerships for Livable Cities,*
https://doi.org/10.1007/978-3-030-40060-6_1

1

emphasized in the United Nations' Sustainable Development Goals. Goal 11 states that: 'Making cities sustainable means creating career and business opportunities, safe and affordable housing, and building resilient societies and economies. It involves investment in public transport, creating green public spaces, and improving urban planning and management in participatory and inclusive ways.' (UNDP 2015).

As a response to these challenges, urban governments have sought to share responsibilities: unable to address these major challenges on their own, they seek cooperation with other governments, companies, civil society organizations, and citizens. For example, governments seek private sources of funding to finance investments, or they cooperate with citizens and civil society organizations for better service provision (Rosol 2010). In this book, we aim to explore how partnerships between public and private actors contribute to the livability of cities. Under what conditions are partnerships successful, and when do they fail to yield the desired results? To find an answer to these questions, we discuss real-life instances of, often innovative, forms of collaboration and interaction in cities all over the world. The central question in this book is:

How do partnerships between public and private actors contribute to the livability of cities?

1.2   Livability

The concept of *livability* is very broad and often encompasses a wide range of dimensions (i.e., social, physical, economic) and an array of issues, including health, convenience, mobility, recreation, and safety, affecting the elements of home, neighborhood, and metropolitan area (Woolcock 2009; Leby and Hashim 2010; Kashef 2016). Since the concept of livability is too comprehensive and multidimensional to study in all its aspects, the focus in this book is on three specific dimensions:

(a) Green (aimed, among others, at environmental sustainability and climate adaptation)
(b) Safety (including preventing or fighting crime and health risks)
(c) Affordable (social) housing

In addition to this, we discuss examples of neighborhood revitalization and urban living labs where public and private actors work together in a more integrated way on many dimensions at the same time in order to create a more livable urban environment. We focus on these dimensions and practices because they all concern the direct living environment of residents, that is, the physically built environment. As a result, we exclude other areas such as infrastructure (transport), natural resources (water) or socio-economic developments (cultural facilities, economic growth or employment).

In this book, we are interested in how partnerships contribute to livability. It is important to note that partnerships may contribute to a short term realization of plans or projects in the field of livability, but that these projects need to be consolidated or have a longer-term spin-off in order to make a long-term contribution to the livability of the city.

1.2.1 Livable for Whom?

'Green', 'affordable housing' and 'safety' are not independent characteristics of livable cities. There can also be trade-offs between these three aspects. For example, a greener and safer environment can lead to higher prices for housing and thus to less affordable housing for lower-income groups (Donovan and Butry 2010); on the other hand, a green environment might also contribute to feelings of unsafety and, as a consequence, to declining housing prices.

Livability, therefore, is not a neutral concept (see also McArthur and Robin 2019) nor a stable entity (Wait and Knobel 2018). The question is not so much whether a city is livable, but rather *for whom* it is livable. While livability may improve for some people, others find themselves mainly confronted with negative effects such as higher housing prices. This question closely relates to the debates about gentrification. Gentrification is 'a process that involves the reinvestment of capital after a period of disinvestment, the production of an aestheticized landscape, and lower class displacement followed by middle class replacement' (Bryson 2013, p. 578). Making a city greener unmistakably plays a role in gentrification processes (Bryson 2013, pp. 584–585), but not in a one-dimensional and predictable way. As early as 1961, Jacobs warned against a one-size-fits-all approach to the construction of city parks: the effects of a park or green area on livability depend, among other things, on the design of the park and the socio-economic composition of the neighborhood (Jacobs

1993(1961), chapter 5). Many scholars argue that gentrification is not a natural, predictable or short-term development, but instead should be studied as a long-term process (Zukin 2016; Barke and Clarke 2016), in which complex interactions between public and private actors play a role and local policy is a very important determining factor (Barke and Clarke 2016).

1.3   Partnerships, Co-production, Collaboration and Networks

The idea that the government is fully responsible for taking care of citizens' needs belongs to the past. After the era of traditional public administration with a strong focus on government and vertical steering and control, and with the rise of New Public Management and more recently, New Public Governance, different forms of interaction between government, private sector and or civic society have developed (Considine and Lewis 2003). In the literature, several concepts are used to characterize this development, including governance or new governance (Pierre 2011; Pierre and Peters 2000; Rhodes 1996), interactive governance (Torfing et al. 2012), networks (Koppenjan and Klijn 2004), governance networks (Klijn and Skelcher 2008), network governance (Provan and Kenis 2008), co-production (Bovaird 2007) and hybrid governance (Koppenjan et al. 2019).

In this book, we study the role of partnerships. Partnerships are defined in numerous ways. Mathur et al. (2003), for example, define these as new organizational arrangements that embody a commitment for joint action towards collective public policy goals. Other definitions include a number of characteristics of partnerships. Baud and Dhanalakshmi (2007, p. 135) define a partnership as follows: a partnership involves two or more actors; it refers to a long-term relationship between actors regarding public goods provision; the relationship benefits all actors (without assuming equal benefits); it is expressed in concrete activities, in which actors invest materially or immaterially; the bargaining process can include tension and conflict as well as cooperation; and the partnership concerns the provision of public goods. Sometimes partnerships and co-production are used as interchangeable terms. Co-production, however, tends to be initiated by a government seeking to cooperate with other actors. Therefore co-production is often part of the policymaking process. The concept of partnerships that we use is a broader concept that encompasses all forms of cooperation, including bottom-up initiatives and forms without government.

Especially in the public-private partnership (PPP) literature, the term partnership is often used to refer to long-term contracts between government and private partners to fund investments in public infrastructure. This connotation of partnerships with formal contracts and an orientation on national policy goals is for some authors, including Sullivan and Skelcher (2002), a reason to prefer the use of the term collaboration as the overarching concept. In this book, we have chosen to stay with the term partnership but to use it in a much broader way. We think that narrowing the discussion about public—private partnerships to these long-term formal contracts between government and private partners does not do justice to the opportunities and possibilities of public-private partnerships. If we wish to understand the full potential of public-private partnerships, it is important to include horizontal, flexible, dynamic and informal partnerships as well. In this book, the authors of the different chapters present a number of the different types of partnerships that appear in practice.

What the definitions of partnerships mentioned above have in common is that they emphasize the goal-oriented and public character of partnerships: the joint action in partnerships is aimed at collective public policy goals or the provision of public goods. This makes a partnership approach different from *a network approach*. Although no sharp distinction can be made between a network and a partnership, networks are, to a lesser extent, based on common interests (a), while mutual interdependency is a more important driver for cooperation than the willingness to realize a common goal (b) (except for *purpose-oriented networks*, Nowell and Kenis 2019); moreover, network relations are, in general, more lasting than partnerships (c) (Kickert et al. 1999, p. 31). At the same time, debates about partnerships and networks often address the same issues, for example, the discussion about when and for whom a network or partnership is successful, or the question of how the discretionary space of a network or partnership relates to the political power of democratically elected bodies.

1.3.1 *Various Forms of Partnerships*

Partnerships between public and private actors come in various forms: some are based on legally binding rules or contracts (such as PPPs, see Hodge and Greve 2005), while others are more loosely organized; some focus on just one activity, while others are involved in many activities; and sometimes the partnership can vary within one single project according to the different functions a partnership may have, such as financing, organization, and day-to-day management (so-called 'layered partnerships').

In this book, we have adopted a broad concept of partnerships, taking the relationship between state, market, and civil society as a starting-point (Brandsen et al. 2005). Within this triangle, multiple types of partnerships are possible, see Fig. 1.1 (van Montfort et al. 2014, p. 10).

It is important to note that a partnership is not static but that it may change over time. For example, initiatives sometimes start as a grassroots or community-based initiative by residents and citizens' organizations (type F or G), but often these projects later develop as a collaboration between civil society, private sector and (local) government (type H) in which public organizations become responsible for facilitating or funding the project. Examples of dynamic partnerships are discussed in many chapters in this book. Also, partnerships can differ in their degree of formalization. Type C public-private partnerships are often formalized in contracts that lay down responsibilities between government(s) and private companies or consortiums, while type E public-private partnerships frequently have an informal structure in which partners are loosely coupled via declarations of intent, covenants, etc.

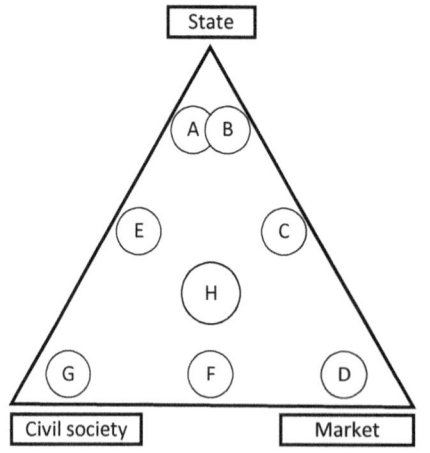

A.   Public organizations
B.   Public-Public Partnerships
C.   Public-Private Partnerships
D.   Private companies
E.   Partnerships between civil society and public organizations
F.   Partnerships between civil society and private organizations
G.   Grassroots civil society organizations
H.   Partnerships in which civil society, market and state are involved

Fig. 1.1   Various types of partnerships

The triangle in Fig. 1.1 characterizes partnerships on the basis of the partners' status as public or private sector stakeholders. Other authors characterize partnerships on the basis of a 'bottom-up – top-down' continuum or on an 'equality – dominancy' continuum. Skelcher et al. (2005) for instance, distinguish between an *agency, club* and *polity-forming* type of *partnership*. The agency type has a formal character, is imposed by the government and intended to realize policy goals. The club type refers to a goal-oriented informal cooperation between elites. Finally, a polity-forming partnership is a bottom-up cooperation in which different public and private stakeholders work together.

Bradford and Bramwell (2014) make a distinction between three *urban governance types*: (1) institutionalized collaborative, based on a long term shared vision, (2) sector networks that are structured around different local networks representing economic actors on the one hand and social actors on the other hand without cross sectoral links or boundary crossers and (3) project partnerships in which different economic and social actors come together around a specific project. These project partnerships are less formalized than the others.

Another typology emerging from the network literature is, for example, that of Provan and Kenis (2008), who distinguish between networks in which the participants are equivalent ('participant governed networks'), networks in which one player is dominant ('lead organization-governed networks') and networks that are governed from outside by a specific governing body ('network administrative organization'). The role of government and criteria for good governance, success, evaluation and for supervision differ for each type.

We consider these typologies to be refinements of the global types of partnerships mentioned in Fig. 1.1. Every partnership in the triangle could be redefined in terms of the typologies from Skelcher et al., Bradford and Bramwell, or Kenis and Provan. For this book, however, the most important feature is the public or private character of the participants and the interaction between them within the partnership.

1.4 Partnerships and Livability

How partnerships contribute to livability may be influenced by two sets of factors. A first set of factors relates to the characteristics and the management of the partnership. Previous research suggests that the following conditions are essential for partnerships to be stable and effective (e.g.

Huang 2010; Dempsey et al. 2016; Foo et al. 2015; Sørensen and Torfing 2018):

- legitimacy: all partners must feel strongly committed to the partnership and its goal. All partners should feel convinced that participation in the partnership is better than not participating.
- responsiveness: it is important that the partnership stays responsive to the (changing) needs and wishes of the public and private partners and/or users.
- stable funding: stability in public and private funding is an important factor for success (continuity, innovation) in the long run.
- leadership: vision and positive energy are, at least at the start of the project, crucial to convince possible new partners to join the partnership or to gain political commitment.

A second important set of factors in understanding the relationship between partnerships and livability refer to the role of context. Relevant context factors include the political environment, the aspect of good governance, socio-economic factors, the role of history and path dependency, and demographic factors. In this book, examples will be presented from different countries and different parts of the world. Context first of all defines the type and scale of livability problems that the city faces. And, secondly, context defines the space within which partnerships can develop and function. Hence, in addition to conclusions about the factors that determine the success or failure of a partnership, this book will also offer insights into what kind of contexts are relevant and which types of partnerships are most promising in a specific context.

In the concluding chapter of this book we will see that the effectiveness of a specific type of partnership depends on a combination of the nature of the specific problem to be solved, the organizational and cultural characteristics of the partnership, the specific political or societal context and the role of government.

1.5   Outline of This Book

The book is divided into five parts, each of which consists of two to four chapters.

Part I analyzes partnerships in relation to the 'green' aspects in cities.

In Chap. 2, *Jeroen van der Heijden and Seung-Hun Hong* explore four experiments in which the Seoul Municipal Government has partnered with local stakeholders and that underlie a series of urban climate governance experiments in the city of Seoul. They discuss the different understanding of the relationship between government, civil society and the business sector in state-guided economies such as South Korea, and the liberal capitalist economies in the West. They also show the fluid character of partnerships when participants and types of partnerships change at different points in time.

Kate Dayana de Abreu, Zilma Borges, Lya Porto and Peter Spink analyze in Chap. 3 examples of partnerships between the public sector and local communities in urban agriculture, which include such activities as local food production, community gardens, and school-based vegetable plots. Using examples from São Paulo (Brazil) and Montreal (Canada), and Orizânia (Brazil), they show how urban agriculture can point to new forms of collective construction and more inclusive governance, thus making substantial contributions to the livable quality of cities.

In Chap. 4, *Ank Michels and Cor van Montfort* explore examples of cities, including Tilburg (The Netherlands), Melbourne (Australia), San Jose (USA), and Cape Town (South Africa), that have successfully been transformed into green cities. They investigate the role played by partnerships between the city government, companies, non-governmental organizations, and citizens in this transformation. The analysis shows that a clear government vision for the future of the city, with a leading role for the city government in the implementation of the plans, are relevant factors. Moreover, engaging the community in the formulation and implementation of the plans contributes to more durable effects.

In Chap. 5, *Haiyan Lu, Li Sun, and Martin de Jong* discuss the role of public and private actors in three eco city projects in China. Although these eco city projects are often state-led, the chapter shows how planners, experts, private investors and citizens are becoming increasingly involved in financing these projects and in knowledge sharing.

In **Part II** of the book, the focus shifts to the role of partnerships in creating affordable housing in the city.

Chapter 6 by *Mary Muthoni Mwangi* highlights some of the negative sides of informal partnerships. She shows how informal collaboration in Nairobi between planners and developers in housing paves the way for non-compliance with planning laws and regulation, with as a result the loss of lives when buildings collapse. She argues that housing needs could be better served by forms of formal collaboration between government, developers and other stakeholders.

In Chap. 7, *Valesca Lima* examines the role of housing associations in shaping effective responses to housing affordability problems. Taking the city of Dublin (Ireland) as a case study, Lima shows how these associations have been able to put forward innovative forms of collaboration and new interaction between public and private actors (NGOs, local authorities, and financial institutions) that play a role in delivering affordable housing.

Zhi Liu and Desiree Chew, in Chap. 8, discuss how rapid urbanization is causing enormous challenges in finding affordable housing in Chinese cities. They discuss the effects of urban spatial processes, driven largely by the real estate market, on gentrification and spatial inequalities which, in the end, cause social tension. After an assessment of recent policy interventions on housing affordability, the chapter concludes with the lessons learned from recent experiences with public-private collaboration in improving housing affordability.

Part III of the book will focus on the role of partnerships in relation to aspects of safety in the city.

Chapter 9, by *Carola van Eijk*, examines the collaboration of local governments and the police with citizens and civil society organizations in order to keep cities safe and livable. Examples include Dutch neighborhood watch schemes, digital tools such as Burgernet, and volunteering networks in Belgium. Reflecting on the implications of the initiatives, van Eijk brings up the questions how and under which conditions these partnerships contribute to safety and livability. She also reviews some positive and undesired effects of partnerships on safety.

In Chap. 10, *Anna Berti Suman* focuses on environmental risks and safety, discussing aspects such as air quality and noise. An emerging practice—that of citizen sensing (citizens-initiated monitoring initiatives based on ICT)—shows that citizens are increasingly willing to monitor these risks themselves. Comparing an example of a successful cooperation between citizens, public and private actors (in Eindhoven, the Netherlands) with an example of conflict between the citizens and the institutions (Fukushima, Japan), Berti Suman examines the conditions under which citizen sensing can unleash its full potential for achieving co-governance of shared risks in the city.

In Chap. 11, Martijn Groenleer, Sanderijn Cels, and Jorrit de Jong focus on yet another aspect of safety in the city, namely, the fight against marijuana production and trade as a form of organized crime. Their contribution investigates the partnerships that have emerged in the Netherlands between the public prosecutor's office, the police, the tax office, local government and the electricity distribution company to fight this form of organized crime and its subversive effects for local neighborhoods. The chapter analyzes how these parties have overcome initial hurdles for coordination and cooperation, the subsequent generation of legitimacy and the building of capacity, as well as the management of performance.

Part IV of the book presents in three chapters a more integral perspective on neighborhood revitalization.

In Chap. 12, *Madeleine Pill* discusses the policy of neighborhood revitalization in the city of Baltimore. City government has long been engaged in seeking partnerships with private (corporate and non-profit) actors in developing a range of livability policies and initiatives. By considering the challenge of making Baltimore 'livable' in terms of by whom, for whom, and where, Pill reveals the city's deep inequities and exclusionary governance.

Taking up the case of the young people growing up in the French *banlieues*, *Simone van de Wetering* and *Femke Kaulingfreks* discuss in Chap. 13 how livable the city is for the young in marginalized urban areas. The authors illustrate how young people often express their civil engagement at a micro political level in everyday activities and establish a sense of belonging to the city through informal processes of place-making. Exploring the activities that the younger generation undertakes to 'make the city', this chapter teaches us not only that young people can be vital actors in partnerships for livable cities, but even more how these partnerships can be effective and legitimate from the perspective of marginalized urban youths.

In Chap. 14, *Niels Karsten, Carlo Maria Colombo, and Linze Schaap* investigate the system of *Quartiersmanagement* (QM) in Berlin where, under the supervision of the Berlin 'Land', or state authorities, private companies develop and implement public policies in conjunction with neighborhood residents and civil society organizations. The authors evaluate the effectiveness, legitimacy and robustness of the QM governance model, focusing on a specific case: the redevelopment of the inner-city Wiesenburg area. The results indicate that hybrid governance is not always a solution, since it can produce tensions between the logics of the state, the market and civil society that are present in a partnership. At the same time, their analysis shows that some of these tensions are not necessarily the result of institutional aspects of the cooperation but also relate to how the people involved perceive and take up their roles in such governance arrangements.

Part V of the book consists of two chapters, both dealing with partnerships within the context of a relatively new phenomenon, that of urban living labs.

In Chap. 15, *Lieke Oldenhof, Sabrina Rahmawan-Huizenga, Hester van de Bovenkamp and Roland Bal* investigate how public-private partnerships between citizens, policymakers, local entrepreneurs and public organizations in Urban Living Labs in a Dutch city deal with their liminal *in-between* position to create livable cities, and which new institutional rules emerge in order to deal with trade-offs in urban development.

In Chap. 16, *Giorgia Nesti* discusses the experiences with the Turin Living Lab, later transformed into Turin City Lab (TCL). The Turin City Lab is an urban living lab aimed at reducing red-tape and promoting collaboration with companies interested in testing innovative solutions for urban living in a real-life context. The experiences with these city labs are, on the one hand, an example of a successful experience with multi-stakeholder partnerships because they created a safe, reliable, and trusty environment for innovation. But on the other hand, there are concerns about the degree in which citizen participate in the project and about the contribution of the partnerships developed for the Labs to the livability of the city.

In the concluding chapter of the book, Chap. 17, *Ank Michels and Cor van Montfort* summarize the main patterns from the various chapters of the book. They start with some observations about the variation in partnerships with respect to the degree of regulation, dynamics and fluidity. They conclude that the specific characteristics of partnerships are closely related to the social, political or economic context in which they arise and develop. They also note that the criteria for success or failure are different in most of the examples discussed in this book. Finally, they discuss the different roles that the government may have in developing and sustaining partnerships that contribute to livability.

References

Barke, M., & Clarke, J. (2016). Residential growth in Newcastle upon Tyne's city Centre: The role of the public and private sectors. *Journal of Housing and the Built Environment, 31*(1), 141–166.

Baud, I., & Dhanalakshmi, R. (2007). Governance in urban environmental management: Comparing accountability and performance in multi-stakeholder arrangements in South-India. *Cities, 2*(2), 133–147.

Bovaird, T. (2007). Beyond engagement and participation. User and community co-production of public services. *Public Administration Review, 67*(5), 846–860.

Bradford, N., & Bramwell, A. (Eds.). (2014). *Governing urban economies. Innovation and inclusion in Canadian city regions.* Toronto: University of Toronto Press.

Brandsen, T., Van de Donk, W., & Putters, K. (2005). Griffins or chameleons? Hybridity as a permanent and inevitable characteristic of the third sector. *International Journal of Public Administration, 28*(9–10), 749–765.

Bryson, J. (2013). The nature of gentrification. *Geography Compass, 7*(8), 578–587.

Considine, M., & Lewis, J. M. (2003). Bureaucracy, network, or enterprise? Comparing models of governance in Australia, Britain, the Netherlands, and New Zealand. *Public Administration Review, 63*(2), 131–140.

Dempsey, N., Burton, M., & Duncan, R. (2016). Evaluating the effectiveness of a cross-sector partnership for greenspace management: The case of Southey Owlerton, Sheffield, UK. *Urban Forestry & Urban Greening, 15*(1), 155–164.

Donovan, G. H., & Butry, D. T. (2010). Trees in the city: Valuing street trees in Portland, Oregon. *Landscape and Urban Planning, 94*(2), 77–83.

Foo, K., Martin, D., Polsky, C., Wool, C., & Ziemer, M. (2015). Social well-being and environmental governance in urban neighbourhoods in Boston, MA. *The Geographical Journal, 181*(2), 138–146.

Hodge, G., & Greve, C. (2005). *The challenge of public-private partnerships.* Cheltenham: Edward Elgar.

Huang, S. L. (2010). The impact of public participation on the effectiveness of, and users' attachment to, urban neighbourhood parks. *Landscape Research, 35*(5), 551–562.

Jacobs, J. (1993; 1961). *The death and life of great American cities.* New York: The Modern Library.

Kashef, M. (2016). Urban livability across disciplinary and professional boundaries. *Frontiers of Architectural Research, 5*(2), 239–253.

Kickert, W., Klijn, E.-H., & Koppenjan, J. (Eds.). (1999). *Managing complex networks. Strategies for the public sector.* London: Sage.

Klijn, E. H., & Skelcher, C. (2008). Democracy and governance networks: Compatible or not? Four conjectures and their implications for theory and practice. *Public Administration, 85*(3), 587–608.

Koppenjan, J., & Klijn, E.-H. (2004). *Managing uncertainties in networks: A network approach to problem solving and decision making.* London: Routledge.

Koppenjan, J., Karré, P. M., & Termeer, K. (Eds.). (2019). *Smart hybridity. Potentials and challenges of new governance arrangements.* The Hague: Eleven.

Leby, J., & Hashim, A. (2010). Liveability dimensions and attributes: Their relative importance in the eyes of neighbourhood residents. *Journal of Construction in Developing Countries, 15*(1), 67–91.

Mathur, N., Skelcher C., & Smith, M. (2003, March). *Towards a discursive evaluation of partnership governance.* Paper presented at the European consortium for political research, joint sessions, Edinburgh, Scotland.

McArthur, J., & Robin, E. (2019). Victims of their own (definition of) success: Urban discourse and expert knowledge production in the Liveable City. *Urban Studies, 56*(9), 1711–1728.

Nowell, B. L., & Kenis, P. (2019). Purpose-oriented networks: The architecture of complexity. *Perspectives on Public Management and Governance, 2*(3), 191–195. https://doi.org/10.1093/ppmgov/gvz012.

Pierre, J. (2011). *The politics of urban governance.* Basingstoke: Palgrave Macmillan.

Pierre, J., & Peters, G. (2000). *Governance, politics and the state.* Basingstoke: Palgrave Macmillan.

Provan, K. G., & Kenis, P. N. (2008). Modes of network governance: Structure, management, and effectiveness. *Journal of Public Administration Research and Theory, 18*(2), 229–252.

Rhodes, R. (1996). The new governance: Governing without government. *Political Studies, 44*(4), 651–667.

Rosol, M. (2010). Public participation in post-fordist urban green space governance: The case of community gardens in Berlin. *International Journal of Urban and Regional Research, 34*(3), 548–563.

Skelcher, C., Mathur, N., & Smith, M. (2005). The public governance of collaborative spaces: Discourse, design and democracy. *Public Administration, 83*(3), 573–596.

Sørensen, E., & Torfing, J. (2018). Co-initiation of collaborative innovation in urban spaces. *Urban Affairs Review, 54*(2), 388–418.

Sullivan, H., & Skelcher, C. (2002). *Working across boundaries. Collaboration in public services.* Basingstoke: Palgrave Macmillan.

Torfing, J., Peters, G., Pierre, J., & Sørensen, E. (2012). *Interactive governance.* New York: Oxford University Press.

UNDP. (2015). *Sustainable development goals.* https://www.undp.org/content/undp/en/home/sustainable-development-goals.html. Accessed 27 Aug 2019.

van Montfort, C., Michels, A., & Frankowski, A. (2014). *Governance models and partnerships in the urban water sector: A framework for analysis and evaluation.* http://dspace.library.uu.nl/handle/1874/303566. Accessed 23 Sept 2019.

Wait, G., & Knobel, H. (2018). Embodied geographies of liveability and urban parks. *Urban Studies, 55*(14), 3151–3167.

Wolch, J. R., Byrne, J., & Newell, J. P. (2014). Urban green space, public health, and environmental justice: The challenge of making cities 'just green enough'. *Landscape and Urban Planning, 125*, 234–244.

Woolcock, G. (2009, November 24–29). *Measuring up?: Assessing the liveability of Australian cities.* Urban Research Program, Griffith University. Paper presented at The State of Australian Cities conference.

Zukin, S. (2016). Gentrification in three paradoxes. *City & Community, 15*(3), 202–207.

PART I

Partnerships and Green in Cities

CHAPTER 2

Partnerships in Experimental Urban Climate Governance: Insights from Seoul

Jeroen van der Heijden and Seung-Hun Hong

2.1 Urban Climate Governance Experimentation and Partnerships

In this book, a liveable city is considered to be a city that is safe and green and has affordable housing. To many urban scholars and practitioners, the combination of 'safe and green' is at the core of one of the most challenging questions we are facing today: how can we mitigate and adapt to climate change at the city level? This question has provoked a wealth of research and scholarship on the technical and behavioural changes that are required to make cities more environmentally, socially and economically sustainable and more resilient to human-made and natural risks. Key in this literature is the conclusion that current modes of urban climate governance (that is, the processes undertaken by governments and others to

J. van der Heijden (✉)
School of Government, Victoria University of Wellington,
Wellington, New Zealand
e-mail: Jeroen.vanderheijden@vuw.ac.nz

S.-H. Hong
Korea Institute of Public Administration, Seoul, South Korea
e-mail: seunghun.hong@kipa.re.kr

© The Author(s) 2020
C. van Montfort, A. Michels (eds.), *Partnerships for Livable Cities*,
https://doi.org/10.1007/978-3-030-40060-6_2

steer the actions and behaviours of individuals and organisations to achieve desired climate mitigation and climate adaptation goals at a city level) have fallen short in achieving their desired results. Globally, scholars have called for—and policymakers, business leaders, civil society champions and others have begun to engage with—urban climate governance experiments to trial new forms of urban climate governance.

Following a global trend in such experiments, the literature on urban climate governance experimentation has grown rapidly over recent years (Turnheim et al. 2018). The literature is particularly vocal about the relevance of including local actors and organisations in such experiments. Particularly high hopes are expressed about partnerships in experimental urban climate governance that bring city governments together with local businesses or citizens or both. It is expected that this allows to the tacit knowledge of stakeholders to be used in future governance interventions (Greenberg and Schroder 2003; Holley et al. 2012). Furthermore, collaborative and consensus-based development processes that include a wide range of stakeholders may increase the legitimacy of instruments used for urban climate governance in the eyes of those who are subject to them (Holley et al. 2012; Kwon et al. 2014). However, there is also criticism of this novel approach to governing urban transformations. While there are advantages in allowing a range of stakeholders to take part in urban climate experimentation, there is also a risk of an overrepresentation of narrow and vested interests (Birnbaum 2015; Scott 2015; Sprain 2016). Partnerships attract a specific set of stakeholders—those with the time and means to be involved in experiments—and give them a disproportionate voice (Evans et al. 2016; Van der Heijden 2016, 2017).

To increase our understanding of the role of partnerships in experimental urban climate governance, this chapter studies a series of partnerships that form the base of four urban climate governance experiments in Seoul, South Korea.[1] Case data were obtained from websites, reports, and other sources. New data were obtained through a series of interviews held from 24 May to 23 June 2016, and follow-up email correspondence with selected interviewees in 2017 and 2018. The interviews sought to fill the

[1] The cases in Seoul were studied as part of two larger research projects funded by the Netherlands Organisation for Scientific Research (VIDI project, *Joined-up governance for low-carbon cities*, grant number 06165322) and the Australian Research Council (DECRA project, *Collaborative governance for low-carbon and resilient cities*, grant number DE 15100511). Professor van der Heijden acted as primary investigator in these projects, and Dr. Seung-Hun Hong provided essential research support.

gaps in the data obtained from other sources, to resolve conflicts in those data, and to gain additional insight into the experiments under scrutiny. A total of 38 interviewees from various backgrounds, including policymakers, bureaucrats, property developers, architects, engineers and property owners, were interviewed for insights into the experiments studied here. The data were processed following conventional practice for this type of research (Creswell and Creswell 2018). The interview data and additional data were coded using a systematic coding scheme, and they were then processed using data analysis software (Atlas.ti). Using this approach, the data were systematically explored, and insight was gained into the 'repetitiveness' and 'rarity' of the experiences shared by the interviewees and the insights provided by the additional sources.

2.2   RESEARCH CONTEXT: THE CITY OF SEOUL

The city of Seoul houses 10 million people over some 600 square kilometres—a population density of 17,000 people per square kilometre. This high population density is, in part, a result of strict planning policies introduced in the 1970s: in 1971, the national government established green belts around the city of Seoul to limit urban sprawl and to preserve the natural environment (Cho 2005; Rii and Ahn 2002). The city faces two main urban climate challenges. First, the existing building stock is dated and shows poor environmental performance as a result of its high resource intensity—specifically, energy to heat and cool buildings. Second, the city faces considerable congestion of its infrastructure, particularly for road transport, resulting in high levels of air pollution (Cervero and Kang 2011; Moon 2006). Other pressing problems for Seoul are an aging population who are not likely to have the financial means to retrofit their properties, an ongoing transition to smaller households asking for ever more urban development, and a highly fragmented property market, with most buildings (more than 70 per cent[2]) owned by individual homeowners and small and medium-sized enterprises (OECD 2012a, b; Seo 2016). Approximately 60 per cent of the city's greenhouse gases can be related to its current building stock, and approximately 20 per cent to city-related transport.[3]

[2] Data from: http://kosis.kr/statHtml/statHtml.do?orgId=116&tblId=DT_MLTM_560&vw_cd=MT_ZTITLE&list_id=116_11611&seqNo=&lang_mode=ko&language=kor&obj_var_id=&itm_id=&conn_path=E1 (20.05.19).
[3] Data from: OECD, 2012a (20.05.19).

Since the early 2000s, the city of Seoul has included environmental sustainability and low-carbon city development and transformation in its city master plans (Lee et al. 2014; SMG 2009). The city of Seoul has been particularly active in trialling innovative governance arrangements to reduce greenhouse gas emissions from its existing built environment and transport systems. Most of the arrangements currently in place align with the *One Less Nuclear Power Plant (OLNPP)* policy of 2012 (Lee et al. 2014; SMG 2012, 2014b). The development of the OLNPP policy was largely driven by Mayor Park Won-Soon, who set the ambition for Seoul to replace the capacity of one nuclear power plant (2 million TOE, tonne of oil equivalent) with energy produced from new and renewable sources by 2014.[4] The first phase of the policy was successfully finalised in 2014. Building on this success, the second phase of the policy has successfully increased the proportion of self-supplied energy in the city to 20 per cent by 2018 (representing 4 million TOE produced from new and renewable sources) (SMG 2014b; Sustainia 2015).

What is of particular interest about the OLNPP is that both phases have been developed in partnership with citizens and businesses, and that they allow for citizen involvement in the implementation of urban climate actions. To achieve and maintain this involvement, local *community centres* have been set up. These provide a range of social services, but they are also places where citizens meet to discuss policy development and implementation at the borough level. Local citizens provide information and suggestions to these community centres, and these are then moved up the hierarchy of the Seoul Metropolitan Government (SMG). The community centres can best be understood as Type G partnerships in how they interact with local citizens, Type F partnerships in how they interact with local small businesses, and Type E partnerships in how they interact with the SMG (see the introduction to the book for an explanation of these types).

This level, close to citizens' homes, was relevant for the success of the first phase of the OLNPP policy, as a senior advisor to the SMG explained: 'It is a centrally organised process, with local ones that reflect local circumstances. A central system, with local adaptations' (int. 4). In addition, the community centres act as essential breeding grounds for novel ideas that

---

[4] This ambition aligns with one of the ambitions of Seoul's current long-term development strategy, *Seoul Plan 2030*. See further: https://www.seoulsolution.kr/en/content/2030-seoul-plan (20.05.19).

can be brought from the local level to the central city level: 'the community centres act as incubators', the advisor continued (int. 4). This approach to policymaking and implementation, which is novel for Seoul, has won the city the 2018 Lee Kuan Yew World City Prize for good urban governance and the 2016 Gothenburg Award for Sustainable Development. Within the traditional approach of state-guided economic development in Korea, partnerships tend to be between major corporations and government—Type C. State-guided economic development (also referred to as the developmental state) is a development paradigm typical of the Asian Tiger economies (Hong Kong, Taiwan, South Korea and Singapore) and of Japan (Guk Jeon 1995). It refers to a model of capitalism in which the state has more independent autonomous power and control over the economy than in economic liberalism. Typical of South Korea is that, in the early stages of modern development, a handful of corporations were 'picked' by the government as economic partners in development partnerships. These old partnerships still resonate in South Korea, as does the idea of state-guided participation between the state and stakeholders of the private sector and civil society (Moon 2006; Park et al. 2016).

2.3   RESEARCH FINDINGS

Four cases are illustrative of the trend in partnerships for urban climate governance experimentation in Seoul: Energy Self-Sufficient Villages, Eco-Mileage, the Building Retrofit Programme, and the No-Driving Day. These are all part of the OLNPP Policy. Table 2.1 provides an overview.

2.3.1   Energy Self-Sufficient Villages

As part of its national green growth policy, the government of South Korea started experimenting with the development of *green villages* in 2002. These villages were heavily reliant on renewable energy, and their development was subsidised by the Ministry of Knowledge Economy. In 2010, the national Green New-Deal Policy intended to develop 600 such villages through the Low-Carbon Green Village Project, but, because of various setbacks, this ambition was later scaled down to 40 villages. The project, nevertheless, inspired the SMG to launch a related project: the Energy Self-Sufficient Village Project. Here the word *village* should be understood as a group of houses and associated buildings within the administrative boundaries of Seoul (i.e., precincts and neighbourhoods).

Table 2.1 The four cases compared

	Energy self-sufficient villages	Eco-mileage	Building retrofit programme	No-driving day
What is the goal of the governance intervention?	Energy saving, energy efficiency, and renewable energy generation at village level; and more grass-roots activities in communities	Energy saving and energy efficiency by households and businesses	Energy efficiency and renewable energy generation at building level	Reduction of car use in the city. The benefits that flow from this are less congestion, less energy consumption, and improved air quality
Who are the partners?	SMG,[a] local communities and households ('villages')	SMG, civil society groups, businesses (for the development of technology and software underpinning the programme)	SMG, Clinton Foundation, finance providers, property developers, property owners	SMG, civil society groups, businesses (petrol stations, repair services, insurance companies)
What type of partnership(s)?	Type E and Type G	A transition from Type E and Type G to Type H to Type C	Type C and Type E	A transition from Type E to Type H to Type C
What is novel about the governance intervention?	It rewards village residents for working together on energy efficiency and renewable energy	It rewards participants with points that can be used for purchasing goods and services	It provides low-interest loans, and participants compete for these loans.	It rewards car owners for not using their car one day a week
How is the experiment controlled?	SMG receives information on energy savings from the utility companies	SMG receives information from the utility companies on participant behaviour	SMG receives information from the utility companies on participant behaviour	SMG has developed a monitoring system, using tags in participating cars

(*continued*)

Table 2.1 (continued)

	Energy self-sufficient villages	Eco-mileage	Building retrofit programme	No-driving day
How are performance and change measured?	SMG works closely with village communities in the implementation of energy efficiency initiatives and technology for energy upgrades. Results achieved over time are reported in OLNPP policy documents	SMG keeps track of the number of participants and their energy consumption. Results achieved over time are reported in OLNPP policy documents	SMG keeps track of the number of retrofits carried out under the programme. Results achieved over time are reported in OLNPP policy documents	SMG collects data from the radio frequency identification system
What changes are made to the experiment over time?	To increase participation, tailored free-of-cost energy consulting is now offered to prospective participants	To increase participation and to improve participant behaviour, town hall meetings were organised and early champions in the programme received additional rewards	To increase participation, tailored free-of-cost energy consulting is now offered to prospective participants	To improve compliance the monitoring system was updated. To improve participation synergies are sought with the Eco-Mileage programme

(*continued*)

Table 2.1   (continued)

	Energy self-sufficient villages	Eco-mileage	Building retrofit programme	No-driving day
When were major changes made to the experiment?	2002 (introduction of comparable experiments at national level), 2012 (introduction of programme in OLNPP), 2014 (introduction of energy consulting)	2009 (introduction), 2010 (introduction of Eco-Mileage credit card), 2012 (incorporation in OLNPP), 2014 (expansion of collaboration with private sector)	2008 (introduction), 2011 (incorporation in OLNPP), 2014 (loans capped at 80% of retrofit costs), 2014 (introduction of energy consulting), 2016 (increase in cap to 100%), ongoing (reduction of interest rates; expansion of property types that can apply for loan)	2003 (introduction), 2011 (incorporation in OLNPP), 2014 (improvement of tags), 2015 (pilot studies to explore linkages with Eco-Mileage)

ªSMG = Seoul Metropolitan Government

Working in close collaboration with citizens to generate initial ideas for energy efficiency improvements at the village level, and after different rounds of public consultation, the SMG decided to include Energy Self-Sufficient Villages in the OLNPP Policy in 2012 (SMG 2014a), reflecting a Type E partnership. The project strives to induce participating communities to make gradual progress from energy conservation to renewable energy production in three stages: practising energy savings, improving energy efficiency, and producing renewable energy. The original motivation was to create a model for citizen-led voluntary energy self-sufficiency activities in local communities, which reflects a Type G partnership. Each village is supposed to come up with a plan to change its everyday practice from an energy consumption focus to an energy conservation focus. The SMG subsidises the planning and implementation by the villages. Of particular interest is that the Energy Self-Sufficient Villages project seeks to strengthen the grass-roots governance and resilience of city communities.

As an advisor to the Mayor explained: '[This] would be very hard without the One Less Nuclear Power Plant policy. Citizens did their best. Local policymakers did their best. It was much experimentation in the beginning. Now they have formal policy backing' (int. 8).

A village comprising more than 50 households can apply.[5] An SMG committee reviews the application and conducts an on-site review and interviews. Those villages where residents show a particularly strong wish to participate are supported over a multi-year period with the aim of gradually improving the village's performance. The Energy Self-Sufficient Villages project provides financial and administrative support for tailored energy consultation and advice, the implementation of energy conservation management and techniques, and technology for improving energy efficiency and generating renewable energy. It also supports cultural activities and festivals to improve citizens' awareness of energy issues, foster energy-saving habits, and share stories of best practice. Over time, administrators involved in the project have come to realise that it is essential in South Korea to increase citizens' awareness of energy issues. 'Compared to conventional energy, the cost of renewable energy is high', an administrator explained (int. 25). The costs of conventional energy at national level are kept down through subsidies. '[Therefore,] you have to add a value dimension [to the programme]. To make sure that people understand it is not just about economic benefits, but serves other values as well' (int. 25).

In 2012 only seven villages were selected by the SMG to receive support. Since then, the number of supported villages has increased significantly, reaching 80 in 2017. In 2018 the SMG announced that it planned to expand its support to 100 villages.[6] The interview accounts and other sources point out that the outcomes achieved and the lessons learnt are highly context-dependent. No two energy self-sufficient villages are alike. One of the villages assumed to be most successful is Seongdaegol village, which we explore here as an illustration. Seongdaegol has a population of approximately 50,000 people. A citizen-led self-governing community was started in Seongdaegol in 2009, when community members established the Seongdaegol Children's Library—a Type G partnership. This community became interested in energy conservation after the Fukushima

---

[5] This condition was later moderated to a village comprising at least three households.
[6] See http://spp.seoul.go.kr/main/news/news_report.jsp#view/249158?tr_code=snews (14.08.18).

Daiichi nuclear disaster, and a local voluntary energy self-sufficiency movement was started in 2011. Various minimally-intrusive activities are undertaken to increase people's awareness of energy savings, including awarding the title of Energy Efficiency Queen or Prince of the Month to those showing best performance, comparing and ranking monthly energy bills on the library wall, and holding a series of open lectures on energy efficiency at the local middle school. A next step will be to raise awareness of low-cost technological solutions to increase energy efficiency at the household level.

2.3.2   Eco-Mileage

Eco-Mileage is a voluntary programme that seeks to reduce greenhouse gas emissions by improving energy efficiency and saving energy.[7] It builds on earlier incentive programmes, such as the national Carbon Point Programme that was run by the Ministry of the Environment. It was introduced in Seoul in 2009, and was later incorporated into the OLNPP by the SMG at the request of civil society groups as a means to support citizens' energy conservation efforts. In the development of Eco-Mileage, the SMG was first *lobbied* by civil society groups and later partnered with businesses to deliver the programme (including developing technology and software to monitor and reward participants). Here we should understand *lobbying* as falling within a long-standing tradition in which the SMG and civil society groups interact and discuss current and future governance interventions; in European and Anglo-Saxon countries this would be looked upon as public participation driven by civil society. The development of Eco-Mileage thus reflects a Type H partnership (which originated from a Type E partnership), whereas the implementation of Eco-Mileage reflects a Type C partnership.

Eco-Mileage seeks to raise awareness of energy consumption at household and business level, and provides rewards to those who seek to reduce their energy consumption. To participate, a household or business creates an account on an online platform. The SMG then collects the participant's data, including consumption of electricity, water, liquid natural gas, and district heating. These data are made available to the SMG by the utility companies (a system is in place to protect personal data), and, through the

---

[7]For a general description, see https://seoulsolution.kr/en/content/eco-mileage-system-1 (09.08.18).

online platform, SMG provides participants with relevant data so that they can track their consumption over time.

A central aspect of Eco-Mileage is *mileage points*. These are awarded to participants if they reduce their carbon emissions by 10 per cent or more compared to the previous two years (the online platform translates resource consumption into carbon emissions). Participants can use these points to buy eco-friendly products (such as LED lights) or to pay for journeys by public transport, or they can redeem them with merchants who are cooperating with the programme. To ease the usage of the mileage points, the SMG introduced Eco-Mileage credit and debit cards in 2010. Another core aspect of Eco-Mileage is information sharing and information supply. Participants can share their experiences through the Eco-Mileage website, and this is a valuable source of information for other participants who are seeking to reduce their energy consumption. In addition, the SMG runs an 'energy clinic service' in which a trained energy specialist visits a household, carries out an energy audit, and provides advice on how that household can reduce its energy consumption. Similar advice is provided to businesses. Between 2009 and 2014, close to 1.5 million households, 1600 schools, 2000 multi-unit housing complexes, 3500 public institutions, and over 30,000 commercial and general purpose buildings (mainly used by businesses) signed up to Eco-Mileage. Over this period, the SMG issued mileage points with a total value of 7 billion Won (US\$ 6.6 million) to nearly 150,000 households that had achieved a 10 per cent reduction in their energy consumption. SMG reports indicate that between September 2009 and December 2017 a total of 930 k TOE of energy was saved by the participants.[8]

Interview accounts and other sources point out that the key conditions for this success are the collaboration of the SMG, civil society groups and businesses in developing the programme (that is, analysing the problems underlying energy consumption in Seoul, proposing possible solutions, and finally developing and implementing Eco-Mileage), the strong support for and marketing of Eco-Mileage by Mayor Park, and the efforts of the SMG in participation rates in its early stages. Without such efforts it would seem that Eco-Mileage would be difficult to replicate, interviewees argued. However, it has also encountered difficulties, they explained. Eco-Mileage initially had problems with attracting participants, mainly because

[8] See http://spp.seoul.go.kr/main/news/news_report.jsp#view/262649?tr_code=snews (14.08.18).

of citizens' low awareness of climate change. Awareness of climate change and of Eco-Mileage was raised through town hall meetings at district offices and training sessions. To create further awareness, early leaders (those achieving the 10 per cent energy reductions) were awarded plaques and certificates by the Mayor in a ceremony that was highly publicised by the media. In addition, to increase the uptake of the Eco-Mileage programme the city of Seoul runs marketing campaigns, targets newcomers to Seoul for participation in the programme, and has made participation mandatory for Building Retrofit Programme (BRP, see below) participants. Also, the utility companies were initially wary about sharing their clients' energy consumption data because they thought this information was confidential. People without internet access have been found to encounter participation problems because they cannot log on to the online platform. Finally, because of the success of Eco-Mileage, the city budget was strained by the SMG providing financial rewards (in the form of mileage points) to successful participants.

In the light of these challenges, some interviewees questioned the value and the transition of the Eco-Mileage programme over time. 'There is a gap between desire and action. [Because of the many changes made,] good ideas may get lost in translation. Eco-Mileage was a promising idea [for energy reductions] but its purpose was lost', an advisor to the Mayor explained (int. 8). The effort put in to attract participants almost undoes the voluntary nature of the programme, she concluded.

2.3.3   Building Retrofit Programme

Like Eco-Mileage, BRP is a voluntary programme. It seeks to incentivise building owners to retrofit their buildings or to build new ones with higher levels of environmental performance than is required by the building codes. Low-interest loans are offered to support them in doing so.[9] The BRP was introduced by the SMG in 2008 for public buildings, initially with support from the Clinton Foundation, and was rolled into the OLNPP policy (both phase 1, 2011–2014, and phase 2, 2014–2018). In 2012, the city offered its first BRP loans for public and commercial buildings as well as for homes. The city enters into partnerships with finance providers so that it can provide low interest loans—Type C partnerships.

---

[9]For a general description, see https://seoulsolution.kr/en/content/building-retrofit-program (09.08.18).

The interest on BRP loans was reduced from 2.5 per cent in 2012 to 2 per cent in 2013, and again to 1.75 per cent in 2014. These rates are well below market interest rates—for example, the market interest rate in 2014 was around 3.8 per cent. Loans are issued for eight years and are capped at 2 billion Won for commercial projects and 10 million Won for homes (US$ 1.8 million and US$ 9400 respectively).

The BRP is announced publicly every year, and only the most suitable beneficiaries are selected, through a series of evaluations. Depending on the intensity of the retrofit suggested, up to 100% of the costs of the retrofit can be borrowed as a BRP loan. Under the BRP, buildings follow eco-friendly construction practices, such as energy conservation, reduction of pollutants, and renewable energy production, throughout the whole process of construction from designing, building, and maintenance, through to demolition. Under the BRP, new buildings are subject to stricter energy standards throughout their entire construction process, while existing buildings are required to improve their energy efficiency in cases of renovation or maintenance. Households and businesses are targeted with information on the benefits of the BRP.

By 2014, the BRP had achieved retrofits of 1200 high-energy consuming buildings, and energy upgrades of 10,000 detached houses and 83,000 units in apartment blocks (more recent data were not available at the time of writing this article). Interview accounts and other sources point out that the key conditions for the success of the BRP are the financial assistance to the owners of houses and condominiums for retrofits and the provision of information on the advantages of building energy retrofits and upgrades. Initially, developers and citizens were reluctant to make use of the BRP because of the high initial costs. The cost of electricity in South Korea is kept low by the national government in support of industry, but this makes it difficult for property owners to reap the returns of a building retrofit in the short term. Seoul confronted this challenge by gradually reducing the interest rate for BRP loans. The SMG also commissioned research projects on energy policies and technological trends worldwide, both to reform and improve the BRP and to further raise the awareness of property owners about the advantages of energy retrofits of buildings. These projects include partnerships between leaders in the BRP and the SMG to develop best practice case studies and share these with other property owners—a Type E partnership.

2.3.4   No-Driving Day

No-Driving Day is a programme and campaign aimed at citizens. It incentivises them to drive less and use public transport more.[10] In short, citizens commit to not using their car on at least one day a week between Monday and Friday, and they are rewarded if they stick to their commitment. In 2003, No-Driving Day was launched to respond to various problems. It was later incorporated in the OLNPP Policy, and synergies have been sought with the Eco-Mileage programme discussed above. No-Driving Day provides a practical approach to reducing household energy costs, the congestion on Seoul's roads, and the city's high level of air pollution. Participants receive an electronic tag to be installed in their car. This tag helps to monitor compliance through a radio frequency identification system located throughout Seoul. All non-commercial vehicles in Seoul with fewer than ten seats can join the programme. Through an online platform, participants indicate their no-driving day (7 am-10 pm) and can keep track of their performance. The development of No-Driving Day reflects that of Eco-Mileage: a Type E partnership, in which citizen groups engaged with the SMG to understand the problems of car use in Seoul, which merged into a Type H partnership when businesses joined to develop solutions to the problems identified. From then, it merged into a Type C partnership in which businesses develop instruments and software and are involved in the implementation of the programme.

Car owners who join the programme are given a five per cent reduction in car tax and a 50 per cent discount on toll fees when using specific toll routes. No-Driving Day is further linked to the on-street residential parking permit system, and vehicles participating in the programme are given priority over non-participating vehicles when applying for a parking permit; different discounts apply in different districts, and range from 20 to 30 per cent. Other incentives include discounts at participating petrol stations and repair services, and discounts in monthly car insurance fees. The programme works with a *three strikes and you're out* enforcement mechanism. Non-complying car owners get two warnings (text messages to their registered phone) for their first two breaches and are disqualified from receiving benefits after the third breach. In 2015, the SMG began a

---

[10] For a general description see: https://www.seoulsolution.kr/en/content/no-driving-day-campaign-one-day-week (09.08.18).

pilot study to reduce the number of miles driven by car by rewarding people with Eco-Mileage points. If this pilot study proves to be successful, it may ultimately replace No-Driving Day. A related initiative, the Bicycle Mileage App, was introduced in 2015 by the citizen-led organisation Networks for Green Transport. This telephone application allows cyclists to keep track of their bicycle use. Based on the distance they cycle and their related carbon emission savings, they are awarded mileage points under the Eco-Mileage programme. 'By mid-2016, 27,000 people throughout Seoul were using the app. The ambition is to have 200,000 people to use the app', a representative of the organisation said (int. 6). Networks for Green Transport can best be understood as a Type G partnership, but in its linkage with the Eco-Mileage programme we observe a Type E partnership.

Approximately 30 per cent of Seoul's vehicles were registered and tagged under the No-Driving Day programme in 2014 (some 750,000 vehicles). This is a considerable decline from the almost 45 per cent of vehicles that were registered in 2012 (some 1 million vehicles). It was estimated that in 2014 No-Driving Day helped to reduce traffic volume by 1.1 per cent, corresponding to a 0.36 per cent reduction in traffic-related carbon emissions. Interview accounts and other sources point out that the compliance rate with No-Driving Day is limited. Car owners indicate that No-Driving Day does not provide enough (attractive) incentives, and argue that it is too rigid because once the No-Driving Day is set, it cannot be altered. The link with Eco-Mileage may be more attractive as it rewards an overall reduction in the number of miles travelled by car on any day and at any time. While compliance rates may be low, the programme still imposes a heavy burden on the SMG. The accumulated income loss resulting from reduced car tax revenue, and reduced toll and parking fees, was 40 billion Won (US$ 38 million) from 2009 to 2013. During these years, the SMG experienced considerable technical problems with the programme. The tag could easily be removed from the car, and determining whether or not a car had its tag installed could only be done visually, resulting in a time-intensive enforcement process. To resolve this, additional incentives (such as reduced toll fees) were introduced that only work for installed tags, and car owners are now required to renew their tag every five years.

2.4   Discussion

The four cases have recorded different degrees of success. While the differences in participation and performance rates are of relevance in themselves, more interesting insights stand out when one takes a step back from considering these direct outcomes and looks at the four cases and the OLNPP policy more broadly. First, the partnerships discussed in this chapter were all initiated by the SMG to implement public policy more effectively and achieve public policy goals. Because of this, the partners in the partnerships are not fully of equal standing, with the SMG having what can be considered the role of a powerful principal, and the partners that of an agent with limited power. Interviewees were of the opinion that the SMG was truly committed to the partnerships, because it has opened up decision-making processes to citizens and other stakeholders, but they were also clear that at the end of the day the final decision-making power in the development and implementation of the experiments lies with SMG. While this limits the power of the non-SMG partners to see their interests served, it allows the SMG to take an approach of relatively quickly rolling out the OLNPP policy and achieving the desired results in the area of urban climate governance (which we earlier located as the interaction between the 'green' and 'safe' dimensions that are central to this book).

Second, when asked what may explain the high rates of participation in Eco-Mileage and No-Driving Day, and the high levels of compliance by participants in BRP and Energy Self-Sufficient Villages, interviewees generally provided two complementary insights. They explained that the system of state-guided economic development combined with strict punishments of violations of law in South Korea had nurtured a culture of obedient citizens. Many citizens, the interviewees continued, consider the experimental interventions as an extension of mandatory governance regulations, and thus something that they should naturally participate in and follow. For other participants, those who are perhaps somewhat critical of the heavy involvement of government in many aspects of South Korean life, it may be precisely the voluntary nature of the interventions that is attractive. For them, the interventions may show a willingness of the SMG truly to open up and involve them in policymaking and implementation (even though, as mentioned above, the SMG keeps the upper hand). The interviewees concluded that, for this group, participation in the experiments may be considered as a way of showing their approval of this new stance of the SMG towards its citizens. When looking at partnerships in countries that are not European or Anglo Saxon, provided by the heuristic sketched in the introduction of this book, it is of relevance to keep in mind that the notion of *partnership* varies across countries and cultures. What is considered as a partnership in one country or culture may be considered as a traditional principal–agent relationship in another.

Third, an aspect that binds together the four cases is that over time the interventions have begun to combine different approaches and incentives to attract participants and reward them for their performance. The combination of raising awareness through educational and consultancy activities with some form of direct or indirect financial reward is now central to the four cases studied. Interviewees pointed to a very specific situation of necessity and sufficiency in the set of incentives on which the cases now build: education or consultancy and direct or indirect rewards appear by themselves necessary but insufficient to achieve the overall goals of the cases studied. They are not complementary to or alternatives for each other but appear to work in conjunction in attracting participants and affecting participant behaviour. Interviewees held the opinion that it was because of the close collaboration between the SMG and other stakeholders in the development and implementation of the experiments that these essential lessons were learnt.

Notwithstanding everything that has been said in favour of the OLNPP, the SMG representatives were careful not to consider these outcomes an overall success yet: 'The main outcome of the OLNPP is that we have achieved public participation and energy savings at citizen level. What we have not achieved is a meaningful change of regulation. To make the policy work well, regulatory requirements need to be tightened', an advisor to the Mayor said (int. 8). Also, the leadership of Mayor Park has been essential in realising system-wide change, but this causes a core risk, the interviewees stressed. If a future mayor were determined to undo Park's signature OLNPP policy, she or he would not find it difficult to dismantle the OLNPP and quickly roll back many of the (experimental) programmes under the OLNPP. As one of the interviewees mentioned: 'One of the big questions now is whether Mayor Park will leave an institutional legacy. He has introduced regulations and a strong institutional framework, but a next mayor might change all this. People know this' (int. 37).

2.5   Conclusion

This chapter set out to gain a better understanding of the partnerships that lie at the base of a series of urban climate governance experiments in the city of Seoul, South Korea. In doing so, it has uncovered some core insights that are of interest to policymakers who are keen to experiment with urban climate governance interventions and who wish to enter into partnerships with businesses and citizens to do so. In this brief conclusion, we touch on three insights that have broader resonance with the literature on partnerships and urban climate governance.

First, having analysed the four cases in Seoul, we wonder how well (or poorly) the notions of urban partnerships travel between geographical locations (see also Turnheim et al. 2018). The literature on these topics has largely emerged over the last two decades from studies on cities in post-industrial, western societies that have largely been carried out by scholars based at universities there. Aspects considered central to partnerships by these scholars, such as the far-reaching participation of citizens and the private sector in the development and implementation of experiments, may simply not resonate with deeply entrenched institutional and governance structures elsewhere. The development strategy that drives state-guided economies such as South Korea, but also Japan and Singapore, has an inherently different understanding of the relationship between government, civil society and the business sector from that in, for example, liberal capitalist economies (Ha 2011; OECD 2012b). What is considered as a far-reaching partnership with a strong commitment from the municipal government in Seoul could, seen through the lens provided by western scholarship, be critiqued as tokenistic (cf., Arnstein 1969). Here we call on scholars—from western societies and elsewhere—to be sensitive to these cultural, political and institutional differences between world regions.

Second, partnerships of the kind discussed in this article are very likely to be a luxury that many cities across the world cannot afford. The cases studied indicate that partnerships require considerable capital investment; in Seoul this investment was made by the SMG using tax revenues and other forms of income, and the SMG allowed for considerable numbers of staff members to be freed up to enter actively into partnerships with stakeholders. While many cities in the world are lauded for being involved in the trend of urban climate governance experimentation, and particularly for the partnerships they have set up in these experiments, many others are not actively experimenting with novel governance interventions and processes (Bulkeley et al. 2015). This does not necessarily indicate an unwillingness of these cities to change and ramp up their climate governance interventions and ambitions, or to work with local stakeholders, but may simply be a result of them lacking the funds to explore how to change things for the better. Urban climate governance scholarship needs to be sensitive to the limitations and challenges faced by these cities. There are limits to what can be achieved through partnerships for experimental urban climate governance, not only in the cities that are involved in the trend of experimentation, such as Seoul, but more broadly because it is likely that so many cities are not able to partner with stakeholders and experiment at all.

Third and finally, the four cases studied point to a hitherto underexplored aspect of partnerships. Most of the partnerships studied in this chapter were fluid, or, at the very least, within in each case we observed different types of partnerships at different points in time. For example, in both the Eco-Mileage and the No-Driving Day programmes we observed that the experiments were initiated through a Type E or even a Type G partnership, were then taken up and worked out in a Type H partnership, and were ultimately implemented in a Type C partnership. There is an intuitive appeal in the assumption that moving in and out of partnerships allows optimal use to be made of the qualities and capacities of the parties involved, without them burning out or losing interest in the long run. Could it be that the best partners know when it is the right time to join a partnership, and, equally importantly, when it is the right time to let go again? Could it be that the best partners know when it is the right time to attract others, and when it is the right time to tell them to leave again? Whatever the case, these Hegelian insights that partnerships are likely to be in flux rather than static partly explain why it is often so hard to 'capture' and learn from what is going on in a partnership. The timing of the research matters considerably for the observations made about the success or lack thereof of a particular partnership; this timing is equally important for classifying a partnership as one of the types described in the introduction to this book.

References

Arnstein, S. A. (1969). A ladder of citizen participation. *Journal of the American Planning Association, 35*(4), 216–224.

Birnbaum, S. (2015). Environmental c-governance, legitimacy, and the quest for compliance: When and why is stakeholder participation desirable? *Journal of Environmental Policy & Planning.* https://doi.org/10.108 0/1523908X.2015.1077440.

Bulkeley, H., Castan Broto, V., & Edwards, G. (2015). *An urban politics of climate change: Experimentation and the governing of socio-technical transitions.* Abingdon: Routledge.

Cervero, R., & Kang, C. D. (2011). Bus rapid transit impacts on land uses and land values in Seoul, Korea. *Transport Policy, 18*(1), 102–116.

Cho, J. (2005). Urban planning and urban sprawl in Korea. *Urban Policy and Research, 23*(2), 203–218.

Creswell, J. W., & Creswell, J. D. (2018). *Research design: Qualitative, quantitative, and mixed methods approaches.* London: Sage.

Evans, J., Karvonen, A., & Raven, R. (Eds.). (2016). *The experimental city.* London: Routledge.

Greenberg, D., & Schroder, M. (2003). *The digest of social experiments* (3rd ed.). Washington: Urban Institute Press.

Guk Jeon, J. (1995). Exploring the three varieties of East Asia's state-guided development model: Korea, Singapore, and Taiwan. *Studies in Comparative International Development, 30*(3), 70–88.

Ha, S.-K. (2011). Chapter 6: Seoul as a world city: The challenge of balanced development. In S. Hamnett & D. Forbes (Eds.), *Planning Asian cities: Risk and resilience.* London: Routledge.

Holley, C., Gunningham, N., & Shearing, C. (2012). *The new environmental governance.* London: Routledge.

Kwon, M., Jang, H. S., & Feicock, R. (2014). Climate protection and energy sustainability policy in California cities: What have we learned? *Journal of Urban Affairs, 36*(5), 905–924.

Lee, T., Lee, T., & Lee, Y. (2014). An experiment for urban energy autonomy in Seoul: The one 'less' nuclear power plant policy. *Energy Policy, 74*(November), 311–318.

Moon, T. H. (2006). Sustainable development in Korea, key issues and government response. *International Review of Public Administration, 11*(1), 1–18.

OECD. (2012a). *Compact city policies: Korea; towards sustainable and inclusive growth.* Paris: OECD Publishing.

OECD. (2012b). *OECD urban policy reviews: Korea.* Paris: OECD Publishing.

Park, K.-K. P., Lee, W., & Lee, S.-H. (2016). *Understanding Korean public administration: Lessons learned from practice.* London: Routledge.

Rii, H. U., & Ahn, J.-S. (2002). Urbanization and its impact on Seoul, Korea. In I. Douglas & S.-L. Huang (Eds.), *Urbanization, East Asian and habitat II.* Taipei: Chung-hua Institution for Economic Research.

Scott, T. (2015). Does collaboration make any difference? Linking collaborative governance to environmental outcomes. *Journal of Policy Analysis and Management, 34*(3), 537–566.

Seo, J.-K. (2016). Housing policy and urban sustainable development: Evaluating the process of high-rise apartment development in Korea. *Urban Policy and Research, 34*(4), 330–342.

SMG. (2009). *Urban planning of Seoul*. Seoul: Seoul Metropolitan Government.
SMG. (2012). *One less nuclear power plant*. Seoul: Seoul Metropolitan Government.
SMG. (2014a). *City energy cultivators*. Seould: Seoul Metropolitan Government.
SMG. (2014b). *One less nuclear power plant – Phase 2*. Seoul: Seoul Metropolitan Government.
Sprain, L. (2016). Paradoxes of public participation in climate change governance. *The Good Society, 25*(1), 62–80.
Sustainia. (2015). *Sustaina 100: A guide to 100 sustainable solutions*. Sustainia: Copenhagen.
Turnheim, B., Kivimaa, P., & Berkhout, F. (Eds.). (2018). *Innovating climate governance: Moving beyond experiments*. Cambridge: Cambridge University Press.
Van der Heijden, J. (2016). Opportunities and risks of the 'new urban governance' in India: To what extent can it help addressing pressing environmental problems? *Journal of Environment and Development, 25*(3), 251–275. https://doi.org/10.1177/1070496516642500.
Van der Heijden, J. (2017). *Innovations in urban climate governance: Voluntary programs for low carbon buildings and cities*. Cambridge: Cambridge University Press.

CHAPTER 3

Livable Cities and Daily Life: Local Level Urban Agriculture in Orizânia, São Paulo and Montreal

Kate Dayana de Abreu, Zilma Borges, Lya Porto, and Peter Spink

3.1 Introduction

The image of partnerships in public affairs usually brings to mind significant arrangements between public, private and/or community based or non-governmental organizations formed with the purpose of improving or contributing to some specific area of action or concern. As they are seen as significant, it is often assumed that they have formal arrangements (Rhodes 1996; Ansell and Torfing 2016). This chapter leads the

K. D. de Abreu • Z. Borges • P. Spink (✉)
Fundação Getulio Vargas, Escola de Administração de Empresas de São Paulo, São Paulo, Brasil

L. Porto
Fundação Getulio Vargas, Escola de Administração de Empresas de São Paulo, São Paulo, Brasil

Université de Montréal, École des Hautes Études Commerciales, Montréal, QC, Canada

© The Author(s) 2020
C. van Montfort, A. Michels (eds.), *Partnerships for Livable Cities*,
https://doi.org/10.1007/978-3-030-40060-6_3

discussion towards the more informal part of the broad arena of partner-ships, as set out in the introductory chapter, and to those relationships that emerge from ways of connecting interests that help to move things forward. This happens, for example, when an urban park committee says 'fine – let's try it' to a local horticultural activist group looking for a place to set up a demonstration plot for discussing flat roof-top gardening and suggests, in turn, that a nearby school might also like to get involved. Every day (or ad-hoc) *connectivity* often starts with what people can do within the possibilities available to them and may grow into more consoli-dated forms of partnership or not.

Our research concern with micro-level connectivities[1] has come from a number of studies on local government innovations (Farah and Spink 2008) and more recently an ongoing project in urban vulnerability. These raised doubts about the effectiveness of the common assumption that gov-ernment action should and does take place by policies, programs, direc-tives or other instruments being developed and applied or implemented through actions in different places; that is, proceed from the general to the specific. This may make some kind of sense when the variety of circum-stances is within what could be called the 'transferrable'. But what hap-pens in those settings where this is not possible or when the demands of immediate connections have very little to do with the broader policies, programs and directives around. Does that mean that public affairs cease to exist, or does it suggest the importance of another type of public affair; those public affairs that are created by publics themselves (Dewey 1927; Marres 2007; Spink 2019). The tensions between these different approaches to public affairs and their implications for the development of effective partnerships forms the basis for this chapter. It does so through an emerging theme in the discussion of the green and the livable: urban agriculture.

Urban agriculture is an expression that covers a wide variety of activities taking place for all sorts of economic, social, educational, health, commu-nity, collective or individual reasons. They range from (usually small) industries on the fringe of towns and cities to window boxes full of herbs for neighbors to use. In the same way that small farms on the urban-rural fringe are not often seen as being part of the city—despite appearing at the library car park for the weekly farmer's market—so the many micro-scale enterprises that are happening in everyday life are often dismissed as

---

[1] The plural emphasizes heterogeneity.

eventual, without impact and certainly not seen as partnerships within the more restrictive use of the term. Yet, to return to an earlier use of the word *industry*, the volunteer street level gardener taking care of fruit trees so that birds can find food, is being just as industrious as the church group making marmalade from the neighbor's orange tree, the medical staff taking care of the raised bed vegetable patch at the health center, the fair price distribution center for vegetables from family collectives or an office building with green-roof allotments.

Whilst we don't want to fall into the trap of romanticizing the less formal aspects of the local, we do want to suggest that they deserve more space in the discussions about urban development. Indeed, if given more attention and support, our studies suggest that these every day connectivities may help to avoid the more negative effects that have resulted from many well intentioned top down planning and open market initiatives.

The chapter begins with a brief discussion of the variety of forms that urban agriculture can take before looking at possibilities and challenges in three urban settings. The first is a small Brazilian rural-urban municipality Orizânia (Brazil pop. 7700) which is part of a study of the Brazilian Federal government program to incorporate family smallholdings into local school meal supply chains (Abreu 2014). It involved field visits and fifteen in-depth interviews with local government officials and family farmers. Here the tensions between the program and local possibilities highlighted the role of local actors in negotiating possibilities.

The second is the municipality of São Paulo (Brazil pop. 12 million)[2] where urban agriculture is still at an early stage, but where a variety of different relationships have already appeared and where flexibility in actions and mechanisms of support will be key. Here research has been taking place since 2016 in contact with local associations, community groups and place based public officials. As well as visits to agricultural activities and participation in local forums, some fifty-eight semi-structured interviews have been carried out.

The third is Montreal (Canada pop. 1.7 million), where urban agriculture, traditionally an activity linked to socialization, leisure and alternative life styles, has become more activist and environmentally focused, leading to changes in municipal food policies and new forms of sub-municipal services. Here civil society is playing a major role in forming the issues.

[2] Study being carried out at the M'Boi Urban Research Station by the four authors (www.fgv.br/ceapg).

Research involved an initial visit in 2016 with thirty-six in depth interviews (Porto de Oliveira 2017) and a second visit in 2019 involving further participation in public meetings, councils and the actions of community-based organizations.

Despite their differences, from the small rural municipality of Orizânia where a mayor and nutritionist were key in 'fitting the bits together', to the densely populated São Paulo with its urban farmers growing under transmission lines and then to the developed and advanced setting of Montreal with its community activists and Universities, we have found there are similar lessons to be learned. That perhaps the best chance we have to avoid the dangers of green and safe becoming unaffordable and, in civic terms, unlivable is not to start from the general, the plan, the policy, the model, the major intervention, but from the specifics and potentials of hundreds and thousands of everyday connections and micro transformations that will create different forms of partnership as they go along. That is to move away from major approaches to financial engineering, urban compensation and formally designed inter-organizational governance mechanisms and provide much more space and support to different bits and pieces of action; block by block, road by road and district by district, which have as their underlying motto: *let's try.*

3.2   ALL OF THIS IS URBAN AGRICULTURE

Urban agriculture is a simple reference to many different ways of integrating formal and informal agricultural activities, food supply chains, commercial and leisure activities, while at the same time providing solutions for environmental issues in cities. The Food and Agricultural Organization of the United Nations (FAO) defines the term as follows: 'Urban and peri-urban agriculture (UPA) can be defined as the growing of plants and the raising of animals within and around cities. Urban and peri-urban agriculture provides food products from different types of crops (grains, root crops, vegetables, mushrooms, fruits), animals (poultry, rabbits, goats, sheep, cattle, pigs, guinea pigs, fish, etc.) as well as non-food products (e.g. aromatic and medicinal herbs, ornamental plants, tree products). UPA includes trees managed for producing fruit and fuelwood, as well as tree systems integrated and managed with crops (agroforestry) and small-scale aquaculture' (FAO www.fao.org/urban-agricuture/en). The concept is multidimensional, and the many different activities can result in products and services that are created or produced for self-consumption, barter or sale. Urban agriculture involves a significant part of the world's population which FAO, using a relatively restricted definition, places at some eight hundred million practitioners and if back garden activities are added, can easily be doubled. Studies carried in settings that include Canada, France, Argentina, Ecuador, Mexico, and Brazil, tend to the conclusion that urban agriculture can contribute to many cross-cutting urban issues such as food safety, individual income generation, food education, environmental awareness, recuperation of green areas and public spaces, as well as boosting local economies (Deelstra and Girardet 2000; Nugent 2000).

The increased use of the term serves not only as a stimulus for new possibilities, but also as a way of making visible the many activities already present. The result, involving everything from commercial enterprises through street collectives, neighborhood food sharing and roof gardens, inevitably raises a number of challenges for public administration. How to rethink policy given the specificities of many singular experiences; how to rethink food flow and supply logistics, provide support for urban-rural businesses and how to link what goes in with what goes out in terms of the integrated management of 'urban waste'? Working to support basic conditions can lead to questions of access to land, farming supplies and credit for investment; can involve issues of urban zoning and a more hybrid use of urban space. Distribution may not just involve farmers markets and other similar outlets, but also rethinking street level activities and permissions for trade. Sustainable development may also involve access to technical support and training on food farming; themes that are not normally on the urban educational agenda. But it can also involve risk management, with a search for feasible solutions for working in areas where there is possible contamination of soil and water, or problems of land slippage and flooding.

Whilst all of this requires actions by communities, civil society, different levels of government as well as different market and commercial actors, there is no one best way of bringing the different sectors together, for the degree of organization and the nature of specific interests varies immensely. What is more, these are not themes where consensus can be guaranteed. How then can public, private and community-based organizations build up the links that are necessary for new patterns of sustainable urban development that actively produce some very basic forms of 'green' and 'livable'.

3.3   Orizânia, Minas Gerais, Brazil

3.3.1   Background and Starting Issues

Orizânia has 7700 inhabitants and is located in the interior of the State of Minas Gerais, 320 kilometers from the state capital. It was originally part of a rice producing area and became an independent municipality in 1997, by which time rice was giving way to coffee as the dominant local crop. Coffee has a seasonal cycle in which there is plenty of hard work and money during three to four months but, when this finishes, life for the coffee farms and for those family farmers that supplement their own small coffee holdings with work as seasonal laborers, is largely a matter of living off what has been saved and a few staple crops such as beans, corn and rice. Despite the availability of land, broader based market gardening either for personal or commercial objectives is not a tradition. Apart from food habits, there is also the fact that market gardening requires constant, seven days a week attention; a work pattern very different from that of coffee. Income flow is also very different and there is less support from the state-wide agricultural extension service, which in this region is heavily focused on coffee, one of Brazil's important export commodities. More important, however, is the question of markets. People may be persuaded to produce a broader range of crops for their own consumption but producing vegetables for commercial purposes requires thinking about demand and supply. The case would probably end at this point if it wasn't for changes taking place in three other spheres of government action: education, food security and family farming.

A key part of local education funding takes place through Federal grants and one of these areas is an often-ignored part of the back stage of education: school meals. School meals need ingredients which require purchasing contracts and suppliers. For many years this process was centralized at either state or national levels. Huge sums of money were involved, and industrial firms competed amongst themselves to provide 'nutritious' biscuits, noodles and other prefabricated foodstuffs that could be stocked in large quantities and distributed throughout this continental sized country.

Following the return to democracy in the 1980s, there was much debate about the quality of school meals, especially after poverty studies on food security pointed out that for many children it was, to all effects, the only meal of the day. This led the National School Food Program

(PNAE)[3] to place a special emphasis on fresh ingredients and suggested local sourcing in order to stimulate local economic development. In parallel, there was much discussion—and indeed conflict—in the agricultural arena about the lack of attention being given to the key role of small farmers or, to use the Brazilian expression, family-based farming in providing the everyday food requirements for the country. Eventually the two would come together in 2009 with a ruling that 30% of the funds passed by the National Educational Fund for school meals were to be supplied by small family farmers and local collectives.

3.3.2   Processes: Actions, Actors and Connections

Orizânia has about 1800 children in its eight schools, many of which are set in semi-rural or peri-urban locations. This might not seem a large market but in a setting where its inhabitants either depended on coffee, on local commercial activities or on working for the municipality, it was a potentially significant intervention in local economic life. As the then secretary of education said in 2013, 'we had children fainting in class because they had spent the whole week eating only rice and noodles; or who we had taken to the health center with severe headaches, only to find out they hadn't eaten anything'.[4]

The municipality already sourced most of its ingredients from local commerce which bought on the regional market and now needed to source 30% of this from local small holdings without a market gardening tradition. As well as dealing with the (negative) impact on local commerce, it also required creating new mechanisms to bring together individual smallholders as collective suppliers. Public sector purchasing depends on contracts which require legally registered parties; none of the small farmers had any form of business registration. Key here were two areas of action and connection. First, the mayor needed to learn how to balance the different interest within the municipality, those of the local commerce and those of the small local family farmers. Family farmers needed to be persuaded to change their habits and farming practices and there had to be a way of making formal and accountable purchases to follow the general laws of public sector finance and also to report back to the Federal

---

[3] PNAE is the Portuguese abbreviation for Programa Nacional de Alimentação Escolar.
[4] Secretary of Education of Orizânia in interview with Abreu, 23 October 2013.

Government. Second, someone had to organize the daily provision of school meals in the school kitchens.

As it turned out, it was somebody in this second arena who enabled this almost impossible set of factors to connect and move ahead: the municipal education department's school nutritionist. She was able to build bridges between those very different interests and turn everything into a 'plate of food'. Once she explained to farmers what she wanted, they went ahead and learned how to produce the different ingredients. Once the demand made sense and in doing so created a market, it was much easier to move on the question of purchasing rules and requirements. In this case it was the Orizânia branch of the Rural Workers' Trade Union that helped to provide the legitimate basis, and the physical space, for a newly formed Orizânia Rural Producers' Association, which became the bridge between farmers and the municipality; consolidated by the use of open public tendering calls.

3.3.3   Outcomes: Benefits, Difficulties and Successes

This all led to a change of culture where it became normal that children were eating food that had in part been produced by people they knew. The local commerce began to readjust itself around a new economy that included different vegetables and fruit; children and parents were nudged to appreciate a variation in different types of meals and new relationships were formed. The local commerce, that had previously been the sole suppliers, lost income but the income that was transferred to the family farmers generated other externalities. Convincing the farmers to diversify production in a setting where there was little support from the regional agency of the state-wide agricultural extension service was not easy. Here the ability and enthusiasm of the nutritionist to talk to everybody about the importance of program was a significant part of the success. The municipal Secretary of Education was another key actor in providing support for the nutritionist and in encouraging the Mayor to find a way through the conflicts and the public accounting requirements. A final piece in the jigsaw puzzle was the Secretary's offer of a single delivery point for nearly all the products purchased, thus reducing greatly the transport costs for farmers who, otherwise, would have to deliver different batches individually to each of the eight schools.

The Orizânia case involves a small population in which conversations and interviews are more directly linked to individual actions and decisions.

In bigger cities and more complex urban-rural settings much of the day today is out of sight and research studies have to rely on other bases of information, reports, documents and more general interviews. However, as we will argue in moving from just under 8000 inhabitants to São Paulo and Montreal, similar processes exist: specific ways of balancing possibilities and resources, identifying and translating the potential of policies, and creating mechanisms to move forward are key to building the connectivity that holds partnerships together. They are neither top down nor bottom up but, as we will show: side by side.

3.4   Urban Agriculture in São Paulo

3.4.1   Background and Starting Issues

São Paulo is marked by problems of socio-spatial distribution, resulting from very rapid population growth in the 1950s, 1960s and 1970s followed by high inflation and a financial crisis in the 1980s which led to firms either closing down or moving to other parts of the State. Over this period there was increasingly informal occupation of outlying districts, referred to as the periphery (see for example Holston 2009), with a lack of services and high degrees of social and material vulnerability. Here, poverty is higher and, as a result, food security has always been an issue.

The municipality has had a small urban agricultural program since 2003, but only launched its first food plan in 2016. Implementation has taken place in a disjointed manner, with problems of continuity and lack of clarity over the public involved. There is very little decentralized municipal government and different services adopt their own models of territorial administration. The thirty-two district administrations (sub-prefectures) have little responsibility apart from basic maintenance tasks. What advances have been achieved are mainly a result of the collective action of civil society and the links created between local leaders and urban farmers in specific regions. Where territorial based farmers associations exist, there is better access to public funding. But there are also neighborhood activities that connect community-based organizations, local services and street level public workers in settings where other sorts of resources are involved; those derived from the possibilities provided by individual professional jobs and personal time.

Urban agriculture also appears as part of varied public and civil society agendas each with their own action networks, consultative committees, policy proposals and pressures on budget priorities. These include activists and forums organized around food and nutrition security; around citizenship, rights and social inclusion; adequate housing; environmental education in schools; better living conditions; the right to the city; community health; general environmental stewardship as well as those concerned with urban agriculture for its own intrinsic reasons. What then, can this somewhat fragmented and at the most very loosely coupled arena tell us about partnerships and the development of more livable cities. We look at two areas: the first in the eastern periphery (*Zona Leste*) and the second in the Southern periphery (*Zona Sul*).

3.4.2   Processes: Actions, Actors, and Connections

3.4.2.1   São Paulo's East Zone

The East Zone Farmers' Association was founded in 2009 and brings together forty families and farmers in 14 areas of market gardens on public land and other idle areas. The initiative dates back to 2002 when farmers were informally growing vegetables along the banks of streams or under the public utility company's high-tension transmission lines. By chance, they came into contact with technical staff from the municipal urban planning department who were surveying the area as part of a new city-wide master plan. Not only was the master plan to be a key tool for urban planning, but the method that had been developed by the then progressive government included meetings with local residents to discuss their interests. Two themes emerged from the meetings: the possibility of using urban agriculture as a tool to preserve the environment and the importance of creating income generation projects that could include the existing farms. The result has been a more organic approach to farming which is important for preserving water sources[5] and raising nutritional standards, but also allows farmers to get a much better price for their produce. Today through engaging with different public, private, social and community actors and building up a variety of connections, the association supports other ecological farming enterprises and has created various sales outlets including four organic markets in the eastern zone and links with

---

[5] São Paulo, is 750 meters above sea level in the middle of a major hydrographic water basin.

organic shops and collectives located in wealthier areas of the city, operating on fair trade principles.

The city government provides support in two ways. First, since 2010, through the Ecological Agriculture Center set up by the Municipal Secretary for Economic Development which provides technical services, support, and guidance for product certification as well as special scholarship training grants for up to a year. Second, through a fund for the environment and sustainable development which supports NGO projects focusing on the sustainable use of natural resources, including maintenance, improvement, and/or restoration activities, environmental research and promotion.

Probably more important than the grants and technical support, have been the partnerships developed in the area of land-use. Legislation prohibits housing or any other permanent building underneath the high-tension power lines that run through different parts of São Paulo. These form unused green ribbons of land that are ideal for market gardening. The former state utility company, which is now privatized, agreed to cede the land to the farmers on a loan-for-use basis. Increased visibility has also helped connections with NGOs working on environmental and food security issues and, more recently, some of the more centrally located Universities have begun to carry out extension and research projects in the region.

3.4.2.2 São Paulo's South Zone

Land occupation in the peripheral south zone is more recent that in the east zone and happened more rapidly and even more chaotically. A great deal of the growth took place during the period of military government in the late 1960s and 1970s when local government and public services were far from a priority. The south zone as a whole, surrounds a reservoir that supplies 40% of the city's drinking water and includes a number of environmental protection areas. Part of it is traditionally rural, part also has indigenous Guarani communities and part is characterized by high density, flat roofed, semi-formal and self-built housing.

It is in the last area that our research is taking place. The subprefecture of M'Boi Mirim is home to nearly 680,000 people. Very different to the east zone where associations were being formed and there was visible government activity, here initial questions about agricultural practices led to blank expressions. Fortunately, by working through rights-based community organizations it was possible to get closer to some of the activities taking place. These included commercial allotments, community gardens, and school and domestic gardens. In terms of actors, projects, and networks, we found local social organizations, associations, incubators, individual educators, farmers, and street-level public sector workers. Everything was very local and often fragmented. This led to two lines of analysis: one looking at the connections between urban agriculture practices (commercial, social, school and domestic) and the different policy arenas such as food education, preventive health and local development, and the second to the organizational processes involved.

The results suggest that here, urban agriculture is emerging through other public agendas: in education, as part of health-support activities, addressing environmental issues, in income generation, and in community development and social activities. Each of these different settings has its own logic that guides the everyday work of government officials, street level workers and local leaders, not in programs, projects and much less policies, but through the informal use of everyday resources and institutional structures to drive public actions.

For example, the state and municipal educational authorities have optional programs that support school gardens in which probably around 20% of schools take part. Those involved suggest that success depends on school gardens being seen as part of a teaching approach that integrates the garden into the classroom and integrates the school into the community. Critical here is the engagement of school principals and educational counselors who are part of local social movements dedicated to reducing urban vulnerabilities.

Whilst the idea of gardens in schools and linking food to education may seem more straightforward (although there are still many schools in Europe sitting on empty plots of land), the relationship between health and environment is less direct. In 2008, the São Paulo Health Secretariat created the Healthy and Green Environment Program (PAVS)[6] as a joint effort between the city's Environment, Health, and Social secretariats. The program is designed to create a combined agenda for health and environmental policies, guided by strengthening inter-sector work at the local level. Key has been a new street level professional who works in each of the local health centers alongside the community health agents (street level health workers that act as a liaison between the clinics and families). PAVS uses a similar idea in linking environment with health and doing so on a

[6] PAVS is the Portuguese abbreviation for Programa Ambiente Verdes e Saudáveis.

territorial basis, fitting actions to circumstances. Here health center gardens are beginning to appear as places to talk about healthier ways of life and, along with some of the school gardens, are serving as points for local activists to connect to public sector organizations.

On the environmental front, the region is increasingly being caught in the tensions between the need for housing and the need to preserve the water catchment sources of São Paulo's largest reservoir. Here early initiatives came from civil society organizations active in the environmental arena but more recently more hybrid forums of public, community movements and at times private and public-private enterprises have taken a lead (Borges 2018; Callon et al. 2011). One such is the Water Forum set up in 2017 by local schools, residents associations and community groups with the support of various universities. It is still at an early stage and the contradictions and conflicts between informal land invasions, social housing demands, local residents and environment are many, but at least the different groupings are beginning to listen to each other. Its recent annual seminar (2018) brought some 150 people together and as was commented: 'we might not have got very far, but at least we are prepared to accept that housing issues and environmental issues are on the same page'. Here urban agriculture begins to gather support as a potential boundary maintaining activity for green areas.

3.4.3   Outcomes: Benefits Difficulties and Successes

São Paulo is still at an early stage as a green city; but as the above examples show, things are happening. That most of the initiatives come from either civil society or, when public, come from those most directly linked to the every-day of public action, might provide a clue as to the importance of supporting flexible, local actions, including here the provision of other street level professionals, rather that investing in major investment projects.

Different from the more direct approach in Orizânia, in São Paulo we see urban agriculture gradually becoming visible as part of a number of different policy areas (education, health and environment). Territoriality is important and making land usable and public has wider implications. In the *East Zone* the partnership with the Electricity Company was key to using the land under the high-tension pylons, which if left would probably become informal rubbish deposits. The *South Zone* has yet to come to terms with this question; the situation here is more complex because the area is a water catchment area. In both regions, territorial based civil society organizations are important, but equally so is the way in which street level public service workers use the flexibility and discretionary autonomy of their work roles to help support local actions, a usually undervalued resource.

3.5   Urban Agriculture in Montreal, Canada

3.5.1   Background and Starting Issues

Montreal has a multi-level governmental arrangement which includes the wider Montreal Metropolitan Community; the Urban Agglomeration of Montreal (a smaller inter municipal arrangement) and the municipality of Montreal with its 19 boroughs each with its own legislative and political processes. The boroughs are in charge of managing local affairs, including social issues, culture, sports, leisure, and parks. Some public services, such as transportation, policing, water resources, and economic development are the joint responsibility of the Metropolitan Community and the Urban Agglomeration. However, if Montreal's decentralized administration helps relationships with non-governmental organizations and other community organizations, it also presents a challenge for integrated planning.

In Montreal, Urban Agriculture was traditionally a leisure activity supported, since 1973, by the local government Community Garden Program, now managed in partnership with community groups. These began to expand in the 1990s to include collective gardens, greenhouses, beekeeping, mushroom cultivation, rooftop gardens, and different initiatives that mixed technology, innovation and entrepreneurship (Duchemin and Vermette 2016). In expanding, they grew to include ideas of environmental and food education, community development and also lead to entrepreneurial activities with positive impacts on employment generation and the local economy.

Montreal faced three challenges with urban agriculture. The first, common to many other areas of government action, was that major policies that imply changes to law cannot be brought in as a single legislative act but must be negotiated with each of the 19 boroughs. The second, more specific, is that, unlike other Canadian provinces which have decentralized health budgets and policies to the cities, the province of Quebec retains central control. Given that many cities structure their urban food policies around the health sector, the lack of a decentralized health structure created additional difficulties. Finally, the province traditionally considered agriculture as a rural issue linked to mainline commercial farming. Seen from the side of government, the result was an institutional void for urban agriculture, and it was the local collectives and community organizations, as well as Montreal's Universities that were to turn urban agriculture into a public issue and change public, environmental and food practices. Today an estimated 43% of the population practices some kind of urban agriculture; in backyards, on sidewalks, in schools and public spaces.

3.5.2   Processes: Actions, Actors and Connections

While community gardens in Montreal are partnerships between citizens and the district government, collective gardens are managed through a partnership between citizens and community organizations. The first collective garden in Montreal was created by 'Action Communiterre' in 1998, in the Notre-Dame-de-Grace neighborhood, and later merged with the neighborhood's food bank (Now the Depot Community Food Centre)[7] which has been working since 1986 to tackle issues of food security. After this, the idea of collective gardens began to spread under the coordination of local community organizations that manage the land, organize access, tools and help coach community gardeners.

Some still remain gardens, others have created connections with food hub[8] activities, such as collective kitchens, marketing and composting. For example, the Santropol Roulant[9] food-hub describes itself as an intergenerational community, with some two thousand volunteers brought together by 'food and community engagement for a healthy, well-fed and close-knit city'. The hub consists of a collective garden, a kitchen, a 'meals on wheels' service, food baskets, a market and a farm in the peri-urban region of Senneville. Carrefour Alimentaire Centre-Sud[10] is another example that works not only as an internal food hub, but also in partnership with eleven other organizations to build what they term an edible

---

[7] www.depotmtl.org/en/. Accessed on 25 September, 2019.

[8] Food hubs in commercial agriculture are distribution arrangements concerned with: supporting local economies at fair trade prices; environmental and farmland preservation; expanding access to fresh food and more humane animal practices. The expression is used in Montreal in the same way at the micro level of inner-city districts and even blocks.

[9] www.santropolroulant.org.en. Accessed on 25 September, 2019.

[10] www.carrefouralimentaire.org. Accessed on 25 September, 2019.

neighborhood (Notre Quartier Nourricier[11]), starting from the community green house, expanding to gardens, kitchens and local social economy markets.

Apart from the community garden initiatives, the main local government response to strengthen the civic culture on gardening was the Éco-quartier Program, established in 1995 by the city of Montreal to promote environmental initiatives focused on education and community life. The program offers finance and guidelines for action by non-governmental organizations that have experience with community, social, and environmental projects. It is funded by the municipality, but there is no centralized coordination and neighborhood CSOs are responsible for their implementation. To bring these together, an independent forum, the Regroupement des Éco-quartiers, was created as a space for discussion between all the different organizations involved.

> *The Eco-quartier Program has two fronts, one environmental and the other social. We try to combine these two dimensions to improve the lives of Montreal residents. Most of the Eco-quartiers indeed offer urban agriculture projects. The focus is not on intensive production, but rather on improving community relations and provide tips and techniques on urban agriculture*[12]. (Coordinator of the Regroupement des Éco-quartiers—Group of Montreal Éco-Quartiers, Interview June 2016)

The program works in four areas: cleaning up alleys and public roads; the ecological management of solid residues, which includes recycling containers, selective garbage collection and composting workshops; distributing and planting flowers; and promoting urban agriculture, planting trees and replenishing vegetation in vacant areas. The emphasis is on supporting ongoing citizen-based projects which can be local or even international in inspiration. Examples are the 'Incredible Edible' and 'Le Mange Trottoir' movements, which have sprouted in Montreal and other cities worldwide to create food gardens on city sidewalks (Giacchè and Porto 2018). The program also supports social entrepreneurship initiatives in the area of environmental and community services, many of which are run by young citizens.

---

[11] www.quartiernourricier.com. Accessed on 25 September, 2019.
[12] Translation from French by authors. www.eco-quartiers.org/programme_ecoquartiers. Accessed on 25 September, 2019.

Important contributions have come from the four Montreal universities, all of which have urban agriculture projects with applied research centers as well as undergraduate and postgraduate students working on urban agricultural questions. This has led to many links with community organizations, as well as encouraging young professionals to create social businesses. One of the early University—community initiatives started in 2004 at the McGill Campus as a partnership between two community service organizations, the Santropol Roulant and Alternatives, and a network from the Distance Learning University of Quebec (TÉLUQ) (Duchemin and Vermette 2016). The purpose was to produce fresh food for people facing social vulnerability. Starting on the rooftop of the TÉLUQ building, it later moved to the central campus of McGill University and became the Edible Campus project. McGill University also manages a rural property in Montreal's agricultural zone, as well as gardens and a greenhouse on its campus. Its Biology College works in partnership with a local social food hub. Another example is the University of Quebec at Montreal (UQAM), where the School of Environmental Studies has two research centers linked to urban agriculture. As well as applied research, consultancy and the incubation of social and technological projects with young professionals, they are also active in promoting courses, workshops, networks and policy discussions in partnership with community-based organizations. Projects being incubated in partnership with the Ministry of Agriculture, Fisheries and Food, include wine growing, micro-greens, composting with insects and aquaponics. Yet another example is Concordia University which has two key areas of action: the Concordia Greenhouse, which is open from September to April when Montreal often experiences freezing temperatures, and the Loyola City Farm School which is open from April to September. The two projects are integrated and allow contact with urban agriculture throughout the year. Even in the midst of the winter, the Greenhouse offers education activities, prepares seedlings, and grows mushrooms. Finally, the Université de Montréal, has a student initiative focused on sustainability and environmental sciences. Students work voluntarily in gardens, with beekeeping, and mushroom cultivation and in other partnerships with community projects, workshops and courses.

3.5.3   Outcomes: Benefits, Difficulties and Successes

As can be seen from the examples, the Montreal case is a broad-based front of loosely articulated partnerships moving along different routes but in the same overall direction towards a greener, more equal and livable city. It is not one, but many movements. There are micro—connections at a very local level, community—non-governmental partnerships, local government financing initiatives and different kinds of private sector and university engagement. The university initiatives have initiated a number of entrepreneurial social and commercial enterprises and at a micro-level there have been a number of income-generating enterprises. There have been difficulties, some of them structural and others about learning to cooperate across different organizational cultures and forms of economic intervention. But there have also been successes. Below, we would like to concentrate on some of the bottom-up initiatives that have created forums for planning and public action.

Firstly, at the neighborhood level, two initiatives play an important role in gathering citizen collectives and community organizations together. The first is Cultiver Montreal,[13] an urban agriculture festival that takes place in 14 different neighborhoods, organized by the City of Montreal in partnership with NGOs. The festival includes workshops, sales and exchanges of plants and produce, information booths on gardening and spaces for local collectives to showcase their projects. The second is through the Neighborhood Table (Table de Quartier),[14] an initiative by the Public Health and Social Development departments to build inter sectoral collaboration and planning at the neighborhood level. The Neighborhood Table is a network coalition that involves direct citizen participation as well as organizations for health, education, environment, social service and culture of which urban agriculture and food are becoming increasingly important.

At the municipal level, the Food Policy Council has become the main organization for partnerships, participative planning and coordination of territorial food systems in Montreal as a whole. The council was formed as a public health initiative and later incorporated a community-based movement to strengthen existing networks and planning initiatives: the Working Group on Urban Agriculture (Martorell 2017). The Working Group had

---

[13] www.cultivermontreal.ca. Accessed on 25 September, 2019.
[14] www.tablesdequartiermontreal.org. Accessed on 25 September, 2019.

collected 29,000 signatures on a petition to demand public authorities to carry out open consultations on 'The State of Urban Agriculture in Montreal' (Montreal 2012). The aim was to use the study to help government thinking on the place of urban agriculture in the city and to develop plans and initiatives that included urban agriculture as a strategic activity in building a sustainable city. With the Working Group being incorporated in the Food Policy Council, bottom-up planning became an official strategy for the city.

3.6   CONCLUSION

Public action, as many authors have argued, refers not just to the actions of governments for and on behalf of the public, but also to those actions initiated by the public to put pressure on governments to adopt new agendas, as well as those actions that people initiate by and for themselves. This certainly is the conclusion based on the three cases that we have presented in this chapter. In each case, we have seen a variety of partnerships, including different ways of working together, and of connecting opportunities and using resources. Some are more formal than others, some create new organizations and institutions and others just agree on a *modus vivendi*.

If there are some underlying conclusions these are firstly, that these different bits and pieces are territorial, rooted in places and part of the day to day of those involved. Secondly, that those involved have discretionary power; they have the resources which they can use as citizens, neighbors and professionals. Finally, that despite we are inclined to believe that policies and projects come from somewhere 'up there', in fact they come from somewhere 'over there' (in the interaction between different stakeholders) and have to be made sense of 'here'.

REFERENCES

Abreu, K.D. (2014). *A implementação do Programa Nacional de Alimentação Escolar (PNAE) em Municípios de Pequena Porte: implicações práticas e teóricas.* Unpublished masters dissertation. Programa de Administração Pública e Governo, Fundação Getulio Vargas, São Paulo.

Ansell, C., & Torfing, J. (Eds.). (2016). *Handbook on theories of governance.* Cheltenham/Northampton: Edward Elgar Publishing.

Borges, Zilma (2018). Perspectivas Territoriais na Produção da Ação Pública entre Sociedade e Estado. *Revista Nau Social,* v. 9, pp. 24–32.

Callon, M., Lascoumes, M., & Barthe, Y. (2011). *Acting in an uncertain world: An essay on technical democracy.* Cambridge, MA: The MIT Press.

Deelstra, T., & Girardet, H. (2000). Urban agriculture and sustainable cities. In N. Bakker, M. Dubbeling, S. Guendel, U. S. Koschella, & H. de Zeeuw (Eds.), *Growing cities growing food: Urban agriculture on the policy agenda* (pp. 43–65). Feldafing: DSE: German Foundation for International Development.

Dewey, J. (1927). *The public and its problems.* New York: Holt.

Duchemin, E., & Vermette, J. P. (2016). Montréal, ville nourricière. In J. Cockrall-King (Ed.), *La revolution de l'agriculture urbaine* (pp. 282–298). Québec: Éditions Écosociété.

Farah, M. F. S., & Spink, P. K. (2008). Subnational government innovation in a comparative perspective: Brazil. In S. Borins (Ed.), *Innovations in government: Research, recognition and replication* (pp. 71–92). Washington, DC: The Brookings Institution.

Food and Agricultural Organization of the United Nations (FAO). www.fao.org/urban-agricuture/en. Accessed 13 May 2019.

Giacchè, G., & Porto, L. (2018). The incredible edible movement. *Nature and Culture, 13*(1), 93–112.

Holston, J. (2009). *Insurgent citizenship: Disjunctions of democracy and modernity in Brazil.* Princeton: Princeton University Press.

Marres, N. (2007). The issue deserves more credit: Pragmatist contributions to the study of public involvement in controversy. *Social Studies of Science, 37*(5), 759–780.

Martorell, H. (2017). The evolution of city-region food governance in Montreal food politics. *Policy and planning under Quebec's neoliberal Turn.* Master Thesis presented at Concordia University, Montreal, Canada.

Montreal. (2012). *État de l'agriculture urbaine à Montréal.* Office de Consultation Publique de Montréal. Agence pour la santé et des services sociaux à Montréal.

Nugent, R. (2000). The impact of urban agriculture on the household and local economies. In N. Bakker, M. Dubbeling, S. Guendel, U. Sabel Koschella, & H. de Zeeuw (Eds.), *Growing cities growing food: Urban agriculture on the policy agenda* (pp. 67–95). Feldafing: DSE: German Foundation for International Development.

Porto de Oliveira, L.C. (2017). *Redes, idéias e ação pública na agricultura urbana: os casos de São Paulo, Montreal e Toronto.* Unpublished doctoral thesis: Programa de Administração Pública e Governo, Fundação Getulio Vargas, São Paulo.

Rhodes, R. A. W. (1996). The new governance: Governing without government. *Political Studies, 44*(4), 652–667.

Spink, P. K. (2019). *Beyond public policy: A public action languages approach.* Cheltenham/Northampton: Edward Elgar Publishing.

CHAPTER 4

From Gray to Green Cities: Tilburg, Melbourne, San Jose, and Cape Town

Cor van Montfort and Ank Michels

4.1   INTRODUCTION

In recent decades, many cities have transformed from 'gray' into 'green' cities. Some are former industrial towns, where air and noise pollution used to be commonplace; others are fast-growing cities where numerous stakeholders compete with one another for the use of space for

We wish to thank Florent Beurret, Xander de Vries, Florence Li, Julia Neuenhaus, Nne Amakar Oguejiofor and Nick Rurangwa Nshimiyen, for their outstanding research for the Outreaching Lab 'From gray to green' at Tilburg University in The Netherlands. This chapter is largely based on their research but the authors are fully responsible for any possible mistakes in the text.

C. van Montfort (✉)
Tilburg Center for Regional Law and Governance (TiREG),
Tilburg University, Tilburg, The Netherlands

Vrije Universiteit Amsterdam, Amsterdam, The Netherlands
e-mail: c.j.vanmontfort@tilburguniversity.edu

A. Michels
Utrecht University School of Governance, Utrecht, The Netherlands
e-mail: a.m.b.michels@uu.nl

© The Author(s) 2020

C. van Montfort, A. Michels (eds.), *Partnerships for Livable Cities*,
https://doi.org/10.1007/978-3-030-40060-6_4

infrastructure, housing, and green areas. Whatever the circumstances, the result has been a growing awareness of the value of green space in the city; urban nature and green rooftops filter the air, and parks and green corridors offer city residents relatively quiet places of refuge, where they can walk and relax.

In this chapter, we explore the interaction between municipalities and other actors in four cities that have been successful in the transformation from a gray into a green city: Tilburg (The Netherlands), Melbourne (Australia), San Jose (USA), and Cape Town (South Africa). Compelling questions are: what were the drivers for this transformation (why), what has been done to make the city greener (what and by whom), and what are the main factors that contributed to this transformation (factors). We are particularly interested in the role of context and of the characteristics of the partnership.

The selected cities all exhibit some form of partnership between the government and other parties when it comes to establishing and maintaining green spaces. Furthermore, in order to be better able to study the role of context in the transformation towards a greener city, we selected four cities in different parts of the world: Tilburg in the Netherlands, Melbourne in Australia, the Californian city of San Jose in the United States, and Cape Town in South Africa. All are relatively wealthy cities, but differ in other respects, including the impacts of climatological, geographic, and socio-demographic factors.

We take the plans, policies, and initiatives of the municipal governments as a starting point and explore how government interacts with other parties in order to achieve a greener city. The findings presented in this chapter are based on documents (such as policy documents, coalition agreements, and reports by non-governmental organizations) and websites.

We start with a brief discussion of the literature on partnerships and green spaces. In Sect. 4.3 we describe how the transformation into a green city started in each of the cities. In Sect. 4.4, we describe recent developments in plans, policies, and initiatives for a greener city. The final sections present an explorative analysis of the main factors that have contributed to this transformation and a conclusion.

4.2 Urban Green Spaces and the Role of Partnerships

The planning and maintenance of urban green spaces were traditionally the responsibility of the municipality or local governments (James et al. 2009). However, over the past decades, both the role and responsibility of governments in green space development have changed (Leroy & Arts 2006). Environmental governance is no longer purely government dominated, but also involves civic society, as well as the market (Fors et al. 2015, p. 723). Urban governments are urging for shared responsibilities and facilitating or seeking partnerships with other actors (Leroy and Arts 2006). Within the scope of the triangular relationship between the different stakeholders—state, market, and civil society—presented in the introductory chapter (Fig. 1.1), multiple forms of partnerships can be distinguished (see also: Van Montfort et al. 2014, p. 10).

In the majority of cases, local government is still heavily involved in the creation or regeneration of urban green spaces, although with different partners varying from, for example, social housing trusts (see Dempsey et al. 2016; O'Brien, 2006) to residents (see Drake and Lawson 2015; Marche 2015; Bendt et al. 2013), businesses (see Pincetl 2010; Clement and Kanai 2015), other governmental bodies (see Slater et al. 2016; Shafer et al. 2000; Kabisch 2015) and various NGOs (see Nastran and Regina 2016; Moskell and Allred 2013; Kozová et al. 2018).

Yet, the bulk of all such partnerships are between public and civil society organizations (e.g. O'Brien 2006; Nastran and Regina 2016). What sometimes starts as a bottom-up initiative taken by residents and citizens' organizations, often later develops as a collaboration between civil society, private sector and (local) government in which public organizations become responsible for facilitating or funding the project (e.g. Kabisch 2015; Shafer et al. 2000). Finally, more formal forms of public-private partnerships are also seen. Characteristic for these is that responsibilities between government(s) and private companies or consortiums are formalized in contracts (e.g. Clement and Kanai 2015).

The role of partnerships in establishing and maintaining green spaces is usually seen as a positive one. Partnerships contribute to the creation of green spaces where, without the involvement of other parties, this would not have been possible. As funding becomes tighter, it helps if volunteers or private companies form a partnership with the local authorities to improve facilities. Also, by involving the local community, urban green spaces can become more tailored to their needs and people value them more. The literature reveals a broad array of improvements stemming from the participation of other parties, from simply cleaning up the park, installing benches, restoring playgrounds, putting up information signs, to (volunteer-run) services such as walking tours or a café (Dempsey et al. 2016; Mathers et al. 2015; Barnes and Sharpe 2009; Kozová et al. 2018; Barker & Kenney 2012; Sipilä and Tyrväinen 2005; Huang 2010; Slater et al. 2016; Lutafali and Khoja 2011).

The literature also shows that bottom-up initiatives, such as community gardens, are clearly associated with high levels of self-reported social cohesion (Marche 2015; Bendt et al. 2013; Rosol 2010). Volunteers valued the time they spent together, viewing this as an important aspect of their involvement (Barnes and Sharpe 2009). This is less so for top-down initiatives. O'Brien (2006) found that some respondents in her study saw more community involvement in the partnership as a means to regain a community spirit. Various projects were designed to regenerate urban green spaces in poor neighborhoods and involved the community to build a greater social cohesion (Dempsey et al. 2016; Slater et al. 2016; Lutafali and Khoja 2011). According to Chanan (2003), this fits into a more general trend for community engagement in deprived areas to be part of a structured intervention by local authority-led partnerships.

Although local authorities sometimes initiate partnerships to improve the overall conditions in impoverished neighborhoods with the aim of building more social cohesion, an adverse effect may also occur, namely, gentrification. The presence of urban green space has a positive effect on estimated property values (Donovan and Butry 2010). Tree canopy cover is found to correlate with median household income; the tree canopy cover in poor neighborhoods is therefore lower in comparison to that of wealthier communities (Pincetl 2010). Hence, as Wolch et al. (2014) state, the challenge is to make the city green 'enough' without necessarily pushing the original residents out of their neighborhoods.

4.3   How It Started

4.3.1   Tilburg

Tilburg flourished during the age of the Industrial revolution. The city was essentially a patchwork of individual neighborhoods that each were home to a number of wool factories. Tilburg, in 1881, counted as many as

145 woolen mills. The woolen textile industry dominated in Tilburg and gave the city its identity. Tilburg was heavily impacted by the Second World War, during which a large part of its built heritage was destroyed by enemy bombings. The city managed to retain its status as the wool capital of the Netherlands after the war, but in the decades following, the wool industry slowly disappeared, a process that lasted until the 1980s. In addition, upon his inauguration as mayor in 1957, Cees Becht set in motion a process of urban renewal. He sought to future-proof the city by tearing down many of the old wool factories and replacing these with housing projects or roads. The city's built heritage, already in a precarious state, was not spared by mayor Becht, during whose tenure innumerable historical buildings and monuments were destroyed to make way for the city ring and to accommodate the future growth of the city.

In the following decades, urban greening as a policy issue failed to strike a chord in Tilburg, even though smaller local efforts and projects were already under way in an effort to turn Tilburg into a greener city. The Dongevallei is one such project, which involved creating a green valley that crossed straight through a residential neighborhood.

In 2010, Tilburg's first Climate Program was drafted at the request of the municipality of Tilburg (Gemeente Tilburg 2010a) by the Hotspot core team. This initial report provided some of the starting points for Tilburg's transition into a green city. Pinpointing the exact moment of the transition is a difficult task; nevertheless, arguably, the seeds were planted somewhere in the 1990s, when, following the urban renewal projects carried out in the inner city area, for the first time conscious thought was given to making Tilburg a greener city. The true transition began to take shape after 2010, a process that especially accelerated in 2014, when the left wing-center political coalition in the municipality declared its commitment to making the city of Tilburg more attractive, inter alia in terms of aesthetics. One approach was to increase the amount of urban green space, a proposition that was also mentioned in the coalition agreement (2014). The first major green project was initiated soon after: the Spoorpark, which will be elaborated on later.

4.3.2 *Melbourne*

The colonial administration of Melbourne, especially in the time of the famous Governor Charles La Trobe, set aside significant tracts of land in the nineteenth century and turned these into green open spaces. These areas, mostly in the form of city gardens and parks, generally surrounded the central city area, which therefore formed a green city ring. The lands on which the parks were established were inhabited by the indigenous Kulin Nation Groups before the settlement of Melbourne.

These parks, created in the nineteenth century, still exist today and their appearance is highly influenced by the colonial interest at the time in the potential of trees and plants from around the globe. Most of the parks, including the Fitzroy Gardens and the Royal Park, are now protected heritage sites, listed on the Victorian Heritage Register or even UNESCO.

However, these green spaces have not always been protected. The original nineteenth century green inner-city ring established by the colonial administration endured continuous erosion in the twentieth century due to the expansion of the city. To counter the erosion, the city of Melbourne has, in the last 40 years, tried to implement an urban planning policy based on a twin spatial application of green wedges; rural non-urban spaces at the edges of urban Melbourne, separating radial urban growth corridors. Through the application of this policy, the green wedges were connected to each other and have formed a true green city belt (Gurran and Miller 2008, p. 62).

From 1993 until 2002, a neo-liberal governance regime caused urban planning to erode Melbourne's green wedges. However, from 2002 onward, Melbourne has continued to implement its green planning policy and has rapidly grown into one of the greenest cities in the world (Gurran and Miller 2008, p. 61). And in 2012, the Melbourne City Council initiated its Open Space Strategy: the overarching strategy when it comes to green open spaces for the next 15 years. Open spaces are publicly owned land used for nature conservation, passive outdoor enjoyment and recreation. Examples are public parks, waterways, major sporting venues, public gardens etc. (City of Melbourne 2012a, pp. 3–4; b). The main goal of this strategy is to make sure that green open spaces are within walking distance of the community, which poses a significant challenge as the population continues to grow. Green spaces are considered important to promote social connectedness, mental health and wellbeing, physical health and wellbeing, biodiversity, etc. Changing (climate) conditions, which brings a new set of challenges to the management of green spaces, is the second main reason for establishing the Open Space Strategy.

4.3.3   San José

San José was originally an agricultural community but has since transformed into a developed urban area. In an effort to accommodate a burgeoning population after World War II, the city expanded rapidly, which resulted in a badly structured suburban community that was lampooned in an article called How Gray is My Valley (Brown-Goebeler 1991) that appeared in the 1991 November issue of Time Magazine. Since the 1990s, San José has striven to improve its urban planning and to focus on smart growth. The goal was to optimize the existing space, rather than growing outward and expanding physically, in line with the concept of smart growth; hence to avoid urban sprawl by providing walkable urban centers, foster sustainable development and to strengthen natural and cultural resources with the focus on public health, thereby facilitating a sense of community.

Over the past decades, San José has been working on various plans and visions that focus on innovation, sustainability, greening etc. One example is the general Green Vision, which was adopted in 2007, with ten goals related to economic growth and environmental conservation to be achieved by 2022. While most of these goals focus on environmental efforts in general, goal 9 and 10 of the plan include practical efforts to construct more trails and to plant trees to make the city greener. One specific plan that San José is currently focusing on is the Greenprint, which encompasses tangible green aspects and their implications for the community rather than environmental aspects in general. In early 1999, San José started the planning process to work towards this comprehensive urban greening goal. The Greenprint is a long-term strategic framework that focuses on the community's needs and guides the city's Recreation and Neighborhood Service Department in planning and developing parks, trails, and community facilities over the next twenty years with the primary goal of defining their sites and how they will operate. Its mission is '[t]o build healthy communities through people, parks and programs' (City of San José 2011).

The Greenprint was adopted in September 2000 and was updated in 2009, and again in 2018 (the name has been changed into 'Activate SJ'). These updates were made to reflect the progress attained to date and to elaborate on the City Council's current and future goals to provide its citizens and the community with the best possible 'natural, educational, social, cultural and economic environments in which one can live, work and play' (City of San José 2009).

4.3.4   Cape Town

In 1840, the City of Cape Town was officially recognized as a municipality. An industrial revolution soon followed, involving the construction of railways, the mining of gold and diamonds and the emergence of a port that steadily gained in importance on the continent of Africa. Due to the growing port, the town gradually transitioned into a modern naval base possessing various establishments such as fish-smoking, wool processing and boat building establishments. The growth of the port brought with it a demand for fresh produce from farms. This demand for fresh products led to a chain reaction that caused an increase in the value and use of farmland, and the number of dairy farms, poultry farms, vegetable farms and flower farms climbed. During the world wars, overseas manufacturers established branches and factories in the Cape Colony.

In the seventeenth century, the Dutch East India Company decided that the colony should become a refreshment outpost for the VOC ships on their way to Asia (South African History Online). It was this decision that led to Cape Town's development into a leading city for the production of fresh produce and to its emergence as a wine producer. This initiative aided the settlers of Cape Town, possibly unknowingly, in promoting a green environment.

In 2001 the city of Cape Town introduced the Integrated Metropolitan Environmental Policy (City of Cape Town 2017), a city-wide environmental initiative aimed at promoting a green transformation. This plan was revised in 2008 and in 2017 replaced by the Environmental Strategy for the City of Cape Town. This strategy aims to 'enhance, protect and manage Cape Town's natural and cultural resources for long term prosperity, in a way that optimizes economic opportunities and promotes access and social well-being' (p. 11). One of its guiding principles is the promotion and prioritizing of the education and empowerment of all citizens of Cape Town (p. 18), designed, among other things, to 'enable citizens to engage with the City on an ongoing basis on ways to improve implementation of the City's environmental principles.'

In summary, the beginning of a transformation towards greening the city was mostly due to a felt sense of urgency, fueled not only by economic reasons—the need to make the city more attractive for investors—but also by the desire to fight urban sprawl, or to adapt the city to the ongoing process of climate change. In recent decades, cities have also felt the need to boost the level of livability in terms of health, an attractive environment, and recreation.

4.4   Policy, Plans, and Initiatives

4.4.1   Tilburg

From the 1990s onwards, a lasting and accelerating trend towards urban greening has emerged. In Tilburg, the city council drafted in 2010 its 'Nota Groen. Dichter bij Groen' (Gemeente Tilburg 2010b) memorandum based on input from its citizens, which laid down one of its earlier visions for structuring green areas in the city. More concrete steps were taken after the council's coalition agreement in 2014. Several parties were involved.

The city council, most notably the Socialist Party and the Dutch green party, GroenLinks (Green Left), set the process in motion by ordering investigations into the structure and locations of green space in Tilburg, and later by drawing up reports on the way urban green space in Tilburg ought to look in the future. The council has played a continuous role; in fact, were it not for the council, a transition may never have been initiated, let alone sustained.

Moreover, the role of Tilburg's citizens has been equally important, as, especially in recent years, they gave added impetus to Tilburg's green transition. For example, one of the larger projects, the Spoorpark project was essentially initiated by a group of local citizens who wanted to do something with the empty area behind their apartment building. Today, right next to the train rails, a large city park is being created. Initially, the zoning plan had specified only very generally that the land was to be developed as a green open space for recreation. However, the coalition agreement of 2014–2018 included a declaration that involving local citizens in that the city's development plans was a priority for the city council (Gemeente Tilburg 2014). Not long afterward, the local government set up a team to develop more concrete ideas for the park and to take into account the wishes of the residents. The team consisted of multiple stakeholders, including neighborhood councils, the local beach volleyball association, and Midpoint, an alliance whose members include (local) entrepreneurs, the government and educational institutions. In addition, the city of

Tilburg created a website where citizens could submit their ideas and input on the new city park. In a later phase, this citizen input became much more important. 82 different plans for the Spoorpark were put forward by (groups of) citizens and implemented in Spoorpark. Among these were initiatives from the local boy and girl scout troops, and ideas for a city camping area and beach volleyball court. The project initially progressed only due to the efforts of the citizens. The result of the inclusive process is a city park in which the preferences of the residents have been implemented but which is also congruent with the initial use of the area allocated by the Tilburg city council. While the project was originally driven forward by the people, during the later stages, as the project expanded, this proved no longer feasible. From that point onwards, professional organizations, i.e., construction companies and landscape architects were contacted to take the project to the next level. The local government paid € 8.2 million for the construction of the park and contributes € 200.000 per year towards its maintenance. The government also tries to attract local volunteers, provincial subsidies and private money from local companies for maintenance and the further development of the park (Jongerius 2019).

In addition to this, many small-scale green initiatives from citizens are financially supported by the municipality. For example, over 500 *geveltuintjes*, or façade gardens, have been planted in the city after the municipality earmarked resources for this in 2015 (Gemeente Tilburg 2015). These are small garden strips at the front of houses lacking a front yard. Another initiative is seeking to make 1000 gardens in Tilburg more water friendly, with more green as an integral part of this.

Finally, the civil organization CAST (Centre for Architecture and Urban Planning) has been an important linking factor between the municipality and citizens. By organizing plenary sessions with citizens on a regular basis to discuss the future of the Green City of Tilburg, CAST has unquestionably accelerated the transition by engaging with the citizens and encouraging active thinking about the need for green.

4.4.2   Melbourne

As in the past, Melbourne's local government is still responsible for most of the projects which help sustain Melbourne's transformation into an even greener city. On the website of the Melbourne municipality, many of the plans can be found that the city council has introduced to make Melbourne one of the greenest cities in the world.

Currently, there are multiple ongoing projects initiated by the City Council. The most important in terms of urban green is the aforementioned 2012 Open Space Strategy. As the name suggests, this is more of a long-term policy strategy, an overarching project, than an individual project in the traditional sense of the word. The Open Space Strategy aims to provide direction on:

1. 'the unprecedented demand for open space as Melbourne's population continues to grow;
2. climate change—a decade of drought, water restrictions and extreme weather and the predicted impacts of climate change provide additional challenges in the management of parks and reserves and the role they can play in climate change adaptation;
3. ensuring open spaces can provide for and adapt to differing needs and uses, providing people with the opportunity to connect with nature' (City of Melbourne 2012a).

The Open Space Strategy (City of Melbourne 2012a) is intended as an overarching strategy for city planning for the coming 15 years. The strategy was formulated after an intensive consultation of and feedback from the community, agencies and stakeholders (City of Melbourne 2012b).

The overall direction of the Open Space Strategy is to expand the already existing green open spaces and to connect them to each other, but also to create new green open spaces. This would promote one of the initial goals of the strategy, namely assuring that green open spaces are within walking distance for most of the community. Ensuring that more people have access to green open spaces is expected to increase the health and wellbeing of the community, for example, by encouraging people to go jogging, walking or cycling. For the implementation of the strategy, a detailed plan has been drafted for every neighborhood in Melbourne to expand their green open spaces, connect the existing green spaces and create new green spaces (City of Melbourne 2012a, pp. 8–28).

Currently, the City of Melbourne also has multiple smaller projects for greening the city. One of these is the *Rooftop Project*. The Rooftop Project invites building owners, both individuals and businesses, to apply for the transformation of their roofs into green, cool or sun roofs. Melbourne's rooftops together span some 800 hectares—more than the total number of hectares of green space in the city. The Rooftop Project aims to make a more efficient use of this area. Instead of using the roofs for storing air conditioners and heating equipment, they could help to cool the city, for example by being transformed into green, cool or sun roofs. The City of Melbourne, as the initiator, made a map of all the roofs in Melbourne, giving recommendations for each roof on whether and how this could be transformed into a green roof. However, the success of this project depends on the willingness of the residents to realize this.

A second major project for greening the city is the *Green Your Laneway program*, in which laneways are turned into leafy, green and usable spaces for everyone to enjoy. Melbourne is funding four laneways out of the 800 nominated options. Residents whose laneways were not selected may still apply and work together with the municipality. Here again, the municipality is the initiator, but residents are invited to contribute.

4.4.3   San José

The Greenprint (now: 'Activate SJ', City of San José 2018) is a strategic plan that aims to make the city of San José greener and improve its community facilities to enhance livability. Various San José city departments and community organizations have contributed to the transformation to a green city and the development and elaboration of the Greenprint. This interdepartmental planning procedure involves representatives from the San José City Council; Parks and Recreation Commission; Parks, Recreation and Neighborhood Services Department (PRNS); Conventions, Arts and Entertainment (CAE); and General Services (GS) (City of San José 2001, p. 1). The Parks and Recreation Commission, which is currently managing the second update of the Greenprint document, was supported by a Community Advisory Task Force consisting of 60 members who were actively engaged throughout the process.

As the Greenprint aims to integrate public input and the community's feedback, a community needs assessment was conducted in 2001 to involve the population that is ultimately supposed to profit from the improvements at first hand. This assessment included, amongst others, telephone surveys of the city's population, the strategic identification of focus groups and different neighborhood workshops aimed at these. In addition, a Steering committee, consisting of different groups and organizations representing the community and some businesses, has regular meetings in which findings, process and challenges are discussed. The

Steering committee serves to guide the Greenprint and is responsible for reviewing the accomplishments. It elaborates on the plan's current goals as well as future goals of the city. It is also responsible for reaching out to the community and organizes and schedules the intercept events, and therefore plays a main role in involving other parties and sustaining the transformation. Members of the Steering committee include e.g. members of the Senior Citizens and the CommUniverCity, both private organizations, as well as public organizations such as the Parks and Recreation Commission, the San José State University, the Santa Clara County Public Health Department and, finally, the San José Parks Foundation, which is a community-based nonprofit organization.

As part of the project, citizens' initiatives are also encouraged. San José's citizens are invited to get involved personally, e.g. as part of a community group and are given the opportunity to suggest possible improvements or suggestions for potential partners online. They can also adopt a trail or a park to support its maintenance or become voluntarily involved in keeping green spaces clean (San José Parks, Recreation and Neighborhood Services). San José is not unique in this initiative; there are many other examples of Adopt-A-Park or Trail Programs, especially in Canada and the United States. In addition, San José launched a design competition in 2017 to redesign one of its parks, which is another example of how the government tries to foster the communities' participation in the transformation.

4.4.4   Cape Town

Although the process of turning Cape Town into a green city commenced as a government initiative, the Integrated Metropolitan Environmental Policy, article 1.2.2 states that the civil society is expected to aid in this project through actively supporting, monitoring and making sure that the policies are being implemented (City of Cape Town 2017). Corporations, non-governmental organizations and civilians are expected to play a role in enhancing and improving the greening of Cape Town, although there are no mandates or regulations in place explicitly requiring them to do so. Nonetheless, private parties, including non-governmental organizations, community groups, trusts and even United Nations-endorsed entities, have taken it upon themselves to advocate a greener society and to promote a greater green awareness. The relationship between the public and private parties in Cape Town is not one where the municipality dictates what the organizations should do but rather an unrestrictive relationship that allows the organizations to implement and carry out programs and projects that aid in the promotion of greening the city of Cape Town.

An important step being taken by both the private and the public sector to sustain this transformation is the education of young children and youths about the environment and ecosystem. Schools work hand in hand with various organizations, both governmental and non-governmental, to ensure that students are educated about how to plant trees, how to maintain them and the importance of doing so. A major actor is the Environmental Management Department of the city, who is actively working to sustain the green transformation through managing over 16 nature reserves in the city. Furthermore, the Department is involved in the development of the environmental education programs, the planning and implementation of conservation schemes and in developing skills on how to be effective in promoting and maintaining the green transition. An important step in sustaining the transformation is ensuring that the actors involved and in particular the governmental actors, comply with the laws and regulations relating to the greening of the city.

Furthermore, a factor contributing to the endurance of the transformation is the Cape Town Environmental Education Trust (CTEET). The aim of this trust is to support and push forward conservation initiatives within the city of Cape Town. The CTEET's goal is to promote the conservation of Cape Town's unique and bio diversified natural heritage through means such as education, trainings and conservation initiatives. The funding mainly comes from private companies, but in managing and promoting conservation they work together with both public (the city of Cape Town) and private parties (such as Eco-Schools, an international organization).

In addition to the above, a Cape Town Green Map was created in 2010 as part of the Green Map Movement, a community of over four thousand local green living sites around the world. The Cape Town Green Map is a social movement in the green sector. Since 2010, there has been a tangible increase in green consciousness. The Green Map initiative in Cape Town was launched as part of the Green Goal 2010 program, the environmental program created as a way to green the World Cup, which was hosted that year by South Africa. This program was modelled on Germany's 2006 program and took into account the impact that an enormous event such as the World cup would have on the environment. The Green Map community shares green sites such as biodiversity hotspots, green spaces, markets, eateries, responsible tourism, green accommodation, eco products and services, green attractions and many more (www.capetowngreen-map.co.za).

4.5   An Explorative Analysis of the Main Factors

In all cases, there is a growing awareness of the importance of green space for the future of the city and the wellbeing of its citizens which has led to the development and implementation of a host of urban greening projects. In this section, we explore a few of the main factors that contributed to this transformation. In doing so, we make a distinction between context factors and factors related to the form of the partnership. We start with the context factors.

Sense of Urgency: Population Growth, Economy or Climate
The transformation towards a greener city is in the most cases triggered by a felt sense of urgency, for example, in response to explosive population growth. In San José, extreme population growth gave rise to an unrestricted and unstructured outward expansion of the city (urban sprawl), which ultimately forced the city to reconsider its urban planning and to focus on improving the quality of the existing space. In recent decades, cities have also felt the need to make the city more livable in terms of health. In Cape Town, because of the fast-growing population, the city sought to create a healthy and sustainable environment for both the advantaged and disadvantaged groups in its society. Also, the need for measures to adapt to changing (climatic) conditions can create a sense of urgency, such as bouts of severe draught in Melbourne or extreme rainfall in Tilburg.

Political Constellation
Specific context factors also impacted on the transformation process. In Tilburg and Melbourne, the political climate played a major role. In Melbourne, the greening of city was hampered at the beginning of the century by the neo-liberal governance regime, while in Tilburg, momentum for green initiatives was generated by the coalition of mostly center and left wing parties that gained power in 2014 and who made the implementation of a green policy a top priority.

Historical Legacy

A third, important factor is historical legacy. The early development of green space in the nineteenth century in Melbourne gave Melbourne a head start when it came to transitioning into one of the greenest cities of the world.

Corporate Strategy: Economic Development, Tourism and Reputation Management

A fourth factor, finally, relates to tourism and reputation management. By enhancing the livability of a city, in terms of an attractive environment and recreational facilities, cities become more appealing to investors and citizens. In that context, Melbourne has a reputation to uphold as the frontrunner in urban green planning. In 2017, Melbourne was named the most livable city in the world for the 7th year in a row. For Cape Town, tourism is an important economic sector. Tourists are attracted by the beauty and biodiversity of the environment of Cape Town, an advantage Cape Town is intent on maintaining.

While these context factors may be considered the main drivers that set off the transformation towards a greener city, how have the governments of these four cities interacted with other parties and how has that influenced the transformation into a greener city? We found that in each case, the cities we reviewed chose a different path. In Melbourne, it was the municipal government that took the lead from the very start. From 1929 onwards, top-down management and strategic planning have worked to turn Melbourne into a livable green city. This does not mean that citizens and organizations are not involved. However, the municipality is the initiator; residents and other parties are invited to contribute. In Tilburg, the municipal government collaborated closely with the citizens. For example, the realization of the Spoorpark plans was a relatively easy and smooth process, thanks to the reciprocal relationship between the local government and the residents and their organizations: on the one hand, the residents actively initiated and developed ideas and on the other, the municipality showing itself to be open and recipient to the ideas. In a latter phase, professional organizations were involved to further advance the projects. San José combined strategic planning with a strong involvement of the community, businesses and public organizations, with the Steering Committee providing an institutional basis for the partnership between the municipal government, local business, community groups, and the

Table 4.1 Factors contributing to a green transformation of the city

City	Context	Characteristics of partnership
Tilburg	• Sense of urgency: Climate • Political constellation	Co-creation with civil society
Melbourne	• Sense of urgency: Climate • Political constellation • Historical legacy • Corporate strategy: Reputation	Top-down planning; citizens and others are invited to contribute
San José	• Sense of urgency: Growing population	Strategic planning combined with a strong involvement of civil society and business
Cape Town	• Sense of urgency: Growing population • Corporate strategy: Tourism	Modest role for government; extensive networks of public and private organizations

public. Cape Town, finally, opted for again a different route. The relationship between the municipality and the public and private parties is much less top-down compared to the other cities. The municipality of Cape Town does not dictate what the organizations should do but rather supports and allows the organizations to implement and carry out programs and projects that aid in the promotion of green space in the city of Cape Town. The city encourages participation from all citizens, corporations and NGOs and suggests ways to promote the green transition within the society. Table 4.1 provides a summary of the main factors.

Thus, in all four cities, the municipal government had an important role in initiating the policy towards the greening of the city. Their role in supporting green policies is still important. However, their approach to interaction with citizens, the community, and business organizations differs and, as a consequence, the opportunities available to these parties to initiate, develop, and implement plans for more green in the city also differ.

4.6   Conclusion

To conclude, both the role of the government and the involvement of other parties are important if cities are to achieve a green transformation. However, municipal governments each interact differently with residents, social organizations, and business, which leaves us with one question: what is the added value of the involvement of citizens, civil society organizations, and businesses in the greening of the city?

Part of the answer to this question is that partnerships, in particular with citizens, local entrepreneurs, and civil society organizations, contribute to establishing green spaces at sites and in ways that would not have been possible without the involvement of these parties. For example, the project Spoorpark in Tilburg would never have evolved as it has now without the involvement of the neighborhood residents. Likewise, the strategic plan for greening the city, the Greenprint, in San José served as a framework for a further development of more concrete plans and only attained its ultimate form with the involvement of the population, groups and organizations representing the community and local businesses.

And second, although hard evidence is lacking, the findings suggest that partnerships with citizens and civil society organizations in particular serve to reinforce these parties' feelings of responsibility for their own environment. This might boost the green consciousness of the residents of the city, possibly generating more support for green initiatives in the city and a greater willingness to participate in or take the initiative for future projects.

References

Barker, E. J., & Kenney, W. A. (2012). Urban forest management in small Ontario municipalities. *The Forestry Chronicle, 88*(2), 118–123.

Barnes, M. L., & Sharpe, E. K. (2009). Looking beyond traditional volunteer management: A case study of an alternative approach to volunteer engagement in parks and recreation. *VOLUNTAS: International Journal of Voluntary and Nonprofit Organizations, 20*(2), 169–187.

Bendt, P., Barthel, S., & Colding, J. (2013). Civic greening and environmental learning in public-access community gardens in Berlin. *Landscape and Urban Planning, 109*(1), 18–30.

Brown-Goebeler, S. (1991). How gray is my valley. *Time.* http://content.time.com/time/magazine/article/0,9171,974295,00.html. Accessed 1 July 2019.

Chanan, G. (2003). *Searching for solid foundations: community involvement and urban policy.* London: Office of the Deputy Prime Minister.

City of Cape Town. (2017). *Integrated Metropolitan Environmental Policy (IMEP).* http://resource.capetown.gov.za/documentcentre/Documents/Bylaws%20and%20policies/Environmental%20Strategy.pdf. Accessed 26 Sept 2019.

City of Melbourne. (2012a). *Open space strategy.* Planning for future growth. https://www.melbourne.vic.gov.au/SiteCollectionDocuments/open-space-strategy.pdf. Accessed 26 Sept 2019.

City of Melbourne. (2012b). *Open space strategy*. Technical Report. https://www. melbourne.vic.gov.au/about-council/committees-meetings/meeting-archive/meetingagendaitemattachments/579/9974/5.3%20open%20 space%20strategy%20(pages%2041%20to%20332).pdf. Accessed 26 Sept 2019.

City of San José. (2001). *Greenprint strategic plan*. http://www.sanjoseca.gov/ DocumentCenter/Home/View/64. Accessed 26 Sept 2019.

City of San José. (2009). *Parks, recreation and neighborhood services*. Draft strategic plan update. https://www.sanjoseca.gov/DocumentCenter/Home/ View/28. Accessed 26 Sept 2019.

City of San José. (2011). *Parks, recreation and neighborhood services*. Our greenprint vision. http://www.sanjoseca.gov/DocumentCenter/Home/View/21. Accessed 26 Sept 2019.

City of San José. (2018). *Parks, recreation and neighborhood services*. Greenprint update (now Activate SJ). http://www.sanjoseca.gov/index.aspx?nid=560. Accessed 26 Sept 2019.

Clement, D., & Kanai, M. (2015). The Detroit future city: How pervasive neoliberal urbanism exacerbates racialized spatial injustice. *American Behavioral Scientist, 59*(3), 369–385.

Dempsey, N., Burton, M., & Duncan, R. (2016). Evaluating the effectiveness of a cross-sector partnership for greenspace management: The case of Southey Owlerton, Sheffield, UK. *Urban Forestry & Urban Greening, 15*(1), 155–164.

Donovan, G. H., & Butry, D. T. (2010). Trees in the city: Valuing street trees in Portland, Oregon. *Landscape and Urban Planning, 94*(2), 77–83.

Drake, L., & Lawson, L. J. (2015). Results of a US and Canada community garden survey: Shared challenges in garden management amid diverse geographical and organizational contexts. *Agriculture and Human Values, 32*(2), 241–254.

Fors, H., Molin, J. F., Murphy, M. A., & van den Bosch, C. K. (2015). User participation in urban green spaces – For the people or the parks? *Urban Forestry & Urban Greening, 14*(3), 722–734.

Gemeente Tilburg. (2010a). Eerste klimaatprogramma Tilburg. *Naar een klimaatneutrale en klimaatbestendige stad*. Periode 2009–2012. http://docplayer.nl/5598449-Eerste-klimaatprogramma-tilburg-naar-een-klimaatneutrale-en-klimaatbestendige-stad.html. Accessed 26 Sept 2019.

Gemeente Tilburg. (2010b). *Nota Groen 'Dichter bij Groen'*. http://www. moerenburg.info/files/nota-groen-april-2010_klein.pdf. Accessed 26 Sept 2019.

Gemeente Tilburg. (2014). *Coalitieakkoord 2014–2018* voor de Gemeente Tilburg. https://www.tilburg.nl/fileadmin/files/stad-bestuur/bestuur/coalitieakkoord-gemeente-tilburg-2014-2018.pdf. Accessed 26 Sept 2019.

Gemeente Tilburg. (2015). *Stimulering van geveltuintjes en regels geveltuintjes en beplanten boomspiegels*. https://zoek.officielebekendmakingen.nl/gmb-2015-19076.pdf. Accessed 26 Sept 2019.

Gurran, N., & Miller, D. (2008). *Urban green belts in the twenty-first century* (1st ed.). London: Routledge.

Huang, S. L. (2010). The impact of public participation on the effectiveness of, and users' attachment to, urban neighbourhood parks. *Landscape Research, 35*(5), 551–562.

James, P., Tzoulas, K., Adams, M. D., Barber, A., Box, J., Breuste, J., et al. (2009). Towards an integrated understanding of green space in the European built environment. *Urban Forestry & Urban Greening, 8*(2), 65–75.

Jongerius, S. (2019, March 18). Spoorpark: Tilburg loopt nog eens 7 ton mis. *Brabants Dagblad.*

Kabisch, N. (2015). Ecosystem service implementation and governance challenges in urban green space planning—The case of Berlin, Germany. *Land Use Policy, 42*, 557–567.

Kozová, M., Dobšinská, Z., Pauditšová, E., Tomčíková, I., & Rakytová, I. (2018). Network and participatory governance in urban forestry: An assessment of examples from selected Slovakian cities. *Forest Policy and Economics, 89*, 31–41.

Leroy, P., & Arts, B. (2006). Institutional dynamics in environmental governance. In B. Arts & P. Leroy (Eds.), *Institutional dynamics in environmental governance* (pp. 1–9). Dordrecht: Springer.

Lutafali, S., & Khoja, F. (2011). Economic and ecological partnerships revitalizing urban slums: A case study of Cairo. *International Journal of Ecology & Development, 18*(11), 29–45.

Marche, G. (2015). What can urban gardening really do about gentrification? A case-study of three San Francisco community gardens. *European Journal of American Studies, 10*(3), 1–13.

Mathers, A., Dempsey, N., & Molin, J. F. (2015). Place-keeping in action: Evaluating the capacity of green space partnerships in England. *Landscape and Urban Planning, 139*, 126–136.

Moskell, C., & Allred, S. B. (2013). Residents' beliefs about responsibility for the stewardship of park trees and street trees in new York City. *Landscape and Urban Planning, 120*, 85–95.

Nastran, M., & Regina, H. (2016). Advancing urban ecosystem in Ljubljana. *Environment Science & Policy, 62*, 123–126.

O'Brien, E. (2006). Social housing and green space: A case study in inner London. *Forestry, 79*(5), 535–551.

Pincetl, S. (2010). Implementing municipal tree planting: Los Angeles million-tree initiative. *Environmental Management, 45*(2), 227–238.

Rosol, M. (2010). Public participation in post-Fordist urban green space governance: The case of community gardens in Berlin. *International Journal of Urban and Regional Research, 34*(3), 548–563.

San José Parks, Recreation & Neighborhood Services. http://sanjoseca.gov/index.aspx?NID=589. Accessed 27 Sept 2019.

Shafer, C. S., Lee, B. K., & Turner, S. (2000). A tale of three greenway trails: User perceptions related to quality of life. *Landscape and Urban Planning, 49*(3), 163–178.

Sipilä, M., & Tyrväinen, L. (2005). Evaluation of collaborative urban forest planning in Helsinki, Finland. *Urban Forestry & Urban Greening, 4*(1), 1–12.

Slater, S., Pugach, O., Lin, W., & Bontu, A. (2016). If you build it will they come? Does involving community groups in playground renovations Affect Park utilization and physical activity? *Environment and Behavior, 48*(1), 246–265.

South African History Online. *The Dutch settlement.* https://www.sahistory.org.za. Accessed 25 Oct 2019.

Van Montfort, C., Michels, A., & Frankowski, A. (2014). *Governance models and partnerships in the urban water sector: A framework for analysis and evaluation.* Accessible through: http://dspace.library.uu.nl/handle/1874/303566

Wolch, J. R., Byrne, J., & Newell, J. P. (2014). Urban green space, public health, and environmental justice: The challenge of making cities 'just green enough'. *Landscape and Urban Planning, 125,* 234–244.

CHAPTER 5

The Impact of Public and Private Partnerships on the Liveability of Eco-Cities in China's Pearl River Delta

Haiyan Lu, Li Sun, and Martin de Jong

5.1   Introduction

In the past decades, many countries have experienced unprecedented rates of urban growth. This remarkable urbanization has also created challenges for the ecological environment, and many cities reflect the future direction by promoting eco-city, smart city, and low carbon city development. Eco-city is a concept widely adopted among cities in China (Yu 2014). The concept of the eco city was initially promoted by urban planners, aiming to balance between environmental impact and economic benefits on the city scale (Kenworthy 2006; Richard Register 2002). According to the academic literature, its main principles include: to revise land-use priorities

H. Lu
Institute of Sinology, Free University of Berlin, Berlin, Germany

College of Urban and Environmental Sciences, Peking University, Beijing, China
e-mail: haiyanlu@pku.edu.cn

L. Sun
School of Sociology and Social Policy, University of Leeds, Leeds, UK
e-mail: L.Sun2@leeds.ac.uk

© The Author(s) 2020
C. van Montfort, A. Michels (eds.), *Partnerships for Livable Cities*,
https://doi.org/10.1007/978-3-030-40060-6_5

to create compact, diverse, green, mixed-use communities near transit nodes and to support local agriculture, urban greening projects and community gardening (Roseland 1997). Later on, these ecological initiatives were promoted in urban planning in different countries (Rapoport 2014). Following the countries in Europe and North America, the eco-city phenomenon was picked up fast in Asian countries in the early twenty-first century, especially in China. In 2003, the Ministry of Environmental Protection (MEP) initiated an eco-cities program, and more than one hundred cities claimed to be eco-cities in the 2010s (de Jong et al. 2016). The development of eco-cities was initially more focused on environmental aspects in cities. Later on, during their expansion, cities began to experiment with ecological initiatives in new towns, and labelled them 'eco-city', 'smart city' or 'low carbon city' projects. Although going by various names, the focus of these projects is to realize green technological innovation (Hult 2013). In this chapter, we use the term eco-city projects to refer to these projects.

Compared with newly built areas of cities in other countries, eco-city projects in China tend to be substantially larger (Zhan and de Jong 2017). As China is still in the process of urbanization, eco-city projects are still under construction (Lu et al. 2018). Additionally, it is noticeable that these eco-city projects cover various aspects, such as environmental protection, energy efficiency, a carbon-efficient economy, and social aspects. All these initiatives aim at liveability of some sort. The liveability resulting from eco-city projects encompasses a wide range of issues, such as health, convenience, mobility, recreation, and safety. However, in the early stages of eco-city development, urban planning and infrastructure provision are two core phases influencing its vision for sustainable development (Yin et al. 2016; Zhan and de Jong 2017). The urban planning of eco-city projects affects the land use in the whole area, while infrastructure provision determines the accessibility of services for residents for a relatively long time to come.

M. de Jong (✉)
Erasmus School of Law, Erasmus University Rotterdam,
Rotterdam, The Netherlands

Rotterdam School of Management, Rotterdam, The Netherlands

Institute for Global Public Policy, Fudan University, Shanghai, China
e-mail: w.m.jong@law.eur.nl

Although most eco-city projects in China are led by governments, developing partnerships with private developers or urban planning institutions has become more and more prominent in the urban planning and infrastructure provision phases (Wu 2015). These partnerships with private actors influence the knowledge input in the urban design of eco cities. Partnerships with private actors affect the design, financing, construction, and operation of the infrastructure provision. In China, governments and/or developers assign most of the urban planning tasks in eco-city projects to urban planning institutes. Additionally, the funding of infrastructure provision in eco-city projects is complex, and sources can be private developers, state-owned developers, and local governments (Wu 2012). Therefore, the partnership between developers, governments, and urban planning institutes is an important issue. Consequently, apart from those governments and other public actors, the interests and resources of private urban planners and developers are also relevant in eco-city development.

This chapter discusses the impact of formal public-private partnerships among state, market, and civil society players in three eco-city projects (newly built area) in the Pearl River Delta in China. We examine how public-private partnerships of urban planning institutes, developers, and governments have an effect on the liveability of eco-city projects in the urban planning and infrastructure provision phrases. As liveability is a broad concept and difficult to measure, we focus on the greenery of eco-cities in this study. Our main aim is to investigate *how public and private partnerships affect the liveability (greenery) of eco cities in the Pearl River Delta in China*. Section 5.2 first reviews the literature about public-private partnerships, and its impact on the liveability of eco cities. Section 5.3 presents the research method. Section 5.4 then demonstrates the PPP model in the overall project, the urban planning and infrastructure provision stages. And Sect. 5.5 discusses the findings and draws some conclusions.

5.2   Literature Review

5.2.1   Public-Private Partnerships

In this chapter, we take the relationship between the state, market, and civil society as presented in Chap. 1 (Fig. 1.1) as a starting point. We focus on the ones formalized in contracts in which parties realize products, services or policy outcomes jointly, and the risks and costs are also shared (Klijn and Teisman 2005), which is type C (Chap. 1, Fig. 1.1).

Public private partnerships (PPPs) can be narrowly defined as cooperative institutional arrangements between the public and private sectors (Hodge and Greve 2007). Some scholars regarded them as a tool in public management, which will replace the traditional methods for public service delivery, especially in infrastructure provision and project finance (Vincent-Jones 2000). However, the difficulties arise when developing a regulatory framework for PPPs, due to different and often conflicting objectives, interests and strategies of public and private actors (De Bruijn and Ten Heuvelhof 2012; Ke 2010). Therefore, applying PPPs in specific cases requires negotiating among the actors involved in contract formulation (Mu et al. 2011).

Each actor should bring valuable skills, knowledge, and resources to the partnership to provide better public services. The public and private sectors also need to achieve a balance in responsibility and risk distribution (Ke et al. 2010). However, the interactions between governments and private actors were complicated by the growth in private and public partnerships without robust institutional arrangements. According to a study by Sagalyn (2007), mistakes easily arise due to lack of experience by public and private partners and their consultants. In practice, some PPP projects show cost overruns, unrealistic prices, and income projections, as well as disputes between private operators and governments (Kumaraswamy and Zhang 2001; Boers et al. 2013). In the end, the governments and the general public tend to have to shoulder the responsibilities (Tang et al. 2010). Therefore, partnerships are not static but may change over time. For example, collaboration initiatives with the private sector at the beginning of the project may later become the responsibility of governments alone or vice versa.

5.2.2 *Partnerships in Eco-City Projects*

In this chapter, eco-city projects usually revolve around newly built areas, which incorporate some technological and ecological features to create better environmental, social, and economic conditions. In China, eco-city projects were initially focused on improving environmental quality in general, adopting green buildings and clean technologies in projects (Hult 2013). Against a background of clean technology development, cities in China more recently have begun to explore solving urban problems through applying engineering solutions in infrastructures, such as buildings, traffic systems, and waste treatment (Joss 2011). For instance, Tianjin eco-city promotes the use of renewable energy sources by innovative technologies on 34.2 km² of non-arable and deserted salt land (Baeumler et al. 2009).

The partnership of eco-city projects in China is a public-private partnership because both private developers and urban planners are involved next to governments and other public actors. The private developers and urban planning institutions began to boom from 1978 on. Private developers and urban planning institutions are also active in the market, ranging from large and medium to small companies. However, public sector planners and developers still contribute hugely to China's real estate market. Some state-owned urban planning institutions and developers evolved from the former type of central or provincial administration units, but have become profit-oriented. In addition to this, investment platforms, which are another form of state-owned developers, are established to manage the construction of new town projects.

5.3   Research Method

The rapid urbanization and industrialization of the Pearl River Delta (PRD) makes it a valuable case to study in terms of eco-city development. The permanent population of PRD has increased from 23.70 to 615.05 million in the years between 1990 and 2017 (National Bureau of Statistics of China 2018). This region is still urbanizing, and many eco cities are under construction. It consists of nine cities in the Pearl River Delta, including two provincial-level cities (Guangzhou and Shenzhen) and seven prefecture-level cities (Foshan, Dongguan, Zhongshan, Zhuhai, Huizhou, Jiangmen and Zhaoqing).

For our research, the selection of eco-city projects within the Pearl River Delta Here is based on the representation of different city types and PPP categories in the PRD. Sino Singapore Guangzhou Knowledge City (SSGKC) and Shenzhen International Low Carbon City (ILCC) were chosen since they represent provincial-level cities. Moreover, the former involves the participation of a private developer, and the latter that of a state-owned developer. Among the eco-city projects in prefecture-level cities, Zhuhai Western Eco-city was selected because of the active engagement of private actors in the project.

Two methods were used to collect the data: one is document analysis, and the other is expert interviews. Firstly, we analysed various urban plans and regulations introduced by urban planning institutes or municipal governments regarding eco-city projects. Secondly, the first author conducted fieldwork in Guangzhou, Shenzhen, and Zhuhai in April 2016, June 2016, and July 2017. Sixteen expert interviews were held, including government officials, urban planners, developers, and other stakeholders. The questions focused on the role of and interactions among public and private actors and the difficulties they experienced during the partnership in eco-city development. Each interview lasted from 30 to 60 minutes. Additionally, in 2018, an interview with one urban planner was conducted in Guangzhou in order to update the Guangzhou Knowledge City project.

5.4   Findings: PPP in Eco-City Development in China

In this study, the public-private partnerships are further analysed based on the engagement of various actors in the eco-city projects in the Pearl River Delta. First. These actors are identified as public or private actors. Public actors include governments, or state-owned enterprises and institutions. The private actors refer to profit-oriented companies, including for-profit organizations owned by individuals, shareholding cooperatives, shareholding corporations, and foreign-funded enterprises.[1] Secondly, the actors are further distinguished as local or external actors according to the location of their headquarters. Thus, we categorised the actors into four types, which are local public actors, local private actors, external public actors, and external private actors.

This section will discuss three eco-city projects, located in Guangzhou, Shenzhen and Zhuhai. For each case we discuss the PPP model used in the stages of urban planning and infrastructure provision. These two stages are analysed in depth since the partnerships began to appear after the agenda-setting stage. The agenda-setting stage is dominated by public actors in the Chinese context, including the national, provincial, municipal, and district governments.

---

[1] Source: All-China Federation of Industry & Commerce: www.acfic.org.cn, accessed in June 2019.

5.4.1 Guangzhou

Guangzhou sees itself as a 'Provincial capital' and 'International Commercial Trade Center', which can be explained by its key position in the national strategy. The Sino Singapore Guangzhou Knowledge City (SSGKC) project was jointly initiated by leaders from Guangdong and Singapore to serve as a strategic development platform and a model for economic transformation and industrial upgrading. SSGKC is positioned as a unique, vibrant, and sustainable city that is highly attractive to both talents and knowledge-based industries. The SSGKC project started in 2010, and most of the infrastructure provision in the initial zone has been completed. Many enterprises and research institutes have settled in the initial zone, such as Tenfei company, Tianyun company, Kaide property company, and Sun Yat-Sen University. Until 2030, SSGKC is expected to provide an attractive area of 123 km^2 for 500,000 residents to live and work.

5.4.1.1 Overall PPP Model in the Eco-City Project

The SSGKC partnership has the Guangzhou government and Singapore investors as its main partners (see Fig. 5.1). The Guangzhou government invested in SSGKC by providing land in the initial area. The Knowledge City Administrative Committee is the bureau established to promote the development of SSGKC. The Knowledge City Administrative Committee was assigned with 20 provincial approval rights. Under it, Guangzhou Knowledge City Investment & Development Co. Ltd. is a financial platform, responsible for negotiating with villages and preparing the land, as well as to build an artificial lake within the initial zone. It was rewarded with the land revenue of half of the initial zone by the Guangzhou Government. Besides these tasks, Guangzhou Knowledge City Investment & Development Co. Ltd. is also responsible for attracting enterprises and other investors.

Guangzhou Knowledge City Investment & Development Co. Ltd. and Singapore investors established a joint venture, named SSGKC Investment and Development Co. Ltd. In 2017, the JTC and Jiuyong Road were merged into a developer to improve the development efficiency. In general, SSGKC Investment and Development Co. Ltd. has introduced the Singapore experience, such as urban design, residential management, and industrial incubation. The strategic collaboration, training, and social management also required coordination between Guangzhou and

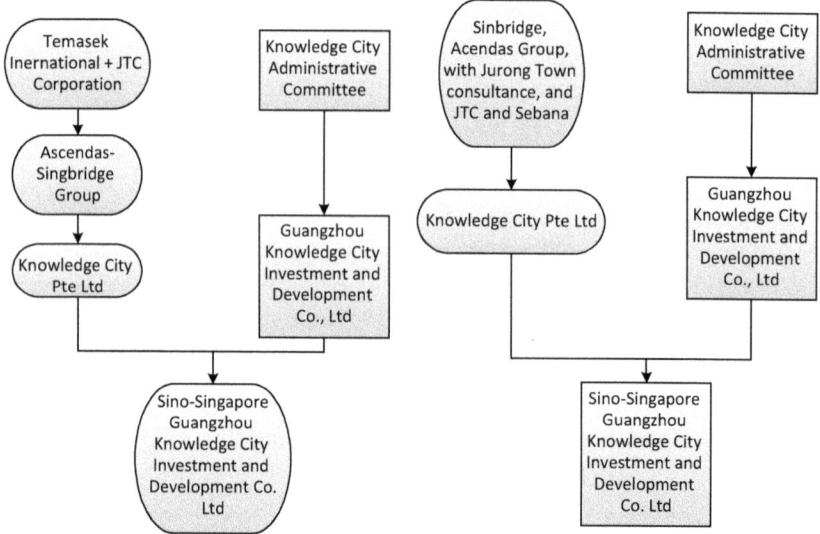

Fig. 5.1 The partnership between the Guangzhou government and Singapore investors in Sino-Singapore Guangzhou Knowledge City (left) before 2017; (right) after 2017. Note: the round-shaped boxes represent private actors and the square-shaped boxes represent public actors

Singapore. The international urban planning institutions also participate in the urban design process of the SSGKC project. We classify the public and private partnership in Guangzhou Knowledge City as the combination of public actors with external private investors (see Table 5.1).

5.4.1.2 PPP in the Stage of Urban Planning

The eco-low carbon master plan of the SSGKC states that the greenery coverage was 40% in 2015, and should increase to 45% in 2020. As industrial and residential lands are essential components in this project, SSGKC tries to learn from Singapore to make use of its land efficiently. The knowledge transfer from international planning institutes can be found in the urban design of the project. The SSGKC joint venture was responsible for the overall urban planning. It contacted Singapore's IDA International company to design a Smart City Master Plan. SSGKC also had an Eco-city Master Plan, which was guided by Green Building and Districts Standards & Guidelines from Singapore.

Table 5.1 Public and private partnerships in Sino-Singapore Guangzhou Knowledge City

	Public	Private
Local	Guangzhou governments	
External		Singapore developers and urban institution

On a small scale, some land plots also attracted international architects and designers through international competitions. SSGKC also transferred the Singapore neighbourhood centre concept. These neighbourhood centres provided social and cultural services to the residents, such as libraries or community centres. SSGKC established a relationship with the neighbourhood centres located in Suzhou and Singapore to learn from their experience. The joint venture played an essential role in attracting knowledge from these actors.

However, difficulties still exist in communication with governments in the urban planning process. For instance, the metro and bus stops in the extension line of metro line 3 belonged to provincial and municipal governments, respectively. This misalignment made it more difficult for urban planners to communicate with different government bureaus.

5.4.1.3 PPP in the Stage of Infrastructure Provision

The infrastructure provision of SSGKC also progressed rapidly in recent years. The supporting facilities include the family service centres, smart library, integrated business park, smart grid, metro, hospital, international school, and neighbourhood centres. These infrastructure services are also attractive for enterprises and residents to locate in SSGKC. Land development is also rapid in SSGKC because the Guangzhou municipal government only guarantees the land development rights for five years. It means the lands will be returned to the government by the developers if the land is not under construction within five years. The developers are also eager to develop due to their pressure to collect revenues from their investment.

5.4.2 Shenzhen

Shenzhen is positioned as 'the national high-tech industry base and cultural industry base' in its urban master plan, and 'International Innovation City' in its 13th Five Year Plan. It is the first demonstration zone for innovation in China and tops the list of innovation cities in mainland China three times in Forbes. Shenzhen is also in the top seed of low carbon cities in China; it aims to be 'National Low-Carbon Eco Model City' in its 12th FYP. This eco-city development strategy has been adopted in its new town projects. One typical example of new construction projects is the Shenzhen International Low Carbon City (ILCC), located in the Longgang District. It is supported by the National Development and Reform Committee as a flagship project for national low carbon development in China.

Between 2012 and 2016, most of the infrastructure in the initial zone was completed, and ILCC is still in the process of attracting business. Until now, a conference centre and a small number of high-tech institutes are located in the initial zone. In 2018, the usage of most available land has not been decided, and a few promising projects are in process, such as the headquarter of Shenzhen Institute of Built Research.

5.4.2.1 Overall PPP Model in the Eco-City Project

ILCC was officially kicked off in 2012 by the Shenzhen municipal government, which was the main project leader. The other key actors involved include Shenzhen municipality, Longgang district government, and a developer named Shenzhen Construction and Development Group (CDG).

Shenzhen municipality is the initiator of the ILCC (see Fig. 5.2). Municipal ILCC Office, the leading organization, is an organization under the Shenzhen municipal government. This office is composed of members representing different departments within the Shenzhen municipality and other key players within ILCC, with the Vice Mayor as the head. Due to this hierarchy, it did not have decision-making power on the land preparation and infrastructure provision in the project. In the past few years, the project progress was reported in the 'Conference Memos', which are signed by the Vice Mayor periodically. Special attention to low carbon emission has been paid in this project.

The Shenzhen Construction and Development Group, a State-Owned financial platform, was responsible for providing a considerable part of the finance used for the development of ILCC. Until 2017, CDG had invested three billion Yuan in ILCC (475 million USD). As an executive and financing organ of Shenzhen municipality, CDG did not have the pressure to earn profit as it can be compensated by land or revenues from Shenzhen municipality directly. The Longgang district government, where the ILCC project is situated, played a more critical role at the later stages. The

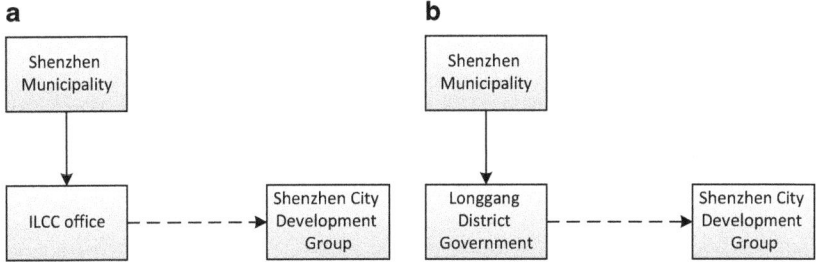

Fig. 5.2 The partnership between municipal government and developers in Shenzhen International Low Carbon City (**a**) before 2017; (**b**) after 2017

Table 5.2 Public and public partnerships in Shenzhen International Low Carbon City

	Public	*Private*
Local	The Shenzhen municipal government	
	State-owned developer and urban institution	
External		

Longgang district government had more knowledge and experience with the local conditions. The urban planning institute involved in the Shenzhen ILCC is the Urban Planning Design Institute of Shenzhen (UPDIS). UPDIS is also a local state-owned enterprise, invested by the Shenzhen Municipal Assets Committee. As a type of public-private partnership in Shenzhen ILCC is a combination of local actors without involvement from private actors (see Table 5.2).

5.4.2.2 PPP in the Stage of Urban Planning

67.23% of the ILCC area is dominated by forest, river or farming land. Therefore, governments need to consider how to make use of available land efficiently. They try to make use of small land plots to increase their greenery, such as rooftop farming, linear parks along with residential areas. Compared with SSGKC, ILCC relies more on local urban designers rather than international design companies. In the initial stage of urban planning for ILCC, Dutch experts prepared a research report for ILCC project, but the overall urban plan was drafted by UPDIS in the end. As the ILCC office is under the Shenzhen municipal government, UPDIS is in a favourable position to make plans for the ILCC. Although UPDIS is a local planning company, its design concepts also refer to the international cases, such as the SMART principle, including Sequestration, Micro-Climate, Architecture, Recycle and Traffic (interview 3).

5.4.2.3 PPP in the Stage of Infrastructure Provision

The Shenzhen municipality has a tight grip on the developer choice within ILCC. The municipal government allows the financial platform, the CDG, to develop the initial zone of the project as it can bear the financial risk with government support. However, in the cooperation between the Shenzhen municipal government and the CDG, not all promises from the Shenzhen municipal government were delivered. The CDG also does not want to invest incessantly in low carbon development. Under such circumstances, private developers would be reluctant to participate in this project. To avoid this dilemma, CDG requires the Shenzhen municipal government to transfer land to it first.

In 2017, the Shenzhen municipality offered more freedom for the Longgang District government to participate in the project. In 2017, the Longgang district government signed a contract with the Overseas Chinese Town (OCT) to develop the 5 km² expansion area, which is another state-owned developer from Shenzhen. It is difficult to tell at this stage how the partnership with OCT will influence the infrastructure provision.

5.4.3   Zhuhai

Zhuhai borders the Macau Special Administrative Region, and it became one of the Special Economic Zones in the 1980s. Zhuhai is a tourism city, and it makes use of the advantage of neighbouring Macao, which is famous for its historical centre and the gaming industry. Zhuhai has emphasized its environmental protection rather than rapid economic growth from manufacturing since 1980. The pursuit of eco-city initiatives can be found in its newly built areas, such as Zhuhai Western Central Eco-city. Zhuhai Western Central Eco-city occupies 200 km² with an initial zone of 10 km². It acquired the status of provincial-level eco-city from the Guangdong Provincial Government. The Zhuhai municipal government also began calling itself 'sponge city' from 2016 on.

5.4.3.1 Overall PPP Model in the Zhuhai Eco-City Project Development

The Zhuhai municipal government established the Western City Development Bureau to organize the project, which was directly led by

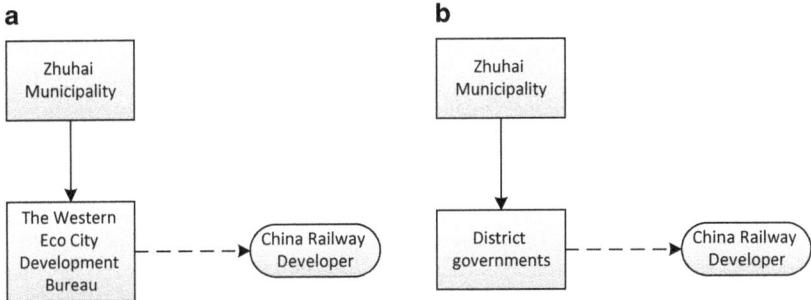

Fig. 5.3 The partnership between municipal government and developers in Zhuhai Western Eco city (**a**) before 2017; (**b**) after 2017

Table 5.3 Public and public partnerships in Zhuhai Western Eco-city

	Public	*Private*
Local	Zhuhai governments, the state-owned urban institute	
External	State-owned developer	

the Zhuhai municipal government (see Fig. 5.3). The Western City Development Bureau had various functions, with among them the discretion to organize land bidding and auctions, without municipal and district governments being involved.

Unlike Shenzhen, the developer involved in Zhuhai is an external state-owned enterprise, which is the China Railways Group. The urban planning institute involved in Zhuhai is also a state-owned enterprise. Therefore, the type of public and private partnership in Zhuhai Western Eco-city is a combination of public actors with an outside private actor (see Table 5.3).

5.4.3.2 PPP in the Stage of Urban Planning

As for Zhuhai Western Eco-city, it should follow the greenery standard of Zhuhai municipality, which says that is more than 60% of the area should be covered by greenery. The urban planning of Zhuhai Western Eco-city relies on the Zhuhai Institute of Urban Planning & Design, which is a local urban planning institute under the Ministry of Housing in Zhuhai. It is a capable urban planning institute dominating the Zhuhai planning market. It has adopted concepts from Western countries, such as transit-oriented development and the eco-city. As Zhuhai was selected as a Resilient City pilot in 2016, the concept of resilient city has been applied in the civil engineering design and construction. Located in Zhuhai, the institute has easy access to local information and performs many local urban planning tasks.

5.4.3.3 PPP in the Stage of Infrastructure Provision

In the implementation process, the initial project goals had to be compromised during the negotiations with state-owned developers. The Zhuhai municipal government preferred to achieve a balance between the Western Construction Bureau and China Railways. The cooperation contract was signed between the Zhuhai government and China Railways. According to the contract, the project can only be continued if both parties reach an agreement regarding the financial budget and technical requirements. The western construction bureau was responsible for the initial design, and China Railways was in charge of detailed project implementation. However, decisions on the budget and engineering projects were jointly made by both parties, which occasionally resulted in conflicts between demands from Western City Development Bureau and what China Railways delivered. China Railways tended to use internal bidding to choose construction companies from the China Railway Group to reduce construction costs and increase benefit. The close relationship between construction companies and China Railways resulted in delays and low-quality products. However, the Western City Development Bureau cannot insist on its requirements because China Railways was an equal partner in the decision making in the project. In this public-private partnership, the Western City Development Bureau was unable to implement its will in the project, resulting in suboptimal quality. After 2017, the role of the Western City Development Bureau had been replaced by district governments. China Railway Company has assigned contracts with district governments directly to ensure their support in the project.

5.5   Discussion and Conclusions

5.5.1   Discussion

Previous research suggests that the stability and effectiveness of partnerships require certain conditions, including legitimacy, responsiveness, stable funding, and leadership (Huang 2010; Dempsey et al. 2016; Foo et al. 2015). The three cases we discussed in the previous section showed three important conditions for an effective partnership in an eco-city context: knowledge transfer, awareness of the local context and strong incentives for responsiveness to ecological considerations.

In eco-city projects, *knowledge transfer* plays a vital role in urban planning, which also influences the greenery aspect of liveability. International planners have advantages in urban design knowledge and world-wide experience. The commitment cannot be established in the short term but demands lots of negotiation and interaction in the agenda-setting stage. For instance, SSGKC in Guangzhou was set up by both Chinese and Singapore as players, which are also in line with Sino-Singaporean predecessors, including Suzhou Industrial Park and Tianjin Eco-city. As for the urban planning stage, the eco-city project in Guangzhou involves private urban planning institutes, while Shenzhen and Zhuhai invite local urban planning institutes to the board (see Table 5.4).

Compared with international urban planning institutes, local planners know more about the local context. However, the difference is less significant in the planning concepts in the above three cases, as local urban planning institute can also provide knowledge input, and the eco-planning depends on the local context. Therefore, the private (even international) urban planning institutes can play a positive role in green development, but public (local) urban planning institutes can also realize this as they have an advantage in their *awareness of the local context*.

As for the infrastructure provision, even in projects where private developers were involved, the municipal government ensured its control

Table 5.4 Actor categorization of urban planning institutes in three eco-city projects

Cases	Urban planning institution	Actor category	Knowledge input in urban planning
Sino-Singapore Guangzhou Knowledge City	Singapore urban planning institute	External private actor	Singapore urban planning concepts, such as neighbourhood Centre
Shenzhen international low Carbon City	Shenzhen UPDIS	Local state-owned urban institute	Rooftop farming, linary parks
Zhuhai Western eco-city	Zhuhai Institute of Urban Planning & design	Local public actor	Eco-city, resilient city

through more than 50% ownership of the shares in the project (Guangzhou and Zhuhai). As for the *responsiveness*, the investment platforms established by governments are compelled to implement the eco-city projects if the municipal government requires them to do so (Shenzhen). In contrast, the responsiveness to ecological considerations from private actors can be undermined by their profit pursuit when the revenue of real estate development is the main income from this project, such as in the Zhuhai case. Compared with Zhuhai, SSGKC also involves private developers from Singapore, but their revenue sources are more diverse, including investment in incubator centres and neighbourhood centre services. This makes them less sensitive to the income from property development. The overall quality of the project matters, more to Singapore investors, which also ensures their dedication.

5.5.2   Conclusion

Although eco-city projects in China have to fulfil an environmental policy agenda in line with original Western ideas, realizing economic growth through real estate investment and attracting investors and residents remains a vital element. We have investigated the impact of the formal public-private partnerships on the greenery aspect of liveability in eco-city projects, and the influence varies according to the actor category and their engagement.

Generally speaking, the leadership of private-public partnerships is still in the hands of public actors. In Zhuhai and Guangzhou, public actors hold dominant shares in the project companies. In Shenzhen, the dominant role of government also exists in the partnership between the municipal government and state-owned enterprises. These state-owned enterprises have easy access to state-owned bank credit and project opportunities, which can ensure the financial credibility of eco-city projects. However, bureaucratic features in the administrative system and lower market competitiveness also undermine the innovation and knowledge transfer in eco-city projects.

The involvement of private urban planning institutes and developers can benefit eco-city projects through knowledge transfer and project experience. However, the impact of private urban planning institutes is still restricted to the planning process. As the developers have a stronger say in the projects, responsiveness to liveablility arguments requires their willingness to pursue ecological initiatives. Compared with state-owned developers, the private ones are more sensitive to profit. The greenery aspect of liveability may be sacrificed when the primary income of development depends on real estate development. When private developments have a broader orientation extended, they care more for the overall quality of projects, which also increases the possibility to ensure the its liveability standard. Above all, it is challenging to state that the different actor categories in public-private partnership result in various practices in urban planning and infrastructure provision. However, the actor categories do have some impact on the knowledge transfer and actor interaction in the planning and implementation process of eco-city development.

REFERENCES

Baeumler, A., Chen, M., Dastur, A., Zhang, Y., Filewood, R., Al-Jamal, K., Peterson, C., Randale, M., & Pinnoi, N. (2009). *Sino-Singapore Tianjin Eco-City (SSTEC): A case study of an emerging eco-city in China*. Working paper no. 59012. Washington, DC: The World Bank.

Boers, I., Hoek, F., Van Montfort, C., & Wieles, J. (2013). Public-private partnerships: International audit findings. In P. de Vries & E. B. Yehoue (Eds.), *The Routledge companion to public-private partnerships* (pp. 451–478). London/New York: Routledge.

De Bruijn, H., & Ten Heuvelhof, E. (2012). *Management in networks: On multi-actor decision making. Management in networks: On multi-actor decision making*. Abingdon: Routledge.

De Jong, M., Yu, C., Joss, S., Wennersten, R., Yu, L., Zhang, X., & Ma, X. (2016). Eco city development in China: addressing the policy implementation challenge. *Journal of Cleaner Production, 134*(Part A), 31–41. https://doi.org/10.1016/j.jclepro.2016.03.083.

Dempsey, N., Burton, M. & Duncan, R. (2016). Evaluating the effectiveness of a cross-sector partnership for greenspace management: *The case of Southey Owlerton, Sheffield, UK. Urban Forestry & Urban Greening, 15*(1), 155–164.

Foo, K., Martin, D., Polsky, C., Wool, C. & Ziemer, M. (2015). Social well-being and environmental governance in urban neighbourhoods in Boston, MA. *The Geographical Journal, 181*(2), 138–146.

Hodge, G. A., & Greve, C. (2007). Public-private partnerships: An international performance review. *Public Administration Review, 67*(3), 545–558.

Hult, A. (2013). Swedish production of sustainable urban imaginaries in China. *Journal of Urban Technology, 20*(1), 77–94.

Huang, S. L. (2010). The Impact of Public Participation on the Effectiveness of, and Users' Attachment to, Urban Neighbourhood Parks. *Landscape Research, 35*(5), 551–562.

Joss, S. (2011). Eco-city governance: A case study of Treasure Island and Sonoma Mountain village. *Journal of Environmental Policy and Planning,* *13*(4), 331–348.

Ke, Y., Wang, S. Q., Chan, A. P. C., & Lam, P. T. I. (2010). Preferred risk allocation in China's public-private partnership (PPP) projects. *International Journal of Project Management, 28*(5), 482–492.

Kenworthy, J. R. (2006). The eco-city: Ten key transport and planning dimensions for sustainable city development. *Environment and Urbanization, 18*(1), 67–85.

Klijn, E.-H., & Teisman, G. (2005). Public–private partnerships as the management of co-production: Strategic and institutional obstacles in a difficult marriage. In G. A. Hodge & C. Greve (Eds.), *The challenge of public-private partnerships: Learning from international experience* (pp. 95–116). Cheltenham: Edward Elgar Publishing.

Kumaraswamy, M. M., & Zhang, X. Q. (2001). Governmental role in BOT-led infrastructure development. *International Journal of Project Management., 19*(2001), 195–205.

Lu, H., de Jong, M., & ten Heuvelhof, E. (2018). Explaining the variety in smart eco city development in China-what policy network theory can teach us about overcoming barriers in implementation? *Journal of Cleaner Production, 196*(2018), 135–149.

Mu, R., de Jong, M., & Koppenjan, J. (2011). The rise and fall of public-private partnerships in China: A path-dependent approach. *Journal of Transport Geography, 19*(4), 794–806.

National Bureau of Statistics of China. (2018). China Stastistics Year Book 2018. Retrieved July 8, 2019, from https://doi.org/data.stats.gov.cn/.

Rapoport, E. (2014). Utopian visions and real estate dreams: The eco-city past, present and future. *Geography Compass, 8*(2), 137–149.

Register, R. (2002). *EcoCities: Rebuilding cities in balance with nature – Richard Register.* Berkeley: Berkeley Hills Books.

Roseland, M. (1997). Dimensions of the eco-city. *Cities, 14*(4), 197–202.

Sagalyn, L. B. (2007). Longer view: Public/private development: Lessons from history, research, and practice. *Journal of the American Planning Association, 73*(1), 7–22.

Tang, L., Shen, Q., & Cheng, E. W. L. (2010). A review of studies on public – Private partnership projects in the construction industry. *International Journal of Project Management, 28*(7), 683–694.

Vincent-Jones, P. (2000). Contractual governance: Institutional and organizational analysis. *Oxford Journal of Legal Studies, 20*(3), 317–351.

Wu, F. (2012). China's eco-cities. *Geoforum, 43*(2), 169–171.

Wu, F. (2015). *Planning for growth: Urban and regional planning in China.* New York: Routledge.

Yin, Y., Olsson, A. R., & Håkansson, M. (2016). The role of local governance and environmental policy integration in Swedish and Chinese eco-city development. *Journal of Cleaner Production, 134,* 78–86.

Yu, L. (2014). Low carbon eco-city: New approach for Chinese urbanisation. *Habitat International, 44,* 102–110.

Zhan, C., & de Jong, M. (2017). Financing Sino-Singapore Tianjin Eco-City: What lessons can be drawn for other large-scale sustainable city-projects? *Sustainability, 9*(2), 201. https://doi.org/10.3390/su9020201.

PART II

Partnerships and Affordable Housing

CHAPTER 6

Production of Middle-Class Residential Developments in Nairobi: Informal Collaboration Between Developers and Urban Planners

Mary Muthoni Mwangi

6.1　Introduction

Urban planners have historically played a vital role in shaping the growth of towns and cities by assigning development zones and overseeing developments. Unmet demand for housing can be said to be at the heart of the phenomenon of non-compliance with planning laws and regulations. Planning for sub-Saharan Africa, which was adopted from the Global North, has been mainly spatially oriented, concerned with the orderliness of the physical environment in cities (Watson 2009a, b; Berrisford 2011). It has also been influenced by political and other vested interests (Schilderman and Lowe 2002). These influences, coupled with limited resources and poor administrative systems, have greatly undermined the role of planning in those cities (Rakodi 2001; Schilderman and Lowe 2002; Anyamba 2011). Planning systems in sub-Saharan Africa were

M. M. Mwangi (✉)
Kenyatta University Nairobi, Nairobi, Kenya
e-mail: Muthoni.mwangi@ku.ac.ke

© The Author(s) 2020
C. van Montfort, A. Michels (eds.), *Partnerships for Livable Cities*,
https://doi.org/10.1007/978-3-030-40060-6_6

developed in different contexts in the Global North, and have thus failed to address the problems of a developing City like Nairobi, where there is a split between formal and informal settlements (Onyango and Olima 2015; Watson 2009b; Anyamba 2011) and the *de facto* standards of most developments are contrary to the *de jure* standards of planners' normative views.

It is evident that the population explosion in sub-Saharan African cities poses major housing challenges (see for example Rakodi 1992; Tipple 1994; Rakodi 1995; Schilderman and Lowe 2002), but it is also presenting investment opportunities to opportunist developers. Nairobi is among the fastest growing cities, not only in sub-Saharan Africa, but in the world. As in other cities, the government is not ever likely to meet the supply of housing needed for its population, which continues to grow. For the middle-income group, private developers have stepped into the breach and are housing a substantial proportion of the population in apartment blocks (Photo 6.1).

This chapter shows that unlike in developed countries where a strict adherence to planning laws deters private developers who are seeking to

Photo 6.1 Some middle-income rental properties in Eastlands, Nairobi, flouting ground coverage and plot ratio regulations. Poor waste management is also noticeable. (Source: Photo made by the author, 2014)

maximise profit at the expense of neighbourhood decline (Adams and Watkins 2002), private developers in sub-Saharan Africa have ways of 'negotiating' with the system and are relentless in the provision of housing, albeit outside the formal guidelines. This chapter is aimed at answering the question: What are the characteristics of the relationships between planners and developers, and why do they foster non-compliance?

This chapter is based on a PhD research which investigated working relationships between planners and developers in Nairobi. First, in Sect. 6.2, the chapter address informality as a mode of governance. Section 6.3 presents the findings and shows three shortcomings in planning governance in Nairobi. Section 6.4 then, discusses the findings with respect to (1) Informality as a mode of governance; (2) the existence of formal and informal partnerships between private developers, public planners and other government agencies, and (3) and the production of middle-income residential developments in Nairobi. Section 6.5 presents the main conclusions.

The research relied mostly on qualitative data from participants. Information was gathered from interviews with senior planners, frontline planners and developers. In total, there were qualitative interviews with 44 participants, comprising 14 planners, 4 planning consultants, 4 relevant government agents, and 22 developers (or their agents). It was a challenge to recruit developers since the research was investigating non-compliance with planning regulations, which made culprits potentially vulnerable to incrimination. The research therefore used a combination of recruitment methods; questionnaires and direct referrals helped to get optimum samples for qualitative interviewing. Once reassured of confidentiality, participants talked freely about the challenges faced in efforts to apply the planning system. All participants were given codes to preserve anonymity (see Table 6.1 for codes).

Table 6.1 Participant codes

Participants	Code
Senior planners	SP
Operational planners	OP
Planning consultants/advisors/other government agents	PA
Developers	DV
Developers' agents	DVA

The chapter shows that cooperation is necessary for developing livable, affordable housing. However, for economic reasons, informal partnerships between private developers and public planners develop.

6.2   INFORMALITY AS A MODE OF GOVERNANCE

6.2.1   *Political Economy Drivers in Planning and Housing Developments: The Rise of Informality*

Becker (1978) inferred that human actors tend to engage in maximising behaviour, whatever the commodity. With regards to landed property, Guy and Hanneberry (2008) affirm Becker, arguing that capitalism requires buildings to be produced profitably, and operations towards this are determined by how people interpret their positions within a given social system. Healey (1991) asserts that the process of private property development is a passive reflection of the demands of industry, commerce, and households for accommodation. Healey (1992) points out that property investment is opportunity driven, and developers look for returns which reflect perceived risk-reward profiles. Adams and Watkins (2014) concur; they point out that developer behaviour is governed by market conditions, current and expected. However, property investment calls for high levels of capital investment, from which substantial returns are realised in the long term (Healey 1992). Berry et al. (1993), echo this, pointing out that real estate assets realise high rates of returns on invested capital, providing value appreciation and protection against inflation. It is therefore not surprising that many developers emerge in periods of boom, when speculation in landed property seems more certain. However, developers' reaction to market forces is not without criticism. Pure unadulterated greed (and sometimes ego) has been blamed for developers' actions, with developers being labelled as predatory, profit driven and ruthless in their pursuits (McDonald and Sheridan 2009).

Healey (1998) has noted widespread negative views among politicians and other public officials, who reason that since developers generate a lot of profit from their investments in real estate, they should contribute some of those profits to help counteract the adverse effects of their developments, for example towards provision of infrastructure and community facilities. About practices in Britain, Crook and Monk (2011) have defined this as planning gain, whereby planning policies enable planning authorities to negotiate with private developers who are seeking building approval for provision of physical and social infrastructure connected to their developments.

Although planners in a market economy have *de jure* dominance over land and resources, with powers to implement ordered space in given jurisdictions, plans do not necessarily precede *de facto* land use. Planning powers have therefore been perceived as 'negative' in that they seek to prevent development. The role of planners seems limited to implementing a predefined '*rational planning order*', setting and trying to enact a vision, devoid of recognition of the '*realpolitik*' of the political economy (Andersen et al. 2015: 347). In a capitalist setting, where developers' investments are shaped by market forces, their realities and rationalities (and those of the population being provided for), and those of planning, are often mutually exclusive. Resourceful developers might not be willing to accept guidance in their quest for profitable investment, and yet planning does not always have 'positive' powers to ensure development. Whatever their motivations, private property developers play an important role in shaping urban growth.

6.2.2 Corruption in Governance

If a country has laws and institutions, but these do not adequately constrain the state ... corruption is likely to be pervasive since state custodians are not fully constrained by existing laws and hence, can easily abuse their public positions for private gain. (Mbaku 2010: 71)

A widespread system of informality is known to exist in African societies, and corruption is among the most rampant informal practices. It is embedded in daily governance, and routine administrative practices foster and accommodate the practice (Blundo and Olivier de Sardan 2006).

There is consensus that corruption is the abuse of public power for private benefit; a practice that hinges on practices by people attempting to subvert or undermine existing rules to generate extra-legal income (Nye 1967; Khan 1996; Friedrich 2002; Bayart 2009; Mbaku 2010; Transparency International 2015). This chapter uses Friedrich's (2002) definition of corruption; '...corruption may therefore be said to exist whenever a power holder who is charged with doing certain things, that is a responsible functionary or office holder, is by monetary or other rewards.... induced to take actions which favour whoever provides the reward and thereby damage the group or organisation to which the functionary belongs, specifically the government' (p. 15). This definition is echoed by Transparency International (2015) in their definition '...the abuse of entrusted power for private gain. It can be classified as grand, petty and political...'. This definition encompasses anyone entrusted with power, from those in high offices, to low level officials. It covers widespread and systematic corruption, which has become a basic mode of operation in some states. This definition is especially apt for this chapter, because as Chabal and Daloz (1999) have noted, '...corruption is not just endemic but an integral part of the social fabric of life in the African continent' (p. 99). Suffice to say, corruption in urban growth management systems impacts on the effectiveness of the systems in promoting and steering private developers.

6.2.3   Types of Corruption

Blundo and Olivier de Sardan (2006) have coined the term *'complex of corruption'* for 'all practices involving the use of public office that are improper – in other words, illegal and/or illegitimate from the perspective of the regulations in force or from that of users – and give rise to undue personal gain' (p. 6). Such corruption includes practices such as nepotism, abuse of power, misappropriation, and influence-peddling, among others. Alam (1989) noted that state regulators may exempt entrepreneurs from compliance with laws and regulations to reduce their costs, in exchange for proportionate monetary rewards.

According to Blundo and Olivier de Sardan (2006), impunity, another form of corruption, mostly arises from clientelism. Goodfellow (2013) found that persistent political interference in Uganda impacted on the effectiveness of planning, with impunity extended to elite and popular groups who could give financial or electoral incentives to the politicians. In systems where impunity prevails over sanctions, implementation of laws and regulations is ridiculed; isolated implementation of laws and regulation is a penalty for failure to show allegiance, or refusal to pay up, or any other motivations that have little to do with just enforcement.

Just as there are rules in formal practices, there are multiple rules in informal practices. Corruption in governance is an informal collaboration between state agents and the public, which undermines the functionality of government systems. It is a complex informal system lurking under the formal system, a mode of governance that works according to its own moral compasses and ethical codes. It is acknowledged that corrupt transactions are by mutual agreement by the givers and the takers, an out-come of a market with informally developed structures (Anders 2005; Blundo and Olivier de Sardan 2006; Olivier de Sardan 2008; Mbaku 2010).

This chapter considers whether non-compliance with planning laws and regulations can be understood not as the individual acts of those 'short-circuiting' planning regulation, but rather as a systemic effect of gover-nance practices that deliberately produce 'grey areas', within which there are possibilities for future developments of uncertain legal status.

6.3   Three Shortcomings in Planning Governance in Nairobi

6.3.1   Political Influence and Impunity

... 'Orders from above' is messing up this city; it's messing up this country.... (Interview SP7)

Political interests do not necessarily foster good practices in the plan-ning system – these are interests that serve a few, but do not necessarily represent the desires of most of the affected population. It is like an invis-ible governance system working alongside the official systems, and plan-ners have been rendered helpless by political interference at many levels. Impunity appears to be an accepted way of life:

In this country ... you find that you're in a fix you find somebody to assist you. And most probably you'll not run to a bishop, you'll not run to a pastor, you'll run to a politician... who will fix things for you.... (Interview PA13)

Political interference seems to know no bounds and comprises even those at senior levels in the planning offices. As one private planner and consultant expressed:

The director.... of City Planning works with the mayor ...., and the mayor asks for a favour for a friend – asks the director to assist in approving a six-storey development in Kileleshwa. The director knows it's bad but not too bad, and through her boss's request "...can you please, assist my friend..." she gets compro-mised by the political environment she's working in...The mayor uses polite language but sends a strong signal to the director to do what he wants "...kindly assist this person and give him what he wants…"… it's implied that she needs to do what he wants. (Interview PA14)

Most of the impunity is extended because money has changed hands, compelling planning officials to turn a blind eye to malpractices by developers, while developers and their agents have become seasoned to making informal payments to buy protection.

Owners 'talk' to the council officials before the building works start. You pay about 60,000 to 100,000 shillings to the council workers, so they will not bother the builders. For example, behind Thika Road Mall I have constructed buildings with seven floors, yet the approval was only for two to three floors…. (Interview DV10)

It is indeed difficult for planners to enforce planning laws and regulations when some developers have 'protection' from people in positions of power and influence, and the remaining developers follow suit in defying planning laws and regulations. Planners and developers believed the penalties on developers for non-compliance are not hefty enough to deter developers in their ventures. The Physical Planning Act specifies a maximum penalty of KSh100,000 (about $1149), and the court takes into consideration any mitigating circumstances before making a judgement. A developer expressed:

…If you're investing 20 million and you're charged only 100 thousand, you can pay. You can even be charged three times and you keep paying and you continue building…. (Interview DV9)

DV9 is a serial developer, and a contractor for other developers, and was talking about official penalties once non-complying developers are arrested. Weighed against the likely returns, the official penalties do seem puny. In a planner's words, the planning authorities have been proved to be 'barking dogs' with no bite.

There is another element to impunity, which is also a force in its own right, but compounds impunity – corruption. The section below will look at this practice further, and how it stimulates harassment by planners (towards developers).

6.3.2 Corruption and Harassment

Kenyans have thought that if they want something and they cannot get it, then they can buy their way out. (Interview SP2)

Engrained corruption was a common theme among participants. According to a planning consultant, more than 90% of the middle-income apartment blocks in Eastlands, for example, are owned by rich and powerful people who live in high end residential developments such as Runda, Lavington and Kitsuru – they are the ones with hundreds of million shillings to put up such developments, and who can afford to persuade planning officials to look the other way (interview PA17). Regarding planning efforts, even government-initiated housing projects, such as the Site and Service schemes, were riddled with this practice – appointed officers turning a blind eye while those allocated serviced plots ignored type plans for single dwellings in favour of storied multiple dwellings. However, when the plots were bought by rich and powerful individuals, who developed storied apartment blocks (interview OP4X), other developers, by default, benefited from the same impunity that the powerful people enjoyed. Planners at City Hall were of the view that Ward Officers in the field were in most cases turning a blind eye (interviews OP1, SP3). They attributed this to the fact that remuneration for subordinate staff is pathetically low, and so there is no official (as opposed to informal) financial motivation. This pushes them to harass developers and their agents for side payments.

Planners reckoned that such officers have limited technical knowledge of the planning requirements and are easily 'persuaded' by developers or their agents to look the other way (interviews OP1, PA5). This notion was reinforced by developers, who expressed that those officials did not seem to have the technical knowhow to inspect or monitor developments. A contractor, who deals with them regularly, lamented:

> ....*They don't know the building codes but they know about simple issues like dumping, helmets for workers, scaffolding. They don't know the technicalities of building requirements. They harass developers on the minor stuff.* (Interview DV10)

Such officers feed on the power and fear (of being brought to book) they generate over developers.

Planners in City Hall also perceived their remuneration to be relatively low compared to other government sector workers, and several believed that unless salaries were reviewed, they would remain easy targets and prone to temptation by developers (interviews SP2, SP7, OP3).

> *...a lot of the development we saw in this Upperhill area, we found the council officer is aware of the provisions of the law and regulations, but when he's put against the developer and the type of financial power the developer seems to command, the council officer simply melts, and it comes to a level where you're saying "...so what do you want?"....* (Interview PA4)

At times the quid pro quo is not only in terms of instant rewards, but a long-term game with high stakes. Whatever the case may be, such officers are happy to look the other way:

> *...This guy is the owner of Equity Bank. He wants offices up there and he buys a big plot, even for one billion, to build his office headquarters. And he asks somebody to approve his plans. And he will ask what is happening to my plans. And this guy [in the planning office] will need to go to that big office to get a loan and so forth...*[1] (Interview OP4X)

Malpractices sometimes cause conflict between planners; there are those who want to do right but are either compromised by political influence and/or pressure, or out of a sense of loyalty to their colleagues. One planner disclosed how, following a field survey, they discovered malpractices by colleagues, which put them in a moral dilemma:

> *.... now I'm in a place I'm not able to analyse data because if I analyse the data I will put so many people into problems, and they might even lose their jobs.* (Interview SP7)

Corruption is not one-sided though, and developers have a large part to play in it. According to DV10 (contractor/developer), when developers are complying and are not afraid to challenge harassment from the field officers, they are left alone. There is evidently joint working with the planners to beat the system, and together they seem to be chipping away at it, while at the same time demonstrating consciousness of general guidelines.

> *.... they will only support you if you're working within the harmony of the area. For example, even if you pay them and you want to put up apartments in*

---

[1] It implied a **quid pro quo** arrangement.

Karen, they'll not allow you because their job will be on the line. They'll turn a blind eye within the realm of what is allowed in the area. They're not totally blind.... (Interview DVA6)

Indeed, they are not totally blind, and there are lines that cannot be crossed in terms of development. As DVA6 pointed out, for example, it would be difficult to ignore apartment blocks in an exclusively single dwelling residential area like Karen. Therefore, there is selective blindness, more pronounced in some areas than others.

One planner aptly said:

.... City hall will not bribe itself; the officers who are being bribed will not bribe themselves, and they will not be bribed by other officers – they will be bribed by developers.... (Interview SP4)

A senior planner told of how one developer went berserk in the planning office because he could not understand how the planner could say no to his 'gift' of money, which was more than the planner makes in several months (SP7). However, there are those planners who will not turn such an offering away, and this fuels developers' belief that they can buy planners' loyalties.

Attempts have been made to eradicate corruption in the city county. Evidence of these attempts was seen in the county planning offices; for example, notices to members of the public cautioning them against paying bribes, and cautioning planners against accepting bribes. The posters were put up amid cries of 'reforms' after the new Constitution came into effect in 2010. The posters are all well and good, but as witnessed in one of the offices in the course of this research, they are ineffective; one developer was expressing anger at a planning official because he had apparently informally paid KSh200,000 (about $2299) to a planning officer who had been recommended by a councillor to process and progress his application for approval, but this had not materialised. What was interesting about this case was that the developer was not upset because he had paid extra informal money for the approval, but because he had not got the approval. Thus, the same people who were crying 'reforms' were the ones behind corruption, even when reforms are implemented.

Surprisingly, planners acknowledged corruption as a cancer that devours integrity and ethical practices in the planning system. What was even more surprising was the high level of tolerance by the public, despite open invitations to object to such practices. And there lies the difficulty; on the one hand are the developers, who even while complaining about corrupt officials seem to have developed a mind-set that it is the only way to get results, and on the other hand there are planning officials who are only too happy to oblige. From small bribes to poorly paid officers looking to supplement their incomes, to sophisticated backhanders to those in positions of power, who ultimately want to accumulate and protect their wealth and positions – the cancer that is corruption persists and spreads.

6.3.3   Poor Joint Working with Developers, Other Government Agencies and Departments

.... the challenge is to develop more inclusive and effective forms of planning, rather than to give up on it all together. (Goodfellow 2013: 84)

Developers aired their frustrations that planners did not seem to pay any heed to their concerns, and so the planning department did not complement their efforts. According to them, they were not effectively consulted for suggestions, and their complaints were ignored. A Kenya Property Developers Association (KPDA) representative complained that, although they were supposed to have meetings with planning officials twice a year, the meetings were not happening.

According to a KPDA representative, the organisation writes policy review documents and provides capacity training for its members i.e. it responds to the different capacity needs of the industry. Regular consultation meetings with the planners could therefore be quite productive for both planners and developers. Although there is some scepticism amongst planners that KPDA members just lobby for their own interests, it cannot be denied that even as they pursue their interests, they would be pushing planners to come up with good policies and general practices in planning that could benefit all. A senior planner acknowledged:

They can lobby for infrastructure, they can lobby for quicker approval processes, they can lobby for efficient and effective enforcement mechanisms. (Interview SP4)

It is through such forums that civil society organisations and other professionals in the industry could contribute to the evaluation and review of the planning system. As one developer aptly noted:

I don't think that in the building industry, that development is a preserve of the planner. There are times when the engineers are right, there are times when the architects will be right....and a developer often has a respectable view about what he thinks ought to be. (Interview DV1)

Developers' agents also complained that there are no avenues to give feedback to planners or to appeal decisions:

.... planning in Kenya is still housed within the government. We have not really become a planning society where we are so informed about the structure of planning and where, when you feel aggrieved, where you can go...... (Interview DVA4)

Making developers' agents, especially architects, structural engineers and even building contractors, more accountable would help to reduce the number of county planning staff required to monitor developments. However, at present there is no code of ethics for these professionals. One suggestion by a senior planner was to require:

..... that every development ... has an architect on record. Just the way if you go to court you wouldn't find any case going on without an advocate on record.... [then] if one architect pulls out and puts it very clearly why he's pulled out.... then any other architect will find it very difficult to come in because the guidelines are very clear to all and sundry.... (Interview SP3)

Developers' agents are potentially a powerful ally for planners in that they are in contact with developers, but may be more inclined to make sense of reasonable laws and regulations, than their clients. It is in the interest of such agents for developers to seek and gain approval, because then they are more likely to get commissioned for their input. As one agent put it:

.... if you [a developer] come to me [because] you want to develop a plot, I should have a question "...have you attended the council training before you came to me?" And I can't draw a plan for a person who has not attended, because the plan will not be approved by the council.... (Interview DVA5)

The theme of poor consultation is also visible between the planning department and other government agencies and departments that work towards similar ends. For example, it appears there is substantial overlap of remits between the functions of the Physical Planning Department at the

Ministry (whose remit includes land management, physical planning and implementation), the City Government (which houses another Department of Physical Planning), the Ministry of Local Government (mandated with developing urban development policies and assisting with planning), and the Ministry of Nairobi Metropolitan Development (mandated to give technical support and resources for planning and implementation). More coherent joint-working and amalgamation of resources could mean increased efficiency in service provision. For example, the Physical Planning department at the Ministry of Lands, Housing and Urban Development has a total of 31 qualified physical planners, spread out in Development Control, Policy Planning, Local Planning, Regional Planning, Forward Planning, Research and Development (interview PA11). So, whilst the Planning Department at City Hall is struggling due to a shortage of qualified staff (with a lot of employees doing the wrong jobs), the Physical Planning Department at the Ministry, which is privileged to have graduate planners, has a duplicate section, which unfortunately works independently from that at the county planning department.

Developers do not necessarily apply for development approval because they believe in the relevance of guidelines for a sustainable environment or the effects of their development on infrastructure, but because getting approval may be a prerequisite for, for example, funding applications to financial institutions (interview OP1). Planners would therefore do well to forge and foster relationships with such institutions. Such institutions need not be involved for technical reasons, but because of their ability to exercise leverage over their clients and to liaise with the relevant planning section if they have any concerns.

What frustrates developers and their agents is that the different departments, such as water, public health, electricity and roads, are aware of developments, yet when it comes to guidance and the provision of infrastructural services they are not very proactive or supportive. This begs the question why planners have not attempted to rectify it by improving coordination between the departments involved in planning approval. For example, the planning department gives approval, subject to approval by the National Environment Management Authority (NEMA). But every so often NEMA has been known to turn down applications due to environmental implications, after the planning department has given development approval.

Developers thought the process would work better if all departments, including NEMA, gave their approval before the final approval from the planning department. They felt that there was an overlap in the departmental roles and that the process could be more streamlined to avoid duplication. NEMA does its own research, for example, on alternative means of sewage disposal, so could advise and guide the planning department in zoning guidelines reviews, but does not (interview OP2). This is frustrating, not only to forward thinking developers, but also to planners. One operational planner commented:

> ... *there are these things we're calling the bio-digesters; those are things we're supposed to look at. If there is no trans-sewer and the developer is willing to use them...NEMA has studied those things and it has several models that they have approved....* (Interview OP2)

Occasionally such technology is applied, for example in parts of Kileleshwa in zone 4 (where there is no sewer line) (interview OP2), but it could easily be rolled out to different areas to meet the needs of the growing population.

6.4   Discussion of the Findings

6.4.1   Informality as a Mode of Governance in Nairobi

The quagmire that is corruption is a product created by both planners and developers, and the powers that be are aware of this. Whichever side corruption emanates from, it has eroded the values of the planning function in Nairobi. It is not just that the majority of contravening developers are not known to the authorities, but also that those known can get away with it. Even when they are called to face the consequences, for example with planned demolitions, they run to the politicians for protection.

The negative impacts of corruption are known, yet it is accommodated and tolerated by the same people who claim to hate it. It would take a change in culture between the stakeholders to eliminate this practice. Developers' agents should not have to factor in 'kickbacks' to planning officials while negotiating their fees, and those messages of anti-corruption practices which line the walls in county offices should count for something. For any fight against this practice to be effective, it would have to start from the people in powerful positions. They need to lead by example, because otherwise it becomes difficult to advocate changes in culture and to enforce from within if conviction is not demonstrated. The question is, do people want to change the culture or they are happy and comfortable with it (the human inertia referred to by Connor (1998)?

There are myriads of reasons for this practice; for example, planners capitalising on fear and the possibility of retribution to hold power over developers, impatient developers who are happy to 'buy' their way through the system, and the ignorance of field staff, coupled with a desire to supplement their low incomes. Whatever the reason, this practice has permeated the planning institution, undermining the role of the state. The parallel organisation referred to by Anders (2005) and Mbaku (2010) has strongly rooted itself, undermining any efforts to eradicate corruption.

6.4.2   The Existence of Formal and Informal Partnerships Between (Private) Investors and (Public) Planners and Other Governing Agencies

Conflicting interests within and between different departments have so far undermined effective joint-working. There seems to be lack of trust between planners and other stakeholders: developers do not believe that planners have their best interests at heart, planners feel undermined by other professionals, and other professionals believe planners want to hold all the power for selfish gains.

The planning system has created a 'new normal' of ignoring rules and regulations, and developers' agents are turning a blind eye as much as the planners—in practice, developers are aided and abetted by professionals who should be guided by their professional ethics, but are not in part because planners do not acknowledge their value in influencing actions (or non-actions) by developers.

There is room for consultation and feedback, which if accommodated could help to foster relationships between planners and developers. Streamlining links and mechanisms with non-governmental stakeholders and developing mechanisms to share planning responsibilities appropriately could positively impact on the number of developers voluntarily engaging with the system. However, this calls for trust in the planning institution, and between planners and other stakeholders.

6.4.3 Production of Middle-Income Residential Developments in Nairobi

The research has revealed that in Nairobi developers are responding to demand by exceeding the allowable development capacities on their land, while the city planners turn a blind eye for various reasons, ranging from low staffing capacities to financial inducements to planning officers. These findings echo those of Gatabaki-Kamau and Karirah-Gitau (2004), about developers leading in setting trends contrary to planning expectations. In Nairobi, these developments, which give the impression that they are formal because they do not display the same obvious symptoms of informality as slum areas, have spread and have clearly been tolerated. There is clearly a need for them—they serve a purpose.

There is a spirit of entrepreneurship amongst developers in and for middle income group, as well as resources (finance, skills and influence) that could be accessed by planners to complement their planning efforts. Partnerships between the private parties (developers) and the public (planners) are necessary for developing affordable houses for the middle-income group. However, for economic reasons informal partnerships between developers and planners develop. Although there is no trust between planners and developers in Nairobi, they do, nevertheless, collaborate informally and have developed a 'parallel order' (as alluded to by Anders 2005), which tolerates non-compliance. This is not a function working type of partnership; because of corruption and impunity, non-compliance with planning laws and regulations in the development of middle-income residential housing has become the norm.

6.5 Conclusion

'.... there is a role for planners in balancing the workings of the capitalistic market in property development for the middle-income group' (Mwangi 2015: 325). Governance of the planning system in Nairobi is clearly not effective, and the results are visible for all to see. The 'weak nature of the state and governance regimes' alluded to by Jenkins and Andersen (2011) is clearly at play.

Forester (1982) aptly noted that planners find it difficult to ignore those in power, because to do so may render them powerless. His argument that private economic actors and/or politics can overwhelm planners has been affirmed in this chapter; politicians and other influential people do often undermine planning efforts. The impunity for developers that results affirms that planning responds to pressure from various sources (Adams and Watkins 2002; Rydin 2011). Also, as noted by Chabal and Daloz (1999), 'the big man' patronage system (and the manipulations it allows), which is characterised by interdependence between leaders and the general population, is present in Nairobi, like elsewhere in Africa.

Corrupt practices are two-sided and deeply engrained: developers offer informal payments to expedite the approval process, while middlemen and poorly paid planning staff are only too willing to oblige. Self-serving interests breed corruption and impunity, and unfortunately, influential people in positions of power have been implicated in such practices. It is indeed difficult to enforce or mete out justice if there is selective toleration of corruption and impunity. It is even more difficult when the very people who are entrusted with power are making a mockery of the best practices they are supposed to be promoting and are involved in violations.

There is an inherent lack of trust between planners and developers in Nairobi: planners on the one hand strictly lay down the law but are frustrated because developers are defiant of the regulations, and on the other hand developers (and their agents) are bewildered and frustrated because they do not understand or follow the rationale of planning. The two groups have not developed common ground to discuss and resolve development control issues and concerns, and neither is happy with the workings of the other, to the detriment of the city-scape.

Whilst the ideology of planning purports that local authorities have power over development, the reality is that private capital drives and directs what happens in the city. It stands to reason that developers present an untapped resource that could work collaboratively with planners and policy makers—incorporating them strategically by respectful inclusion could change cityscapes for the better. Partnerships can contribute to affordable housing and a livable city if there is good governance in government, which directs private capital to complement planning efforts. In the Nairobi case, the informal form of partnership has not worked because of the dominance of economic drivers, corruption at all levels, and the lack of trust between stakeholders. Such partnerships require trust between the stakeholders, which can only be cultivated by consensus legitimatisation of what the system is trying to achieve.

REFERENCES

Adams, D., & Watkins, C. (2002). *Greenfields, brownfields and housing development.* Oxford: Blackwell Science.

Adams, D., & Watkins, C. (2014). The value of planning. RTPI research report no.5. Retrieved August 31, 2015 from http://www.rtpi.org.uk/value of planning

Alam, M. S. (1989). Anatomy of corruption: An approach to the political economy of underdevelopment. *American Journal of Economics and Sociology, 48*(4), 441–456.

Anders, G. (2005). *Civil servants in Malawi: Moonlighting, kinship and corruption in the shadow of good governance.* PhD manuscript, Law Faculty, Erasmus University Rotterdam, 15.

Andersen, J. E., Jenkins, P., & Nielsen, M. (2015). Who plans the African city? A case study of Maputo: Part 1 – The structural context. *International Development Planning Review, 37*(3), 329–350.

Anyamba, T. (2011). Informal urbanism in Nairobi. *Built Environment, 37*(1), 57–77.

Bayart, J. F. (2009). *The state in Africa: The politics of the belly.* Cambridge: Polity Press.

Becker, G. S. (1978). *The economic approach to human behavior.* chicago, illinois: University of chicago press.

Berrisford, S. (2011). Why it is difficult to change urban planning laws in African countries. *Urban Forum, 22*(3), 209–228.

Berry, J., MCgreal, S., & Deddis, B. (Eds.). (1993). *Urban regeneration: Property investment and development.* London: E. and F. N. Spon.

Blundo, G., & Olivier de Sardan, J. P. (2006). *Everyday corruption and the state. Citizens and public officials in Africa.* London: Zed Books.

Chabal, P., & Daloz, J.-P. (1999). *Africa Works: Disorder as Political Instrument.* Oxford: James Currey.

Crook, T., & Monk, S. (2011). Planning gains, providing homes. *Housing Studies, 26*(7–8), 997–1018.

Forester, J. (1982). Planning in the face of power. *Journal of the American Planning Association, 48*(1), 67–80.

Friedrich, C. J. (2002). Corruption concepts in historical perspective. In A. Heidenheimer & M. Johnston (Eds.), *Political corruption: Concepts and contexts* (pp. 3, 13–3, 23). New York: Routledge.

Gatabaki-Kamau, R., & Karirah-Gitau, S. (2004). Actors and interests: The development of an informal settlement in Nairobi, Kenya. *Reconsidering informality: Perspectives from urban Africa,* 158–175.

Goodfellow, T. (2013). Planning and development regulation amid rapid urban growth: Explaining divergent trajectories in Africa. *Geoforum, 48,* 83–93.

Guy, S., & Hanneberry, J. (Eds.). (2008). *Development and developers: Perspectives on property.* Oxford/Malden: Blackwell.

Healey, P. (1991). Urban regeneration and the development industry. *Regional Studies, 25*(2), 97–110.

Healey, P. (1992). The reorganisation of state and market in planning. *Urban Studies, 29*(3–4), 411–434.

Healey, P. (1998). Regulating property development and the capacity of the development industry. *Journal of Property Research, 15*(3), 211–227.

Jenkins, P., & Andersen, J. E. (2011, June 15–18). *Developing cities in between the formal and informal.* Conference paper. ECAS 2011 – 4th European Conference on African Studies. Uppsala, Panel 85.

Khan, M. (1996). A typology of corrupt transactions in developing countries. *IDS Bulletin, 8*(5), 12. https://doi.org/10.1111/j.1759-5436.1996.mp27002003.x.

Mbaku, J. M. (2010). *Corruption in Africa: Causes, consequences, and cleanups.* Maryland: Lexington Books.

McDonald, F., & Sheridan, K. (2009). *The builders: How a small Group of Property Developers Fuelled the building boom and transformed Ireland.* London: Penguin Ireland.

Mwangi, M. M. (2015). *Urban growth management in sub-Saharani Africa: Conflicting interests in the application of planning laws and regulations in middle income residential developments in Nairobi.* PhD thesis. http://etheses.whiterose.ac.uk/15563/

Nye, J. S. (1967). Corruption and political development. *American Political Science Review, 61*(2), 417–427.

Olivier de Sardan, J.-P. (2008). State bureaucracy and governance in Francophone West Africa: An empirical diagnosis and historical perspective. In G. Blundo (Ed.), *The governance of daily life in Africa: Ethnographic explorations of public and collective services.* (pp. 39–71). Leiden: Brill.

Onyango, M. O., & Olima, W. H. (2015). *Housing transformations in Nairobi, Kenya: A strategy towards sustainable urban development.* http://erepo.usiu.ac.ke/11732/1091

Rakodi, C. (1992). Housing markets in third world cities: Research and policy into the 1990s. *World Development, 20*(1), 39–55.

Rakodi, C. (1995). Rental tenure in the cities of developing countries. *Urban Studies, 32*(4–5), 791–811.

Rakodi, C. (2001). Forget planning, put politics first? Priorities for urban management in developing countries. *International Journal of Applied Earth Observation and Geoinformation, 3*(3), 209–223.

Rydin, Y. (2011). *The purpose of planning: Creating sustainable towns and cities.* Bristol: Policy Press.

Schilderman, T., & Lowe, L. (2002). *The impact of regulations on urban development and the livelihoods of the urban poor.* Conference paper. Second RGUU international workshop held at Bourton on Dunsmore, UK, March 2001.

Retrieved from: www.gov.uk (Department for International Development; Research For Development Outputs).

Tipple, A. G. (1994). The need for new urban housing in sub-Saharan Africa: Problem or opportunity. *African Affairs, 93*(373), 587–608.

Transparency International website. (2015). http://www.transparency.org/what-is-corruption/#define. Accessed 8 Aug 2019.

UN-Habitat. (1996). *The habitat agenda goals and principles, commitments and the global plan of action*. Istanbul: UN Habitat.

Watson, V. (2009a). Chapter one: Urban challenges and the need to revisit urban planningIn UN Habitat. In *Planning sustainable cities. Global Report on Human Settlements 2009*. https://unhabitat.org/wp-content/uploads/2010/07/GRHS.2009.0.pdf

Watson, V. (2009b). Seeing from the south: Refocusing urban planning on the globe's central urban issues. *Urban Studies, 46*(11), 2259–2275.

CHAPTER 7

Innovations in Affordable Housing in Dublin: Lessons from Not-for-Profit Housing Developers

Valesca Lima

7.1 INTRODUCTION

Much has been written about how poor-quality and insecure housing is associated with low levels of health problems, poverty, educational achievements and wide inequality (Gibson et al. 2011). As the lack of affordable housing in Ireland continues to soar into a housing crisis, reports call for thousands of more houses to be built to address the country's housing shortage. The shortage of affordable housing in the Greater Dublin Area, where the rents prices are more expensive, is one aspect of a sharp deterioration of the living condition experienced by a broad sector of the population. Affordable housing is an important aspect of livability in cities, and in this chapter, I examine housing innovation from an affordability perspective. Ireland's recent history is marked by boom and bust of the housing market, caused by problems in the private housing and financial systems (Byrne and Norris 2018). The financial crisis that stroke Ireland in

V. Lima (✉)
Maynooth University Social Sciences Institute, Kildare, Ireland
e-mail: Valesca.Lima@mu.ie

© The Author(s) 2020
C. van Montfort, A. Michels (eds.), *Partnerships for Livable Cities*,
https://doi.org/10.1007/978-3-030-40060-6_7

125

2008 stemmed from a real estate bubble, and it has had damaging effects on social housing, producing a crisis across the whole Irish housing system. The housing crisis in Dublin is due to both a market failure and policy failure, since the government has neglected the provision of social housing to low income families, in an implausible expectation that market will provide affordable housing for this group.

The term *affordable housing* is broad and includes specific meanings in different contexts. Throughout the text, the term is used to refer to housing that is delivered directly by not-for-profit providers, funded by a combination public and private finance for social rent at below the market prices to families who cannot afford to pay private sector rents or buy their own homes. The Irish case provides useful and unique insights into the role of not-for-profit affordable housing developers—henceforth, housing associations—in shaping effective responses to housing affordability problems. The housing crisis has challenged governments to increase the social housing supply but the implementation of a larger plan to deliver social housing has not been effective, as evidenced by the growing homelessness and long social housing waiting lists. In this context, housing associations have adapted their policy responses to the housing problem while maintaining their advocacy agenda. Their experiences signal their potential to facilitate pathways to housing security for tenants. Housing associations have been able to put forward innovative forms of partnership between civil society and public organizations: NGOs, local authorities, and financial institutions (Type H, see Fig. 1.1, Chap. 1). Those are concrete practices that may contribute to a better understanding of the functioning of specific types of partnerships that play a role in the production and management of affordable housing in urban centers.

This chapter examines the role of not-for-profit affordable housing developers in shaping effective responses to housing affordability problems in Ireland. Taking the experience of housing associations based in Dublin, I explore their participation in delivering affordable housing, as I attempt to respond the following question: can housing affordability goals be achieved through public-private partnerships? I assess the factors and conditions for success in delivering social housing, while I analyze whether affordability goals can be achieved through public-private collaborations. In this manner, the chapter investigates the social housing solutions and accomplishments of notable not-for-profit housing developers in Dublin. My main objective is to understand the current operating environment of those entities and identify directions for policy that could enable these or similar organizations to make larger scale contributions to the provision of affordable housing in Ireland. It is worth mentioning that this chapter is not intended to support a market solution for the housing crisis. Housing associations are one of the main government partners in the provision of social housing, but it has itself also suffered with cuts in government funding, thus they need to find funding and credit elsewhere. These associations are making it possible to provision dwellings that are low-cost than the ones built by the for-profit sector. They alleviate the distress of homeless families or on the verge of homelessness, sometimes providing emergency accommodation and other times by acquiring debts before vulture funds (hedge funds that buy distressed debts) can buy their debt. I argue that there is sufficient evidence to prove that housing affordability is possible, and despite their valuable role in direct housing provision, higher rates of local authorities housing input is still needed.

This chapter is organized as follows: In Sect. 7.2, I introduce the issue of lack of affordable housing in Dublin/Ireland and the current rise in family homelessness. My analysis starts from the transformation the housing sector has gone through since the property bubble in 2008/2009, as I look at the impact of the Irish government's austerity policies and privatization of housing over recent years. In Sect. 7.3, I move to the discussion of the voluntary housing sector in Ireland and their increasing role in the provision of affordable housing. In Sect. 7.4, I introduce the housing associations promoting innovative social housing policies, which combine a new model of financing that include partnerships between local authorities, non-profit housing bodies (housing associations) and private banks. In this part of the chapter, I present the cases of 'Clúid Housing' (innovating the finance of social housing); 'Ó Cualann Cohousing Alliance' (innovation in low-cost housing), and 'iCare Housing' (innovation in the prevention of family evictions). I seek to explain novelty practices brought by these new types of partnership and which lessons can be taken from public-private partnerships to address the lack of affordable homes and the housing crisis. In the final part of the chapter, I reflect about current housing dynamics that provides new opportunities to housing associations to be innovative, as they embrace new financial alternatives and collaborate with new actors; also, on the limits of their contribution to the alleviation of the housing crisis.

7.2   Financial Crisis, Housing and Homelessness

Dublin has been painted by many as 'the poster child of Europe' for its discipline and compliance in implementing a rigorous austerity program (Gaynor 2020; Roche et al. 2016). Despite the severity of the social cuts meted on its population, post-crash Ireland has seen a rapid growth in employment, increasing number of international students, expanding Foreign Direct Investments (FDI) and net migration, all indicators of economic prosperity. However, this economic recovery is not for everyone. The impact of austerity and welfare reform is heavier on the most vulnerable groups, and this impact was felt mainly by people relying on disability support, children, caregivers and those reliant on public services (Roche et al. 2016). The consequences of the 2008 economic crisis and the debt that followed have deepened inequality and increased poverty levels in Ireland. For example, child poverty almost doubled during the economic recession from 6.3% in 2008 to 11.2% in 2014 (TASC 2016). According to the same report, key factors contributing to economic inequality in Ireland comprise low paid jobs, precarious employment and unemployment.

What started as a bank crisis spiraled into a crisis of public debt, which then became a crisis of investment that gave birth to a relentless social crisis. In the critical evolution of the crisis, political institutions addressed the crisis with rough intervention oriented towards countercyclical policies. The most significant was the government intervention to guarantee the liabilities of Irish banks with an investment of 29% of the GDP (Della Porta et al. 2017). The austerity measures implemented in Ireland were one of the most severe in the European Union (EU). Among the changes in welfare state functions associated retrenchment of public spending, social housing was one of the most affected, as the high level of homelessness and poverty indicates the gravity of the social crisis (Considine and Dukelow 2009). Government spending for housing provision fell by 94% between 2008 and 2013 (Norris and Hayden 2018). Since then, the spending related to social housing has increased, but associated with a significant in reliance on housing allowance in the private sector to low-income households, with a sharp decline in the provision of mainstream social housing's traditional role as the main source of accommodation for this cohort (Byrne and Norris 2018). The changes in social housing provision have weakened the already tenuous social welfare protection. An increasing number of working families are becoming homeless, the majority of them coming from rent increases and evictions in the private housing sector.

The current housing crisis affects the whole nation in many aspects (street homelessness, housing shortage, soaring rents and housing insecurity), although it has particularly pernicious effects in Dublin, where rents prices have been increasing 11.3% on a yearly average. The average national monthly rent was €1300 in the third quarter of 2018 (DAFT 2018) and an average of 34,000 new units are needed each year to supply the current demand (Initiative Ireland 2018). While the investments in homeless services have more than doubled since 2015 (Lima 2018), the number of homeless families has sharply increased over the past years. There were 9759 people living in homeless accommodation in December 2018, 3559 of those are dependent children, an increase of 36% on the number of people facing homelessness compared with the same period in December 2016 (DHPLG 2018, 2019). These numbers might be even higher, since government data does do not take into account the 'hidden homelessness': those sleeping at a friend's couch, unsuitable accommodation and families receiving social housing supports (i.e. Housing Assistance Payment—HAP and the Rental Accommodation Scheme—RAS). In December 2018, there were 71,858 households in the waiting list for social housing in Ireland (Housing Agency 2018).

While not the first housing crisis in the Irish history (Kenna and O'Sullivan 2014; Byrne and Norris 2018), this time people are experiencing a particularly severe supply constraint due to the depth of the economic crisis which collapsed the construction industry (Dunne 2016). As a consequence of market-oriented neoliberal policies, the Irish government has moved from core delivery to regulating or coordinating the delivery of welfare. It has adopted a private-market solution to the crisis, where private rental market subsides have played an increasing role in the provision of social housing, as the market is seen as the ideal provider and allocator of housing.

The private housing market, in turn, has not been able to respond to the lack of affordable homes. According to Drudy and Punch (2005) the current Irish housing policies treat housing as a commodity, an approach that minimizes the direct provision of housing by the state. Many European countries have different approaches to housing, with a mix of state-led and market-led housing solutions. Ireland has substantially moved to a heavily market-led housing approach, designed to produce robust and larger market-based housing finance models. This financial model has been highly pro-cyclical, with cash available during boom times to build homes when construction costs are at its highest and little or no construction when during periods of recession when, but building is much cheaper (Byrne and Norris 2018). Even after property prices have lowered by 5% at the end of 2018, buyers still cannot afford homes. Affordability has become a serious issue for home buyers on lower incomes or who are in distressed mortgage debt. Many young people are forced to stay longer living with parents or to rent indefinitely (the "rent generation"). Unsurprisingly, home-ownership has dropped from 80% in 1991 to 67% in 2016 (CSO 2018).

The flagship housing policy program, *Rebuilding Ireland*, intends to achieve progress in housing affordability by trusting the private sector to provide 85% of the 134,000 new social housing (Housing Agency 2018). However, the costs of an average three-bedroom semi-detached house nearly doubles when provided by for-profit sector. Private housing developers set prices by adding to construction costs the profit they seek. As a result, their asking prices are clearly unaffordable for many families. For example, a report published by the Society of Chartered Surveyors Ireland (SCSI) pointed that the construction cost of a whole three-bedroom semi-detached house is €150,250, but when VAT, developer's profit, land costs and other fees are added, the cost of the house is €330,493. For this reason, many activists, progressive politicians, NGOs and housing associations have called for the state to build houses directly, through local authority grants.

A key element to housing affordability is income. If housing prices are rising faster than wages, affordability becomes a problem. In many EU countries, including Ireland, wages lag behind house price growth. A recent report that monitors housing affordability has placed Dublin as one of the least-affordable places to buy a home (see Fig. 7.1). When we look at the ratio of real house price growth compared to real income growth, it is possible to observe that Dublin has experienced a 61.9% fast rate house price growth over the last five years, with a relatively higher rate of income growth over the same period if compared to other countries, 13.2%. This finding suggests a large gap between the increase rates of increase. Interestingly, Dublin has a higher real income growth than London and Berlin, but five years of double-digit house price growth has pushed the cost of owning a home unaffordable for most families.[1]

---

[1] In the third quarter of 2018 In Dublin, the average house price was €365,000, and the average national income of €38,496.

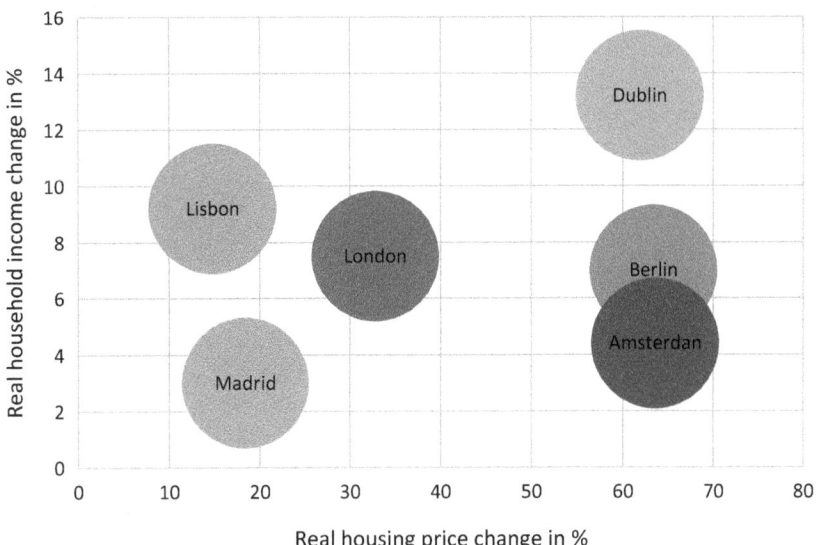

Fig. 7.1 Real house price growth and household income in six European cities since 2014. (Author's elaboration. Source: Knight Frank affordability monitor (2019))

Housing activism has been strong in Ireland in the past four years. In this period, diverse housing movements emerged in response to the challenges of economic recession and neoliberal austerity policies since 2014 (Mallon 2017). From the successful Right2Water movements that stopped the introduction of water charges to a number of protests and direct action around the right to housing, the country has seen an intensified level of dispute around the housing issue. There are up to 40 different grassroots housing groups across Dublin at the time of this writing. Those activists' groups challenge the current political decision through institutional politics (motions in the parliament), social protest and direct action. In 3th October 2018, about 10,000 attended the 'Raise the Roof' rally demanding change in the government responses to the crisis and in support of a motion calling for housing crisis to be declared a national emergency, which was approved by the parliament. Some movements are oriented towards direct forms of resistance, in contestation of rising rents, housing insecurity and to stop evictions, such as the 'Take Back The City' group. One of the main demands of the housing activists relates to the use of vacant properties in arrears that were put into receivership or were repossessed by banks and investment funds. They demand vacant buildings to be turned into social housing and reintegrated into the space of the city.

The recent rise of anti-eviction activism has targeted the discrepancy between properties that are kept lying vacant while evictions and homelessness grows. The increasing real estate prices result in intensification of housing unaffordability and growing number of evictions, but financial actors are more concerned in resolving the problem of distressed assets (O'Callaghan et al. 2018). As shown in Fig. 7.2, at end-September 2018, there were 728,075 private residential mortgage accounts for principal dwellings held in the Republic of Ireland, to a value of €98.2 billion (Central Bank 2018). Of this total stock, 63,246 accounts were in arrears, which represents a decline if compared to previous years. However, in the post-crisis context, international investors, such equity funds firms, buy billions of distressed assets and loans (Aalbers 2016). In Ireland, they have been increasingly interested in the mortgage arrears crisis, which saws NAMA and other banks selling loans and property assets to hedge funds

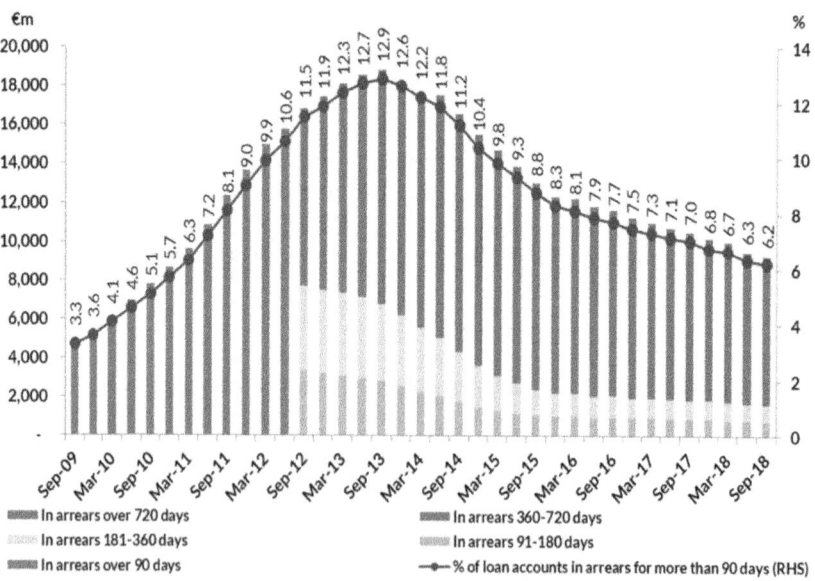

Fig. 7.2 Private home mortgage accounts in arrears over 90 days. (Source: Central Statistics Office (CSO) 2018)

(called 'vulture funds' in Ireland), mainly from the United States.[2] Many Irish banks were left with a large portfolio of mortgages in arrears and vulture funds buy this 'distressed debt' to sell it on a profit and potentially repossess the property to put it back in the market.

Years of government retreat for the provision of social and the reduced support for affordable housing policy have created a hiatus in the response to the population housing needs. Next, I present the changes in the provision of social housing, including the new role of local authority and housing associating in providing affordable housing.

7.3   Housing Associations: Non-profit Sector Providers of Social Housing in Ireland

Local authorities have been the main provider of social housing in Ireland. Social housing is a rented accommodation supplied by a local authority or a housing association. Since the end nineteenth century, local authorities have provided 365,350 housing units, which counted for the 22.2% of the total Irish housing stock in 2016 (CSO 2018). In the past 30 years, a significant reduction in the role of local authorities as the primary provider of affordable housing has been observed, especially after the 2008 financial crash, when the number of local authorities' tenants declined by nearly 50%. This reduction is due to two main reasons: first, the reduction of funding available for social housing output, which declined by 93% between 2008 and 2013. Second, the tradition of local authorities selling social council housing to long term tenants without reposition (Norris and Hayden 2018). Housing associations are different from local authorities in that tenants cannot buy their homes, so they have retained their stock over the years.

In spite of being the main provider, local authorities rely on other suppliers of social housing, such as housing associations and housing welfare benefits. The delivery of social housing involves three main types of providers: local authority, housing associations, and private landlord that rents to tenants in receipt of housing subsidies, such as the Housing Assistance Payment (HAP).

---

[2] NAMA is Ireland's National Asset Management Agency, set up in 2009 to acquire property loans from banks. Ninety percent of NAMA sales of distressed loans were made to US-based hedge funds firms in 2013 (O'Callaghan et al. 2018).

Housing associations are AHBs ('Approved Housing Bodies'), which are non-profit providers of social rented housing in Ireland. They are independent and registered not-for-profit charities. Until 1991, housing associations were a minor provider of social housing, delivering affordable, specialist housing for people with disabilities, the homeless and the elderly. But from 1991 on, housing associations started to participate in a range of rental schemes subsided by the Irish state, changing their status from small-scale housing provider to the point where they own and manage over 32,000 houses and apartments (CSO 2016). Around 140,000 social houses in Ireland are provided by local authorities and non-profit housing associations, allocated on the basis of need and let at a below marker rent value (Norris 2011). The decline stated-provided housing reflects the long-term re-arrangements of governmental policy towards the provision of social housing to low-income groups. The non-profit sector today is composed by over 540 AHBs registered with the Department of the Environment, Community and Local Government (DECLG). Housing Associations are in the process of being regulated by a statutory regulator, as set in the voluntary code of practice, 'Building for the Future – A Voluntary Regulation Code for Approved Housing Bodies', created in 2013.

Housing associations have played an increasingly important in the provision of social homes, and Almost 10% of Irish households live in social housing. In the last census (2016), nearly 30% of all occupied dwelling were rented. The rate of home €35,000 owner ship dropped from 69.7% to 67.6%, while the growth in rented accommodation continues (See Fig. 7.3). The delivery of social housing became more elaborated and varied over the years, as local authorities no longer is the sole provider of social housing. In 2017, for example, the 2245 social housing output comprised of 1058 houses constructed by local authority and 799 (nearly 35%) of new build social housing in 2017 was provided by housing associations (See Fig. 7.4). The remaining 388 social homes delivered that year were delivered through a Public Private Partnerships (PPPs) mechanism, the 'Part V' of the Planning and Development Act, 2000. This mechanism enables local authorities to require that up to 10% of new houses private estates are set aside for social housing. As showed by Norris and Hayden (2018, p. 62), local authority and housing associations dwellings procured using 'Part V' of the Planning and Development Act, 2000, have dropped. They argue this is evidence the marked decline in total private sector house building since the recent economic crisis, and that despite the benefits of having council housing in mixed tenure developments, it also means that when market supply falls local authority housing output falls too.

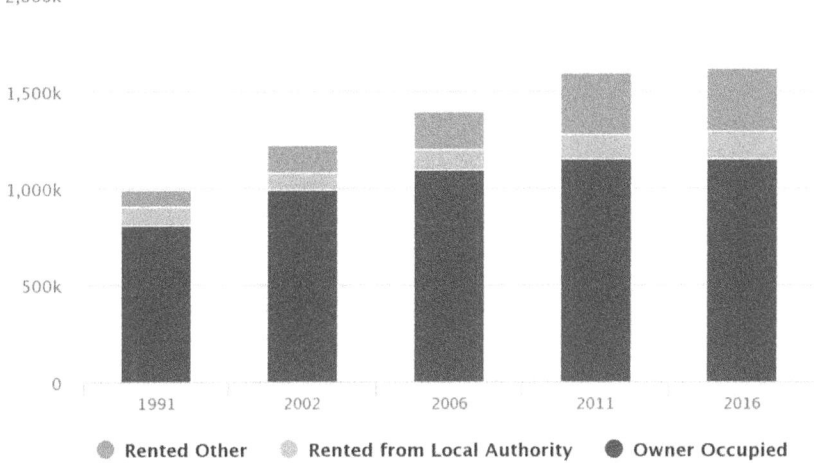

Fig. 7.3 Households tenure status in Ireland (1991–2016). (Source: Central Statistics Office (CSO))

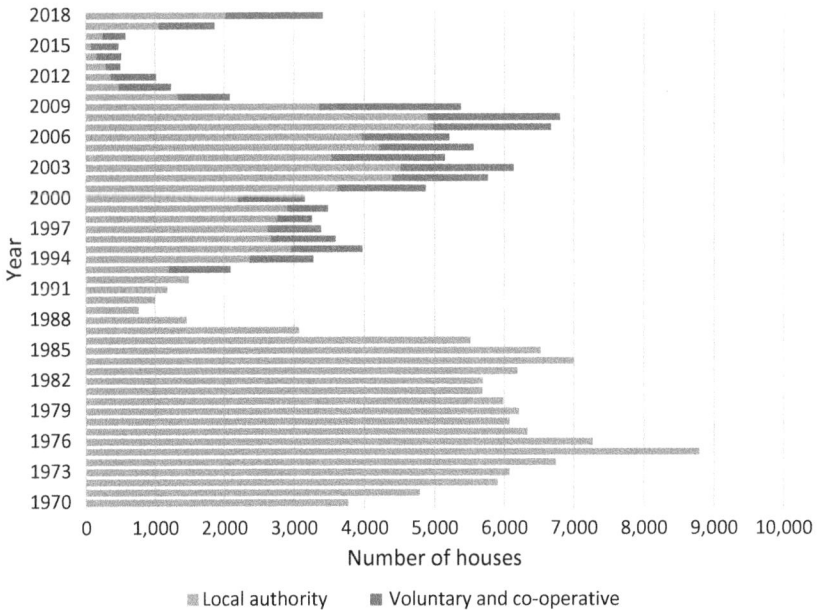

Fig. 7.4 Housing completion by sector. (Author's elaboration. Source: CSO Ireland (2018))

7.3.1   Housing Associations Finance Models

The social housing system in Ireland has experienced different funding models' arrangements since the 1930s (Norris 2011). Initially, the financing of local authority housing was based on loans which were then paid back through rental payment from tenants and generous interest. Since the early 1990s, funding was provided from central government grants, which has made the social housing supply dependent on central government funding allocations (Murphy and Dukelow 2016). With the 2008 economic collapse, the state funding for social housing was drastically reduced, as was with the direct housing provision by local authorities (Fig. 7.4). Concerns about the funding options after the financial crisis focus on the significant reduction of housing provisions. But as already pointed by Byrne and Norris (2018), the defunding of local authority housing is a long-term phenomenon, indicating that funding problems are not solely related to the recent fiscal and economic crisis but that successive policies have tried to find new options for the funding and delivery of social housing with less input of state resources. In practice, it means an attempt to withdraw the state as the main provider of social housing, passing that responsibility to housing associations, private landlords and private developers through housing assistance benefits. At the moment, the funding system has now returned to a borrowings/revenue model in which social housing providers can raise funds off balance sheet, in particular through the Social Housing Capital Expenditure Programme (Murphy and Dukelow 2016).

The changes in funding have not affected the model where social rents are connected to household income. From a management point of view, this system leaves a level of income gap between rental income from tenants and outgoing housing management and maintenance costs (Murphy and Dukelow 2016). For example, a house where a family would pay €1000 a month renting housing privately (€250 weekly), their average rent is about €50 weekly in the not-for-profit sector. Therefore, housing associations need to balance their books, and they attempt to fill the gap between what tenants can afford to pay and what they need to pay for the loans of the house bought or constructed. Instead of conceding grants the government provides housing associations with loans to cover for a percentage of the house they buy or construct. In many cases, housing associations fund their housing scheme using a government loan of 30% of the total purchase price to leverage a larger bank loan, normally from the

Housing Finance Agency (HFA). As the state is playing a limited role in the provision of credit, the funding reduction pushes housing associations to find novelty financial solutions.

In the next section, I explore how three housing associations have devised alternative funding ideas and interesting solution for the provision of affordable housing and avoidance of evictions.

7.4 The Making of Possibilities for Affordable Housing

As discussed above, local authorities remain the major provider of social housing, but their delivery is followed by the housing association, which from 2011 to 2015 delivered more houses than local authorities (See Fig. 7.4). The not-for-profit housing sector has gone through different funding models, especially after the austerity measures that reduced the capital spending on housing (Bergin et al. 2011). Basically, it changed the way of housing associations are funded. In turn, housing associations have attempted to develop an alternative model to respond to the scarcity of government funding. Largely, this chapter identified that these new models include partnerships with the private sector, alternative funding and sustainable development. This section starts with the case of Clúid, the largest housing association in Ireland.

7.4.1 Innovation in the Finance of Social Housing: Clúid Housing Association

Clúid Housing provides over 6000 affordable homes to nearly 16,000 tenants all over the country. They work in partnership with local authorities to provide housing to households registered on the social housing waiting list. In 2017, Clúid worked in partnership with 23 local authorities to deliver 595 new homes to 1976 people across the country. As of December 2017, 15,900 people were living in 6300 properties either owned or managed by Clúid. They have been a prominent housing association not only due the number of affordable housing they deliver and manage, but also by their ability to raise funds for new housing construction and regeneration projects.

For the construction 595 houses in 2017, Clúid financed this delivery in the following ways: 92.6% from private finance (bank loans), 2.5%

management contracts, 4% 'Capital Assistance Scheme' (CAS), and 0.8% 'Capital Loan and Subsidy Scheme' (CLSS).[3] In order to continue delivering new social housing, Clúid has to actively obtain new sources of funding that can ensure the supply of units. Most of their lending is provided by the Housing Finance Agency (HFA), a self-financed government agency that offers loan finance to local authorities and housing associations. In fact, the Irish government has encouraged housing associations broaden their funding sources, highlighting the tangible benefits of having access to more than one lender (Clúid 2018). It is discernible here the government approach to incentivize housing associations to embrace new financial alternatives with the private sector, reinforcing the withdraw of the state in the direct provision of housing. Remarkably, Clúid has a strong balance sheet, maintained through a sustained project-based funding programme, largely due to government grants but with support from private sector loans.

Housing associations, such as Clúid, have a strong need to balance their books. Thus, housing associations have to raise funds from a combination of sources: loans from HFA, loans from banks and capital grants. In other words, the state has a limited role as a provider of credit, offering loans at friendlier rates but those still need to be repaid. Housing associations have a mortgage, such similar to a private household. They make repayments on that loan and receive regular funds in the form of grants to repay those loans.

Funding is crucial for housing associations, and the cuts in the overall grants has forced Clúid to deal with third-party actors, such as private banks. With the shrinking of housing funding schemes, housing associations reach to banks to obtain funding, and housing associations shape themselves into their new financial context. In an interview with a representative of Clúid, I was told about their need to develop a relationship with new organizations in order to obtain the funding they need: 'What has been done by us is that we have had to work very hard at establishing a relationship with organizations that we were not so familiar with before, such as banks, and convincing them that we know what we are doing and that we are a good organization to lend money to. The banks are very

---

[3] The Capital Loan and Subsidy Scheme (CLSS) and Capital Assistance Scheme (CAS) provide capital funding to housing association to meet the cost of constructing units of accommodation.

cautious, because they are afraid to be defaulted on the loan' (Clúid staff).[4] It has increased their amount of work, since banks have to be convinced to lend money and have several eligibility criteria. With this diversity of funding options Clúid's has developed the necessary capacity to construct and manage a larger portfolio of housing units.

Has this combination of financial sources—as exemplified in Clúid's case—been sufficient to achieve housing affordability goals? The scarcity of credit has made it more difficult to finance a new supply of affordable housing. While the housing association sector has become bigger in Ireland—due to the government withdrawal of direct provision of affordable housing—the scale of new housing units delivered by housing associations still limited. It is important to point out that the majority of small housing associations do not have access to loans because the finance model is focused on government funding and private banks do not grant them credit (Norris and Hayden 2018).[5] Ninety-five percent of housing associations own less than fifty housing units. In some cases, small housing associations have little possibility of starting new housing projects. Despite having a good tracking record provision and management of housing units in Ireland, housing associations still have limits to deliver the units required.

7.4.2 Innovation in Low Cost Housing: Ó Cualann Cohousing Alliance

In June 2017, Ó Cualann Cohousing Alliance (Ó Cualann) made the headlines for featuring homes at 30% below market value, with units starting from €140,000 for a 1-bed apartment. The families moving into of the 49 homes in the Poppintree development Ballymun in Dublin paid considerably less than the usual price of new houses in this area. Ó Cualann is a voluntary housing co-operative, with Approved Housing Body status, meaning that despite being a housing co-op, they enjoy the same status as

---

[4] As part of my research on housing mobilization in the post-crisis context, financed by the Irish Research Council, I interviewed several activists and representatives of housing association about the impact of austerity measures on housing policies. Interview conducted in January 2019 in Dublin.

[5] Small housing associations are more dependent on state funding, and they encompass the majority of the AHB in Ireland. Most of its staff are volunteers and those small entities provide houses in small and scattered projects, attending to specific social groups (such elderly people and people with disabilities).

any housing associations. Ó Cualann runs its own affordable purchase scheme. It reduced the cost of housing by lowering the minimal income for mortgage loan, eliminating profit margins and acquiring land at a lower value from local authorities.

The maximum household net income to qualify for social housing is €35,000 for a single person in Dublin, and where the median salary is €38,000 (Revenue Commission 2018). It means that this segment of workers does not qualify for social housing and might have trouble in accessing a mortgage with a private bank. Ó Cualann facilitates mortgage to buyers, which is around €900 per month for a three-bed house, instead of the average rental price of €1452 in the area (DAFT 2018). In the Ó Cualann scheme, the maximum combined income for housing was €79,000 and a 4% deposit was required, as well as bank mortgage approval for the remaining total.

Their houses are cheaper than the market average for two reasons: first, Ó Cualann eliminated all developer's margin, reserving a maximum of 5% surplus to be used in new projects. In the private sector, developers seek a profit margin of about 15% to 30% (DHPLG 2018). Second, because Ó Cualann is a not-for-profit AHB, Dublin City Council waived construction levies, greatly reducing the price of the land. Ó Cualann also provides a mix of social and affordable homes, to avoid segregating the community around income levels.

The cost of land, development levies and developer's margins have a substantial weight determine housing prices. The case of Ó Cualann demonstrates that non-profit bodies can provide low-cost accommodation, and development costs can be reduced when the state stop considering at land as a commodity to be profited from. There are two potential downsides in this scheme: a 'clawback' clause, prohibiting house owners to sell the house for ten years, and an over-reliance on land being available at minimum cost and infrastructure, such as roads and drainage, funded by the state or local authority.

7.4.3   Innovation in the Prevention Evictions: iCare Housing

iCare Housing is a registered AHB (Approved Housing Body) established to provide outcomes to indebted households. In addition to the growing social housing lists and the homeless crisis, there are also those families who are in mortgage difficulties and cannot repay their mortgage, thus at risk of becoming homeless. iCare helps families by purchasing their homes from banks where the mortgage holder is not able pay the mortgage and is eligible for social housing. In another words, iCare prevents families from being evicted. Until the end of 2018, 571 deals have been made with private banks to buy homes and keep the former owners living in them. The family pays rent as social housing tenants.

iCare joined the existing Mortgage-to-Rent scheme and created partnerships with support from the HFA (Housing Finance Agency). They obtained funds from private banks under normal commercials agreements and obtained loans from HFA that covered 30% of the purchase to acquire the houses. Mortgages in arrears are sold to iCare at a significant discount. In turn, iCare rents the house back to the previous homeowner and their debt is written off. After signing a 30-year lease with iCare, the tenants in this scheme can buy the house back at the same price paid by the entity. The deals are negotiated in case-by-case basis among iCare, the bank, and the Irish Mortgage Holders Organization (IMHO). In addition to preventing families to be evicted, iCare is also frustrating the plan of vulture funds planning to acquire distressed debt in Ireland.

This scheme has been an effective alternative solution to keep families in their homes, and it also alleviates pressures on social housing. However, not all banks or vulture funds are willing in engage in negotiations. In August 2018, for example, Ulster Bank ignored iCare's proposal to restructure or purchase 5200 mortgages in arrears, which were them sold to an American private equity fund, Cerberus.[6] AIB, ESB and other private banks have engaged with iCare and IMHO to restructure debts and negotiate the mortgage-to-rent scheme, but there is little evidence lenders are willing to cooperate in any significant way to avoid evictions. Banks often fail to communicate adequately and timely with indebted customers and there are numerous reports that vulture do not engage properly with costumers in arrears (Cox 2018). As the number of properties that have fallen into arrears still high, iCare joined the anti-eviction movements discourse that want regulation to prevent landlords from evicting tenants before their own loans are sold to vulture funds.

The key implication of the three cases above is that housing associations are indeed key players in providing housing to low income groups. They have raised prominence not just for delivering as many houses (sometime more houses) as the government; these associations have showed capacity

---

[6] See article at: https://www.thejournal.ie/ulster-bank-vulture-find-4210181-Aug2018/. Accessed 6 August 2019.

to be inventive in the provision of affordable housing. They operate under clear principles, and their not-for-profit approach has demonstrated to be cost-effective when incentives are in place. Thus, while the case studies presented examples of innovation and commitment towards alternative approaches to the housing crisis, in all cases further efforts were thwarted by a policy model that restrict funding and move to the private sector the responsibility of providing affordable housing. A key driver of homelessness in Ireland is that low income earners and housing subsidy recipients have great difficulty in securing private rented accommodation, a problem that can only be resolved with the provision of more social rented housing (Norris and Hayden 2018). Local authorities acknowledge that housing associations are playing an important role in delivering additional social housing, but they also acknowledge that the sector does not have yet the capacity, funds, and scope to deliver housing in the required development scale. The private sector has demonstrated no significant interest in supply houses at lower costs and rent pressures only grow stronger. The local authorities are better placed to provide the required housing output, but the government policy of over-reliance on the private sector has disincentivizing efficient state direct housing delivery.

7.5   Conclusion: Innovations in Affordable Housing

The delivery of affordable housing by not-for-profit developers provides an important contribution to the stock of social housing in Ireland. The role of local authorities in the direct provision of social housing started to change in the 1980s, and the path towards the withdrawal of the state from the direct provision of social housing was consolidated after economic meltdown in 2008. This crisis has ramifications that initiated a major adjustment of how to provide social housing. Since then, the state has trusted private developers to provide much need housing units, while expanding housing assistance benefits to enable low-income households to rent private housing. Simultaneously, housing associations have assumed an important position in the provision of affordable housing.

This chapter has identified some of the new financial alternatives and new strategies for affordable housing. The cases presented demonstrate that cheaper housing is possible and that some component costs can be reduced. The analysis of innovations suggests that there would be value for the government to restructure the incentives and strategies needed to foster a better output of affordable housing. Many other changes are necessary, such as the suspension of the tenant purchase scheme and the introduction of efficiency incentives, but the prospect of improving the financing of affordable housing and having a more enabling role in land and incentives still lays with the government. Considering the discussion in the sections above, there is little evidence that not-for-profit housing providers are capable of adding to affordable housing supply at the required scale in the long term, mainly due to the inadequate commitment of public finance for new social housing at the level required.

In the current context, social housing is more a tool for global investment rather than the provision of home and shelter (Aalbers 2016). Within this process of commodification of housing, the government is complicit to varying degrees. A significant finding of the study is the key role incentives for construction—such as the elimination of levies and profit margins—play in the construction of lower-cost affordable homes. Affordable housing policy in Ireland, while obstructed by the lack of sufficient funding, is remarkably adaptable and subject to innovations. For a more diverse, just, and livable city, a long-term policy framework that allows progressive expansion and inclusion of deprived households is essential to undertake market and state failures.

REFERENCES

Aalbers, M. B. (2016). *The financialization of housing: A political economy approach.* New York: Routledge.

Bergin, A., Gerald, J. F., Kearney, I., & O'Sullivan, C. (2011). The Irish fiscal crisis. *National Institute Economic Review, 217, R47.*

Byrne, M., & Norris, M. (2018). Procyclical social housing and the crisis of Irish housing policy: Marketization, social housing, and the property boom and bust. *Housing Policy Debate, 28*(1), 50–63.

Central Bank. (2018). *Residential mortgage arrears & repossessions statistics.* Dublin: Central Bank of Ireland.

Clúid. (2018). *Clúid Housing annual report* (p. 72). Dublin: Clúid.

Considine, M., & Dukelow, F. (2009). *Irish social policy: A critical introduction.* Dublin: Gill & Macmillan.

Cox, A. (2018, April 22). So, a vulture fund bought your mortgage, what's next? *Raidió Teilifís Éireann RTE.*

CSO, Central Statistics Office. (2016). *Housing and households reports*. Statistical Release, Ireland: CSO.

———. (2018). *Housing and households reports*. Cork: CSO.

DAFT, R. (2018). *The DAFT rental price report*. Dublin: Daft.

Della Porta, D., Andretta, M., Fernandes, T., O'Connor, F., Romanos, E., & Vogiatzoglou, M. (2017). *Late neoliberalism and its discontents in the economic crisis: Comparing social movements in the European periphery*. Cham: Springer.

DHPLG, Department of Housing, Planning and Local Government. (2018). *Review of delivery costs and viability for affordable residential developments*. Dublin: Department of Housing, Planning and Local Government.

———. (2019). *Homelessness report*. Dublin, Ireland: Department of Housing, Planning and Local Government Homelessness.

Drudy, P. J., & Punch, M. (2005). *Out of reach: Inequalities in the Irish housing system*. Dublin: TASC.

Dunne, T. (2016). *The crisis in housing has deep roots and supply alone will not resolve*. Annual Conference The Housing Agency, Dublin Castle.

Gaynor, N. (2020). Governing austerity in Dublin: Rationalization, resilience, and resistance. *Journal of Urban Affairs, 42*(1), 75–90.

Gibson, M., Petticrew, M., Bambra, C., Sowden, A. J., Wright, K. E., & Whitehead, M. (2011). Housing and health inequalities. *Health & Place, 17*(1), 175–184.

Housing Agency. (2018). *Annual summary of social housing assessments*. Dublin: Housing Agency.

Initiative Ireland. (2018). *Initiative Ireland Housing 2031* (p. 12). Dublin: Initiative Ireland.

Kenna, T., & O'Sullivan, M. (2014). Imposing tenure mix on residential neighborhoods: A review of actions to address unfinished housing estates in the republic of Ireland. *Critical Housing Analysis, 1*(2), 53–62.

Knight, F. (2019). *Knight frank global affordability monitor 2019*. https://www.knightfrank.com. Accessed 6 Aug 2019.

Lima, V. (2018). Delivering social housing: An overview of the housing crisis in Dublin. *Critical Housing Analysis, 5*(1), 1–11.

Mallon, B. (2017). A radical common sense: On the use of direct action in Dublin since 2014. *Interface: A Journal for and about Social Movements, 9*(1), 46–71.

Murphy, M., & Dukelow, F. (2016). *The Irish welfare state in the twenty-first century – Challenges and change*. London: Palgrave Macmillan.

NAMA, National Asset Management Agency. (2013). *NAMA Annual Statement 2013*. (No. Section 53). Retrieved from https://www.nama.ie/fileadmin/user_upload/NamaAnnualStatement2013.pdf

Norris, M. (2011). Funding social housing: Time for a radical revamp. *Eolas, 4*, 24–25.

Norris, M., & Hayden, A. (2018). *The future of council housing: An analysis of the financial sustainability of local authority provided social housing* (p. 101). Dublin: The Community Foundation of Ireland.

O'Callaghan, C., Feliciantonio, C. D., & Byrne, M. (2018). Governing urban vacancy in post-crash Dublin: Contested property and alternative social projects. *Urban Geography, 39*(6), 868–891.

Revenue Commission. (2018). *Individualised gross incomes – 2016.* Dublin: Revenue Office.

Roche, W. K., O'Connell, P. J., & Prothero, A. (2016). *Austerity and recovery in Ireland: Europe's poster child and the great recession.* Oxford: Oxford University Press.

TASC, Think-tank for Action on Social Change. (2016). *Cherishing all equally 2016 report* (p. 98). Ireland: TASC.

CHAPTER 8

Emerging Public-Private Partnership in the Provision of Affordable Housing in China's Major Cities

Zhi Liu and Desiree Chew

8.1 Introduction

Developing livable cities has long been a major pursuit of national policy makers, urban leaders, and urban planners in China. In 1996, China was among the signing parties of the United Nations Istanbul Declaration on Human Settlements and the Habitat Agenda (also known as UN Habitat II). The declaration endorsed the universal goals of ensuring adequate shelter for all and making human settlements safer, healthier, and more livable, equitable, sustainable and productive (United Nations 1996). These goals have been widely accepted in China. The Urban Master Plan of Beijing Municipality (2004–2020), for example, set livability as one of the city's development objectives. In 2007, the Ministry of Construction adopted a set of evaluation criteria to guide cities to plan, implement and

Z. Liu (✉)
Lincoln Institute of Land Policy, Beijing, China
e-mail: zliu@lincolninst.edu

D. Chew
Peking University Post-Graduate, Singapore, Singapore

© The Author(s) 2020
C. van Montfort, A. Michels (eds.), *Partnerships for Livable Cities*,
https://doi.org/10.1007/978-3-030-40060-6_8

manage livability (People's Daily 2007). One criterion is the comfort of living conditions, measured by adequate and affordable housing for all and healthy communities with adequate infrastructure services.[1] In 2018, the central government called for a transition of the national economic objective from rapid growth to high-quality development. In terms of urban development, the concept of high-quality development implies better urban living conditions and access to high-quality urban services.

Despite the long-standing policy emphasis on livability, however, the major cities in China have struggled in providing adequate and affordable housing to their low-income households. This is not surprising, as many countries around the world, rich and poor, encounter the same challenge. Like many growing cities around the world, the major cities in China have seen the rapid increases in housing prices over the last two decades, which result in declining housing affordability and increases in the fiscal burden for municipal governments to meet the need of affordable housing. Moreover, unprecedentedly rapid urbanization has made the provision of affordable housing especially challenging in China. Over the last four decades, hundreds of million people have migrated from rural areas to cities; many of them are concentrated in the major cities, creating a huge demand for urban affordable housing.

The modality of urban housing provision has evolved over time. In the era of planned economy from 1949 to 1978, China's urban housing was mainly publicly provided. After a series of housing reform actions taken during 1988–98, China eventually privatized most of the existing public housing units to the occupying households, and created a commodity housing market as the main mode of urban housing provision.[2] Despite the housing marketization reform, affordable housing remained a policy concern. Significant effort has been made by municipal governments to provide affordable housing to the low-income urban households with local urban residential status (also known as urban hukou, see Box 8.1). However, the migrant workers, who constitute the social group most in

---

[1] Affordable housing in this chapter refers to the housing units provided by the government, or through the intervention of government support policy, to the low-income households at below-market prices. It is interchangeable to the term "social housing."

[2] The term "commodity housing" is a translation of the Chinese term "shang pin fang" which literally means the housing units commercially supplied by the market and sold as a commodity, as opposed to the welfare housing supplied by the government or employers to their employees as a fringe benefit.

need of affordable housing, hold rural hukou and do not have access to the municipal affordable housing programs.

> **Box 8.1 The *hukou* System**
> Hukou is a system of household registration in China. Every citizen has a household registration record, which identifies the person as an urban or rural resident of a local jurisdiction, depending on the householder's employment (urban or rural) at the time of registration. The system is also used to control access to social services/programs. As social services/programs are better in larger cities than in smaller cities, and are better in urban areas than in rural areas, an urban hukou, especially hukou of a major city, is a valuable ticket to social services/programs, such as affordable housing and local public schools.

As the need for affordable housing far exceeds the government fiscal resources available, some municipal governments have explored alternative ways to provide affordable housing in recent years. These include various forms of public-private partnership (PPP), or various forms of cooperation among the government, market and communities. One particular form is a contractual arrangement between a local government and a real estate developer (or enterprise) for the developer to finance and deliver affordable housing for the government. It is largely similar to the PPP contract often seen in the infrastructure sector. Other forms are broadly cooperative arrangements for affordable housing provision between the municipal government and real estate developers, and sometimes among the government, developers, and communities. These are not necessarily a legally binding contract between the public and private parties for the delivery of public services, as those often seen in infrastructure PPP projects.

This chapter attempts to describe the affordable housing challenges in China and the transformation of affordable housing provision from purely public sector intervention to the emerging PPP arrangements. The chapter first provides a brief overview of the urban and land context in China, before highlighting the history of urban housing reform and the achievement and disappointments of the government's affordable housing programs. The chapter then describes several emerging PPP practices that are aimed at improving housing affordability for the low-income households, especially migrant households—an important component of livability in the major cities of China.

8.2   The Urban and Land Context

To understand the urban affordable housing issues in China, it is important to first understand the context of urban development and land policy. Since 1978, the year when the economic reform started, China has experienced unprecedented rapid urbanization. Between 1978 and 2018, the total population grew from 963 million to 1.39 billion, and the share of the urban population grew from 18% to almost 60%. Today, about 850 million of China's population lives in cities.

There are 661 cities and over 20,000 townships in China. The real estate sector loosely groups the cities into four tiers based on the city's administrative rank, size of the economy, and the size of population. Tier 1 includes Beijing, Shanghai, Guangzhou, and Shenzhen; these are the global cities in China. Tier 2 includes most of the provincial capital cities in the more prosperous eastern and central regions and a few other cities that are considered as the national or regional economic centers. Tier 3 includes several provincial capital cities in the poor and remote western region and a number of prefecture-level cities. Tier 4 includes mainly the county-level cities. The "major cities" as commonly known are the Tier-1 and Tier-2 cities. The four Tier-1 cities are the most economically vibrant global cities in China, and the Tier 2 cities are mostly the national, regional and provincial economic centers. Not surprisingly, these major cities attract a large number of migrant workers from the rural areas each year.

The land management system in China is unique. Urban land is state-owned, and rural land is collectively owned by the villages. There is no private ownership of land. According to the Land Administration Law, only the state has the power to acquire rural land for urban development.[3] At the city level, municipal governments exercise the state power. To accommodate rapid urbanization, they constantly engage in the urban

---

[3] The long awaited Amendment to the Land Administration Law was passed by the China National People's Congress on August 26, 2019. The new amendment allows rural collectives to lease rural construction land for urban development without going through government land expropriation as long as the land use conforms to urban planning. This essentially breaks the monopoly power of the government in urban land supply.

spatial expansion, which involves acquisition of rural land, provision of infrastructure to turn the acquired rural land into serviced urban land, and allocation of serviced urban land for different kinds of urban land use. The land parcels for commodity housing development are allocated through an open bidding process in which all interested real estate developers can participate. The highest bidder will be the winner, who would pay the government a large lump-sum amount known as the land concession fee in order to secure the right to develop commodity housing on the land parcel. The commodity housing units built on the parcel are then sold to urban households who would own the purchased unit itself and the use right of the land underneath for the concession period of 70 years. The concession fee paid by the developer often constitutes over 30% of the financial cost of commodity housing supply and passes onto the buyers through the purchase prices.

The land parcels for affordable housing development are allocated mainly through state land appropriation, instead of the bidding process. Municipal governments would select the sites, acquire the land from the rural sector, appropriate the land parcels for the affordable housing program, procure civil works from construction contractors to build housing units, and then lease or sell (with certain conditions and limitations) the units to eligible low-income households. As this does not involve the land concession process (and fee) i, the financial cost of affordable housing supply is much lower than that of commodity housing supply. Moreover, municipal governments often choose the less attractive locations for affordable housing, as the more attractive locations, such as those near the employment centers, are reserved for commodity housing development, through which more land concession revenues could be generated for the municipal governments.

The land concession (bidding) process for commodity housing development is adopted for the purpose of achieving land use efficiency through market mechanism. However, it also creates the opportunities for municipal governments to raise revenues through urban land supply. Driven by rapid urbanization, most of the Chinese cities have grown fast in recent decades, in terms of population, industries, and gross domestic products (GDP). The growth and the prospect for future growth drive up the urban land value. As a result, the land concession fee bid by real estate developers is often significantly higher than the cost of rural land acquisition, which is assessed on the basis of the agriculture production value, instead of the market value for urban use. The net profits, after accounting for the costs of rural land acquisition and infrastructure provision, become an important source of municipal revenues, which are used to fund capital investments for urban development (including affordable housing construction). Driven by the strong incentive for municipal revenue generation, many municipal governments tend to take advantage of the growing housing demand to enable the land markets to sell high. But this process unfortunately results in the steady rise of land and commodity housing prices (Gao et al. 2019).

The strong incentive for land concession revenues has much to do with the municipal finance system in China (Liu 2019). The current taxation system, known as the tax sharing system, was established in 1994. Under the system, all taxes are divided into three categories: central government taxes, local government taxes, and shared taxes between the central and local governments. The types and rates of all taxes are determined through a central government process, and the local governments—i.e. all governments at the provincial level and under, including all municipal governments—are given little taxing power or tax autonomy. However, municipal governments are mandated to deliver a large number of public services. The needed municipal public expenditures always exceed the municipal tax revenues (including intergovernmental transfers if any). This situation creates a strong incentive for the municipal governments to raise revenues through land concessions. Given the convenience of state ownership of urban land, the municipal governments often use land as collateral for the municipal government-owned local finance vehicles (LFV) to borrow from commercial banks or sell bonds to the capital market, in order to fund more capital investment projects.

Affordable housing is one of the major public services mandated as the responsibility of municipal governments. The construction of affordable housing units is part of the municipal capital investment program, which is usually funded by the land concession revenues and LFV borrowing. From the municipal finance perspective, therefore, the ability of a municipal government to mobilize financial resources to fund affordable housing is closely related to the performance of the commodity housing market. When the commodity housing markets are hot and high, municipal governments will be able to collect more land revenues and borrow more from the capital market to fund affordable housing and other capital investment projects. The dilemma, however, is that the rising commodity market—good news for municipal governments—often makes housing less affordable for more households, fuelling greater demand for affordable housing—bad news for municipal governments.

The desire of the municipal governments to maximize the net revenues from land concessions also contributes to the existence of urban villages in the major cities. Chinese cities are typically surrounded by large rural areas. As cities expand, the municipal governments would first take the farmland, instead of the village settlements, for urban development; this is because the compensation for farmland taking is much cheaper than the total costs of taking settlement land and funding the resettlement. Over the last few decades, the built-up areas of most Chinese cities have grown a few times. In the process of urban spatial expansion, some village settlements have transformed into what is known as urban villages. After losing the farmland, most farmers established their new livelihoods by building multi-story houses on their homestead land plots and leasing out to the new urban entrants. Therefore, the urban villages are typically overcrowded, with high building annd residential densities. They also lack the usual urban public services and amenities, such as standardized urban street networks, modern drainage and sewage, solid waste management, kindergartens, and public space. Because of these poor conditions, rent is relatively cheap and affordable. Therefore, urban villages supply a large number of rental housing units for the migrant households.

8.3   Public Provision of Affordable Housing

In the era of the planned economy during 1949–1978, state-owned enterprises and public sector agencies provided their employees with practically free housing, in the form of a fringe benefit. This system was not financially sustainable, and the shortage of urban housing was acute across urban China. By 1978, the year when China started economic reform, only 18% of the population lived in urban areas, and the housing floor area per person was very low, averaging 6.7 square meters (Chen et al. 2013).

The government started to reform the urban housing supply system in 1988. Through a series of reform actions, the welfare housing system was gradually relaxed to allow the formation of a housing market (Wang 2011). Finally, in 1998, China abolished the old system of housing provision by employers as a fringe benefit to their employees, privatized the existing housing units already allocated to employees, and moved the housing provision to the commodity housing market. Since then, Chinese cities relied on the commodity housing market as the major means of housing provision. For urban housing today, the average floor area per person has reached 38 square meters. However, against the backdrop of rapid economic growth and urbanization, the market-oriented system allows for rapid housing appreciation, especially in the Tier-1 and Tier-2 cities. As the data in Fig. 8.1 indicate, average housing prices for the 35 major cities have increased 3.5 times since year 2000.

The rapid increase of housing prices has resulted in declining housing affordability, which is often measured by the price-to-income ratio (PIR), i.e. the median housing price over the median household income in a city (or a market). If the PIR of a city is 5, it implies that a household with the median income will be able to purchase an adequate housing unit with a total household income of 5 years. By international consensus, the reasonable range for PIR is considered between 4 and 6. As the data in Fig. 8.2 indicates however, average PIR for the 35 major cities has increased rapidly during 2001–2010 and then remained at a level of close to 9 till 2015 (the last year when the cross-city data are available). The PIR for the top level cities are much higher than the average of major cities. According to recent data released by E-house Real Estate Institute (2019), the Tier-1 cities exhibited particularly high levels of PIR in 2018: 34.2 in Shenzhen, 26.1 in Shanghai, 25.4 in Beijing, and 17.5 in Guangzhou. These are the cities that have the most employment opportunities and thus are most attractive to the migrant workers. Over 40% of the total population living

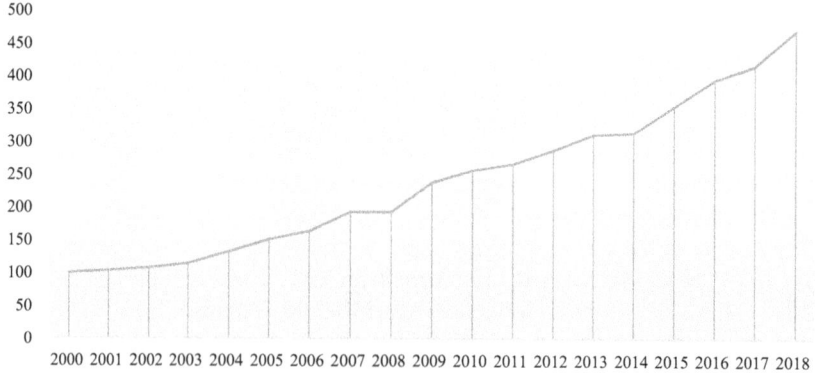

Fig. 8.1 Average residential housing price index for 35 major cities, 2000–2018. (Source: China National Bureau of Statistics (various years). China Statistical Yearbook

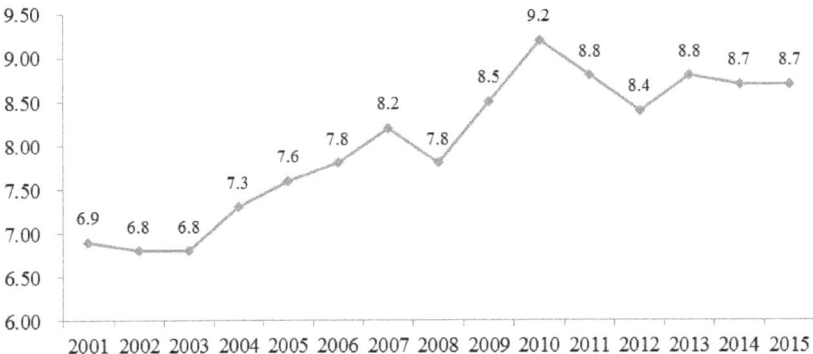

Fig. 8.2 Average price-to-income ratio, 35 major cities, 2001–2015. (Source: E-house Real Estate Institute and the National Bureau of Statistics of China)

in these cities are migrant workers and their families. However, the extraordinarily high housing prices make it practically impossible for most migrant households to own a housing unit there. Even the newly formed young households with local urban hukou and access to mortgage finance would find it financially difficult to come up with sufficient down payment to purchase a housing unit.

The market failure to provide affordable housing to the low-income groups was not unanticipated. Even in the 1998 housing marketization reform, the central government issued guidelines for housing provision to different income groups (State Council 1998). According to the guidelines, the housing needs of the lowest-income group (bottom 20 percentile) will be met by affordable rental housing provided by the government. Furthermore, the 12th National Social and Economic Five-Year Plan (2010–15) set an ambitious target of supplying 36 million affordable housing units to low-income urban households. As a result, a total of 28 million affordable housing units were provided during 2010–15. The number was equivalent to 12.3% of the total number of urban households in China at the time.

While this is an achievement that would be unthinkable in many countries, it is not without flaws. The most significant flaw is that these affordable housing units are pre-dominantly accessible by the low-income urban households with local urban hukou. Most migrant workers still hold their rural hukou and thus are excluded from the municipal affordable housing programs. A few cities, such as Guangzhou, established a point system for migrant workers to access the affordable housing program. Under the system, if a migrant worker has worked and lived in the city for over 10 years, and has paid taxes and social security contributions, then the worker will earn enough points to access the affordable housing. This is certainly a major progress, but it would take many more years for most migrant workers to accumulate enough points.

The second significant flaw lies in the locations of many affordable housing projects. Since municipal governments lack the incentive to allocate lucrative land parcels to affordable housing, these projects are mostly sited in the urban fringe areas or exurbs, where the land is cheap due to the remote locations and a shortage of public services such as public transport, hospitals, and quality schools (Zou 2014). Low-income households end up spending much more time and out-of-pocket costs in daily transport. The remote locations also result in social exclusion of those households. As such, some households who are allocated affordable housing units do not actually live there; instead, they find a place to stay in the central city area close to their jobs and original social network.

The low-end rental housing markets, especially those located in urban villages within the built-up area or rural villages in the urban fringe, play a significant role in housing migrant households. The poor neighborhood conditions, overcrowded buildings, and lack of land use regulations make the housing in these locations more affordable. However, as the urban redevelopment process gradually extends to urban villages, these migrant households are losing their rental housing option and many are forced further out to the urban fringe areas.

8.4   EMERGING PUBLIC-PRIVATE PARTNERSHIP IN AFFORDABLE HOUSING PROVISION

In terms of urban housing provision, municipal governments are caught in a major dilemma. On one hand, they must enable the commodity housing market to meet the housing needs of the majority of the urban population. One the other hand, the rapidly rising commodity housing prices make it more and more difficult for the low-income households to afford or rent a housing unit. Despite significant efforts and fiscal inputs made by the government, the task of affordable housing provision remains daunting in the major cities, where migrant workers continue to urbanize.

The primary constraint for municipal governments in the provision of affordable housing is fiscal. Due to limited budgets, some municipal governments have introduced various forms of public-private partnership (PPP), often on the experimental basis. This section describes some of the PPP practices in affordable housing provision.

8.4.1   Build and Transfer (BT)

The use of BT for affordable housing construction was initiated over 10 years ago, mainly by cities with weaker economies and fiscal capacity. They even found it difficult to borrow through their LFVs. To them, affordable housing was like an unfunded mandate. In order to deliver the mandate, they chose the BT contract, where a real estate developer would come up with the needed capital (mainly through commercial borrowing) to build the affordable housing units on public land given by the municipal government. Then the municipal government would repay the developer a fixed amount every year from its annual budget for an agreed number of years. As affordable housing generates limited revenue for the developer to make a profit from the BT contract, and because the financial viability gap to be covered by public funds could exceed 90%, this practice was essentially another form of municipal borrowing in the name of PPP. There were other problems as well. Due to the lack of clear PPP regulations, the BT contracts were not well enforced. Some fiscally stressed municipalities failed to repay the developers in schedule according to the BT contract, and the interests of the developers were not adequately protected by the regulations. Realizing the financial, fiscal, and administrative risks, the central government stopped the BT practice in affordable housing provision a few years later.

8.4.2   Inclusionary Affordable Housing

In view of rapid housing appreciation, some municipal governments ramped up their commitment to inclusionary affordable housing provision. This policy innovation strives to incorporate affordable housing provision into commodity housing projects. It involves the following steps in the residential land concession process. First, a price cap is placed on any land parcel before opening the bid. Once the bidding price reaches the cap, real estate developers may continue to bid by offering an amount of affordable housing to be developed on the same plot of land. This effectively avails land for affordable housing without compromising much of the land concession revenue. It also improves residential diversity by mixing commodity housing with affordable housing (Zou 2014). There is a caveat, though, that such public housing schemes are only open to the residents registered with local urban hukou.

While the idea of residential diversity is good, it causes some practical issues that should be resolved in the future. In the major cities, a commodity housing project usually contains a number of multi-family residential buildings (mostly high-rise), with a total of a few hundred or even over a thousand of housing units. This makes it possible for the real estate developer to locate the affordable housing buildings in a corner with the least amenities. Moreover, as a common practice, the real estate developer would form or hire a real estate management company to manage the public services of the compound with a fee assessed on the square meters of the floor area. The fee for affordable housing occupants is much lower than that of commodity housing occupants. This prompts the commodity housing occupants to set physical limits (such as a fence), preventing affordable housing occupants from using the public amenities in the commodity housing section. Chu, Nomura and Mori (2019) found that 73% of the mixed housing complexes in Beijing had built-in elements that visibly divide the residential zones, stifling opportunities for interaction and sharing of public spaces; in some cases, affordable and commodity-housing residents used different paths from the gate to their units. Such management practices unfortunately cause social exclusion within a so-called inclusionary housing project.

8.4.3   Leverage on Urban Villages in Affordable Housing Provision

Another policy innovation addressing poor housing affordability is to leverage on urban villages as an affordable housing avenue, instead of pursuing the usual route of demolition and redevelopment. In some cities, simply tearing down the urban village has become a less palatable option due to growing compensation costs. The villagers have increasingly high expectations of compensation. Often, they consolidate and exercise bargaining power via the village committee (Bertaud 2010).

The compensation is given in cash, or in-kind (such as a certain square meters of new housing for a square meter of demolished housing), or a combination of both. A study by Xue (2018) found that cash compensation alone can amount to 20 years of rental fees; in the more prosperous Eastern coastal region, the average compensation per household is over a million yuan. Compensation-in-kind has also proven quite hefty. In some major cities such as Shenzhen and Guangzhou, urban renewal has created a new 'housing class', referring to the urban villagers who hurtle to prosperity after receiving generous compensation in the form of multiple housing units from which they can enjoy asset appreciation and rental incomes (Wu 2016). In a study on five resettlement districts in Beijing, 32.6% of returning households own one housing unit, 40.6% own two, 18.4% own 3 and 8.3% own 4 or more (Xue 2018). It is evident that municipal governments already pay a high price that is bound to increase, to sustain this pattern of urban renewal.

Another concern is that urban village demolition entails the destruction of existing societal and cultural networks and structures. Over the last few decades, many migrant workers have become permanent members of the receiving cities, and they add to the cultural diversity not only in the urban villages, but also in the cities where they live and work. In "The Death and Life of Great American Cities", Jane Jacobs (1961) argues that by nature, cities survive and thrive on diversity; however, large-scale redevelopment plans often reduce human choice and participation, thus denying the city of diversity. Currently, the redevelopment of urban villages does not accommodate for the return or integration of migrant tenants. Following Jacobs' line of reasoning, urban villages once torn down will suffer an irrevocable loss of social and cultural capital, which is ultimately detrimental to the city's organic growth. Even for the urban villagers who do return, they often face difficulties adapting to the newly developed area. This is especially so if the village collective disintegrates, affecting solidarity and strength of the original community. A study on urban villages in 28 provinces and provincial-level municipalities found that 56.8% of returning villagers miss the neighborly relations of the old, and this transition is especially hard for the retired elderly, whose social network is most affected (Xue 2018).

In light of these concerns, many have started to redefine and reinvent urban village redevelopment. There is a new focus on protecting the culture, ecology and character of the urban villages, instead of conducting the usual quick, large-scale and often-expensive projects aimed at garnering the largest economic benefits. For this to happen, the village collectives and real estate developers drive the redevelopment process, while the municipal government assumes a guiding role instead (Xue 2018). There have recently been two main thrusts toward a healthier kind of urban village redevelopment, one that does not involve complete demolition and destruction of the old.

The first is to open a legal pathway that grants legitimacy and stability to housing in urban villages. Before the 2019 amendment, China's Land Administration Law did not permit collectively-owned land to be developed for urban use. The central government now allows some cities with especially high housing prices, including Beijing and Shanghai, to develop public rental housing projects on collectively-owned land. Since commodity housing is expensive and public housing is limited, land policy reform that permits rural communities to build rental units can serve to boost the supply of affordable housing. How it works: there is no land expropriation, meaning that the land is still owned by the village collective. The government's role here is to offset the financial and capability constraints typically faced by the collective, by providing a steady stream of capital and drawing in more real estate developers, both state-owned and privately owned. Without expropriation of land, housing appreciation is constrained. Hence, the migrant tenants (who are unable to buy commodity housing and ineligible for public housing) will be able to afford to stay there even after upgrading and redevelopment (Tian and Yao 2018). Furthermore, the village collective, a bastion of cultural solidarity and continuity, is allowed to remain intact through the renewal of the urban village.

Nonetheless, the central government remains cautious in pursuing this approach. For instance, in compliance with the Land Administration Law, the National Development and Reform Commission (NDRC) has stipulated that collective land can only be used for rental purposes, meaning that housing leases cannot be sold or transferred (Sun 2018). Also, the program is still in the experimental stage; it has only been piloted in certain cities like Shenzhen and Beijing. In 2017, the Beijing municipal government confirmed 39 collective rental programs, of which at least ten are situated in prime and central locations. All units will be fully fitted and ready for occupancy. Rental fees will be determined based on a unified assessment of geographical location, unit fittings and demand. Moreover, public services like schools will be included in the development plan. Altogether, this land reform pilot program serves to increase the quantity and quality of rental supply as well as keep rental fees and terms of lease stable.

The second key thrust is to improve the livability of urban village housing. In other words, enhance the physical and environmental conditions instead of resorting to demolition. This often requires the participation of real estate developers due to the needs for capital and real estate know-how. For example, in 2017, Vanke, a prominent property developer in Shenzhen, launched its transformation project called the 'Million Village Plan'. This project aims to comprehensively improve urban villages by investing in fire protection, pipelines, interior décor, operation and maintenance of housing units. Vanke opened a subsidiary company, Wancun Development Company, to collectively rent the buildings, make necessary modifications, and then lease them out (Hua 2017). Vanke's involvement is crucial given that it has more than 30 years of experience in real estate development. Furthermore, Vanke is both developer and service provider, meaning that it will provide urban commercial functions like property management and educational facilities. As of August, 2018, the Fortune 500 company was working to redevelop 33 villages in Shenzhen, each with a population of 10,000 to 30,000 (Haack 2018).

One example of a Vanke's transformed sites is Dameisha Village. According to Nansha Original Design Studio (2018), five architects hailing from Beijing, Shanghai and Shenzhen were hired to contribute their unique perspective toward creating a dynamic and diversified space. The team discerned that public spaces, including a market, agricultural plot and religious corner with shrines and altars, were important to the community. In addition to retaining and enhancing these sites, they developed a new communal space around a big banyan tree, which had come to epitomize the spirit of the village and the center of living. Inclusive of a bookstore, drama society and social service center, this space was designed in harmony with the surrounding greenery.

Nonetheless, it remains to be seen whether the price of urban village apartments will indeed remain stable post-transformation. While a source close to Vanke claimed that its renovated apartments would be priced 'in a similar range' as before renovation, some researchers and residents beg to differ. According to Haack (2018), in some cases, the new rental fees double or triple the original rates, such that many original tenants fear eviction. The Shenzhen government is in the midst of taking steps to ensure that with redevelopment, urban villages continue to accommodate the residential needs of those they are designed to serve (Haack 2018).

Altogether, the urban village is instrumental in promoting the market-driven provision of affordable housing. This is key to the integration of the floating population, whom as of now cannot access decent housing options. Here a paradigm shift is necessary: a city's diversity, in terms of its migrant communities, should be embraced and encouraged, rather than ignored. Considering the tangible as well as intangible costs of demolition, local governments should elect to pursue a holistic and incremental redevelopment approach, wherein conditions are improved over time without a complete overhaul of the urban village and all that it embodies. The guiding principle is not to resist change, but to temper the speed and means of change.

8.5   Conclusions

Despite the policy emphasis on urban livability, the development of livable cities in China has been seriously compromised by declining housing affordability for the low-income households, especially the migrant workers and their families, who mostly have no access to the state-run affordable housing programs. Rapid housing price appreciation, fuelled by the burgeoning commodity housing market, makes housing less affordable for those who need housing, presenting urban governments the increasingly daunting task of providing affordable housing to their residents.

Significant effort has been made by the municipal governments to supply large quantities of affordable housing, but migrant workers and their families do not benefit from such programs due to their hukou constraint. Those who are given affordable housing are not satisfied due to the remote locations, lack of public services and/or lack of convenient physical access to services. These shortcomings could be overcome with more fiscal inputs and better planning for service delivery, but it would be constrained by the limited fiscal capacity as well.

In many cases, local governments are driven by profit in deciding how and whether to redevelop urban villages. So far, the process primarily benefits developers and the original urban villagers who are handsomely compensated; however, it hurts the migrant workers and their families who rent housing units in the urban villages. They have to relocate to farther locations that require longer commute and suffer poorer access to urban services.

Confronted by such difficulties, some municipal governments adopted PPP models to overcome the fiscal constraint for affordable housing provision, albeit with mixed results. The BT practice by some municipal governments brought serious fiscal and administrative risks, and was ceased by the central government. The experiment of inclusionary housing triggered some disturbing social reactions that served to intensify social exclusion. These may have to be addressed through legal and regulatory reform. It remains to be seen whether the regeneration of urban villages via cooperative arrangements between the governments, developers and local communities is a progressive action or will prove unsustainable amid continuing urbanization and housing appreciation.

In short, it is promising to see the significant effort and emphasis that Chinese municipal governments devote to affordable housing provision. It is also promising to see the emerging PPP practices in this sector. However, there is still a long way to go for the PPP to work effectively and supplement the government's affordable housing programs in achieving the real outcomes of efficiency and equity. The recently amended Land Administration Law, which permits villages to sell the use rights of their land for urban development without undergoing state expropriation, may help pave the way for municipal governments to address affordable housing issues more effectively.

References

Bertaud, A. (2010, May). *Land markets, government interventions, and housing affordability.* Working Paper 18, Wolfensohn Centre for Development. https://www.brookings.edu/wp-content/uploads/2016/06/05_urban_development_bertaud.pdf. Accessed 23 Sept 2010.

Chen, J., Jing, J., Man, Y., & Yang, Z. (2013). Public housing in Mainland China: History, ongoing trends, and future perspectives. In J. Chen, M. Stephens, & Y. Man (Eds.), *The future of public housing: Ongoing trends in the East and the West* (pp. 13–35). Berlin Heidelberg: Springer.

Chu, C., Rie, N., & Suguru, M. (2019). Actual conditions of mixed public–private planning for housing complexes in Beijing. *Sustainability, 11*(8), 1–19.

Gao, H., Liu, Z., & Long, Y. (2019). Residential land supply and housing prices in China. In R. Chiu, Z. Liu, & B. Renaud (Eds.), *International housing market experience and implications for China* (pp. 330–351). London/New York: Routledge.

Haack, M. (2018, August 23). *Hundreds of thousands displaced as Shenzhen 'upgrades' its urban villages.* https://www.theguardian.com/cities/2018/aug/23/hundreds-of-thousands-displaced-as-shenzhen-upgrades-its-urban-villages. Accessed 22 Aug 2019.

Hua, C. (2017, December 13). *China Vanke project improves 'urban village'*. http://usa.chinadaily.com.cn/a/201712/13/WS5a306771a 3108bc8c672b0e5.htm. Accessed 22 Aug 2019.

Jacobs, J. (1961). *The death and life of Great American cities*. New York: Random House.

Liu, Z. (2019). Land-based finance and property tax in China. *Area Development and Policy, 4*, 367. https://doi.org/10.1080/23792949.2019.1610333.

Nansha Original Design Studio. (2018). *Village is a kitchen, play conceals life: Shenzhen Dameisha Village Renovation*. December (in Chinese). https://mp.weixin.qq.com/s/hiSzYs3BbCd7hFn9ehe74w. Accessed 23 Sept 2019.

People's Daily. (2007, June 25). The Ministry of Construction officially announced the scientific evaluation criteria for livable cities. *People's Daily*. http://www.gov.cn/jrzg/2007-06/25/content_660218.htm. Accessed 28 Aug 2019.

Shanghai E-house Real Estate Institute. (2019). *2018 Report on China's urban housing price-to-income ratio*. Report of E-house Real Estate Institute (in Chinese).

State Council of the People's Republic of China. (1998). *Notice of the State Council on further deepening the reform of urban housing system and accelerating housing construction*. State Council Document (in Chinese).

Sun, J. (2018, May 4). *Collective land lease housing loan pilot: Four banks have issued plans*. (A news article in Chinese). http://www.xinhuanet.com/fortune/2018-04/05/c_1122640517.htm. Accessed 22 Aug 2019.

Tian, L., & Yao, Z. (2018). The housing problems of the floating population in China's large cities. *Comparison, 94*.

United Nations. (1996, June 3–14). *Report of the United Nations Conference on Human Settlements (Habitat II)*. Istanbul (Turkey). https://www.un.org/ruleoflaw/wp-content/uploads/2015/10/istanbul-declaration.pdf. Accessed 23 Sept 2019.

Wang, Y. (2011). Recent housing reform practices in Chinese cities: Social and spatial implications. In J. Y. Man (Ed.), *China's housing reform and outcome* (pp. 19–44). Cambridge, MA: Lincoln Institute of Land Policy.

Wu, F. (2016). State dominance in urban redevelopment. *Urban Affairs Review, 52*(5), 631–658.

Xue, F. (2018). *The present and the future of urban villages*. (Power Point Presentation in Chinese). China Construction Engineering Design Group Co Ltd.

Zou, Y. (2014). Contradictions in China's affordable housing policy: Goals vs. structure. *Habitat International, 41*(January), 8–16. https://doi.org/10.1016/j.habitatint.2013.06.001.

PART III

Partnerships and Safety in the City

Partnerships for Safe Cities: Community-Safety Initiatives in Cities in the Netherlands and Belgium

Carola van Eijk

9.1 Introduction

For many decades, local governments and the police in the Netherlands have collaborated increasingly with citizens and civil society organizations in order to keep cities safe and livable (Van Noije and Wittebrood 2008; Van Steden et al. 2011; Van Noije 2012; Lub 2016b; Van Eijk 2018). A similar trend can be observed in Belgium where citizens as well as organizations are encouraged to take responsibility for their own neighborhood (Verlet and Reynaert 2004; Gelders et al. 2009). On the one hand, this development towards more active participation of citizens and civil society organizations is driven by urgency: local governments and the police are

---

The author would like to thank Jan García Olier (research assistant at the Institute of Public Administration, Leiden University) for his help in collecting data on the various co-production initiatives.

C. van Eijk (✉)
Institute of Public Administration, Leiden University, Leiden, The Netherlands
e-mail: c.j.a.van.eijk@fgga.leidenuniv.nl

© The Author(s) 2020   167
C. van Montfort, A. Michels (eds.), *Partnerships for Livable Cities*,
https://doi.org/10.1007/978-3-030-40060-6_9

not able to address the major challenges they are confronted with on their own, without citizens/organizations taking responsibility as well (Martinus et al. 2018). The different actors can strengthen each other by providing joint efforts. On the other hand, the development is also driven by more ideological reasons: in both the political and societal debates emphasis is put upon 'active citizenship' (Dekker 2019). Citizens not only have the right to consume public services, they also have the (moral) obligation to actively contribute to the service delivery process.

As such, the growing contribution by citizens and civil society organizations in the domain of safety fits in a broader trend, labelled under such headings as 'governance' (Pierre and Peters 2000), networking (Koppenjan and Klijn 2004), and co-production (Brudney and England 1983). The insights from co-production literature especially are relevant here. Not only because within this literature the domain of neighborhood or community safety is often studied (cf. Voorberg et al. 2015; Brandsen and Honingh 2016; Brudney and England 1983; Van Eijk et al. 2017), but also because the definition of co-production clearly describes the nature of the collaboration between (local) governments and citizens/civil society organizations. That is, the (local) government and citizens/civil society organizations collaborate with the aim of delivering public services (i.e., 'safety'), based on long-term relationships (cf. Brandsen and Honingh 2016).

The involvement of multiple actors, based on a long-term relationship and with the aim of providing public goods, makes the collaborations in the context of safety a perfect fit with the definition of partnerships as established in the introduction chapter of this book. Although we will see in this chapter that in some instances the market is also involved (Type H, see for the typology Fig. 1.1, Chap. 1), the partnerships mentioned in the chapter can be particularly labelled as Type E: partnerships between civil society and public organizations. We will see that the actors involved are mainly loosely connected; sometimes via covenants but often only via expressing their intention to collaborate.

The aim of this chapter is to examine the collaboration of local governments and the police with citizens and civil society organizations in order to keep cities safe and livable. I will address two questions. First, *what variation in partnerships exists?* After providing an overview of how these partnerships are referred to in the literature on co-production (thereby also linking to the concept of community safety), I present an overview of some concrete examples in the Netherlands and Belgium. Second, *how do these partnerships contribute to safety and as such livability?* To answer that question, I review the positive and negative implications mentioned in the literature and integrate insights on the specific Dutch and Belgian initiatives.

Insights on the existence and characteristics of partnerships in the Netherlands and Belgium are based on earlier research by the author[1] as well as on a (literature) search conducted specifically for this book chapter. Through snowballing, we searched the internet for reports, news items and official websites of concrete initiatives. This (literature) search was also used to find more information about how partnerships contribute to safety.

9.2 WHAT THE LITERATURE TELLS US ABOUT PARTNERSHIPS FOR COMMUNITY SAFETY

This section and the following one address the question of what variation in partnerships exists. The next section will focus on some concrete examples of partnerships in the Netherlands and Belgium. This section provides an overview of what role citizens in particular have in the delivery of safety according to the literature. But before moving to the role of citizens in partnerships for community safety and the idea of co-producing safety more specifically, we first need to get more grip on what is meant by *safety* in this context.

9.2.1 Defining (Community) Safety

In this chapter, I focus on *community (or neighborhood) safety*. I define safety as a broad range of 'community concerns'. These include various forms of crime and actual criminal victimization, but also the fear of crime, perceptions of disorder, quality of life, and various neighborhood conditions that contribute to (feelings of) pauperization (cf. Gelders et al. 2009; Kappeler and Gaines 2015; Cordner 2014). As such, safety refers to more than crime rates per se. It includes all those aspects that make citizens perceive their city or neighborhood as '(un)safe', '(un)comfortable', and so on.

This shows the close link between safety and livability. According to Woolcock (2009), livability is about 'feeling convenient and safe'. In other

---

[1] This research is published in Van Eijk (2017); Van Eijk (2018); Van Eijk, Steen and Verschuere (2017); Van Eijk and Ohler (2018).

words, safety is one of the conditions to experience the neighborhood or city as livable. The broad definition of community safety mentioned above expresses this association between both concepts: when people experience pauperization of the neighborhood they are living in, they will be unlikely to describe it as a livable place. Furthermore, the definition expresses the possible connection between two of the three dimensions of livability as outlined in this book, namely safety and greenery. This might be a connection in terms of a trade-off. That is, a green pedestrian area can improve livability in terms of the dimension of greenery, but might also increase the fear of crime when passing this area at night or feelings of pauperization if the area is not well kept.

9.2.2   Establishing Partnerships

Over the years we can observe some interesting changes in the roles of both governments and citizens in providing community safety (Van Noije 2012; Pridmore et al. 2018). We can observe a wide variety of concrete activities citizens are involved in (see also Sect. 9.3). This ranges from more passive and 'low effort' activities to activities that require a more active attitude of citizens, the investment of greater effort and often an intense interaction between these citizens and the police/municipality. Examples of the first category include putting locks on doors, reporting crime and asking neighbors to watch one's home when one is away on holiday. The second category includes neighborhood watch groups patrolling on streets, prison councils and peer training by offenders for young people at risk (Loeffler 2018; Percy 1978).

Although the initiatives of the first category are considered as '*co-production*', especially in the early co-production literature (cf. Ostrom 1978), I would consider the initiatives of the second category in particular as exemplary co-production cases. This is due to the active attitude required of the citizens involved and the often intense interaction with police professionals (cf. Van Eijk 2018; Van Eijk et al. 2017). The citizens' input is crucial for the police in safeguarding a public service (i.e., public safety), but at the same time citizens can hardly achieve the same result without the professional knowledge and guidance as well as back-up in dangerous situations.

The idea of establishing partnerships in order to improve community safety becomes especially visible when we do not take a public administration perspective of the co-production literature, but instead consider these kinds of initiatives from the disciplines of criminology and policing. Within these disciplines, these initiatives are referred to as '*community policing*'. Community policing can best be described as a collaborative form of policing aimed at problem solving by promoting active partnerships. These partnerships include the police, citizens and (eventually) public/ private agencies like (social) housing offices and schools (Kappeler and Gaines 2015; Cordner 2014; Scheider et al. 2009).

The idea behind community policing is that these different actors are engaged during the entire policing process. This implies that the police will share decision-making authority with the community as well as stimulating the community members to be involved in the implementation phase. Here one can think of reporting and sharing information on crime and developing solutions to problems (Scheider et al. 2009). One of the crucial aspects of community policing is that the police needs to better understand the needs, concerns and desires of the community. To develop a community-based agenda, the police should be in close contact with all the different actors. Possible ways to do so are surveys, holding neighborhood meetings and regularly meeting with potential partners such as community organizations and business groups (Kappeler and Gaines 2015). By establishing a wide variety of partnerships, it will be possible to provide collaborative responses on concrete issues and to achieve ambitious social objectives (Kappeler and Gaines 2015).

In that sense, we might conclude that the difference between co-producing community safety and community policing is that, in general terms, co-production is more focused on citizens' participation, while community policing also emphasizes the participation of public/private agencies. In other words, co-production seems to fit in a Type E partnership (partnerships between civil society and public organizations), while, according to the community policing literature, partnerships (also) fit into Type H (partnerships in which civil society, market and government are involved) or even Type B (Public-Public Partnerships). However, as the next section will show, this distinction is more of an analytical one. In practice, we see that in co-production initiatives like *Buurt Bestuurt* or *Veiligebuurt*, other actors then citizens are also involved, including private organizations such as retailers.

As a further discussion about the (differences between the) concepts of co-production and community policing is beyond the scope of this chapter, in the remainder of this chapter I will use both terms interchangeably and mostly refer to 'partnerships' as the overarching term.

9.3   What Type of Partnerships Exist? Some Concrete Examples from the Netherlands and Belgium

From the literature we can conclude that a wide variety of partnerships may occur. These partnerships can vary in terms of the actors involved: solely citizens, a combination of citizens and civil society organizations or even a network setting including business organizations. Also, a partnership between (local) government / the police and citizens can be based on individual relations (e.g., reporting on crime) or be organized on a group or community level (e.g., a neighborhood meeting).

But what examples of partnerships can be found in practice? Table 9.1 provides an overview of partnerships in the Netherlands and Belgium. This overview does not pretend to be exhaustive, rather it reflects an overview of exemplary partnerships in the context of community safety. As well as the purpose and the activities performed, the table also reflects on the type of partnership (see Chap. 1).

Two observations stand out. First, the number of initiatives is growing rapidly. This popularity can be linked with current societal debates that popularize the idea of active citizenship in which everyone is stimulated and encouraged to actively contribute to service delivery processes and to take up their responsibility (Dekker 2019). Second, there is huge variety among the nature of initiatives and among municipalities. Sometimes, similar kinds of initiatives are referred to differently by different municipalities, or initiatives labelled similarly are organized differently.

9.4   How Successful Are These Initiatives?

The wide variety of cases presented in the previous section reflects the current popularity of partnerships for the delivery of community safety. With more than 2.4 million citizens participating in *Burgernet* (2019) and more than 8600 WhatsApp neighborhood watch schemes (WABP 2019), we can conclude that citizens are willing to collaborate with the police and (local) governments in order to improve the safety in their own cities. This popularity is shared by the police and municipal organizations, who often actively support and promote citizen's participation in these partnerships (Lub and De Leeuw 2019). This raises the question of how successful these initiatives are; do partnerships contribute to safe cities, and, if so, under what conditions?

Table 9.1 Overview of exemplary co-production of community-safety initiatives in the Netherlands and Belgium

Characteristics/Initiatives	Country of presence	Main purpose(s) of the initiative	Activities developed to achieve the main purpose	Actors involved (type of partnership)
Buurtpreventie Teams (BPT) [Neighborhood watch schemes]	The Netherlands	Improve safety in the neighborhoods by actively involving citizens in the prevention and mitigation of safety-threatening situations, and through patrolling the streets	Citizen patrol, sometimes accompanied by police officers Identify suspicious activities (petty crimes and nuisance) Alert the authorities and the neighbors about the unsafe situations Directly (although limited) intervene in situations when possible	Citizens Police Municipalities (including *Stadswachten*) Sometimes fire brigade Sometimes other organizations like housing corporations *(Type E partnership)*
Buurtvaders [Neighborhood Fathers]	The Netherlands (some cities)	Improve safety, social cohesion and life quality in neighborhoods of strong multicultural presence (especially Moroccan) by preventing and addressing nuisance created by young citizens	Citizen patrols Signaling nuisance created by youth (mainly of Moroccan descent) Mediating for and between the young residents Alerting the police of the nuisance when mediating is insufficient	Citizens Municipalities Police *(Type E partnership)*

(continued)

Table 9.1 (continued)

Characteristics/Initiatives	Country of presence	Main purpose(s) of the initiative	Activities developed to achieve the main purpose	Actors involved (type of partnership)
Vuurwerkvrij zones [Firework free areas]	The Netherlands (some cities)	Improve livability in neighborhoods by jointly limiting the use of fireworks during the final days of the year	Reaching agreements between residents regarding the use of fireworks Posting signals of "firework-free zones" Reaching out to citizens using fireworks in order for them to give up on such activities (control task)	Citizens Municipalities (Type E partnership)
WhatsApp Buurtpreventie [WhatsApp neighborhood watch]	The Netherlands and Belgium	Improve safety in the neighborhoods by actively involving citizens in the prevention and mitigation of safety-threatening situations, through digital means	Signal suspicious activities (petty crimes and nuisance) Alert the authorities (mainly the police) through telephone Alert other neighbors through the WA groups Directly (although limited) intervene in situations when possible	Citizens Police Municipalities (Type E partnership)

Veiligebuurt [Safe Neighborhood]	The Netherlands	Improve safety by digitally facilitating the social interaction among citizens, making them aware of the situations taking place in their living environments, and actively involving them in the prevention and mitigation of safety-threatening situations	Safety-related information exchange among residents Safety-related information delivery from the authorities	Citizens Police Municipalities Other public sector organizations like the ministry (*Ministerie van Justitie en Veiligheid*) Private sector organizations (*Type E/H partnership*)
Nextdoor	The Netherlands	Improve safety, livability and social cohesion in neighborhoods by facilitating the social interaction among residents, and making them aware of the situations taking place in their neighborhoods, through an app	Information (including safety-related) exchange among residents and sometimes private organizations in the neighborhood area	Citizens Sometimes local businesses (*Type E/H partnership*)

(continued)

Table 9.1 (continued)

Characteristics/Initiatives	Country of presence	Main purpose(s) of the initiative	Activities developed to achieve the main purpose	Actors involved (type of partnership)
Burgernet [Citizen Network]	The Netherlands	Improve safety in the cities by attending the requests brought up by the police to collaborate in collecting and providing information about safety-related situations. All of this through an app or social media	Communication of safety-related information and alerts to the citizens Request for relevant information collection and provision, as well as its reception Information collection and provision by citizens	Citizens Police Sometimes municipalities (*Type E partnership*)
Wijkschouw [Neighborhood Inspection]	The Netherlands	Improve and maintain safety conditions in neighborhoods through safety inspections, focusing on visibility, accessibility, attractiveness and property delimitation, and by jointly reaching to agreements on responsibility for addressing the issues raised	Safety inspections in designated neighborhoods Responsibility division among co-producers for addressing the issues that are raised Direct intervention (e.g., repairing lights and windows, painting walls, etc.)	Municipalities Police Citizens Private sector organizations (*Type H partnership*)

Buurt Bestuur [Neighborhood Governance]	The Netherlands (some cities)	Improve safety and livability by consulting their residents about the issues that require priority attention in their neighborhoods and attending such situations	Regular meetings; could be monthly Define priorities to be addressed Define the approach and actions to be undertaken Activate citizens	Citizens Police Municipalities (including *Stadstoezicht*) Other public organizations (e.g., housing corporations) Private sector organizations *(Type E/H partnership)*
Buurtinformatie-netwerken (BIN) [Neighborhood Information Networks]	Belgium	Improve safety and life quality in neighborhoods through the exchange of information related to nuisance and crimes, actively involving citizens in the safety mitigation tasks	Signal suspicious activities Alert the police about the suspicious activities Information exchange between the police and the BIN coordinators Information exchange between residents Indirectly intervening in the suspicious activities and mitigation	Citizens Police Municipalities Other public sector organizations (e.g., housing corporations) *(Type E partnership)*

(continued)

Table 9.1 (continued)

Characteristics/Initiatives	Country of presence	Main purpose(s) of the initiative	Activities developed to achieve the main purpose	Actors involved (type of partnership)
Politiecafé [Police Café]	Belgium	Improve safety in neighborhoods by consulting the residents about their perceptions on safety and the police operation	Group discussions between the police and citizens	Police Citizens
Wijkbabbels [Neighborhood talks]	Belgium	Improve livability and safety by consulting the residents about the issues in their neighborhoods regarding livability (including safety), and jointly brainstorming about how to solve them	Group discussions between the municipal civil servants and citizens Brainstorming about the solutions for the issues raised	Municipalities Citizens

Though crucial, this question is at the same time also difficult to answer. Not least because as the label 'successful' is of course highly subjective. To some extent, it depends on the actors' viewpoints and interest, determining the goals to be achieved. 'Reducing crime' will most likely be prioritized highly by the different stakeholders, but previous research shows that other aims are also mentioned. Citizens are, for instance, also focused on increasing social cohesion in their neighborhood or on developing individual skills (Van Eijk 2018; Van Noije and Wittebrood 2008). For the police, increasing trust in the police organization can be relevant, as well as achieving sustainable behavioral change to prevent crime in the near future (Gelders et al. 2009). As such, partnerships can be part of a wider 'nudge approach' (cf. Loeffler 2016).

Furthermore, crime and crime reduction may be impacted by several different factors, making it difficult to distill the potential effects of partnerships on observed crime reduction. Given the complexity and costs of isolating the effects of each initiative on crime reduction, the ambiguity of the concepts of safety and livability, and the number of initiatives in place, a comprehensive and precise assessment of the implications of such initiatives is difficult to make. This could explain why empirical studies on the effects of partnerships are scarce, and why the few studies that do exist show mixed results (Loeffler 2018).

Although empirical insights are limited, the co-production literature as well as literature on community policing elaborate extensively on the potential and theoretically assumed effects of partnerships for community safety, in some instances from a more normative perspective. I will review the positive and negative effects mentioned in this literature and address some conditional factors, where possible, linking these general insights with the Dutch and Belgian initiatives introduced above.

9.4.1   Positive Effects of Partnerships

Given the focus on improving community safety, it is not surprising that in the international literature the effect in terms of crime reduction stands out. Safety co-production initiatives could contribute to crime reduction by deterring potential offenders, limiting the opportunity for crime, and enhancing police action (Lub 2016b, 2018). However, the empirical findings are mixed here. MacDonald (2002, p. 592) uses a variety of databases (including a survey and the FBI's Uniform Crime Reports) for 164 American cities and concludes that 'community policing had little effect on the control or the decline in violent crime'. In contrast with this, Bennett, Holloway and Farrington (2006) conclude that neighborhood watch schemes have a favorable effect on crime reduction. The authors conduct a meta-analysis and narrative review of studies focusing on the effects of neighborhood watch schemes (mainly in the US and UK). Based on this meta-analysis, they conclude that generally speaking the neighborhood watch scheme can be associated with 'a relative reduction in crime of about 16%' (Bennett et al. 2006, p. 453). However, two remarks should be addressed. First, the authors observe that evaluations of neighborhood watch effectiveness stopped abruptly in the mid-1990s; as such it is unclear whether similar reductions in crime can also be observed today. Second, the evaluations included in the meta-analysis were based on either police data or on (citizen) survey data. The authors conclude that evaluations based on police data were associated with a greater positive effect than evaluations based on survey data (Ibid.). This raises the question of what is the best method to measure the effects of safety co-production initiatives.

Within the Dutch context, there are also some studies that investigate the effect of neighborhood watch teams and digital apps in terms of crime reduction. In line with the international literature, here, too, the results are mixed. Akkermans and Vollaard (2015) focuse on how the number of burglaries in different neighborhoods in Tilburg was effected by the implementation of WhatsApp groups. Since the digital groups were implemented at different points in time, the research was conducted in an experimental setting. The authors conclude that the number of burglaries reduced significantly, by on average 40%. A more recent study by Mehlbaum and Van Steden (2018), however, does not confirm these conclusions. Instead, focusing on the number of arrests in a small number of Dutch cities, these authors conclude that the activities of WhatsApp groups are rarely directly linked with concrete arrests.

Linking the presence of co-production initiatives with a concrete amount of crime reduction might in itself not be a very valuable way to reflect the effects of these initiatives. A more useful approach, followed by several authors, may be to focus more on the 'subjective' effects. Eysink Smeets et al. (2013), for instance, study six *Buurt Bestuurt* initiatives taking place in Rotterdam and find that such initiatives increase citizens' level of cooperation and trust in the professionals involved, professionals' levels of job satisfaction and professionals' understanding of citizens' needs and how to address them. The *Buurt Bestuurt* initiatives and neighborhood watch schemes also have a positive effect in safety perceptions and social cohesion among residents (Eysink Smeets et al. 2013; Van der Land 2013, 2014; Bervoets 2014).

We can, therefore, conclude that, regardless of the lack of empirical evidence of a positive relation between neighborhood watches and actual crime reduction, participants in safety co-production initiatives are often positive about the direct effect of the initiative on reducing crime and nuisance, and that the collaboration often results in a shared positive perception of safety among residents, the police and the local authorities (Van der Land 2014; Lub 2016b; Lub and De Leeuw 2019).

For the digital forms of partnerships specifically (e.g., *Burgernet* and WhatsApp neighborhood watch groups), studies often report the positive effects in terms of reducing costs and improving information exchange. *Burgernet*, for example, benefits the police patrol work with wider citizen information sources, reduces the costs of co-producing safety through face-to-face contact, and increases legitimacy (Meijer 2014). WhatsApp *Buurtpreventie* networks (WABP) seem to increase social control (Bervoets 2014) and the number of reports made to the police (Vollaard 2016). As such, Akkermans and Vollaard (2015) argue that the above-mentioned positive effect on the reduction of burglaries is realized through an improved exchange of information between citizens, the police and local authorities.

9.4.2   Negative Effects of Partnerships

Safety co-production initiatives may also have undesirable results. As put by Brewer and Grabosky (2014), there is a 'dark side' to community safety co-production as it may threaten safety rather than enhancing it. These threats can take many forms and apply to both the actors involved in the partnership and the wider community. Regarding threats to the actors involved, one can think, for example, of injuries suffered by citizens who found themselves in a dangerous situation with criminals (cf. Hardeman 2017).

Concerning the community threats, groups of citizens providing community safety can disrupt social harmony in the neighborhood (Loeffler 2018). Tensions and resentment may arise with residents who collaborate ('snitches') and those who do not ('accomplices') (Van der Land 2013). This could be especially relevant for initiatives relying on citizens signaling suspicious activities, as with the Belgian Neighborhood Information

Networks (*Buurtinformatienetwerken*). Research indicates that these initiatives are prone to the stretching of 'perceived safety threats' on the basis of biased perceptions and prejudice, and vigilantism or excessive control with little regard for the privacy of others (Lub 2016a, 2018). As empirical research shows that migrants, women, youths and poorer people are less likely to participate (Martinus et al. 2018; Meijer 2014; Van Steden et al. 2011), partnerships can strengthen social boundaries in society and result in the stigmatization and exclusion of certain groups.

One extreme case is that of a neighborhood watch member in America who shot a teenager, simply because he 'looked suspicious' (Williams et al. 2015). Such extreme cases are not found in the Dutch and Belgian context, but a survey among Dutch municipalities shows that so-called *eigenrichting* is an issue (Lub 2019). This refers to citizens who behave as substitute police officers and as such perform tasks for which they have no authorization. Examples include citizens asking pedestrians or bikers for their ID card (Martinus et al. 2018) and a neighborhood watch scheme that reportedly patrolled with dogs and helicopters (cf. Koch 2017). Furthermore, it is found that the presence and use of digital surveillance mechanisms and social media, and the unclear criteria for identifying and reporting unsafe situations, encourage judgments and actions based on personal perceptions, interests, and stereotypes (Lub 2018).

Another undesired effect of partnerships identified in the literature is that citizen perceptions of safety are negatively affected as residents perceive increasing concerns about safety in their living environments (Pridmore et al. 2018). More attention results in more awareness of potentially unsafe situations. Bervoets (2014), for instance, find that the presence of neighborhood watches in the Dutch municipality of Ede led to decreasing feelings of safety among some residents (particularly those who did not know the neighborhood), increasing tensions between residents and members of the neighborhood watch teams, and increasing nuisance in some neighborhoods as a reaction to the watch schemes.

9.4.3   *Conditional Factors*

The above review shows that partnerships for community safety contribute to safe cities in various ways, although not all assumed effects are supported by empirical research. Yet, partnerships might also be challenging for the local community. In this section, I review what insights we have on the conditions strengthening the positive effects and eliminating or at least reducing the negative consequences. Here, I rely on those conditions and factors mentioned in the Dutch and Belgian context, since what works is highly dependent on the context. The co-production literature especially states this context dependency: what co-production partnerships entail and what is the nature of the interaction between the actors involved highly depend on the context and specific public administration regime (Pestoff 2018). Or, as Loeffler (2018, p. 219) argues: '(...) perceptions of risks and barriers to co-production in public safety and public order are strongly linked to different legal frameworks and administrative traditions.'

Four conditions are elaborated on in detail below: (1) the significant and positive involvement of community members; (2) the motivation, competences and capabilities of the actors involved; (3) the quality of the relations/interactions between the actors involved; and (4) the absence of professional barriers and bureaucratic regulations and procedures.

9.4.3.1 Involvement of Community Members

A first important conditional factor is the *significant and positive involvement of community members*. Although partnerships for community safety are becoming more and more popular, it might be difficult to engage a sufficient group of neighborhood members (Martinus et al. 2018; Eysink Smeets et al. 2013). It is not hard to imagine that when the number of volunteers is too low, those citizens involved have to provide more efforts in order to perform the required tasks. For citizens with busy lives, this could demotivate them to continue their involvement over a longer period of time. Furthermore, given the challenges listed above concerning the unrepresentativeness of partnerships, it is also important for the effectiveness and success of the partnership to involve neighborhood members with diverse backgrounds. This will help increase community support for the initiative (Van der Land 2014).

An interesting discussion in this context is the position of social ties. On the one hand, it is argued that community initiatives related to safety help increase social ties among the neighborhood members (Van Noije 2012). By participating in, for instance, a neighborhood watch scheme, people get to know each other better as well as their neighborhood (Van Eijk 2017; Martinus et al. 2018). As the face-to-face contact between participants and non-participants is often limited (Lub 2016a), such schemes appear to strengthen especially the ties among the participants. As a neighborhood father indicates: the participating fathers 'became friends now' (Gelders et al. 2009, p. 129). On the other hand, empirical research also finds that the presence of social ties is important *in advance* for people to be willing to participate. That is, they need to feel a certain connection with their neighborhood in order to be willing to put efforts in this neighborhood (Van Eijk et al. 2017; Van Eijk 2018). For an initiative like *Buurt Bestuurt* (Neighborhood Governance), this connectedness to the neighborhood where the initiative is in place (mentioned as 'feelings of being home') is found to be one of the most important conditions for success (Eysink Smeets et al. 2013). In the Dutch *Schilderswijk* neighborhood (city of The Hague), the *Buurtvaders* are considered successful by the actors involved because the fathers and youths shared similar experiences and they already knew each other before the initiative started (Boutasmit and Snel 2016).

9.4.3.2 Motivation, Competences and Capabilities

A second conditional factor is the *motivation* of all actors involved, linked with their *competences and capabilities*. To start with the citizens involved, a comparative case study among six different Belgian initiatives indicates that, for five out of these six, attracting 'the right people' is a crucial condition for success (Gelders et al. 2009). Here one can think of having a clear understanding of how the initiative can contribute to community safety, feeling engaged with it and having a sufficient level of competence. Being motivated is important for several reasons. Motivation positively relates to the efforts participants are willing to invest, but is also important to establish a good interaction among the participants (see below) (van Eijk 2018).

Motivation (or rather: the willingness to involve civil society and to collaborate with various actors) is also relevant on the part of the municipal and police organization. Collaboration implies that the organization and professionals need to share decision-making power. Indeed, when professionals want to collect information about the neighborhood members' needs through, for instance, the Belgian *Politiecafé* (Police Café), this can only be successful if the police officers have an open attitude and show willingness to listen (Gelders et al. 2009). As such, we can also conclude that professionals need certain competences, such as being inspiring and having the ability to bring people together (Eysink Smeets et al. 2013).

Furthermore, for the initiative to be successful and sustainable over time, research shows that municipal organizations need to be supportive (Lub 2019; Van Eijk 2017; Gelders et al. 2009). In initiatives like neighborhood watch schemes, it is the municipality that plays a role in establishing covenants with the participants (though this does not happen for all initiatives) and that provides some money. Though the required budget for this kind of partnerships is often small, the participating citizens do need some funds, for instance to buy special jackets and flashlights, and to rent a location for meetings (Van Eijk 2018; Gelders et al. 2009).

9.4.3.3 Quality of Relations/Interaction

Linked to the motivations, the third factor relates to the *quality of the relations/interactions* between the actors involved (e.g., Van der Land 2014). Research on Dutch neighborhood watch schemes shows that for both citizens and professionals, their perceptions of their partner's engagement have an impact on their willingness to invest time and effort (Van Eijk 2018). That is, when citizens feel police officers are not really willing to take their input into account, they will feel less supported and will be unwilling to continue their efforts (see also Eysink Smeets et al. 2013). Similarly, if professionals like local police officers feel the members of a neighborhood watch scheme are less serious about their tasks or do not appreciate the police's efforts, the police officers in turn will be less willing to invest their time and effort, for instance by sharing information (Van Eijk 2018). This might be especially problematic, as information sharing and providing feedback are crucial for the effectiveness of the partnerships (Lub 2019).

9.4.3.4 Absence of Professional Barriers and Bureaucratic Regulations and Procedures

Finally, within the academic literature and reports reference is made to *the absence of professional barriers and bureaucratic regulations and procedures*. Studying community safety programs in Amsterdam, the Netherlands, Van Steden et al. (2011, p. 446) find that police officers 'tend to try to keep their distance from citizens – not in the last place because, explicitly or implicitly, they depict themselves as the experts in instant problem solving'. In the same study, the authors find that citizens often perceive bureaucratic regulations and procedures as obstacles, preventing the initiatives from flourishing. Here, a tension occurs. On the one hand these procedures may be a hindrance, but at the same time we also saw above that there is a potential risk of citizens behaving as substitute police officers (*eigenrichting*). In order to prevent this, training of the citizens involved is crucial, as well as establishing clear instructions and procedures for how to behave in concrete situations (Lub 2019; Van Eijk and Ohler 2018; Van Eijk 2018).

9.5   Concluding Remarks

Partnerships for safe cities are growing in popularity. An increase in the number of partnerships can be seen in both the Netherlands and Belgium. With digital tools, the variety of such partnerships increases even further. Some scholars refer to this trend as 'responsibilization' and 'securitization' (cf. Van der Land 2014). Securitization refers to a development in which all kinds of social issues are increasingly defined in terms of safety, regardless whether there is any actual decrease in safety. Responsibilization, then, refers to the growing emphasis on citizens accepting their own responsibility and taking action to solve problems in society. The idea of securitization especially is relevant in the context of this book on livability, as it might imply that the dimension of safety becomes more important relative to the other two dimensions. That is, issues that were previously perceived as part of the dimension of greenery (e.g., maintenance of green areas) or even housing (graffiti or pauperization) are now perceived as safety issues requiring safety solutions. It is interesting to study how perceptions on securitization have changed in other countries around the globe, and how this impacts the content of the three livability dimensions.

Another important conclusion is that the actual impact of partnerships on the safety and thus the livability of cities is hard to determine. In the first place, this is due to the ambiguity of the meaning of the concept of success. Furthermore, as several factors might impact crime and crime reduction, the potential effects of partnerships cannot be distilled. Nevertheless, if we focus on how the different actors involved perceive the partnerships, some conclusions can be drawn. In this chapter I for instance referred to evidence that partnerships increase citizens' level of cooperation and trust in the professionals involved, professionals' levels of job satisfaction and their understanding of the citizens' needs and how to address them. For digital tools specifically, also cost reduction and improved information sharing are mentioned.

However, based on the materials presented in this chapter, we also must conclude that partnerships come with challenges. Both for the citizens participating, as for the professionals and wider community, I illustrated the potential risk of partnerships disrupting social harmony in the neighborhood. The negative effects of partnerships that result in stigmatization and exclusion of certain groups, stimulate citizens to behave as substitute police officer, and increase citizens' perceptions of unsafety stand out. Yet, based on reports and academic literature on the Dutch and Belgian context, four conditions were identified that help to strengthen the positive effects and can reduce the negative ones.

To conclude, whether it is from a more ideological point of view or for more practical reasons: partnerships nowadays do play an important role for cities to be(come) safe. However, (local) governments cannot easily take the community efforts for granted. In the words of Carr (2012, p. 409): '[b]uilding trust and partnerships takes more time, is always messy, and is not guaranteed to contribute greatly to the law enforcement bottom line, namely, reducing incidents of crime.' Governments do play a role in motivating civil society, and in setting the boundaries to prevent partnerships end up in government producing safety *with* a particular groups of citizens *at the expense* of another group of citizens. Further research is needed to delve into these issues and to study how exactly government should transform to that new 'facilitating' or 'orchestrating' role. Furthermore, partnerships bring new questions on the table, like who is accountable and responsible for the safety of a city in the end. If crime reduction is not achieved; can we as society blame the partnership or do we still believe this to be the sole responsibility of government?

REFERENCES

Akkermans, M., & Vollaard, B. (2015). *Effect van het WhatsApp-project in Tilburg op het aantal woninginbraken – een evaluatie*. Tilburg: Universiteit Tilburg.

Bennett, T., Holloway, K., & Farrington, D. (2006). Does neighborhood watch reduce crime? A systematic review and meta-analysis. *Journal of Experimental Criminology, 2*(4), 437–458.

Bervoets, E. (2014). *Een oogje in het zeil: buurtpreventie in Ede*. Amersfoort: Bureau Bervoets.

Boutasmit, M., & Snel, E. (2016). Buurtsurveillance in de Haagse Schilderswijk – door de ogen van jongeren uit de buurt. *Justitiële verkenningen, 42*(5), 45–58.

Brandsen, T., & Honingh, M. (2016). Distinguishing different types of coproduction: A conceptual analysis based on the classical definitions. *Public Administration Review, 76*(3), 427–435.

Brewer, R., & Grabosky, P. (2014). The unraveling of public security in the United States: The dark side of police-community co-production. *American Journal of Criminal Justice, 39*(1), 139–154.

Brudney, J. L., & England, R. E. (1983). Toward a definition of the coproduction concept. *Public Administration Review, 4*(1), 59–65.

Burgernet. (2019). *Over Burgernet*. Published on https://www.burgernet.nl/about. Accessed 23 Aug 2019.

Carr, P. J. (2012). Citizens, community, and crime control: The problems and prospects for negotiated order. *Criminology & Criminal Justice, 12*(4), 397–412.

Cordner, G. (2014). Community policing. In M. D. Reisig & R. J. Kane (Eds.), *The Oxford handbook of police and policing* (pp. 148–171). Oxford: Oxford University Press.

Dekker, P. (2019). From pillarized active membership to populist active citizenship: The Dutch Do Democracy. *VOLUNTAS, 30*(1), 74–85.

Eysink Smeets, M., Moors, H., Jans, M., & Schram, K. (2013). De bijzondere belofte van Buurt Bestuurt. In *Maakt Buurt Bestuurt in de Rotterdamse praktijk de verwachtingen waar? En welke uitdagingen zijn er voor de toekomst?* Amsterdam: Lokaal Centraal.

Gelders, D., Brans, M., Maesschalck, J., & Colsoul, N. (2009). *Burgers betrekken in lokaal veiligheidsbeleid. Praktijkinitiatieven en succesvoorwaarden.* Brugge: Uitgeverij Vanden Broele.

Hardeman, J. (2017, April 22). 'Omsingel die gasten!', in *Elsevier*, 16, 24–27.

Kappeler, V. E., & Gaines, L. K. (2015). *Community policing. A contemporary perspective.* London: Routledge.

Koch, H. (2017, maart 3). Noem de burgers geen wachters, in *Trouw*, 11.

Koppenjan, J., & Klijn, E.-H. (2004). *Managing uncertainties in networks: A network approach to problem solving and decision making.* London: Routledge.

Loeffler, E. (2016). Co-Production of public services and outcomes. In T. Bovaird & E. Loeffler (Eds.), *Public management and governance* (pp. 319–336). London/New York: Routledge.

Loeffler, E. (2018). Providing public safety and public order through co-production. In T. Brandsen, B. Verschuere, & T. Steen (Eds.), *Co-production and co-creation: Engaging citizens in public services* (pp. 211–222). New York/London: Routledge.

Lub, V. (2016a). Buurtwachten in Nederland: ontwikkeling, mechanismen en morele implicaties. *Justitiële verkenningen, 42*(5), 27–44.

Lub, V. (2016b). *De burger op wacht. Het fenomeen 'buurtpreventie' onderzocht.* Rotterdam: Kenniswerkplaats Leefbare Wijken.

Lub, V. (2018). Neighbourhood Watch: Mechanisms and moral implications. *The British Journal of Criminology, 58*(4), 906–924.

Lub, V. (2019). *De burger kijkt mee. De groei van buurtpreventie en gemeentelijk veiligheidsbeleid.* Utrecht: Het CCV.

Lub, V., & De Leeuw, T. (2019). *Politie en actief burgerschap: een veilig verbond? Een onderzoek naar samenwerking, controle en (neven)effecten.* Den Haag: Politie & Wetenschap.

MacDonald, J. M. (2002). The effectiveness of community policing in reducing urban violence. *Crime & Delinquency, 48*(4), 592–618.

Martinus, E., Van Eijk, C., van Daele, E., Lam, A., Arnold, H., & Arends, W. (2018). Coproductie in het veiligheidsdomein. In A. Meijer, M. Honingh,

T. Steen, B. Verschuere, & T. Brandsen (Eds.), *Coproductie in de publieke sector* (pp. 83–104). Den Haag: Boom bestuurskunde.

Mehlbaum, S., & Van Steden, R. (2018). *Doe-het-zelfsurveillance. Een onderzoek naar de werking en effecten van WhatsApp-buurtgroepen.* Den Haag: Politiekunde.

Meijer, A. (2014). New media and the coproduction of safety: An empirical analysis of Dutch practices. *The American Review of Public Administration, 44*(1), 17–34.

Ostrom, E. (1978). Citizen participation and policing: What do we know? *Journal of Voluntary Action Research, 7*(1–2), 102–108.

Percy, S. L. (1978). Conceptualizing and measuring citizen co-production of community safety. *Policy Studies Journal, 7*(Winter), 486–493.

Pestoff, V. (2018). Co-production at the crossroads of public administration regimes. In T. Brandsen, B. Verschuere, & T. Steen (Eds.), *Co-production and Co-creation: Engaging citizens in public services* (pp. 27–36). New York/London: Routledge.

Pierre, J., & Peters, G. (2000). *Governance, politics and the state.* Basingstoke: Palgrave Macmillan.

Pridmore, J., Mols, A., Wang, Y., & Holleman, F. (2018). Keeping an eye on the neighbours: Police, citizens, and communication within mobile neighbourhood crime prevention groups. *The Police Journal: Theory, Practice and Principles, 92*(2), 97–120.

Scheider, M. C., Chapman, R., & Schapiro, A. (2009). Towards the unification of policing innovations under community policing. *Policing: An International Journal of Police Strategies and Management, 32*(4), 694–718.

Van der Land, M. (2013). Burgers voor/tegen burgers. Buurtwachten in Nederland en hun verbindingen met bewoners, politie en gemeente. *Tijdschrift Voor Veiligheid, 12*(2), 62–78.

Van der Land, M. (2014). *De buurtwacht: naar een balans tussen instrumentalisering en autonomievan burgers in veiligheid.* P&W Verkenning. Apeldoorn/Amsterdam. Politic en wetenschap/VU.

Van Eijk, C. J. A. (2017). *Engagement of citizens and public professionals in the co-production of public services.* Doctoral dissertation, Leiden University, Leiden.

Van Eijk, C. J. A. (2018). Helping Dutch neighborhood watch schemes to survive the rainy season: Studying mutual perceptions on citizens' and professionals' engagement in the co-production of community safety. *VOLUNTAS, 29*(1), 222–236.

Van Eijk, C., & Ohler, D. (2018). *Buurtpreventie binnen lokale veiligheidsaanpak. Handreiking.* Utrecht: Het CCV.

Van Eijk, C. J. A., Steen, T. P. S., & Verschuere, B. (2017). Co-producing safety in the local community: A Q-methodology study on the incentives of Belgian and Dutch members of neighbourhood watch schemes. *Local Government Studies, 43*(3), 323–343.

Van Noije, L. (2012). Coproductie Veiligheid. In V. Veldheer, J.-J. Jonker, L. van Noije, & C. Vrooman (Eds.). *Een beroep op de burger. Minder verzorgingsstaat, meer eigen verantwoordelijkheid?* (pp. 188–212). Sociaal en Cultureel Rapport 2012. Den Haag: Sociaal en Cultureel Planbureau.

Van Noije, L., & Wittebrood, K. (2008). *Sociale veiligheid ontsleuteld. Veronderstelde en werkelijke effecten van veiligheidsbeleid.* Den Haag: Sociaal en Cultureel Planbureau.

Van Steden, R., Van Caem, B., & Boutellier, H. (2011). The 'hidden strength' of active citizenship: The involvement of local residents in public safety projects. *Criminology & Criminal Justice, 11*(5), 433–450.

Verlet, D., & Reynaert, H. (2004). De participerende burger op lokaal vlak in Gent, Brugge en Antwerpen. *Burger, Bestuur & Beleid, 3,* 237–256.

Vollaard, B. (2016). Private bijdragen aan publieke veiligheid: Effecten van Buurt-WhatsApp. *Justitiele Verkenningen, 42*(5), 59–68.

Voorberg, W., Bekkers, V., & Tummers, L. (2015). A systematic review of co-creation and co-production. *Public Management Review, 17*(9), 1333–1357.

WABP. (2019). *Wat is WABP?* Published on https://www.wabp.nl/wat-is-wabp/. Accessed June 2019.

Williams, B. N., Kang, S.-C., & Johnson, J. (2015). (Co)-contamination as the dark side of co-production: Public value failures in co-production processes. *Public Management Review, 18*(5), 692–717.

Woolcock, G. W. E. (2009). *Measuring up?: Assessing the liveability of Australian cities.* Urban Research Program, Griffith University. Paper presented at The State of Australian Cities conference, 24–29 November 2009.

CHAPTER 10

Multi-Stakeholder Cooperation for Safe and Healthy Urban Environments: The Case of Citizen Sensing

Anna Berti Suman

10.1 INTRODUCTION

Residents of the twenty-first century's city are often confronted with challenges to their health and wellbeing deriving from, among others, environmental health risks, such as air pollution, radiation and high noise levels. It has been argued that such risks could be minimized through adaptive urban policies, i.e. policies designed to be responsive to changes in the environment and society (Corfee-Morlot et al. 2011; Berti Suman 2018a), and through multilevel (Corfee-Morlot et al. 2011), integrative and adaptive approaches to risk governance (Renn et al. 2011) aimed at including in the process various networks of public and private, individual and collective actors (Piattoni 2010). Urban actors tend to respond to risk through various innovative solutions when they are in a situation of stress (e.g. air pollution) or shock (e.g. nuclear disaster) that threatens their

A. Berti Suman (✉)
The Tilburg Institute for Law, Technology, and Society (TILT),
Tilburg University, Tilburg, The Netherlands
e-mail: A.BertiSuman@uvt.nl

© The Author(s) 2020
C. van Montfort, A. Michels (eds.), *Partnerships for Livable Cities*,
https://doi.org/10.1007/978-3-030-40060-6_10

safety. In this chapter, I focus on an emerging practice, that of 'Citizen Sensing', which can be framed as a *spontaneous innovation* in response to stressors and shocks[1] in the urban context.

Citizen Sensing is defined as grassroots-driven monitoring initiatives based, in general, on sensor technologies. The practice displays a trend involving citizens that are increasingly becoming willing to monitor urban environmental risks themselves. When lay people take advantage of the city's technological infrastructure (in particular sensors and open access data platforms) or build it themselves to visualize, monitor, report and combat environmental risk factors, two possible outcomes are conceivable. On one side, an outcome could be that the pre-existing institutional patterns for governing such risks are *de-legitimized* and the institutional and grassroots levels *clash*.

On the other side, it is also possible that—eventually—the two systems *converge and strengthen* each other, as illustrated in Fig. 10.1.

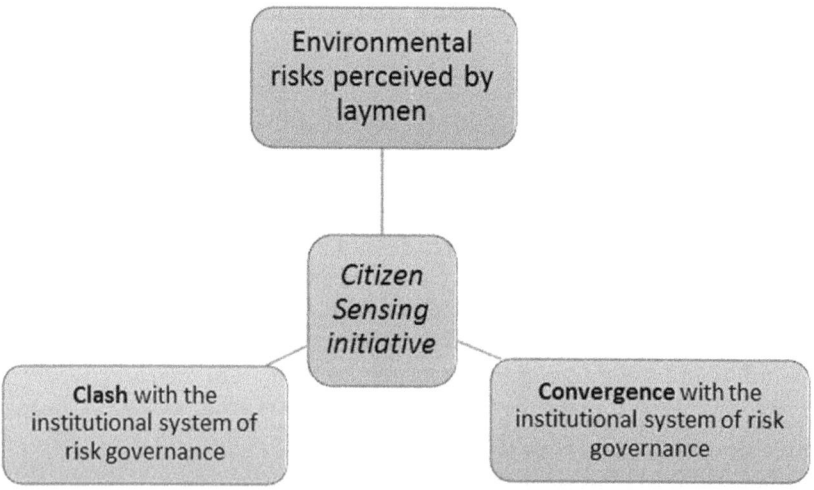

Fig. 10.1 Clash and convergence of Citizen Sensing with institutional risk governance

[1] Inspiration from the Vespucci Training School on "Digital Transformations in Citizen Science and Social Innovation" that the author attended, Fiesole, Italy, January 21–25, 2019. Part of the group work available at https://www.researchgate.net/publication/338422628_What_factors_determine_the_success_and_failure_of_social_innovation_triggered_by_stress_or_shock. Accessed March 8, 2020.

The present contribution will investigate two cases, the AiREAS air monitoring case in Eindhoven (Netherlands) and the Safecast radiation monitoring case initiated after the Fukushima Daiichi nuclear disaster (Japan). The first case stands as an example of multi-stakeholder partnership involving citizens, public and private actors, whereas the second illustrates a conflict between the citizens and the institutions. The latter case, however, at one point seems to also be drifting towards convergence. The success factors and challenges that both initiatives encounter are discussed.

The central question guiding the analysis will revolve around the inquiry of *the conditions under which Citizen Sensing—understood as a form of partnership—can contribute to improving the liveability of the city by stimulating a co-governance of shared urban risks* (specifically, environmental risks to public health). The imaginable result of this enhanced, rather informal, partnership that takes the form of Citizen Sensing is the implementation of joint strategies aimed at realizing safer and healthier urban environments, eventually passing from a situation of conflict to one of cooperation. The inquiry is thus embedded in the central question of this book and resonates with a number of key topics discussed. In particular, it provides two tangible examples of a response (more or less solicited) to the appeal (again, more or less explicit) by urban governments for shared responsibilities between institutions and citizens, with—in this case—the aim of tackling environmental health risks in the city.

10.2   Citizen Sensing as a Form of Partnership

The chapter follows the *broad* concept of 'partnership' that guides this book, including examples of informal types of partnerships between governments, citizens, and companies. In addition, the *public character* of the partnerships at issue is emphasised: both examples discussed are aimed at realizing collective public policy goals and safeguarding specific public goods (in this case, a healthy environment). Yet, it will be also illustrated that the market plays a (more or less) important role in the instances discussed and can bring in opportunities, and also challenges. The *level* at which the Citizen Sensing initiative deploys is also important: the process of influence of the initiative on different institutional and spatial levels (local, regional, national, global) is investigated. Lastly, the *temporal dimension* is considered: both projects studied have been initiated in 2011 and are still ongoing. This 8+ lifespan of the project facilitates the assessment of the project's contribution to the city's liveability in the longer term. The long term spin off is particularly relevant for projects that respond to a sudden shock (e.g. nuclear disaster) rather than to a persistent stress (e.g. air pollution). There is indeed a risk that the first could 'disappear' when the situation of emergency is over. It will be argued, however, that this was not the case for the Safecast case studied.

Overall, in line with the book's approach, Citizen Sensing is inspected as a practice possibly contributing to liveability and, by extension, to innovative practices in urban governance. The barriers that may undermine this contributory potential are also analyzed, inductively drawing findings from the analysis of the two case studies. In choosing a Dutch and a Japanese case, I am particularly aware of the difficulty of reaching generalizable conclusions for the importance of context-factors that may strongly affect the contributory or instead failing outcome of an initiative over the other. Context-dependency has been particularly taken into account.

In targeting environmental risk to public health in the urban context, this chapter is situated in between two dimensions of liveability: that of *greenery* and that of *safety*. The concept of green can broadly be considered as including a healthy urban space, which also falls into the concept of a safe urban environment. Safety is here understood as encompassing specifically non-human threats, i.e. environmental risk factors, such as air pollution, noise and radiation.

The chapter takes the citizen's standpoint in responding to the question '*for whom* the city becomes (more) livable'. Particular attention is indeed devoted to the risk perceived by the citizens, which often frame the risk differently from the institutions responsible for handling it. It has been argued that different risk perception-attitudes influence individual opinions on how a risk problem should be solved (Berti Suman and Van Geenhuizen 2019; Renn and Klinke 2016). In advocating for the inclusion of laymen's knowledge into urban (risk) governance, issues related to false information or perception biases (Renn and Klinke 2016, p. 1) that the citizens may have on the risk should be considered. Yet Citizen Sensing initiatives can be viewed as a way to increase information availability for the citizens (but also for other interested stakeholders) and mitigate risk perception biases. Overall, it will be argued that Citizen Sensing can enhance *liveability of* and *control over* the city for the participating citizens. Nonetheless, for other citizens and, especially, for policy-makers, the practice can also be regarded as a possible source of 'fake' claims, as a reactionary practice and a disturbance to smooth governance. Such negative outcomes are acknowledged. However, due to length constraints, these issues will not extensively addressed in this chapter.

Lastly, it should be noted that the type of partnership that can be considered realized through Citizen Sensing initiatives in this context bridges *three categories* (see for a typology Fig. 1.1, Chap. 1). I refer to Categories 'E. Partnerships between civil society and public organizations', 'G. Grassroots civil society organizations' and 'H. Partnerships in which civil society, market and state are involved'. Throughout the case study analysis, it will be shown that a Citizen Sensing initiative may start as only falling under Category G and later develop in a form of collaboration under H, also involving the private sector and (local) government. Despite the use of categorization, I wish to underline that Citizen Sensing-based partnerships mostly have an *informal structure* and are driven by events, in the sense that partners gather their energy rather spontaneously in response to a situation of shock or stress. For this informal nature of Citizen Sensing-based partnerships, any effort of categorization has intrinsic limits.

10.3 Definition of Citizen Sensing and Its Link to Social Capital

Citizen Sensing has been defined by Gabrys, Pritchard and Barratt (2016, p. 3) as a practice in evolution which developed from the mere 'bottom-up production of geographic information' to a 'wider set of participatory, DIY [Do It Yourself] and digital sensing practices that are proliferating through newer sensor technologies.' The *participatory element* is central and connects the practice with the nature of partnership. More recently, the Citizen Sensing Toolkit (Making Sense 2018, p. 7) defined Citizen Sensing as 'a form of citizen participation in environmental monitoring and action which is bottom-up, participatory and empowering to the community'. The 'empowering' discourse seems underlying a push for having different actors engaged in the city (risk) governance arena. In Berti Suman (2018b, p. 4) by unpacking and combining definitions of the practice, I affirmed that Citizen Sensing 'entails lay people acting as intelligent interpreters through pre-existing networks, or networks created more spontaneously by events (e.g. a public health crisis), on which they actively observe, report, collect, analyse and disseminate information via certain technologies.' The *networked nature* of Citizen Sensing (Berti Suman 2018b, p. 4) resembles a key figure of partnerships: that of being a network of actors.

Citizen Sensing can also be framed a manifestation of social capital's mobilization in response to urban shocks and stressors. More generally referring to the umbrella term of 'Citizen Science', Van Brussel and Huyse defined the practice as a 'catalyst for triggering behaviour change and building social capital around environmental issues' (Van Brussel and Huyse 2018, p. 1). I noted earlier that Citizen Sensing is understandable as *a* sub-set of the broader Citizen Science concept (Berti Suman and Van Geenhuizen 2019). Consequently, Van Brussel and Huyse's definition seems also timely to the present discussion. Citizen Sensing shows traits of what has been affirmed regarding Citizen Science, i.e. the potential of the practice to influence (urban) data collection practices, citizen behaviour and, eventually, policy-making (Berti Suman and Van Geenhuizen 2019; Hallow et al. 2015).

A partnership *through Citizen Sensing* could be viewed as a way to link these concepts together. By being able to partner with other stakeholders, the Citizen Sensing initiative gets broader social support and gains more attention from interested parties. Once the visibility of the initiative has been enhanced, the likelihood that the initiative could also have an influence on policy-makers is higher. Through influence on (urban) policy-making, Citizen Sensing can contribute to bringing in the citizen's perspective on the risk problem at issue. As a result, the governance of the problem conceivably becomes more participatory, more legitimate and the social capital potential deriving from the collaboration between stakeholders is unleashed. If the risk problem regards issues such as air pollution, radioactivity in the city and others along this line, it can be argued that the Citizen Sensing initiative contributed to improving liveability in the city through social capital-building processes. This flow is illustrated in Fig. 10.2.

When discussing social capital, it is worth to devote some consideration to the notion of *trust* and Citizen Sensing, especially as trust has been defined as the 'social capital' of society (Fukuyama 1995; Putnam 2000). One of the pillars of the Social Capital Theory is indeed the notion of trust (Glaeser et al. 2000, pp. 811–812). Trust has been also studied as a 'group

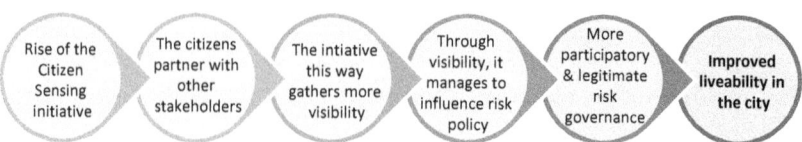

Fig. 10.2 The flow of Citizen Sensing contributing to the city's livability

attribute' (Coleman 1990; Putnam 1993). The existence of a 'social network' among a group of individuals, in this case represented by the act of joining a Citizen Sensing initiative, can suggest the presence of a specific trust bond between the actors (Glaeser et al. 2000, pp. 814–815, 840).

What is worth inquiring is whether this (already existing) trust bonds among the sensing citizens facilitate the building of trust relationships with other actors outside the network or rather discourage it. The act of monitoring environmental risk, may be seen as already showing distrust by the citizens towards the actors institutionally appointed to govern such risk (Berti Suman 2018b). These citizens would have in common this distrustful attitude towards the *outside*, through which they (paradoxically) build trust *internally* to the network of the Citizen Sensing initiative. This configuration is illustrated by the Safecast case discussed. However, another interpretation can also be possible. When the citizens realize that the impact of the network can be enhanced if they obtain the trust of other actors, such as institutions and companies, they may 'invite' other stakeholders to join the initiative, as occurred in the AiREAS case study. The discussion of the cases will shed light on these two possible configurations (among many others) and draw implications for (Citizen Sensing-based) partnerships.

10.4   THE CASE STUDY ANALYSIS

10.4.1   The AiREAS Case

The AiREAS case has been presented in the opening of this chapter as an example of multi-stakeholder partnership through Citizen Sensing, involving citizens, public and private actors. In addition, it has been introduced as an initiative born in response to an urban stressor, i.e. the problem of air quality. The case study is analyzed through a literature review complemented by a web-survey and follow-up, semi-structured interview, that were been performed with the participants and project's founders.[2]

---

[2] The web-survey and (in person and phone/Skype) interviews have been performed as part of the PhD research of the author (start date September 2017, defense date May 8, 2020). The web-survey is available on Qualtrics at https://tilburglawschool.eu.qualtrics.com/jfe/form/SV_37MhcbbyoiU8Qg5. Ethical clearance for the data collection has been granted by Tilburg Law School (TLS-ERB #2018/01 issued on 12 June 2018).

The AiREAS case started with a 'mission': in Close et al. (2016, p. xi), it is stated that the project was started/created with the aim of co-creating 'Healthy Cities'. From the description of the project's founder, it appears evident that there is a 'cooperative' rather than conflictive nature in the initiative. Close et al. (2016, p. xi) refer to "a mission to transform ourselves, citizens of a twenty-first-century post-industrial consumer society driven by self-interest [..] into new men and women, inspired by human values, motivated by *common purpose*, seeking to build a *sustainable* world order, shouldering *shared responsibilities* [..]" [emphasis added]. The ideology behind the initiative is clearly suggesting a partnership approach.

As a matter of fact, AiREAS, differently from the second case analyzed, partnered from an early stage with the private sector, inviting businesses such as Philips Lighting and TomTom. Also academic partners, like ITC University of Twente and the University of Madrid, were invited to join the initiative. Remarkably, from an early stage also the public sector, namely the Province of North Brabant and the City of Eindhoven, were involved. A sign of this involvement is the financial support that the initiative received from the Province of North Brabant: the project received a small funding of €25,000. Overall, the initiative can be categorized as H. Partnerships in which civil society, market and state are involved (see Fig. 1.1, Chap. 1).

In terms of organizational structure of the partnership, it can be noted that a level of *coordination* among the partners is identifiable. However, a formal and clearly definite organization is not found. Hamm et al. (2016, p. 52) in describing the early stages of AiREAS stress the importance of 'the commitment of individual persons from the [engaged] stakeholders' as key to the launch of the project. The element of the individual personalities involved in the negotiation process results in being decisive (the role of 'champions' within organizations that believe in the initiative, GFDRR 2018). Hamm et al. (2016, p. 52) describe how, before entering any discussion about finances, they 'started by *co-creating* a project plan focusing on what has to be done and what are the deliverables' [emphasis added]. Only at a later stage did the partners agree on the cost of the project, 'who would invest and for what would they be paying' (Hamm et al. 2016, p. 52). The principles driving the initiative go beyond the matter of budget and investments. Hamm et al. (2016, p. 52) indeed affirm: 'It is essential to realize that AiREAS projects are not based on traditional customer-supplier relationships, but on *co-creation, mutual commitment and equality*' [emphasis added]. Overall, a considerable part of the finance that supported the project plan came from the provincial and municipal partners. However, as stressed by Close et al. (2016, p. 82), the biggest asset was represented by the mobilization of voluntary time and work of the participants.

Considering the engagement of the Province of North Brabant and the City of Eindhoven, it can be affirmed that the partnership is identified only at a sub-national level. The air quality issue, however, is a 'vertical' problem, tackled both at the central government-level and by local and provincial authorities. If the specificities of the area of Eindhoven in terms of air pollution make it a more concerning topic for the municipal and provincial authorities, yet AiREAS aimed at influencing also the national and even EU-wide political agenda on air quality. A future partnership, engaging state-level actors, could thus also be hypothesized.

Close et al. (2016, p. 83) stress the heterogeneity, yet potential of what I frame here as a partnership through Citizen Sensing: 'We see civilians participating free of charge out of personal interest for a healthy living environment. Or they develop entrepreneurial initiatives around the wellbeing mission which they test in the AiREAS network. (..) All the participants have their own uniquely different *reciprocity expectations* in the project and still *complement each other effectively* in the value-driven process' [emphasis added]. Elements of reciprocity and complementarity emerge, all oriented to a greater goal, that of the city's wellbeing. Close et al. (2016, pp. 43–44) underline that a success factor to align the different actors is to agree 'in an open democratic dialogue' on 'priorities' on the basis of 'equality among all participants', keeping in mind the common purpose of 'healthy city through air quality'.

From this ideology, Close, the project's founder, moved to the creation of the STIR foundation (in Dutch, *Stichting Transformation, Indexation en Research*) and the Sustainocratic Movement, two realities that strived for creating a healthier city, framed as the 'City of Tomorrow' (in Dutch, *Stad van Morgen*). The ideology concretized in a 'Proof of Principle' (Close et al. 2016, p. 109), where participants were engaged in researching the link between air pollution exposure and human health and lifestyle. Air pollution exposure was made visible through a network of sensor technologies and data infrastructure, the Innovative Air Quality Measurement System (ILM, in Dutch *Innovatief Lucht Meetsysteem*) consisting of 35 Airboxes placed at various locations throughout Eindhoven.

The Airboxes measure various air quality and meteorological variables that, after calibration, are made available online in near-real time. The rationale behind the sensors' location was to target the locations of most concern for the citizens. Interestingly, some of the sensors were located where existing municipal and RIVM air quality detectors were already in place. This shows that, despite a convergence-oriented partnership of type H, still a push to cross-check how state actors monitor air quality is present, configuring traits of distrust.

An interview conducted with a participant of AiREAS underlined the concern that governments do not *take* (enough) *responsibility* for air pollution problems. This was, in the respondent's opinion, why the citizens need to activate and mobilize their actions through e.g. Citizen Sensing to push policymakers to care about air quality. The interviewee suggested that, by joining AiREAS, the citizen 'takes' the responsibility for improving her/his city's air quality both through the monitoring, and through behavioural adaptation coming from to the data obtained on pollution in the city. By inviting policymakers to join from an early-stage of the initiative, the participants aim to show to governors that the citizens are not waiting 'silently' for policymakers to take action but want to tackle the shared problem *together*.

One of the achievements of the project was the ability to meet the requirements for data quality and data validation (Close et al. 2016, pp. 58–62), for sensors precision (2016 et al., pp. 73–76) and for data management (2016, pp. 68–72) through the adoption of the related protocols. Despite the support from institutional actors at the municipal and city-level (but not yet national level) and the private sector, one of the challenges of the project was the scaling up in terms of social support by peer citizens. As a matter of fact, the initiative did not manage (yet) to reach the goal of achieving 4000 participants in the city of Eindhoven and up to 4 million participants in Europe (Close et al. 2016, p. 109). However, the project expanded through the deployment of adjacent activities (e.g. 'FRE2SH' for food resiliency and the 'School of Talents' for education).

Another challenge expressed by participants, in interviews, deals with the issue on diverging objectives, values and interests over time. If at the beginning all partners were devoted to a healthier, more livable city, soon 'money-driven reasons hampered real value-driven innovation', noted a respondent. In addition, communication channels between the citizens and the institutions involved were, in certain instances, problematic. All these considerations offer specific sparks for reflection that will be further developed.

10.4.2   The Safecast Case

In introducing the Safecast case, it has been noted that the case is an example of a conflict (more or less manifested) between citizens and institutional stakeholders on the governance of post-Fukushima radiation risk, with specific regard to its monitoring. In addition, it has been referred to as an initiative responding to an (urban) shock, i.e. the nuclear disaster of the Daiichi nuclear power plant in 2011. The shock affected (even more pervasively) the rural areas. However, for the sake of comparability with the other case study and for maintaining the focus of the book, only the impact at the city level will be here discussed. The case study is also inspected through literature review complemented with a web-survey and follow-up semi-structured interviews performed with the participants and project's founders.[3]

The shock is here identified by the nuclear disaster that resulted of the 2011 earthquake and subsequent 15-metre tsunami which destroyed the Fukushima Daiichi plant (Abe 2017). Over 100,000 people were evacuated from their homes to avoid radioactive contamination and over 1000 deaths were registered during the evacuation.[4] The World Health Organization (WHO) estimated the radiation dosage received by the residents of Japan, outside the evacuated areas, for example in Tokyo, were below any levels for concern. However, public discontent was high specifically in relation to 'the inadequacy of official preparation for such a disaster, and the chaotic nature of inter-agency, inter-governmental, and public emergency communication' (Brown et al. 2016, p. S82). The information

---

[3] The web-survey and (in person and phone/Skype) interviews have been performed as part of the PhD research of the author (start date September 2017, defense date May 8, 2020). The web-survey is available on Qualtrics at https://tilburglawschool.eu.qualtrics.com/jfe/form/SV_50e6PvHGAeEKCIB. The survey has also been translated and offered in Japanese (credit: Taisei Tatsumi). Ethical clearance for the data collection has been granted by Tilburg Law School (TLS-ERB #2018/01 issued on 12 June 2018).

[4] See report by 'World Nuclear Association' at http://www.world-nuclear.org/information-library/safety-and-security/safety-of-plants/fukushima-accident.aspx. Accessed September 18, 2018.

provided to citizens through institutional channels on the actual radiation levels was often scarce, incomplete and/or contradictory (Brown et al. 2016, p. S82).

The conflictive nature of the initiative emerges. Safecast can indeed be framed as a response to *information failures* in an emergency and post-emergency situation in which city dwellers are exposed to an uncertain risk. The risk was uncertain as there was confusion on the actual radioactive dosage to which citizens were exposed, outside the directly affected areas. As I noted earlier with regards to haze risk governance (Berti Suman 2019 on 'The role of information in multilateral governance of environmental health risk: lessons from the Equatorial Asian Haze case'), information is a central asset in risk preparedness and response. Information is also the basis to start a dialogue between the citizens, the institutions, and any other actor involved. If the information is not available or not properly provided, the citizens will have to organize themselves to obtain it. As Abe underlines, the discrepancy between the citizens' expectation to information and that actually provided by institutions 'provided opportunities for collective action' (Abe 2019, p. 37).

Bonner, co-founder and global director of Safecast, noted in an interview that the crisis was the trigger for the citizens to act. When the people realized that governmental authorities did not have enough capacity to install/operate existing sensors and deploy sound radiation measurements (at least this is what they perceived, see above discussion on risk perception), the citizens took action to monitor radiation through alternative means. As noted by Brown et al. (2016, p. S82). 'Safecast's effort and others like it are public responses to institutional inadequacy'.

Safecast started from a small group of individuals which began aggregating already publicly available radiation data and published them as online maps. The lack of standardization or consistency in the available data pushed these individuals to gather tools to independently measure the radiation. As the available global stock of radiation detectors were almost depleted, the group started building their own radiation detectors. They deployed a system based on a radiation sensor attachable to a vehicle and linked to GPS, the 'bGeigie Nano', sending data to a map where concerned people could view radiations' patterns.

From the small group of participants, many other people joined. The literature (Abe 2017) and numerous respondents interviewed stress that the high media impact of Safecast stimulated more people to join the initiative. Other, more local initiatives (Safecast was strongly internationally oriented from the beginning) failed to gather such visibility and 'disappeared' soon after the disaster (Abe 2017, p. 69). Brown et al. (2016) note that 5 years after the launch of Safecast around 500 bGeigie Nanos have been distributed over a number of different countries. On the Safecast's map more than 35 million pieces of data are displayed (Baumont 2018) and the number of participants keep increasing (Abe 2015).

In addition, as noted above regarding trust, the bonding element among the participants that stimulated even more grassroots-actors to join was this perceived need of 'cross-checking' or even filling institutional data gaps. The element of distrust emerged among the Japanese respondents. One interviewee affirmed: 'My trust in the government did not change after the accident but I learnt not to rely on the government anymore'. As a typical trait of the Japanese culture, distrust is not openly manifested. However, the decision 'not to rely on the government anymore' can arguably show a distrustful attitude.

In terms of organizational structure, the Safecast case is quite blurred. The Safecast team defines itself as a very decentralized collective, where hundreds of participants from various parts of the world share concerns regarding radiation levels. Anybody who is interested in joining the project can get a bGeige and start adding data points to the Safecast map. Who is also interested in the group's discussions can share measurements and opinions on different channels, from Safecast's social media to its official blog. Yet a (light) form of coordination is found: the smooth development of the initiative and the soundness of the various measurements added by the participants all over the world are primarily checked by a hub based in Tokyo where the founders of the project are located. In this hub, Safecast's agenda is shaped and key decisions for the future of the initiative are taken.[5] In terms of finances, Safecast is essentially a network of volunteers based on crowd sourcing. Yet recently Safecast had to look for financial support from the private sector to ensure the sustainability of the initiative over time. The initiative succeeded in getting funding from the private company Amway,[6] which could actually be viewed as quite controversial.

All in all, Safecast never built a partnership with institutions or the private sector, striving to remain a reliable and independent source of risk information (Hemmi and Graham 2014). In this sense, it can be

[5] Data and observations gathered during fieldwork on the Safecast case (Japan, April–May 2019). Ethical clearance for the fieldwork has been granted by Tilburg Law School (TLS-ERB #2018/01 issued on 12 June 2018).

[6] See https://blog.safecast.org/2018/09/safecast-at-soma-future-lab-2018/; https://www.amway.nl/en/. Accessed September 24, 2019.

categorized as a type G partnership (Grassroots civil society organizations). The initiative indeed relies exclusively on grassroots' resources, both in terms of volunteers, equipment (they build their sensors), and funding (they crowdfund their work). Nonetheless, Safecast cannot be understood as a solely conflictive initiative that stayed in its bubble to criticize official risk governance. As noted by Brown et al. (2016, pp. S82, S90), nowadays Safecast is often contacted by academics and experts, schools, companies, and other community groups. In addition, and even more remarkably, Brown et al. (2016, pp. S82, S84) argued that 'the inclusion of Safecast data and experience in official institutional discourse concerning radiation risk, measurement, and disaster response suggests that the importance and value of providing this kind of option has been recognized by policy makers at many levels'. In addition, over time, the governmental risk communication channels became more trusted by the citizens. Brown et al. (2016) noted that, at first, public data were insufficient or inaccessible, whereas later on the government started releasing comparable data to those published by Safecast.

From the above arguments it appears that even type G partnership can move towards type E (Partnerships between civil society and public organizations) or even H, if the initiative manages to also engage the private sector (Safecast managed to engage in a dialogue also with the nuclear company TEPCO). Although Safecast started as an initiative contrasting the state system, over time a dialogue with interested institutions mitigated this sense of distrust. It could be argued that the trust process was mutual, i.e. from the sensing citizens to the institutions and the reverse, the first receiving valuable data from official sources, the second realizing the complementary potential of the citizen-initiative. Numerous respondents interviewed pointed that, currently, the citizens often consult both official and Safecast information sources. The development of the Safecast case from conflict to (a light form of) converge has implications for the assessment of success elements of partnerships through Citizen Sensing (see 'Discussion').

Two contextual elements have to be considered in terms of assessing Safecast's transition from conflict to convergence, vis-à-vis the AiREAS cooperative attitude from the start: the Safecast initiative raised from a nuclear disaster, an instance where predictably tensions arise between citizens and institutions. The AiREAS case instead responded to a relatively less problematic issue, i.e. that of air pollution in the city. In addition, the Safecast case is inserted in a cultural setting, the Japanese one, arguably based on a *culture of respect* for the institutions and shaped by a sharper division between civic and institutional actors, where the decisions of the second are in general scarcely (perceived to be) influenced by the grassroots. Differently, in the Netherlands a stronger *culture of dialogue* between citizens and institutions is found but also that citizens more often have an attitude to challenge institutional decisions and to engage in a conversation with governmental actors. These context-level differentiations can definitely influence the development and outcome of a partnership.

10.5   DISCUSSION

The analysis of the two initiatives facilitated the process of extracting the conditions under which Citizen Sensing—understood as a form of partnership—can contribute to improving liveability of a city by stimulating a co-governance of shared (urban) risks. The risks discussed in the two cases could well take place in both the urban and in the rural context. An urban lens is chosen here, although some of the conclusions can be extended to Citizen Sensing in rural settings. The following factors seemed to be contributing to a successful partnership when this can be framed as type H and thus cooperative from the beginning:

- Despite internal diversity among the participants, all participants should be committed to a *shared goal*, which has as a trait a public good (e.g. improving liveability in the city through tackling the air quality problem); when such a commitment fails, often the success of the initiative is hampered.
- An early *open attitude* towards policymakers and the private sector from the citizens stimulate engagement and mutual trust on both sides, from which the initiative can benefit.
- This type of partnership should particularly strive to obtain the participation of *peer grassroots-groups* in the initiative (e.g. environmental collectives, associations of concerned citizens) and of the media at both local, provincial and national level. It indeed resulted from the case studies' analysis that they struggle to enlarge the number of participants and to sustain social support and attention from peer citizens and media over time.
- Type H partnerships are expected to be apt for relatively mild health and safety issues, such as air pollution in the city, rather than for disaster response.

- Similar types of partnership are more likely to be found and probably more successful in a context where there is a dominant culture of dialogue between citizen and institutions.

The following factors seem to instead contribute to a successful partnership of type G (in this analysis, 'conflictive'):

- The need for *cross-checking* and the sense of distrust towards institutional actors appear particularly successful to stimulate social support and media attention, which can result in more influence for the initiative.
- Also crucial is the ability of the initiative to stay independent while gaining the attention of other stakeholders, such as the private sector and even the government, showing them the *credibility* of the data produced.
- For enhancing its impact, this type of partnership should be particularly open to *engage in a dialogue with institutional stakeholders*, accepting that valuable data can come from official sources, but also showing to the government the complementary potential of the citizen-initiative.
- Type G partnerships are expected to be fitting (also) for disaster scenarios as they are exactly triggered by a reaction to an emergency.
- Similar types of partnership are appropriate for contexts where a dialogue between citizen and institutions is lacking and rather there is a pronounced distance between the two sides.

Both types of partnership illustrated by AiREAS and Safecast have two conditions for success in common:

- The initiative must arise from an *actual problem*, either a stressor or a shock-related problem, yet showing that there is the need for combining energy and resources to tackle it.
- Citizen Sensing initiatives have to *meet the data quality and reliability standards* to be 'listened' by other stakeholders and ultimately be successful.

Some of these points resonate with what is discussed in the Introduction to this book regarding the conditions that are essential for partnerships to be effective. In particular, *legitimacy* plays an important role: all partners must stay committed to the ultimate goal, in this case enhancing liveability through addressing environmental risk in the city. Also *responsiveness* appears important: as indicated in the Safecast case, the partnership should be able to adapt to changing conditions. By discussing the role of the specific Japanese culture in terms of trust/distrust discourses, I also stressed how *context-factors* are relevant for the successful outcome of a partnership.

By comparing a more local and more global initiative (which yet started locally), I suggested that also *level* and *scale* matter when we asses success. For example, an initiative can be very successful in attracting global attention (e.g. the Safecast initiative is often referred to in international media and figures in numerous international networks), but may lose social support in the local reality from where it originated (e.g. the Safecast initiative struggles to maintain/increase the number of Japanese participants) or the other way around (e.g. the AiREAS case, which is still very successful at the local level but struggles to obtain international visibility). Scale instead refers to the origin of the initiative: success for an initiative started in response to an issue concerning a very limited number of citizens can be considered to have 'scaled-up' if it manages to enlarge its audience to a smaller proportion of citizen than if it was an initiative responding to a large-scale disaster affecting a considerable size of the population of a country, such as a nuclear accident.

10.6   Conclusion

This contribution discussed a rather novel practice, Citizen Sensing, and framed it as a peculiar form of partnership, oriented to tackle environmental risk in the city. The chapter offered a case-based insight into possible conditions facilitating Citizen Sensing's contribution to liveability of the city by stimulating a more participatory governance of the city's environmental risk. Factors that seem particularly favorable to success are the existence of a real problem and a high compliance with data quality and reliability standards. In addition, the commitment to a public good; an open attitude towards stakeholders outside the Citizen Sensing networks; support from media and from peer grassroots-groups are helpful in 'cooperative' types of initiatives. In case of 'conflictive' initiatives, a distrustful attitude and a sense of independence of the initiative from government and companies seem leading to more social support. Also the ability of the initiative to appear credible to other stakeholders is particularly crucial.

It has also been shown that 'cooperative' and 'conflictive' partnerships are blurred categories as the typologies of partnership can move from one to the other. The type G partnership discussed above moved towards a type E and could eventually even become a type H. This shifting is often the result of a mutual trust process, occurring between the different stakeholders interested in the risk. Convergence when the initiative started as conflictive can be considered as an overall success of the initiative as this shows that Citizen Sensing can actually complement (urban) risk governance. In addition, it has been noted that also partnerships of type H, which would arguably be 'cooperative', may show traits of distrust.

Lastly, the decision of a Citizen Sensing initiative on which stakeholders to engage always entails trade-offs. On one hand, the inclusion of governmental and private sector-actors can be at the detriment of a larger social support from grassroots-organizations. In addition, the involvement of a broader array of stakeholders may over time lead to diverging objectives, values and interests that could conflict and undermine the potential of the initiative. On the other hand, a Citizen Sensing initiative that does not 'dare' to engage stakeholders beyond the close network of trusted citizens might fail in unleashing its full contributory power. Future research should target the need to inspect a larger number of cases, to further test the conditions outlined here and investigate deeper the influence of context-dependency.

Overall, both initiatives analyzed resulted in an impact on the surrounding reality in which they were inserted. Such an impact can be framed in terms of improved liveability, in Eindhoven, Tokyo and the cities of the Fukushima prefecture as well as cities around the world where citizens joined Safecast. This outcome can be associated with a twofold process: on one side, the citizens became more aware on the real environmental risk to which they were exposed in their cities and in this way perception biases and uncertainties were mitigated. The participating individuals felt to be 'in control' of their city's air quality and radiation levels. On the other side, the engagement of various institutional and non-institutional actors in the conversation over a shared problem led to a number of concerted actions as well as behavioral adjustments that made the mitigation of the risk possible. Risk mitigation through awareness and dialogue seems to be the key outcome of a successful partnership, where success is associated with enhanced health and safety in the city through Citizen Sensing.

REFERENCES

Abe, Y. 2015. *Measuring for What: Networked citizen science movements after the Fukushima nuclear accident*. Dissertation defended at the University of Southern California.

Abe, Y. (2017). Mina no Data Site (MDS) and the culture of measurement after Fukushima. *Unmediated: Politics and Communication, 1*, 68–72.

Abe, Y. (2019). Making civic media in the post-Fukushima media ecology. In J. Hunsinger & A. Schrock (Eds.), *Making our world: The hacker and maker movements in context*. New York: Peter Lung.

Baumont, G. (2018). Nuclear crisis preparedness lessons learned from Fukushima Daiichi. In M. Bourrier & C. Bieder (Eds.), *Risk communication for the future*. New York: Springer.

Berti Suman, A. (2018a). The smart transition: An opportunity for a sensor-based public-health risk governance? *International Review of Law, Computers & Technology, 32*(2–3), 257–274. https://doi.org/10.1080/13600869.2018.1463961.

Berti Suman, A. (2018b). Challenging risk governance patterns through citizen sensing: The Schiphol Airport case. *International Review of Law, Computers & Technology, 32*(1), 155–173. https://doi.org/10.1080/13600869.2018.1429186.

Berti Suman, A. (2019). The role of information in multilateral governance of environmental health risk: Lessons from the Equatorial Asian Haze case. *Special Issue on Multilateral Governance of Technological Risk*, 1–17. https://doi.org/10.1080/13669877.2019.1617338.

Berti Suman, A., & Van Geenhuizen, M. (2019). *Not just noise monitoring: Rethinking citizen sensing for risk-related problem-solving. Environmental Planning and Management*. https://doi.org/10.1080/09640568.2019.1598852.

Brown, A., et al. (2016). Safecast: Successful citizen-science for radiation measurement and communication after Fukushima. *Journal of Radiological Protection, 36*(2), S82–S101.

Close, J. P., et al. (2016). *AiREAS: Sustainocracy for a healthy city. The invisible made visible phase 1*. Springer Briefs on Case Studies of Sustainable Development. https://doi.org/10.1007/978-3-319-26940-5.

Coleman, J. (1990). *Foundations of social theory*. Cambridge, MA: Harvard University.

Corfee-Morlot, J., Cochran, I., Hallegatte, S., et al. (2011). Multilevel risk governance and urban adaptation policy. *Climatic Change, 104*(1), 169–197. https://doi.org/10.1007/s10584-010-9980-9.

Fukuyama, F. (1995). *Trust*. London: Hamish Hamilton.

Gabrys, J., Pritchard, H., & Barratt, B. (2016). Just good enough data: Figuring data citizenships through air pollution sensing and data stories. *Big Data & Society*, 1–14. https://doi.org/10.1177/2053951716679677.

GFDRR – The Global Facility for Disaster Reduction and Recovery. (2018). *Identifying success factors in crowdsourced geographic information use in government.* Washington, DC: GFDRR.

Glaeser, E. L., Laibson, D. I., Scheinkman, J. A., & Soutter, C. L. (2000). Measuring trust. *The Quarterly Journal of Economics, 3*(115), 811–846. https://doi.org/10.1162/003355300554926.

Hallow, B., Roetman, P. E. J., Walter, M., & Daniels, C. B. (2015). Citizen Science for policy development: The case of koala management in South Australia. *Environmental Science & Policy, 47*, 126–136. https://doi.org/10.1016/j.envsci.2014.10.007.

Hamm, N. A. S., van Lochem, M., Hoek, G., Otjes, R. P., van der Sterren, S., & Verhoeven, H. (2016). The invisible made visible: Science and technology. In J. P. Close, et al. (Eds.), *AiREAS: Sustainocracy for a healthy city. The invisible made visible phase 1.* Springer Briefs on Case Studies of Sustainable Development. Cham: Springer. https://doi.org/10.1007/978-3-319-26940-5.

Hemmi, A., & Graham, I. (2014). Hacker science versus closed science: Building environmental monitoring infrastructure. *Information, Communication & Society, 17*(7). https://doi.org/10.1080/1369118X.2013.848918.

Making Sense Project. (2018). *Citizen Sensing. A toolkit.* ISBN/EAN: 978-90-828215-0. Retrieved May 10, 2019 from http://making-sense.eu/publication_categories/toolkit/

Piattoni, S. (2010). *The theory of multi-level governance: Conceptual, empirical, and normative challenges.* Oxford: Oxford University Press.

Putnam, R. (1993). *Making democracy work: Civic traditions in modern Italy.* Princeton: Princeton University Press.

Putnam, R. (2000). *Bowling alone: The collapse and revival of American community.* New York: Simon and Schuster.

Renn, O., & Klinke, A. (2016). Risk perception and its impacts on risk governance. Oxford Research Encyclopedia of Environmental Science. Oxford University Press USA.

Renn, O., Klinke, A., & van Asselt, M. (2011). Adaptive and integrative governance on risk and uncertainty. *Journal of Risk Research, 15*(3), 273–292. https://doi.org/10.1080/13669877.2011.636838.

Van Brussel, S., & Huyse, H. (2018). Citizen science on speed? Realising the triple objective of scientific rigour, policy influence and deep citizen engagement in a large-scale citizen science project on ambient air quality in Antwerp. *Journal of Environmental Planning and Management.* https://doi.org/10.1080/09640568.2018.1428183.

CHAPTER 11

Safety in the City: Building Strategic Partnerships in the Fight Against Organized Crime

Martijn Groenleer, Sanderijn Cels, and Jorrit de Jong

11.1 Introduction[1]

While marijuana consumption is tolerated in the Netherlands, marijuana production and trade is illegal. Due to the constant crackdowns on marijuana production, marijuana supply is scarce, making marijuana plantations

[1] We are grateful to all our partners from the various public agencies, private entities and societal organizations for their confidence and collaboration. We especially thank the members of the team that figures prominently in this contribution.

M. Groenleer (✉)
Tilburg Institute of Governance, Tilburg Center for Regional Law and Governance, Tilburg University, Tilburg, The Netherlands
e-mail: m.l.p.groenleer@uvt.nl

S. Cels
Harvard Kennedy School's Carr Center for Human Rights, Cambridge, MA, USA
e-mail: Sanderijn_cels@hks.harvard.edu

J. de Jong
Harvard Kennedy School, Cambridge, MA, USA
e-mail: Jorrit_dejong@hks.harvard.edu

ever more lucrative. Increasingly, citizens grow marijuana in their homes, for instance in attics. Many such growers are in desperate financial straits and thus easy targets for criminals who do not shy away from intimidation and violence. Marijuana plantations in homes are difficult for police to detect, and even when detected, the criminal masterminds behind them often elude apprehension. Moreover, because electricity is often illegally tapped to power marijuana plantations, home growing operations can pose major fire hazards, especially in residential areas.

This contribution investigates a partnership that emerged between the public prosecutor's office, the police, the tax office, local government and the public utility company to fight this form of organized crime and its subversive effects on local neighborhoods and beyond in the Netherlands. We ask what obstacles these parties ran into as a team, and how they together overcame the hurdles to cooperation, particularly in relation to the diagnosis and definition of the problem, the formulation of goals, and the development and implementation of an innovative approach. We also seek to find out, in this specific case, how public professionals engaged with a private company and how together they sought to enlist the support and capacity of not only their own organizations, but also law-abiding local residents. Our focus is thus on a partnership that was mostly informal in nature, and that over time came to include public organizations, private parties and civil society actors (for a typology see Fig. 1.1, Chap. 1).

To describe and explain the process of building the partnership, we draw on the literature on both collaborative governance and multidisciplinary teaming. This is a relatively novel combination. In taking this approach, we aim to advance the theory of partnerships, particularly regarding collaborative governance, using the case as an illustration. After a short description of the background to the process of building the partnership, we present a number of common challenges hampering collaboration across organizational boundaries and put forward a set of more general elements for effective teaming. We subsequently apply these challenges and elements to our case of partnership building. The empirical data are drawn from a field lab experiment that we conducted in 2015 and 2016, as well as additional research over 2017–2018. In the conclusions, we discuss the challenges identified in the case and propose that the literature on multidisciplinary teaming could be helpful in future research on collaborative challenges that manifest at the level of teams.

11.2 THE 'SICILY OF THE NORTH'

11.2.1 Organized Crime in the Southern Netherlands

In the summer of 2014, local and regional authorities, the police and the public prosecutor's office in the southern Netherlands sounded the alarm. Organized crime was expanding outwards from the country's central conurbation to the peripheral regions of Zeeland, Noord-Brabant and Limburg. In these provinces, the largest marijuana farms in the country could be found, and most synthetic drugs were produced here as well. For example, in the city of Tilburg alone, almost €1 billion worth of illegal weed was grown annually. Outlaw motorcycle gangs, such as Satudarah and No Surrender, and mobile home parks played a central role not only in local and regional criminal networks, but also in those operating nationally and internationally. Organized crime in the south could spiral out of control, was the message.

The subversive effects of increased organized crime was a particular cause of concern, and not just in the south of the country. Criminals were said to have gained a place in society and the economy. In fact, the business model of many criminal organizations seemed to be highly dependent on conscious or unconscious facilitation by legal organizations, both private and public. In addition, mayors and other authorities that acted against criminal organizations found themselves threatened and intimidated. Organized crime was thus feared to undercut the integrity of the state and weaken trust in the rule of law. In the media, a chief prosecutor with a sense of drama warned of an 'Italian state of affairs'.

11.2.2 Innovations in Collaboration to Fight Organized Crime

In the fight against organized crime in the southern provinces of the Netherlands, there has been intensive cooperation between municipalities, the public prosecutor's office, the national police, the tax authorities and the Royal Netherlands Marechaussee. Collaboration was initially mainly in the preparatory phase, but has increasingly expanded to include implementation of new approaches. The specially established Task Force Brabant-Zeeland, in which the various parties are represented, has played an important role in coordinating this cooperation. The idea is that the government parties should work together to make it as difficult as possible for criminal organizations to operate in the south. To this end, most joint action has focused on criminal leaders and their assets.

After crisis consultations between the public prosecutor's office and the police, a decision was made in 2014 to allocate more capacity to intensify investigations and prosecutions. This was accomplished within the existing legal frameworks and following the appropriate administrative procedures. At the same time, more and more attention was being paid to parties that facilitate crime. The question was asked of how these parties could be encouraged to play a preventive role. In addition to using legal coercion and administrative measures, experiments were conducted with new forms of cooperation and collaboration, such as with housing corporations and public utility companies to tackle illegal marijuana production in neighborhoods. The southern Netherlands therefore became not only a hotspot of organized crime, but also a living lab for innovation in the fight against such crime.

11.3   Cross-Boundary Collaboration and Effective Multidisciplinary Teaming

11.3.1   Challenges to Cross-Boundary Collaboration

It has become almost a platitude to state that complex societal problems, such as organized crime, can no longer be solved by a single government agency. They require the collective efforts of multiple organizations, both public and private, at various levels of governance, from the local to the global (e.g., Weber and Khademian 2008; Head and Alford 2015). To attain societal goals or create public value (Moore 1995, 2013), government agencies need to cooperate as part of multi-agency collaborations. Within these efforts they, while still autonomous, are dependent on other organizations, each with its own interests and ideas. An extensive literature has by now developed on the various forms in which such collective efforts can be shaped, such as collaborative governance (Ansell and Gash 2008; Emerson et al. 2012), interactive governance (Torfing et al. 2012), network governance (Klijn and Koppenjan 2009; Provan and Kenis 2008), co-production (Bovaird 2007) and public-private partnerships (Hodge and Greve 2005, 2007). Much has also been written on the advantages that cross-boundary cooperation can bring, including innovation

(Huxham and Vangen 2005; Sørensen and Torfing 2011; Crosby et al. 2017).

In reality, the advantages are often not realized as working in partnership produces novel governance challenges (e.g., Klijn and Koppenjan 2000; Bryson et al. 2006, 2015; Jacobs 2010; O'Leary and Vij 2012; Getha-Taylor and Morse 2013; Emerson and Nabatchi 2015; Page et al. 2015; Vangen 2017). In previous work (Waardenburg et al. 2019b), we have identified three main categories of collaborative governance challenges that arise from the public management and governance literature: substantive problem-solving challenges, collaborative process challenges, and multi-relational accountability challenges. The first category of challenges comprises 'the technically and politically difficult work of defining the problem a collaboration should work on, developing a collaborative response, and designing measures of success' (see also Waardenburg et al. 2018). The second category pertains to 'reconciling different perspectives and interests and building trust'. The final category of challenges consists of 'tensions between new channels of accountability, including to other organizations and society at large, and old channels of accountability'.

There is limited research, empirical or otherwise, regarding how these collaborative governance challenges manifest in practice at the level of multidisciplinary teams. For example, how do team members navigate the tensions associated with participating in a multi-agency collaboration, while representing the interests and perspective of their 'own' agency, and still with one foot in the known bureaucratic way of working? How do they handle apparently contradictory commitments, and develop effective practices that can overcome collaborative paralysis, to improve networked governance?

11.3.2   Elements of Effective Multidisciplinary Teaming

The collaborations we studied in previous work (Waardenburg et al. 2019b) varied in their responses to the collaborative governance challenges outlined above. But a clear pattern did emerge: those that were able to adopt a 'both/and' (rather than an 'either/or') mindset were able to make more consistent progress. They did not get stuck in analysis, but instead picked a point of entry to the problem and forged ahead. It is not fully clear why some of the collaborations were able to change their mindsets while others remained stuck, but this willingness to dive into the deep seemed to be facilitated by certain elements in the process of collaboration. There was something inherently different in how some of the collaborations managed their team process.

In the business management literature, a distinction is made between 'teams' and 'teaming' (Edmondson 2012a, b). The former refers to structures, boundaries and routines that hold certain people together and are most suitable for long policy lifecycles, and a lot of routine and well-understood work. They are usually carefully designed and last some time before they disband. The latter concerns collaborating 'on the fly', through more fluid, flexible configurations, in line with today's complex societal problems (Emerson and Nabatchi 2015). Organizations that do teaming well gain a collaborative advantage; they effectively harness the problem-solving abilities of their members to develop, design and test innovative solutions. Doing teaming well is not easy, however; it requires learning a new set of skills. Indeed, a new mindset is required to be able to flexibly respond to shifting circumstances.

More specifically, the process of teaming is said to include two elements (Edmondson 2012a, b): the hardware and the software. The hardware of teaming encompasses scoping out a challenge (a learning, not an execution challenge), sorting tasks based on interdependence, and lightly structuring temporary boundaries. The software of teaming involves articulating what is at stake for the team (a compelling purpose), building psychological safety (e.g., to speak up), and adopting a mindset of problem-solving, experimentation and trial-and-error. Teaming thus entails basic team skills, such as establishing trust, asking frequent questions and careful listening, and resolving conflicts early on. Often, there is not enough time, though, to get to know each other and to practice working together. A key teaming skill is thus the ability to get up to speed quickly on each other's perspectives and ideas, in order to act, reflect, analyze, learn to learn, and collaborate effectively.

11.4   A Combination of Action Research and Quasi-Experimental Design[2]

To investigate the collaborative governance challenges and, particularly, how teams dealt with them in practice, we drew on empirical data from a field lab experiment that we conducted in 2015 and 2016. As part of the field lab, we studied partnerships around the particularly wicked problem

[2] This section is based on Waardenburg et al. (2019a).

of organized crime with subversive effects on society, the economy and even the state itself. The partnerships we studied were formed within the framework of the Task Force Brabant-Zeeland, and included representatives of the police, the public prosecutor's office, the tax authorities, and local government.

Our involvement began with the formation of the partnerships in March 2015 and ended, after an 18-month period of facilitating and following their functioning, in August 2016. During this period, we trained and coached the partnerships on how to diagnose and define the problem, formulate goals, and develop and implement an innovative approach. Beyond training and coaching, our involvement enabled us to investigate the challenges that collaborative governance efforts face and study responses to these challenges up close.

To generate data on the case presented in this contribution, that of a partnership to fight illegal marijuana plantations in residential areas, we observed the partnership's decisions and actions in real time, and on various occasions interviewed and surveyed those involved in the partnership building process. Moreover, throughout the 18 months, we gathered documents that the partnership produced as a part of a training program. This served not only to monitor their progress in tackling the substantive problem, but also to enrich our own understanding of their working process. Supplementing this data, we conducted a round of interviews with the individual members of the partnership in 2017–2018, after the field lab experiment had officially ended.

11.5   How a Multidisciplinary Team Took on Illegal Marijuana Production in Residential Areas[3]

11.5.1   *Setting the Scene*

One afternoon in June 2015, five men from different professions met in a room on the campus of Tilburg University in the southern Netherlands (Box 11.1). Along with 35 other professionals and city officials, they listened to an urgent message from leaders of the national police and public prosecutor's office: organized crime was penetrating deeper into Dutch

---

[3] This section is based on Cels et al. (2019).

Box 11.1 Team Members, Their Organizations, Perspectives and Interests

John, a police officer from the city of Breda in the region of Brabant, was used to lead large police operations targeting criminal gangs. Having the capacity, he was eager to crack down on the grow houses through conventional raids.

Richard worked at the national tax office, an organization that did not necessarily feel it had a role in chasing people who rented out their attics and spare rooms to drug criminals in order to supplement their income. His superiors were more interested in the ringleaders who lived in villas in the countryside, and whose tax evasion and financial crimes were worth pursuing.

Peter, from the public utility company Enexis, was chiefly worried about customer safety. Pot growers regularly tampered with the electrical supply, which could cause huge blazes. As far as he was concerned, confronting criminals was a matter for law enforcement.

Joop, director of public safety and security for the city of Breda, had a particular goal in mind. He had seen the limited effect of the city's current approach to tackling grow houses—simply delivering a blow and hoping it would go away. He wanted to come up with a more thorough, systematic approach.

David, a public prosecutor, knew that drugs criminals put enormous pressure on poor and vulnerable people to allow them to set up grow houses in their homes. He was concerned about the impact on the social fabric of neighborhoods if residential grow houses continued to exist with impunity. In the province of Limburg, where he was based, he had been devising plans with Peter, the only member of the team he already knew. But he knew nothing about Breda, located in the province of Noord-Brabant, which was out of his jurisdiction.

society, especially in the south, where the meeting participants were from. 'Time is running out', said Herman Bolhaar, Chief Prosecutor of the Netherlands. 'It's up to you to put a stop to this!'

Everyone in the room had been selected to take part in an 'innovation program' for tackling complex issues that made headlines but were exceedingly difficult to unravel, such as chemical dumping by synthetic drug labs, trafficking in human beings and money laundering. All these organized crime problems had one thing in common: no single organization could confront them alone. In Tilburg, representatives of different organizations were assembled in groups and charged to develop a novel, collaborative approach within nine months and then return to the campus and report on their 'innovations'.

The group of five men, most of whom had not met before, was designated to tackle marijuana 'grow houses'. Evidence suggested that drug gangs were increasingly using the spare rooms and attics of regular home-owners and renters, often in working-class neighborhoods, for illegal marijuana production. The challenge put to the group was both loosely defined and daunting: 'structurally disrupting the criminal homegrown marijuana industry'. They were now supposed to be an 'integrated multi-disciplinary team'. But the individuals at the table certainly did not look like one. They each had their own perspective, their own interests and their own distinct organizations to report to.

11.5.2   Reframing the Problem

The group was instructed to start by considering 'the societal problem' they sought to remedy. For John, the police officer, there was no debate. This was clearly a drugs crime problem, which to him meant simply that the perpetrators had to be found and arrested. What more was there to talk about? John's perspective made the others uneasy. Richard, the tax official, for instance, brought up the plight of low-income residents, for whom this was probably just a way to get a bit of extra cash into their pockets, not a serious offense. To him, the issue was that allowing criminals to grow pot in an attic was somehow accepted as normal. All of the team members struggled with rethinking the problem; the meeting became mostly a lot of talking and not much listening. Each tended to frame the problem, and the solution, from the perspective of his own organization or professional background. When one person proposed something, another would exclaim, 'Well, that has got nothing to do with us!' It went on like this until someone pointed to the clock and said they had better come up with something, soon.

Richard brought up a news report he had recently seen. A father in one of the working-class neighborhoods where pot was grown illegally said that the house next to him had burned down while his daughter was sleeping upstairs. We can do something with this, Richard told the group, 'That man's emotion, the fire risk faced by innocent people.' He went on to say that while the police were adamant about apprehending and arresting criminals, they lacked the capacity to do it everywhere it was needed. He told John, 'You have framed the problem so that only you are responsible for handling the situation, but there are 30,000 grow houses in this country, and the police will never have sufficient resources to take them all on.' Richard felt that by emphasizing the grave fire hazard to homes they were more likely to enlist neighborhood residents to help authorities confront the problem. The others did not immediately have a better plan, so this became the group's entry point. While mitigating fire risk was no one's primary area of expertise, everyone could see a link to the problem as they perceived it.

11.5.3   Developing an Innovative Approach

The next day, the team met again. They had a 'problem definition' that everybody could get behind, more or less. Now they needed to think about tackling it. What could they do? They were only five men. Who were they to come up with an entirely new approach? How far outside of the box were they allowed to go, exactly? Who would provide the support and resources? There were many questions and significant uncertainty. Yet, here they were and because things started to click between them, they simply began mapping the work.

Their point of departure was to see the problem through the residents' eyes. 'We need to consider their interests, and the challenges they face', Richard said, 'otherwise they will never be motivated to help us'. Their goals were now (1) to stop 'pot-fires' caused by illegal growing, (2) to drive out organized crime and (3) to protect vulnerable residents. While Richard had been the catalyst in the group, the 'problem exploration' was drifting away from the core business and mission of the tax office, but that did not bother him much: 'I was hooked and I decided to stay on the team as an individual.'

The approach they developed would involve advanced data analysis to locate at-risk buildings, alongside community engagement focused on awareness and prevention measures and targeted police action. Rather than engaging in a game of 'whack-a-mole', they focused on investing in broad community support to detect and deter grow houses, as these represented a significant fire risk. They came up with a plan: Enexis, the public utility company, would measure power consumption, identifying housing blocks where power was being sucked up in unusual amounts at unlikely times.[4] A team consisting of Enexis, the police, city officials and fire department employees would knock on doors and ask to look inside all of the housing units on these blocks. An official from the prosecutor's office would supervise from nearby. Before any activity, however, the neighborhood council would be informed. Residents would be educated about the fire hazards associated with marijuana cultivation in homes. During and after the door-to-door canvassing, team members would talk to residents and collect feedback. The idea was to combine targeted enforcement of criminal activity with building broad community support for improved fire safety.

At the end of the workshop at the Tilburg University campus, the team left in high spirits. Collaboration had not always been easy, and a certain amount of friction had occurred. At times, they had felt incredibly unproductive, as if they were just going around in circles. They had, however, surprised themselves: none of the men had expected to emerge with this particular problem definition, and a new approach. But now, they had to go back to their own organizations where no one knew what they were working on.

11.5.4   Engaging Stakeholders Back Home

At Enexis, Peter, the company's fraud manager, found that his colleagues were really not that interested in marijuana. Sure, they understood that crime caused misery and that grow houses stole electricity. But illegally tapping power to grow pot in an attic did not affect the company's bottom line. It just meant each customer paid a few more euros each year. Fire safety, however, was a big deal. 'When the growers start tinkering with the heat lamps, the place literally starts to cook. We do need to protect our customers', Peter said. This argument worked: he was given permission to carry out a fire-safety experiment—nothing to do with crime control—in a designated neighborhood. Soon after, Enexis ran a power test on an apartment building. It was a success, but as yet was just one building. 'It was risky', he recalled, 'because we did not know if and how this would work on a larger scale', like a whole neighborhood. But the successful experiment inspired confidence within his organization.

---

[4] Power utilities could measure power usage per housing block, not per individual unit.

Upon his return to Breda, Joop, the city official, discussed the plan with his colleagues to decide on an area or neighborhood where the team could try out the approach. Bringing the fire department into the conversation, he listened as a fire department employee expressed reservations: 'We need to get along with the residents to do our job. Sure, we do prevention, and in fact increasingly so, but we cannot be seen to be doing police work.' After several meetings, they finally agreed that when it came to ringing doorbells, firefighters would not be on the doorstep with the other agencies, but would watch from a distance.

Joop also had to convince his boss, Mayor Paul Depla of Breda. With some 180,000 inhabitants, Breda was the ninth largest city in the Netherlands. Mayor Depla had many questions about social and political risks. He wondered if it would be possible to try the approach in different areas of the city, some suspected of pot-growing and others not. This way, he reasoned, there would be a control group of sorts, and the possibility of stigmatizing neighborhoods and harassing people could be avoided. After all, what if the team burst in on a single mother on welfare who had a few plants in her attic? He did not want it to appear as if the might of the state was being used to target vulnerable citizens.

Joop promised to fine-tune the plan where possible, including picking a neighborhood that would not raise allegations of stigmatization. One would be chosen that was not the likeliest place for grow houses, but where they probably were not entirely absent either. At the same time, he told the mayor that inevitably there would be risk involved, including the possibility that none of the work would make a difference. 'It was an experiment', Joop said, so there will always be uncertainty. The mayor had to accept this. 'We honestly did not know what to expect, if residents would even let us in when we rang the bell. But it sure was exciting', Joop said, as the designated weekend approached.

11.5.5   Testing the New Approach

Mayor Depla gave permission to test the new approach and by the last week of October 2015, everything was ready for the two-day experiment. John, from the Breda police, had his list of apartment blocks from Enexis. They would start in the area known as Muizenberg, with three-story flats. Then, on the second day, they would move to a mobile home park called Kesteren, so it would not appear that any one place had been singled out. The team brought flyers to distribute to residents. The fire department would park one of its vehicles on the street with an officer to explain what was going on.

Over the two days of the operation, no major complications arose. They requested entrance to 400 homes, and were allowed in to all. 'Some even asked us to come have a look right now, as they had to go shopping soon.' Two grow houses were found, including one where they had to climb in through a window and transformers for grow lights were baking at 97 degrees Celsius. John's police colleagues were disappointed however. They were used to a bigger catch with such a sweep. Overall, the reaction in the city was tepid. Mayor Depla told local media that a 'new approach' was being piloted and that he was basically satisfied.

11.5.6   Drawing Lessons

The team of five that had kicked off the pilot felt they had achieved their goal and the approach was shown to have worked. Lessons were also learned, both practical and strategic. For instance, next time the search area should be smaller. 'Twelve-hundred residences is just too much', John said. Enexis concluded that it could repeat the operation once but after that, someone else was going to have to fund the equipment costs.

A key lesson concerned the project's frame or messaging, which proved hardest to control. The media quickly made it about criminality and crooks, not the fire hazard in the neighborhood. 'Residents will say you are re just after bad guys; leave me out of it', John said. But he had to admit, all the organizations had worked well together and stayed firmly on-message: the action was about keeping citizens safe from the fires caused by illegal grow houses. 'We projected a strong and unified image, a common purpose', he said, 'despite our different objectives'. This, it turned out during an evaluation meeting, had also been noticed and appreciated by the city's residents.

11.5.7   Making the Innovation Scalable and Sustainable

In the year that followed, the team launched new operations in other cities, including Tilburg, where the men had originally met. Keeping in mind what his boss, the chief prosecutor, had said at the beginning of the field lab, David, the public prosecutor on the team, thought about what it would take to implement the approach in other regions, and possibly to scale it up nationwide. 'We needed courage, support and commitment from our top managers', he said. 'Enough resources, enough people, from the police, from my office and the cities, to create a structural solution across the country.' The team indicated to their immediate superiors that they wanted to keep working together and make that happen, even if it meant working outside their own region. They asked for permission and time to keep the project active and take it on the road. 'This was a big deal, but top management seemed to agree on it', David recalled, 'which was encouraging'.

Reality turned out to be more complicated. 'The farther we got from our turf', he said, 'the thornier it was'. For example, David and Peter gave presentations in the province of Limburg, where a number of mayors and police chiefs peppered them with questions about operational and financial aspects. The questions were hard to answer, and David realized that the team would not be able to supply all the right information. Their superiors had given them some time and resources, but not enough to make a solid business plan and scaling strategy. Over the course of 2017, having carried out operations for another year, the team began to break up.

11.6   Discussion and Conclusions

In this contribution, we were interested in the obstacles partnerships run into and how they overcome hurdles for cooperation, particularly related to the diagnosis and definition of a problem, the formulation of goals, and the development and implementation of an innovative approach. We also wanted to find out how public professionals engage with private parties and enlist the support and capacity of not only their own organization, but also local citizens. To answer these questions, we presented a number of common challenges that hamper collaboration across organizational boundaries, and put forward a set of more general elements of effective multidisciplinary teaming.

To illustrate how these elements can help deal with collaborative challenges in practice at the level of a team of professionals, we zoomed in on the case of a multidisciplinary team taking on illegal marijuana production in residential areas in the Netherlands. We described the team's process of problem diagnosis and definition, goal setting, and strategy formulation and how it tested and tried its plans. The team partly succeeded and partly failed, but drew lessons and tried again in an attempt to make the innovative approach it developed scalable and sustainable. We found that the team process was far from linear and complete; indeed, it was characterized by an iterative and tentative nature.

At first, the team struggled to define an adequate theory of change to intervene on the broad societal issue of illegal marijuana production in residential areas. With thousands of such marijuana plantations spread across the country, they wondered how such a small group of individuals could make a dent in the problem. Particularly, they wondered how their intervention in one or a limited set of cases could lead to any significant, broader result. To move ahead, they took a leap of faith and narrowed their problem definition to domestic marijuana plantations and related safety and security hazards.[5]

Use of electricity network data enabled the team to hone in on locations where marijuana plantations were possibly illegally tapping electricity. Representatives of several public agencies as well as the public utility company then went door-to-door, raising awareness among residents of the dangers of marijuana production at home, including fire hazards and extortion by criminal networks. This strategy provided an entry point to disrupt criminal networks' opportunity structure. The door-to-door visits and the visible action as collaborative partners also generated support from citizens for the approach and, indeed, created informal enforcement capacity.

We found that the team adopted a 'both/and' way of working rather than an 'either/or' approach (see also Waardenburg et al. 2019b). For instance, it focused on a concrete instance (delineated in time and place), but it did not lose sight of the broader (societal) problem. It framed the problem such that it was both meaningful for society and actionable for the various individual organizations involved. And it made use of both repressive and preventive interventions, engaging professional crime fighting organizations as well as private parties and citizens. We suggest that the team's ability and willingness to adopt such a both/and approach was facilitated by how the team managed its collaborative process.

Looking through the lens of multidisciplinary teaming theory (Edmondson 2012a, b), we conclude that the team was result-oriented, in that individual team members were committed to the joint goals, and they felt responsible for realizing these goals, even if the goals were not entirely in line with their own organization's interests, as was the case with the tax

---

[5] This and the following paragraph are based on the case description in Waardenburg et al. (2019b).

office. Moreover, the team was willing to experiment and learn in order to innovate, and to go beyond taken-for-granted approaches. It was not afraid to take some risks along the way—personal, organizational and political ones—and to have tough conversations within the team and with stakeholders, such as with the fire department and the mayor of Breda.

We thus propose that the literature on teaming can help us analyze how collaborative challenges manifest at the level of teams, and better understand how teams can overcome these challenges. While originating in business management, the elements of effective multidisciplinary teaming (Edmondson 2012a, b) may also be applicable in governance settings. More (empirical) research is necessary, however, into the conditions for effective public sector teaming. Such research would have to include the field lab as both a research method and governance practice, and the extent to which interventions as part of a field lab help teams move away from either/or thinking and unidimensional solutions, and work towards realizing public value.

References

Ansell, C., & Gash, A. (2008). Collaborative governance in theory and practice. *Journal of Public Administration Research and Theory, 18*(4), 543–571. https://doi.org/10.1093/jopart/mum032.

Bovaird, T. (2007). Beyond engagement and participation: User and community coproduction of public services. *Public Administration Review, 67*(5), 846–860. https://doi.org/10.1111/j.1540-6210.2007.00773.x.

Bryson, J. M., Crosby, B. C., & Stone, M. M. (2006). The design and implementation of cross-sector collaborations: Propositions from the literature. *Public Administration Review, 66*(s1), 44–55. https://doi.org/10.1111/j.1540-6210.2006.00665.x.

Bryson, J. M., Crosby, B. C., & Stone, M. M. (2015). Designing and implementing cross-sector collaborations: Needed and challenging. *Public Administration Review, 75*(5), 647–663. https://doi.org/10.1111/puar.12432.

Cels, S., De Jong, J., & Groenleer, M. (2019). *Growing pains: How a Dutch cross-agency team took on illegal marijuana production in residential areas.* Cambridge, MA: Bloomberg-Harvard City Leadership Initiative.

Crosby, B. C., 't Hart, P., & Torfing, J. (2017). Public value creation through collaborative innovation. *Public Management Review, 19*(5), 655–669. https://doi.org/10.1080/14719037.2016.1192165.

Edmondson, A. C. (2012a). *Teaming: How organizations learn, innovate, and compete in the knowledge economy.* San Francisco: Jossey-Bass.

Edmondson, A. C. (2012b). Teamwork on the Fly. *Harvard Business Review*, *90*(4), 72–80.

Emerson, K., & Nabatchi, T. (2015). *Collaborative governance regimes*. Washington, DC: Georgetown University Press.

Emerson, K., Nabatchi, T., & Balogh, S. (2012). An integrative framework for collaborative governance. *Journal of Public Administration Research and Theory*, *22*(1), 1–29. https://doi.org/10.1093/jopart/mur011.

Getha-Taylor, H., & Morse, R. S. (2013). Collaborative leadership development for local government officials: Exploring competencies and program impact. *Public Administration Quarterly*, *37*(1), 71–102.

Head, B. W., & Alford, J. (2015). Wicked problems: Implications for public policy and management. *Administration & Society*, *47*(6), 711–739. https://doi.org/10.1177/0095399713481601.

Hodge, G., & Greve, C. (2005). *The challenge of public-private partnerships*. Cheltenham: Edward Elgar.

Hodge, G. A., & Greve, C. (2007). Public-private partnerships: An international performance review. *Public Administration Review*, *67*(3), 545–558. https://doi.org/10.1111/j.1540-6210.2007.00736.x.

Huxham, C., & Vangen, S. (2005). *Managing to collaborate: The theory and practice of collaborative advantage*. London: Routledge.

Jacobs, K. (2010). The politics of partnerships: A study of police and housing collaboration to tackle anti-social behavior on Australian public housing estates. *Public Administration*, *88*(4), 928–942. https://doi.org/10.1111/j.1467-9299.2010.01851.x.

Klijn, E. H., & Koppenjan, J. F. M. (2000). Public management and policy networks. *Public Management: An International Journal of Research and Theory*, *2*(2), 135–158. https://doi.org/10.1080/14719030000000007.

Klijn, E.-H., & Koppenjan, J. F. M. (2009). *Managing uncertainties in networks: A network approach to problem solving and decision making*. London: Routledge.

Moore, M. H. (1995). *Creating public value: Strategic management in government*. Cambridge, MA: Harvard University Press.

Moore, M. H. (2013). *Recognizing public value*. Cambridge: Harvard University Press.

O'Leary, R., & Vij, N. (2012). Collaborative public management: Where have we been and where are we going? *The American Review of Public Administration*, *42*(5), 507–522. https://doi.org/10.1177/0275074012445780.

Page, S. B., Stone, M. M., Bryson, J. M., & Crosby, B. C. (2015). Public value creation by cross-sector collaborations: A framework and challenges of assessment. *Public Administration*, *93*(3), 715–732. https://doi.org/10.1111/padm.12161.

Provan, K. G., & Kenis, P. (2008). Modes of network governance: Structure, management, and effectiveness. *Journal of Public Administration Research and Theory, 18*(2), 229–252. https://doi.org/10.1093/jopart/mum015.

Sørensen, E., & Torfing, J. (2011). Enhancing collaborative innovation in the public sector. *Administration & Society, 43*(8), 842–868. https://doi.org/10.1177/0095399711418768.

Torfing, J., Peters, B. G., Sørensen, E., & Pierre, J. (2012). *Interactive governance: Advancing the paradigm.* Oxford: Oxford University Press.

Vangen, S. (2017). Developing practice-oriented theory on collaboration: A paradox Lens. *Public Administration Review, 77*(2), 263–272. https://doi.org/10.1111/puar.12683.

Waardenburg, M., Groenleer, M., de Jong, J., & Bolhaar, H. (2018). Evidence-based prevention of organized crime: Assessing a new collaborative approach. *Public Administration Review, 78*(2), 315–317. https://doi.org/10.1111/puar.12889.

Waardenburg, M., Groenleer, M., & De Jong, J. (2019a). Designing environments for experimentation, learning and innovation in public policy and governance. *Policy & Politics, 48*, 67. https://doi.org/10.1332/030557319X15586040837640.

Waardenburg, M., Groenleer, M., de Jong, J., & Keijser, B. (2019b). Paradoxes of collaborative governance: Investigating the real-life dynamics of multi-agency collaborations using a quasi-experimental action-research approach. *Public Management Review, 22*, 1–22. https://doi.org/10.1080/1471903 7.2019.1599056.

Weber, E. P., & Khademian, A. M. (2008). Wicked problems, knowledge challenges, and collaborative capacity builders in network settings. *Public Administration Review, 68*(2), 334–349. https://doi.org/10.1111/j.1540-6210.2007.00866.x.

PART IV

Partnerships and Neighborhood Revitalization

CHAPTER 12

Partnerships in Shrinking Cities: Making Baltimore 'Liveable'?

Madeleine Pill

12.1 Introduction

City governance is undertaken by the local state (city government and its agencies) engaging in a variety of forms of *partnership* with a range of non-state actors to decide and enact policy priorities. Whether these partnerships are perceived as collaborative, co-optative, coercive or contested reflects different normative and ideological perspectives on the extent to which the priorities of those with most power do, and should, predominate. But in practice there is broad agreement that there has been a long-standing shift towards prioritising economic growth over equity, related to wider debates about the extent of city-level policy choice given broader political-economic constraints.

Increased competition between cities for investment has led to an emphasis on making cities more attractive to footloose capital and 'creative' workers who, it is claimed, are increasingly sensitive to the quality-of-life package offered by different cities (Florida 2005). Dominant policy

M. Pill (✉)
Department of Government and International Relations, University of Sydney, Sydney, NSW, Australia
e-mail: madeleine.pill@sydney.edu.au

© The Author(s) 2020
C. van Montfort, A. Michels (eds.), *Partnerships for Livable Cities*,
https://doi.org/10.1007/978-3-030-40060-6_12

231

prescriptions align with the conception of the entrepreneurial, competitive and creative city, interpreted by critical scholars as the neoliberalisation of the state's role to align with and seek to facilitate the priorities of the market and private interests rather than meet the social welfare needs of existing residents. Florida's (2005) creative class thesis, which has had significant policy influence, has been subject to critique as 'cappuccino urban politics' (Peck 2005) given the distributional impacts on other city residents (McCann 2007). But contestation of these governance priorities is nullified through deployment of 'common sense' arguments that the needs of the poor and less powerful will be met once economic growth occurs, despite increasing inequality leading to characterisations of the 'dual city' (Castells 1989).

Debates about the notion of liveability have played out within these broader analyses of city governance and governance priorities. Recent scholarship emphasises the discursive power of this now ubiquitous term within urban strategies and policy documents (Clarke and Cheshire 2018). Liveability is especially useful as it can be imbued with many meanings by different actors and groups, smoothing over conflicts and generating consensus. Who can reject the appeal of making a city more liveable? But the way the notion is deployed reinforces the power differentials of urban governance and the stark socio-spatial inequalities which result, rather than encouraging efforts to improve the lived experience of the majority of residents. What would actually improve quality of life would be to meet the diverse needs of a city's population in its entirety by confronting inequality. Unequal power relations are inherent in which actors get to frame (understand, define, categorise and measure) a policy problem. Such 'power dynamics of knowledge production' underpin how liveability is deployed to frame urban problems in such a way that it bolsters policies that favour the needs of the market over the needs of residents (McArthur and Robin 2019: 1716). Thus liveability as a concept does not confront the conflicts and trade-offs inherent in urban politics and policy making, described by Lasswell (1936) as 'who gets what, when, and how'.

12.2   THE CASE OF BALTIMORE

Baltimore City in the State of Maryland provides a rich location in which to explore the partnerships and power relations of who gets what, along with the vital question of where, in order to interrogate how liveability and its corollaries are deployed amidst the policies being pursued in the city. It reveals that the policies which liveability discourse assists in justifying privilege some and further contain other populations, whilst also precluding debate and contestation about more equitable alternatives.

The analysis is informed by documentary review of City and State government and agency policies, research reports and evaluations, along with those of other key city institutions, plus local media reports. The review combines with primary data gathered via semi-structured interviews conducted with salient actors in the governance of the city, including: political leaders; public officials; philanthropic foundation staff; staff of 'ed and med' (education and medical, or university and hospital) 'anchor' institutions (so-called due to their inability to move and resultant vested interests); non-profit organisations (some neighbourhood-based); community groups and citizen activists. In total, 39 respondent interviews, 5 non-participatory observations, 3 group interviews and a stakeholder workshop were conducted between 2015 and 2017.

Prior to examining current partnerships and policies, further context helps establish the path dependencies of Baltimore's contemporary governance: how it has become a shrinking, segregated city with severe socio-spatial inequality; and how partnerships between key state and non-state actors that formulate policies have changed over time.

The city's current population of 612,000 is over a third smaller than its 1950 peak of 950,000 and nearly a quarter of its residents fall below the federal poverty level (US Census 2017). Its 'population loss, economic downturn, employment decline and social problems' (Martinez-Fernandez et al. 2012: 214) stem not only from deindustrialisation but from a much longer history in which local and federal policies have concentrated and segregated its African American population. Federally-supported suburbanisation in the post-war period exacerbated the city's depopulation and its concentration of African American residents and of poverty. City neighbourhoods vacated by 'white flight' became renters' enclaves for African Americans, who had little choice but to rent substandard housing due to practices of 'financial apartheid' (Coates 2014). The displacement and disruption experienced by the city's communities were aggravated by urban renewal activities, aided by significant federal financial transfers for comprehensive redevelopment projects. As a state government official explained:

in the '60s and '70s what people call 'urban removal' as opposed to neighbourhood-based change making... projects really messed up a lot of neighbourhoods, African American neighbourhoods particularly.

An unsuccessful 1951 petition sought the withdrawal of federal urban renewal funds on the basis that redevelopments 'place[d] the full strength of the Federal government behind a policy of rigid residential segregation' (Williams 2005). It was not until 2005 that the federal Department of Housing and Urban Development (HUD) was found guilty of violating the Fair Housing Act (1968) by unfairly concentrating African American public housing residents in the city's most impoverished and segregated areas, the judge concluding that HUD had treated Baltimore 'an island reservation for use as a container for all of the poor' (Kline 2007). The city's continuing extreme spatial segregation is described as the 'black butterfly' of poor African American neighbourhoods west and east of the central spine of the city (Brown 2016). The city's population loss manifests in its built form, with more than 16,500 vacant residential properties (BNIA-JFI 2016). Unsurprisingly there is a very strong correlation between neighbourhoods with the highest densities of vacant properties and those in the 'black butterfly' which had been subject to 'redlining' (the highly racialised practice of refusing mortgage finance). As an anchor institution officer summarised:

We have a tremendous amount of racism institutionally in how we've been planned as a city, how our institutions function as a city, and the lack of resources and leadership to... address the 50 plus years of delayed investment in... neighbourhoods.

To contextualise Baltimore's contemporary governance it is also important to understand how the configurations of key state and non-state actors—and partnerships between these—have changed over time. These configurations play out in a context of decades of neoliberal urbanism, typified by the withdrawal of federal support for cities. All interviewed in present day Baltimore perceived 'fiscal squeeze' as an imperative for working in partnership. Fiscal squeeze refers to declining governmental revenues (whether derived from the local tax base or inter-governmental transfers) and increasing demands for public goods and welfare supports, as one interviewee explained, 'the needs are so great and the resources have dwindled... there's just not enough resources'. This imperative has long driven city government's efforts to partner with private actors. In terms of partnership types (see for a typology Fig. 1.1, Chap. 1), the principal form is a longstanding, informal (type C) public-private partnership, wherein the local state is the public element, and the private element combines private companies (particularly property developers) and, especially latterly, private organisations with 'non-profit' status. These major non-profits are locally-based philanthropic foundations, which undertake a variety of grant-giving activities, and 'ed and med' institutions with a vested interest in the proximate neighbourhoods in which they are 'anchored'. These partners have long set a broad policy agenda in terms of what types of investments and activities are prioritised where in the city. In undertaking the wide range of activities involved in implementing this agenda, different partners may also engage in other types of layered partnership, such as via grant-giving to smaller, neighbourhood-based non-profit organisations or perhaps grassroots civil society organisations (type F partnerships).

Reviewing the composition and changing agenda of this loosely organised type C public-private partnership over time highlights that its durability stems from its adaptability to changing circumstances. Its membership is determined by the power partners can wield in terms of the resources they have to determine and realise the agenda. Grassroots civil society organisations are excluded from these opaque agenda-setting arrangements, but are enrolled into implementation (via type F partnerships) when deemed necessary by powerful type C partners. Indeed, when discussing partnerships, elite actors did not tend to mention citizens and grassroots civil society organisations, interpreting partnership as being amongst themselves.

12.2.1 Partnering with Local, Private Non-state Actors

Federal withdrawal from cities in the 1980s led to the adoption of more localist practices combined with more privatist city governance (Barnekov et al. 1981) as city government increasingly needed to form alliances with private actors in order to gain 'power to' develop and implement policy agendas (Stone 1993). In Baltimore, the attention of type C elite partners remained focused on downtown and the waterfront, as favoured during the earlier period of federally-supported urban renewal. Other neighbourhoods did not gain elite attention and resource. Wealthier neighbourhoods which had the requisite voluntary capacity increasingly self-provided services. Funding mechanisms enabled by City and State government legislation such as Business Improvement and Community Benefit Districts generated additional funding streams for privatist forms of neighbourhood service provision. But there was also rising awareness of the spatial division between the favoured downtown and waterfront and the need to address the problems faced by the city's poorer, African American neighbourhoods. Calls for action came from BUILD, a community alliance rooted in the power base of the city's black churches. The city's rising philanthropic presence also asserted neighbourhood inattention, as manifested in the Goldseker Foundation's *Baltimore 2000* report (Szanton 1986). In 1987 Schmoke, the city's first African American mayor, was elected on a platform of addressing the long-neglected neighbourhoods.

Private actors such as the city's philanthropic foundations started to rise in importance in the type C public-private partnership given their 'power to' (amidst declining city corporate presence). Several foundations aligned with Schmoke's neighbourhood agenda. An example is the Enterprise Foundation, which partnered with city government and BUILD to sponsor a neighbourhood-targeted initiative (Pill 2018). However, an advocacy organisation officer commented that:

> *To really address the conditions in distressed neighbourhoods… requires something that only the federal government can do… We put 130, 140, 150, nobody really knows, million into Sandtown-Winchester in the '90s… but you can only do that once a decade at that level and it wasn't enough and it took money from all the other neighbourhoods.*

Thus the initiative became regarded as a lesson in the intractability of the city's neighbourhood problems. Schmoke and the philanthropic sector's neighbourhood emphasis did succeed in attracting some federal program funds, albeit subject to much greater (time-limited, market-leveraging) strictures compared to the large federal transfers of the urban renewal era. Under the Clinton administration, Baltimore gained a ten-year federal Empowerment Zone designation and a federal HOPE VI program for redevelopment of six public housing projects – though 'the goal of deconcentrating the poor came largely at the expense of the poorest of the poor' (Stoker et al. 2015: 57) who were displaced, affirming the lack of attention to those most lacking power.

12.2.2 Asset-Based Approach

The advent of Schmoke's successor, O'Malley (in office 1997–2007) represented a disjuncture with emphasis on deprived neighbourhoods. The pivotal moment was the adoption in 2000 of an 'asset-based' (rather than need-based) mode of resource allocation to boost the city's housing market (explained below). Continued reductions in federal aid combined with the city's shrinking tax base led to the justificatory narrative of the 'greater realism' of market-based approaches. The director of a neighbourhood-based non-profit explained:

> In the '90s, Clinton was elected… everybody said, "Oh finally. The federal government's going to help cities again," right? Clinton's like, "I'd love to help but we're broke, we don't have the money". And that's when people started thinking… we're never going to get all the money we used to get. We have to figure out a different approach. And that's where the asset-based approach came from. It was a culture of scarcity.

The approach was adopted by O'Malley and still remains the purported basis for city planning and resource allocation. It is manifested spatially via a typology of housing markets with different policy prescriptions and thus differential prioritisation of city elite resources—ranging from 'stressed' neighbourhoods (subject to demolition for site assembly, especially if aligning with the growth needs of anchor institutions); through 'the middle' (where interventions seek to 'help the market'); to 'regionally competitive' neighbourhoods (not requiring intervention). Crucially, city and foundation resource allocation maintains the asset-based rationale in what is prioritised for support via type F partnerships. The physical development activities of neighbourhood-based non-profits such as Community Development Corporations, and pro-market approaches of other non-profits (such as encouraging homeownership) in neighbourhoods 'in the middle' are favoured. For example, the non-profit organisation Healthy Neighborhoods undertakes neighbourhood marketing to prospective homebuyers, along with provision of some financial assistance and advice for housing purchase and rehab, in thirteen city neighbourhoods 'in the middle'. In emphasising that they 'work "in the middle"', neighbourhood-based non-profit officers affirmed their enrolment into the spatial priorities of their type C funders through layered type F partnerships.

12.3   'CHANGE TO GROW'

The previous review of elite actors (type C partners) who have determined the spatial priorities for investment and attention sets the scene for a critical examination of how liveability has been deployed (explicitly and implicitly) in the city's policies. Liveability as a term is not prominent in city discourse and is not deployed directly in plans and strategies, but it is clearly implied in the governance imperatives which predominate and the policies which have been developed and are pursued as a result. This is best encapsulated in 'Change to Grow' (City of Baltimore 2013), presented as helping to achieve then Mayor Rawlings-Blake's goal (in office 2010–16) to grow Baltimore by 10,000 families in ten years by:

> ... allowing new investments in neighbourhood infrastructure... providing a funding surge for the demolition of more than 4,000 vacant homes; all while reducing homeowner property taxes by more than 20%.

It is notable as a financial reform rather than spatial plan, highlighting the predominance of the strictures of 'fiscal squeeze' as a governance imperative. But beyond its deficit reduction emphasis the plan's policies align with and seek to reinforce the existing spatial policy prescriptions established in the housing typology. That the city's population shrinkage and hyper-concentration of the poor has resulted in a shrinking tax base and rising service needs is cited to reinforce a narrative of 'harsh realities' to frame policy pronouncements. The plan's first aim, to 'eliminate a nine-year $750 million structural budget deficit', is located as the basis to free up funds for realisation of its other aims. As clear in its title, the plan's explicit goal is to attract people to live in the city, thus reversing its decades of shrinkage and decline. It is therefore clearly predicated on a liveability discourse about making the city attractive to potential residents. But what was described by a city official as the 'meta-goal' is to deconcentrate poverty, explicitly sought through attracting new (wealthier) residents through a focus on (some) neighbourhoods and by reducing property taxes (the city has the highest in Maryland). Less emphasised is the poverty deconcentration which results from the displacement of the city's poor through relocation resulting from 'stressed' neighbourhood redevelopment, as well as via housing mobility strategies (explained below).

'Change to Grow' encapsulates the emphasis of Baltimore's type C elites on realising 'the great inversion', or gravitation of a younger, more affluent population to the city (Ehrenhalt 2013). The supposition is that millennials are attracted to urban life given their 'urban values' (Ross 2014). The activities supported in neighbourhoods 'in the middle', such as marketing and provision of financial incentives to homebuyers, are part and parcel of these efforts. The predication of city strategies on attracting and retaining such residents seeks to link the city with its wealthier surrounding region and beyond, with the city framed as providing a cheap housing option despite its relatively high property taxes. As the director of a Community Development Corporation explained:

> *Thirty years ago, Baltimore was in a bad position because it was a city in a small region when you compare it to New York or Boston or Philadelphia. It was squeezed between Washington and Philadelphia. But now that whole thing has merged together and now we're a low-cost alternative in a high-cost region. And that region goes, you know, from Washington to Boston.*

Type C partner emphasis on attracting a younger as well as more affluent population was reflected by interviewees mentioning 'millennials' as a prominent target group. In her 2015 State of the City speech, the Mayor trumpeted Baltimore as the 'fourth fastest growing city for that demographic', expanding on this theme in her 2016 speech:

> *Baltimore is getting national attention for how many millennials are moving here. There are a number of reasons – jobs, of course, being one. But the reason they will stay is because Baltimore is pretty awesome. From musicians to artists to foodies, we have made Baltimore a hip place to be. People want a real city, not a generic landscape. They want to be part of a sustainable city. A walkable city. A city that shaped our nation's history. A welcoming city. A vibrant city in which each neighbourhood has its own unique identity. A city of robust arts and culture.*

This rhetoric encapsulates how liveability discourse has combined with economic development and competitiveness in a way that is seemingly congruent with the creative class thesis (McCann 2007, 2013). In this combination, liveability is narrowly conceptualised as focusing on who the city's type C elites want to attract—a putative population of mobile millennials—rather than incorporating what is needed to improve the lived experience of poorer, predominantly African American existing residents who have been excluded from partnership governance arrangements. As an anchor institution official explained:

Our approach to current challenges has been... to bring more white people back into city, to highlight the good that is existing in a lot of our neighbourhoods... But there's a polarity that I don't think we own as a city, I don't think we own it as a country... we are not addressing the root causes of a lot of the issues of our city.

The narrowed liveability of 'Change to Grow' has implications for the existing poor communities which are contained spatially, socially and economically in the 'black butterfly' of this highly segregated city. It reinforces the housing typology's de facto policy prescription of abandonment for such 'stressed' neighbourhoods deemed unattractive to capital and new residents and thus lacking the asset-based rationale to benefit from what one non-profit official described as even 'basic services'. However, the 'stressed' neighbourhoods do form the focus for one policy which benefited from the 'funding surge' predicated on realisation of the 'Change to Grow' plan's deficit reduction measures. The Vacants to Value initiative, launched by the City of Baltimore in 2010, targets the city's vacant residential properties concentrated in its 'stressed' neighbourhoods. The initiative comprises a more focused type C public-private partnership through which the local state seeks to enrol the private sector in 'fighting blight' through provision of investment incentives, coupled with increased code enforcement and strategic demolition. The program also offers grants to assist buyers purchase formerly vacant, renovated houses (360 awarded as of 2015). A City-commissioned evaluation reported that 513 demolition permits has been issued during its first 5 years of operation. But the analysis concluded that the program could not reverse market trends in terms of reducing property vacancy (BNIA-JFI 2016). Another report sponsored by a city philanthropy (Jacobson 2015) concluded that the program had been successful in code enforcement in some stressed neighbourhoods. But it found that development of vacant properties had been highly uneven and the practice of selling city-owned houses to for-profit developers had not created or maintained affordable housing for current residents. As such, the program demonstrates that narrow framings of liveability such as those contained in 'Change to Grow' not only result in distributional issues given their emphasis on the preferences of the relatively privileged (McCann 2007, 2013), but that the initiatives that result such as Vacants to Value can exacerbate inequality, in this case in terms of reduced access to housing for the city's poorer residents.

12.4   MAKING BALTIMORE LIVEABLE: FOR WHOM, IN WHICH NEIGHBOURHOODS?

A key question which arises when considering the challenge of making Baltimore liveable (or in city parlance, 'changing it to grow') is for whom? In such a starkly socio-spatially divided city this question closely equates to where or which neighbourhoods. Given the city's fiscal squeeze and reliance on localist and privatist approaches, the research reveals an opportunistic practice, albeit one which aligns with the spatial typology of policy interventions determined by the asset-based approach. Indeed, the city's neighbourhood revitalisation efforts have been described as scattered 'improvisations shaped by the pursuit of resources' (Stoker et al. 2015: 69). Neighbourhoods gain the attention of type C elite partners when they intersect with other priorities—most notably economic development and the attraction of wealthier residents.

The city's current waterfront megaproject, Port Covington, illustrates the forms of development prioritised and how 'public-private partnership' is operationalised. The development has approvals for $660 million of tax increment financing (TIF) to assist redevelopment of 80 hectares of railyards and former industrial property in South Baltimore to create a 'city within a city' of fifty new city blocks, with parks, apartments, office space and retail, housing 10–15,000 new residents (Broadwater 2016). Elites acknowledged the project raises 'gentrification and race issues' but did not question the underlying assumptions about the city's development priorities in terms of for whom and where. Citizen activists and advocacy organisations in contrast were united in their disdain, as an activist explained:

> a bajillion-million-dollar TIF... they get these breaks from the city government and they're encouraged to develop these areas... this corporate park in Port Covington... it gets all the funding and all the city benefits.

Sandtown, a 'stressed' neighbourhood located in the West Baltimore part of the 'black butterfly', stands in stark contrast. It is subject to the policy prescription of demolition (ideally for site assembly) given its '33% vacant and abandoned housing' as an anchor institution officer explained. The neighbourhood has latterly gained greater elite attention and resource. The City's ongoing Vacants to Value initiative has been accelerated and expanded by Project CORE (Creating Opportunities for Renewal and Enterprise), a 4000 property demolition and redevelopment initiative principally funded by the State of Maryland. Sandtown's selection as site for the initiative launch was symbolic as it formed the locus of the April 2015 uprising in the city following the death of a young black resident, Freddie Gray, due to injuries sustained whilst in police custody. As a government official explained:

> *It related to the unrest because Mister Freddie Gray... that was his neighbourhood. I think that was also a turning point for [the State Governor], because he wasn't as familiar with what was happening in these neighbourhoods... through the State's role in addressing that unrest, it was startling to him to see the level of vacancy and blight.*

In its first year of operation (2016), 400 properties were demolished in 'stressed' target neighbourhoods. A city official explained how it boosts the city's efforts for more strategic 'demolition in the context of a broader land use plan, and a phasing plan, and a greening plan'. The City's resultant Green Network Plan is described as:

> *a bold vision for reimagining vacant and abandoned properties and transforming them into community assets, creating an interconnected system of flourishing spaces throughout the city. Through a collaborative and community-directed process, the Plan will direct resources to underinvested areas and lay the foundation for the revitalization of some of Baltimore's most challenged neighbourhoods.* (City of Baltimore Office of Sustainability, n.d.)

Another government official explained the perceived opportunities of combining demolition and greening strategies in terms which encapsulate elite emphasis on enhancing the city's liveability to attract wealthier, homeowning residents:

> *A community like Sandtown needs some fairly big interventions... do we need to really think big about bigger parks that rearrange how the city is designed? Back in the 1800s, as the city was growing out... some smart person laid out a series of residential squares which survive today [where there is] strong home ownership... so, there is a power that a park strategy, if we can sort out the politics and community equity issues around how much you'd have to really rearrange the deck chairs to come up with major spaces out of what is now a sea of empty row houses, or half empty row houses.*

In contrast, community activists based in West Baltimore saw these policies as a gentrification strategy displacing poor, current residents, one explaining, 'this community is left with a bunch of holes or green spaces as they like to say… you're proposing all this demolition to lure developers… it's a slow gentrification process'. In terms of the 'meta-goal' of poverty deconcentration, the way in which such neighbourhood clearance contributes is implicit by removing residential properties. But it is accompanied by initiatives which are explicit in seeking the relocation of existing (poor, black) residents of stressed neighbourhoods. These stem from litigation ('fair housing complaints') to counter Baltimore's role as 'a container for the region's poor' (Kline 2007). The outcome, regional housing mobility strategies (now institutionalised as the non-profit Baltimore Regional Housing Mobility Program), involves provision of housing vouchers to former public housing residents to relocate to rental housing in the city's neighbouring counties. An advocacy organisation officer explained that vouchers had been provided to 3300 households, estimated to reach 4400 by the following year (2018). A city government official saw such efforts as vital rather than continuing attempts to improve neighbourhoods 'beyond repair'. The bifurcation between such elite views and those of citizen activists regarding gentrification and displacement underscores the exclusion of existing residents from debates about priorities regarding 'liveable for whom and where'. Thus the city's liveability strategies are targeted at attracting a (wealthy) mobile population rather than improving the quality of life for existing *immobile* residents through making their neighbourhoods *liveable*—in ways that work for those communities. In turn, strategies also seek to boost the mobility of the immobile through removing them from the city, as a result of demolition and displacement, or housing 'mobility' programs. An activist group member described the situation in stark terms as:

> *a scramble for resources and space in Baltimore where essentially white folks are trying to take Baltimore and push black folks out.*

Certainly it is clear that neighbourhoods in Baltimore gain attention when they intersect with the priorities of city elites involved in the broad type C partnership which determines and seeks to deliver its neighbourhood agenda. Port Covington gains top priority due to its perceived economic development and (wealthier) population growth opportunities, and tools (notably tax increment financing) are deployed to seek to realise these. Sandtown as a focus for Project CORE exemplifies city (and State) attention at the other end of the spectrum—a focus for demolition rather than development (albeit envisaged as enabling green infrastructure), linked by existing residents to longer-term gentrification, clearing poor residents as part of the city's 'changing to grow' to attract others. The initiative also serves the political imperative of being seen to take concerted action following the city uprising. But demolition as a reaction to the uprising, which was sparked by the city's inequities and police violence, is not the most needed response to improve the situation for current residents. Indeed, in neither example are the needs of the city's current residents to the fore. Consultation mechanisms are absent or, in the case of the city's Green Network Plan, regarded by resident activists as tokenistic. Whilst some interviewed saw the necessity of neighbourhood prioritisation given resource scarcity, others stressed that neighbourhoods which do not align with elite priorities are 'written off', in the words of a community activist. An official of a West Baltimore anchor institution described its location as a 'containment area', explaining that Baltimore was often described in terms of 'a tale of two cities... one doesn't have anything to do with the other'.

Some neighbourhoods beyond the preceding examples may gain elite attention when they are proximate to the city's major anchor institutions and in which the institutions therefore have a vested interest in seeking to ensure stability and safety. Civil society-private (type F) partnerships ensue between the smaller, neighbourhood-based non-profits and the major, private (but designated non-profit) 'ed and med' institutions (which are also members of the predominant type C partnership which sets the city's neighbourhood agenda). For example, the non-profit Central Baltimore Partnership gains support and resource given its proximity to Johns Hopkins' Homewood campus and its Community Partners Initiative. This in turn encourages other resource flows (such as from Maryland State's neighbourhood initiative and foundation and bank support for its development fund). Another example is the partnership between the city's longstanding community alliance, BUILD, and a community development financial institution to develop housing in the neighbourhood proximate to Hopkins' hospital, a type F partnership which levers from the major investment anchored by this institution. Indeed, it is these partnerships, located in specific anchor-proximate neighbourhoods, which have been most successful in drawing down Vacants to Value resource (Jacobson 2015). Resource allocation therefore continues to reflect the spatial prioritisation of certain spaces in the city, which in turn reflect the power of certain private partners. Potential community partners recognised the need to work with these elite city anchor institutions, especially as support from the city's philanthropic foundations tends to align with anchor resource allocations to enable 'collective impact'. In other words, weak neighbourhood-based organisations seek type F partnerships with powerful private (non-profit) type C partners. Indeed, many interviewed stressed the vital role played by these non-profit actors in contrast with city government's lack of leadership. An officer of a neighbourhood-based non-profit explained 'the City no longer sees itself as a leader in community development'. An elected politician described the necessity of 'outside institutions… working hard with each other because there's a vacuum in city government'. An official of a philanthropic foundation explained it in the following terms:

> *the non-government actors are very committed to this city… the great anchor institutions in our city have really, in my view, stepped up and increased the climate of collaboration. And I think that all of us have realised that without collaboration, again, in spite of city leadership… we won't be able to accomplish our goals.*

12.5 Conclusion

The imperative to increase the City of Baltimore's population and thus alleviate its fiscal squeeze has brought the liveability of this shrinking city to the fore. City government has long been engaged in an informal type C partnership with private (corporate and non-profit) actors to develop and deliver a neighbourhood policy agenda which seeks to stabilise and grow the city. By considering making Baltimore liveable in terms of for whom and where, the challenges posed by the city's deep inequities and exclusionary governance to the realisation of liveability for all its residents are revealed. Baltimore affirms how conceptions of liveability work to elide the conflicts of who gets what and where in urban politics. The city's strategies and plans, particularly 'Change to Grow' and the typology of policy prescriptions for different neighbourhoods, combine with its elite and exclusionary governance to affirm the city's continuing socio-spatial inequality. The strategies deployed appeal to 'common sense' given the city's 'fiscal squeeze', politically useful as this avoids contestation of priorities and obscures the power differentials and inequalities of the city's governance. The city seeks to attract a putative population of the mobile and (relatively) wealthy, whilst the residents of the 'black butterfly' are further contained, lacking voice in envisaging a more liveable, equitable city—on their own terms. Thus Baltimore is set to continue as a 'twin-track' city, aligning with the dual city thesis advanced by scholars considering the increasing inequality of neoliberal urbanism. Citizens and civil society organisations are excluded from the public-private partnership that determines what constitutes 'liveability' in the city.

The predominant partners who determine and seek to realise Baltimore's neighbourhood policies are the local state (city government and its agencies) and Maryland State, along with key non-state actors (philanthropies and anchor institutions) who also partner amongst themselves in the absence of local state leadership. Existing residents are largely excluded from these arrangements, which seek to accommodate the needs of corporate actors and in particular property developers perceived as offering what is needed to attract residents to this shrinking city. The emphasis on attracting millennials by making Baltimore, in the words of the Mayor 'a hip place to be', and a 'low-cost alternative in a high-cost region', are the shrinking city version of how cities compete for internationally mobile capital and people. Millennials are thus shrinking cities' target population in the way that the preferences of 'well-educated, internationally mobile individuals and families' (McArthur and Robin 2019: 1720) predominate in how cities are ranked globally in composite urban liveability indexes.

Baltimore's expression of the widely (ab)used, narrow notion of liveability aligns with critiques which assert that liveability does not acknowledge socio-economic disparities and how these could be addressed through planning, service provision and governance structures and strategies at city level (McArthur and Robin 2019). Elite attention and resource are not targeted in terms of what would be revealed by a 'people-centred' approach of meeting the human needs and capabilities (Fainstein 2014) of the city's existing residents. Resultant policy choices would differ, such as retaining the recreation centres widely used by young 'black butterfly' residents closed as a result of the 'Change to Grow' deficit reduction measures; and shifting the spatial targeting of policy tools such as tax increment financing.

Whilst urban liveability indexes emphasise the preferences of the privileged (and mobile), their underlying metrics point to what would be needed to make Baltimore more liveable in terms of improving the quality of life for all residents, both putative and existing. In their review of six global indexes, McArthur and Robin (2019) identified four metrics that were shared: crime, healthcare, schools and infrastructure. Crime (in terms of the need for improved police-community relations) was emphasised by all those interviewed in Baltimore as a realm which needed to be addressed as a prerequisite for other change in the city. This is unsurprising as the city uprising was in response to the city's socio-spatial containment of its poor, black communities reinforced by violent policing practices. These communities understand that in terms of liveability, basic security and freedom from violence and trauma are key, as explained by a community activist:

> *Police-community relations... I think everything else is so minor... that developer developing Port Covington don't have absolutely nothing to do with my day-to-day existence.*

In terms of current strategies, progress towards achievement of the city's 'meta-goal' of deconcentrating poverty—through attraction of a wealthier, mobile population and spatial mobility (relocation/displacement) of the existing, poor population—remains halting. The 1000 person population increase (indicated by US Census mid-year estimates) trumpeted by the Mayor in her pre-uprising State of the City address (2015) was followed by a post-uprising estimated population decline (of 6000 people in mid-2016 estimates, and a further 3000 decline in mid-2017). In expressing concerns about student recruitment following the uprising, a university anchor institution officer recognised the importance of having a more holistic understanding of quality of life:

> *we've took a hit as far as students coming to Baltimore... [the uprising brought the underlying issues that] we've all known have been there to international attention, like how horrible is Baltimore that the poverty is this, the vacancies... the incarceration, the joblessness.*

Certainly Baltimore—with its extremes of poverty and violence by Global North standards—provides a set of salutary lessons about the meaning of 'liveability' for different groups in society. The city is riven by starkly visible, longstanding and deep inequities. Those interviewed expressed different views on the way forward. Some stressed the need to find 'ways of partnering in a positive manner'. Others stressed the need for an alternative to what a citizen activist described as the 'let's attract corporate dollars to try and create a space where people come to the city' approach. Such an alternative would benefit from clearly specified goals which seek to improve the city's liveability in terms of the actual needs of its current, and especially most disadvantaged residents, rather than the imagined needs of a putative and mobile group of possible residents. Realising this would entail much more open and equal partnerships between citizens, grassroots organisations, the local state and private actors.

REFERENCES

(BNIA-JFI) Baltimore Neighborhood Indicators Alliance-Jacob France Institute. (2016). *Evaluation of the Baltimore City Vacants to value program: Quantitative analysis.* Baltimore: BNIA-JFI.

Barnekov, T., Rich, D., & Warren, R. (1981). The new privatism, federalism, and the future of urban governance: National urban policy in the 1980s. *Journal of Urban Affairs, 3*(4), 1–14.

Broadwater, L. (2016, September 19). City Council approves $660 million bond deal for port Covington project. *The Baltimore Sun.*

Brown, L. (2016, June 28). Two Baltimores: The white L vs. the black butterfly. *The City Paper.*

Castells, M. (1989). *The informational city: Information technology, economic restructuring and the urban-regional process.* Oxford: Blackwell.

City of Baltimore. (2013). *Change to grow: A ten-year financial plan for Baltimore.* Baltimore: Baltimore City.

City of Baltimore Office of Sustainability. (n.d.). *Green Network.* http://www.baltimoresustainability.org/projects/green-network/. Accessed 5 July 2019.

Clarke, A., & Cheshire, L. (2018). The post-political state? The role of administrative reform in managing tensions between urban growth and liveability in Brisbane, Australia. *Urban Studies, 55*(6), 3545–3562.

Coates, T. (2014, June). The case for reparations. *The Atlantic.* https://www.theatlantic.com/magazine/archive/2014/06/the-case-for-reparations/361631/. Accessed 5 July 2019.

Ehrenhalt, A. (2013). *The great inversion and the future of the American city.* New York: Alfred A. Knopf.

Fainstein, S. (2014). The just city. *International Journal of Urban Sciences, 18*(1), 1–18.

Florida, R. (2005). *Cities and the creative class.* London: Routledge.

Jacobson, J. (2015). Vacants to value. *The Abell Report, 28*(5), 1–28. http://www.abell.org/sites/default/files/files/cd-vacants2-value1115.pdf. Accessed 5 July 2019.

Kline, G. (2007). Thompson v. HUD: Groundbreaking housing desegregation litigation, and the significant task ahead of achieving an effective desegregation remedy without engendering new social harms. *University of Maryland Law Journal of Race, Religion, Gender and Class, 7*(1), 172–191.

Lasswell, H. (1936). *Politics: Who gets what, when and how.* New York: Whittlesey House.

Martinez-Fernandez, C., Audirac, I., Fol, S., & Cunningham-Sabot, E. (2012). Shrinking cities: Urban challenges of globalization. *International Journal of Urban and Regional Research, 36*(2), 213–225.

Mayor's State of the City Speech. (2015, March 9). http://mayor.baltimorecity. gov/news/press-releases/2015-03-09-mayor-rawlings-blake-delivers-16th-annual-state-city-address

Mayor's State of the City Speech. (2016, February 29). http://www.baltimorecity.gov/news/general/2016-02-29-seventeenth-annual-state-city-address

McArthur, J., & Robin, E. (2019). Victims of their own (definition of) success: Urban discourse and expert knowledge production in the liveable city. *Urban Studies, 56*(9), 1711–1728.

McCann, E. (2007). Inequality and politics in the creative city-region: Questions of livability and state strategy. *International Journal of Urban and Regional Research, 31*(1), 188–196.

McCann, E. (2013). Policy boosterism, policy mobilities, and the extrospective city. *Urban Geography, 34*(1), 5–29.

Peck, J. (2005). Struggling with the creative class. *International Journal of Urban and Regional Research, 29*(4), 740–770.

Pill, M. (2018). Philanthropic foundations in the city policy process: A perspective from the United States. In W. Xun, M. Howlett, & M. Ramesh (Eds.), *Policy capacity and governance: Studies in the political economy of public policy* (pp. 313–335). Cham: Palgrave.

Ross, B. (2014). *Dead end: Suburban sprawl and the rebirth of American urbanism.* Oxford: Oxford University Press.

Stoker, R., Stone, C., & Worgs, D. (2015). Neighborhood policy in Baltimore: The postindustrial turn. In C. Stone & R. Stoker (Eds.), *Urban neighborhoods in a new era: Revitalization politics in the postindustrial city* (pp. 50–80). Chicago: University of Chicago Press.

Stone, C. N. (1993). Urban regimes and the capacity to govern: A political economy approach. *Journal of Urban Affairs, 15*(1), 1–28.

Szanton, P. (1986). *Baltimore 2000: A choice of futures.* Baltimore: Goldseker Foundation.

U.S. Census Bureau. (2017). *QuickFacts Baltimore City, Maryland.* Retrieved from https://www.census.gov/quickfacts/fact/table/baltimorecitymaryland,US/PST045217#qf-headnote-a. Accessed 5 July 2019.

Williams, R. Y. (2005). *The politics of public housing: Black women's struggles against urban inequality.* New York: Oxford University Press.

CHAPTER 13

Youths Growing Up in the French *banlieues*: Partners That Make the City

Simone van de Wetering and Femke Kaulingfreks

13.1 Introduction

Cities all over the world are growing. Also in Europe more and more people live, work, and spend their leisure time in urban areas (Nabielek et al. 2016). European policy discourses are increasingly focused on urban opportunities for upward social mobility, social cohesion and inclusion. Some authors say that cities are 'the home of prosperity' (United Nations Human Settlements Programme 2013), or that cities are triumphing (Glaeser 2012). However, the spatial segregation of socio-economic and ethnic groups, daily experiences with inequality and a lack of opportunities are also part of city life. Since the rise of neoliberal governance and the decline of the welfare state, the potential of public policies to bridge urban

S. van de Wetering (✉)
Tilburg Center for Regional Law and Governance (TiREG), Tilburg University,
Tilburg, The Netherlands
e-mail: s.a.l.vdwetering@uvt.nl

F. Kaulingfreks
Lectoraat Jeugd en Samenleving, Kenniscentrum De Gezonde Samenleving,
Inholland University of Applied Sciences, Amsterdam, The Netherlands
e-mail: femke.kaulingfreks@inholland.nl

© The Author(s) 2020
C. van Montfort, A. Michels (eds.), *Partnerships for Livable Cities*,
https://doi.org/10.1007/978-3-030-40060-6_13

251

divides is debated and lesser privileged urban residents increasingly struggle to participate in decision-making processes about their living space and the future of their city (Dikeç 2017; PBL 2016; Rodríguez-Pose 2018; Slooter and Diphoorn 2016). How can cities become 'livable' for all urban residents? In this regard, many scholars explore the role of partnerships, in which public, private, and/or civil society partners work together in fostering livable cities (Elwood 2004; Foo et al. 2015; Huang 2010; Koppenjan and Enserink 2009).

New governance arrangements can open up the traditional state-centred approach to policy making and offer citizens ways to have a more direct influence on institutions, but can also reinforce existing democratic deficits (Brandsen et al. 2017; Swyngedouw 2005). For instance, it appears difficult to involve young people and people from cultural and ethnic minority groups in such partnerships (Michels 2012). New initiatives in participatory governance often lead to the participation of selective citizen groups in decision making while not all voices are equally heard. In this chapter, we explore how young people, who are often underrepresented in partnerships for urban governance, participate in practices and processes aimed at revitalizing neighborhoods and the shaping of livable cities. We do so by zooming in on the case of French youths growing up in the *banlieues* of Paris.[1]

Young inhabitants of the French *banlieues* often do not feel represented by policymakers or included in decision-making processes, but they do have an impact on life in the city, albeit often in non-institutional ways (Kaulingfreks 2016). This chapter explores the activities which *banlieue* youths undertake to realize quality of life in their city. Drawing on ethnographic research in Seine-Saint-Denis, a *banlieue* northeast of Paris, we see that youths in the *banlieues* engage in 'making their city' in everyday practices and informal partnerships, even if they do not engage in 'governing their city' through formalized partnerships. Based on our study, we

---

[1] It is important to note here that the periphery of Paris is a highly diverse urban area, both consisting of neighborhoods which could be characterized as deprived and as wealthy. Even the deprived areas form a heterogeneous mixture in terms of urban texture, economic activities and composition of inhabitants (Kaulingfreks 2015; Wacquant 2008). Despite the diverse urban landscape in the *banlieues* and its non-homogeneous identity, we choose to speak of the *banlieues* when addressing the living conditions and experiences of young people as they take place in the poorer neighborhoods, where we both conducted research (Kaulingfreks 2015; van de Wetering 2017).

suggest that attention for informal practices that shape collective life in the city could inform a more inclusive perspective on urban decision making.

We start this chapter with a theoretical discussion of livability as a policy concept and the various ways of 'making the city' in everyday social inter-actions and associations, which tend to be undervalued in the measure-ment of neighborhood livability. Having situated the chapter within these academic debates, we turn to our case study of youths growing up in the French *banlieues*. We explore the ways in which youths 'govern' and 'make' their city, identify a gap between these activities, and examine the role associations play in bridging that gap.

13.2 THEORETICAL DISCUSSION: LIVABILITY AND THE PRODUCTION OF SOCIAL LIFE IN THE CITY

13.2.1 *Livability in Urban Policy*

Since the turn of the twenty-first century the encouragement of 'urban revitalization' and 'social cohesion' in the neighborhood became a focal point of urban policies in order to overcome socio-spatial inequalities and segregation (Cassiers and Kesteloot 2012). Urban policies shifted from a city-wide approach to a neighborhood-oriented approach (van Gent et al. 2009; Musterd, et al. 2006). As Richard Florida suggested, post-industrial cities had to become attractive places for investment, by first attracting a young and creative class working in the service and information sector, in search of 'intense, high-quality and multidimensional experiences' (Florida 2002, p. 166). The quality of life in the city thus became an asset for eco-nomic competition and sparked processes of gentrification to turn work-ing class neighborhoods into vibrant areas of cultural production and consumption that would satisfy the standard of living of the creative class. The 'livability' of the neighborhood became a matter of concern for hous-ing corporations, house owners, city planners and policy-makers because of its key impact on the popularity and economic success of the neighbor-hood (Veenhoven 2000). Despite the highly subjective nature of livability, it became a tested indicator in city-wide surveys among inhabitants, and an important factor in comparing neighborhoods (see for example the Global Liveability Index). The emotional perception of life in the neigh-borhood thus became a quantifiable tool of measurement (Conger 2015), despite the failure of these 'objective measurement tools' to adequately reflect the nuances in how people describe characteristics of 'a good life' or 'a good community' (Salvaris 2012 in Lloyd et al. 2016, p. 364).

With these developments, livability became associated with an ideal image of civic and economic participation within the urban environment. Neighborhoods which do not score well in terms of livability are often associated with a larger number of residents with an immigrant background, a lower level of social cohesion and a higher level of poverty, crime and degradation. The quality of urban life as it is measured by livability indexes is intricately related with the mobility of economic and human capital, and therefore offers a selective perspective, which reinforces social hierarchies and urban segregation (Ruth and Franklin 2014). What is seen as a 'livable' neighborhood reflects upper and middle-class interests and the pursuit of agendas of urban growth (Kaal 2011, p. 534). Both the interests and (civic) activities of marginalized groups run the risk of being underrepresented in efforts to increase the livability of the city. As highlighted in the introduction chapter of this book, the question of the livability of the city is thus not so much whether a city is livable, but rather *for whom* it is livable.

13.2.2   *The Production of Social Life in the City*

Urban geographers and sociologists have taken up the tasks to critically evaluate the unequal attention of local institutions of governance to different parts of the city and different groups of urban residents. David Harvey, who analyses the relationship between global urbanization and capitalism, concludes that the quality of urban life has become a commodity for those with money, since consumerism, tourism, cultural and knowledge-based industries have become major aspects of the urban political economy (Harvey 2008). Harvey revisits Henri Lefebvre's idea of 'the right to the city' as a basic human right of urban residents, regardless of their economic or citizenship status. Not companies or governments, but the inhabitants who bring the city to life, should have the first right to control the development of the city, regardless of their income, citizenship status or profession. Lefebvre (1991) emphasized that urban space is not only an objective, physical substance, but is also socially constructed and subjectively experienced by different residents. However, in the current times of neoliberal governance decision making processes that impact the production of urban space and everyday city life are not equally accessible for all residents, despite efforts to make these processes 'inclusive'.

Lefebvre's work resonates in Richard Sennett's distinction between a fixed notion of the city as a built environment and a more fluid notion of the city as place in which people live, dwell and experience a sense of belonging (Sennett 2018). In line with this distinction, we may refer to different things when we speak about 'making the city'. We may refer to the urban design of houses, office-buildings and infrastructure and we may refer to the social structure of city life as it emerges in everyday interactions and associations. The social production of urban space always partly escapes the intentions and modelling of architects and city planners. Various urban residents produce the city in unintended ways; vacant lots are turned into communal gardens or meeting places, youth hang out with their friends at street corners and homeless people sleep on park benches and in metro stations. The making of the city can never be fully captured by formal modes of city planning and urban governance. If policy- and decision making is to tackle urban segregation and inequality, it should recognize informal human interactions and organic development as important aspects of the process of making the city.

13.3   Youths in the City

What then, does this mean for the most marginalized neighborhoods of France, the cités and quartiers[2] in the *banlieues* that are labeled 'sensitive urban zones'? A variety of policy programs, starting in the 1980s with 'la politique de la ville', a national urban policy with the *banlieues* as its main object, have aimed to improve these neighborhoods that were rapidly constructed after the second world war to house the new working class, but -even so rapidly- degraded into areas of deprivation and social exclusion at the peripheries of French cities (Dikeç 2007; Délégation Interministérielle à la ville 2000). Still today they remain areas with relatively high crime-, unemployment- and poverty rates, much social housing, a lack of public transport and infrastructure, and both a public and political stigma as 'no-go' areas. New efforts to make the *banlieues* 'more livable', like the current Grand Paris-project that aims to include the peripheral areas of Paris

---

[2] Literally 'cité' and 'quartier' translate to 'city' and 'district', but in the context of the *banlieues* these words have a specific connotation, as 'cité' is used to describe the housing projects and 'quartier' as an abbreviation of 'quartiers populaires': working class neighborhoods within the *banlieues*.

in the prosperity of the city center, again underline the question: livable for whom (Enright 2013)?

How do youths growing up in the *banlieue* make themselves feel at home in the city, how do they advocate for their interests and how do they contribute to the production of the city through their daily activities? To find answers to these questions, we delve into the data of ethnographic research conducted in 2014–2015 on growing up in Seine-Saint-Denis (department '93'), a *banlieue* northeast of Paris. This department is home to 1.552.500 '*banlieusards*', many of migrant descent but, because the French government does not collect statistics on ethnicity (or religion), there are no official numbers on that (INSEE 2017). Data was collected in interviews with youths, civil servants, and people working for associations, and field notes based on five months of walking around this area, hanging out with youths, visiting meetings of the municipality and going to events organized by associations. Delving into this data, we elaborate on the ways in which youths engage in 'governing' the city by engaging with institutional structures and services and in 'making' the city in everyday practices and interactions, and we explore possibilities to bridge the gap between these two modes of social production of urban space.

13.3.1   Governing the City: The Youth Council as a Partnership Between Youths and the Municipality

In France, an important way in which citizens can work together with the municipality as partners, in order to impact the vitality of their neighborhood, is through councils. Currently, many towns in Seine-Saint-Denis have a citizen council (Website conseils citoyens 2019). These councils have various functions: from speaking on behalf of the neighborhood, to advising the municipality on policy actions and organizing local events. At the time and place of study a specific youth council (*conseil des jeunes*, CDJ) came together once every two weeks to discuss the organization of activities in the neighborhood. These activities ranged from events especially targeted at youths, like a movie screening and discussion evening, to gatherings for all residents, like a neighborhood dinner. The participating youths were between fifteen and thirty years old, were from a variety of ethnic backgrounds, and were both male and female. The council members were not selected by the municipality but started participating out of own initiative: in principle, anyone could join. The majority of them was following education in high school or college, some of them were working at a social center. According to the council members, the main drive to participate in this council was to do something for their neighborhood and to create a positive image of their neighborhood, on behalf of youths.

Overall, [members of the conseil des jeunes said] it was "because I want to do something for my town, for youths, to make my voice heard'. [...] because [they] wanted to show another side of le 93.[3]*"* (Fieldnotes, October 2014)

These are really youths with a goal. They stand for something. Have a plan. Have the opportunity to study and do something with these plans. It's really cool and especially interesting to see this other, positive side of the neighborhood. I wonder who of the kids [at the social center where I did tutoring] will be here in a few years. (Fieldnotes, October 2014)

The youths that participated in the council were politically engaged. Also outside of the CDJ many of them were embedded, through activities of their family or their own, in the political or associational life of the neighborhood.

I am a political activist. For a political party. [...] And I am also part of an association [..] organizing events at the university. (B., 20 years old, male, member of the Conseil des Jeunes)

Honestly, the Conseil des Jeunes... My mother is part of an association and if she hadn't said that there was something like that I think I would have never known. (N., 15 years old, female, member of the Conseil des Jeunes)

The CDJ is part of the municipality: the youths had their meetings in the city hall, and once in a while the president of the municipality's youth service came by to get informed and show support. However, the day to day business of the CDJ, the meetings, discussions and planning of events, evolved in a pretty informal and unorganized way.

People are not really listening to each other. [...] Everybody is laughing with each other, fooling around, not really paying attention. Meanwhile it is 22.10 and everybody is talking at the same time, interrupting each other. C. [the chairwoman] tries to establish order. We still have to vote on who will be part of

---

[3] 'Le 93' stands for the department nr. 93 of Seine-Saint-Denis. It is an abbreviation of the area code, used by youngsters to speak about their neighborhood.

the board, and on the commissions. This takes a long time and happens in a messy way. But in a sociable way. Meanwhile, coca cola is poured and the food people brought is passed around. (Fieldnotes, October 2014)

A lot of people didn't show up. Some really only came one meeting, and now there is a small 'set' group. (Fieldnotes, December 2014)

With the group I am part of it is going very slowly because the one who came up with this idea in the first place is not here. Nobody is taking the lead. N. proposes that after today's meeting we just set a date to come together in the meantime. (Fieldnotes, December 2014)

The 'messiness' of the meetings and of the organisation of the CDJ shows that, despite this embeddedness within an institutional infrastructure, the council is run by engaged, but non-professional and mainly inexperienced youths, who also come together to just have some fun.

The youth council as a partnership between youths and the municipality offers a well-functioning balance between the informal freedom of young people to bring up their own ideas and initiate their own plans, and the formal structure of an organization serving as institutional interlocutor for the municipality, including yearly funding by the municipality. Participating youths can access and make use of a broad network through the municipality, but the municipality does not impose certain topics or activities on the CDJ. Simultaneously, the fact that the CDJ's right to exist is based on the voluntary participation of young people, impacts its effectivity and stability as an institution. It is the CDJ's task to organize events but the CDJ does not participate in policy making and general decision making processes about the neighborhood, thereby limiting its power to get things done.

In addition, the CDJ as a partnership between youths and the municipality shows a lack of inclusivity in institutional youth participation. Other than average youth in the neighborhood, many council members engage in political or associational activities besides their CDJ membership, which raises the question whether the council sufficiently represents all *banlieue* youths. Youths who do not have family members that are part of the associational life of the neighborhood are less involved. The CDJ therefore seems to enforce already existing 'linking social capital' in the neighborhood, providing youth who are already embedded in networks that interact across vertical levels of social position and institutionalized power with a platform to advocate for their interests, while others who have less institutional connections are underrepresented.

The youth council as a partnership in governance reflects a traditional view of civic and political participation. Farthing (2010) argues that the approach to 'entice and assimilate' youths to traditional processes of democratic politics is inadequate. Many youths, he says, do not engage in traditional forms of participation, like a youth council. However, this does not necessarily mean they are not politically active, do not have ideas about their neighborhoods, or do not undertake other activities that shape the city. Young people are not either 'passive and devoid of political interests' or 'actively political' in a formal way, but often express their engagement in informal ways and in everyday practices (Kaulingfreks 2015). Political participation may include a range of activities and expressions, from local community activism, to online discussions and campaigns, conscious consumerism and the expression of identity politics in popular culture. Rather than engaging in traditional politics, because they distrust the capacity of state authorities to promote real social change, many youth *live* their politics and they practice change in their daily lives (Farthing 2010, p. 189). The youth council then on the one hand serves as an example of a partnership in which youths work together with public partners to contribute to their neighborhood. On the other hand, it shows the difficulties of such institutionalized arrangements to include the perspectives of all citizens and the need to redefine what it means to be 'politically engaged' as a citizen or youth.

13.3.2   *Making the City: The Act of Living Life in the* banlieues

The youths that participate in a youth council are only a small part of the youths living in the *banlieue*. They know how to reach formal institutions and want to work together with the municipality. Many others do not want to—or do not know how to—engage in such formal governance structures, but have opinions and ideas about the quality of life in their city. They may impact social life in their city, albeit in different ways. When we look at the everyday lives of youths in the *banlieues*, we see how they experience their neighborhood, how they value the capacity to move around in the city, and how these movements influence the social production of urban space.

My neighborhood for me is my friends. My family. I like my neighborhood. What I don't like about it is that there is a lot of noise [..]. There is a lot of trash [in the streets]. But I still like my neighborhood. (M., 13 years old, female)

For me, my neighborhood is family. (O., 12 years old, male), and

For me, my neighborhood is my life. It's like my home, I feel good with the people who live there. (E. 12 years old, female)

Many youngsters describe their neighborhoods as a place they like. The neighborhood provides them with a strong sense of community based on both positive and negative shared experiences (Kaulingfreks 2015, pp. 62–63). The sense of belonging and respect they experience in their direct environment makes the city 'livable' for them, and the positive experiences they share in 'their' *banlieue* contradict the negative, stigmatizing image that is predominant in public, political and policy discourse. Dutch anthropologist Luuk Slooter explains how youths in the *banlieues* not only engage in community building, but also in place-making processes; they claim spaces by naming spaces or developing narratives about them, they draw boundaries, appropriate space as their home territory and socially organize the neighborhood by hanging out at the street corner, and they surveil the streets of the *banlieue*, defining who is 'in' or 'out of place'. These practices, he argues, are the everyday discursive and practical routines through which youths maintain and transform places, thereby 'making the *banlieue*' (Slooter 2015, p. 106). While they get older, both their experiences in their living space and their activities start to change.

It starts to be small [here] and it starts to be, it starts a little to be boring. (B., 14 years old, female)

In high school I started going out a bit. With friends we went to the shopping center, to the cinema in Paris. [Here] there is nothing. There is not much choice. (O., 24 years old, female)

They start to go outside of the direct environment of their homes for leisure activities.

I asked him if you could go out here. Not really, he says. The cinema plays the movies only very late after their release, there is no theater [...]. What about drinking a beer? He did that in Paris. (Fieldnotes, October 2014)

I go shopping, I go to the cinema, I go to visit people, friends family. I go to see some shows with the group. [...] I often go in Seine-Saint-Denis, but I also go to Paris and other cities near Paris. (L., 16 years old, female)

While for people living in the center of Paris having to cross the *périphérique*, the highway around the city center, is often seen as an obstacle to go to the *banlieues*, it does not seem to work like that the other way around. Youths describe the possibility to move around from their neighborhood to the city center as a habitual, by some preferred, part of their routine.

I have the tendency to go to Paris [...] It is easy. I take the RER and then in 15 minutes I am in Paris. (B., 20 years old, male, member of the Conseil des Jeunes)

I can go everywhere I want. Because there is a bus, train, it's easy. (L., 16 years old, female)

Another daily routine that youths growing up in the *banlieue* often mention, is dealing with the police. Many young people, especially teenage boys and young men living in the banlieue experience identity checks, being disrespected and approached in a rude way by the police on a daily basis (Schneider 2008, p. 153; Body-Gendrot 2010). While young *banlieusards* have a strong wish to freely move both within and outside of their neighborhood, their encounters with the police have an impact on their mobility and sense of belonging in the city. Common knowledge amongst youths living in the banlieues is that by being black or arab and by moving through the *banlieue*, you are likely to experience troublesome run-ins with the police. Inside of the neighborhood, security police units are often performing stops and searches because they are looking for drugs. Outside of their neighborhoods young *banlieue* residents are often targeted by ethnic profiling because they fit certain 'risk profiles'.

I was looking for my class, my university, and you see I was looking for directions. I was with three friends and me, so four in total. And I turned to a lady. And I said, yes, ma'am, please, can you tell me how to get to the university? I turned around and saw the police directly. Directly (laughing). They said wait, wait, what is this? They searched us and everything, you see, touching you, asking, they take everything you have in your pocket, asking what is this? [...] Because I had 200 euro on me, and they ask me where is this money from? After

that, they took my phone, asking me is this a stolen phone? You see, they do checks
like that. [...] In their heads they say to themselves, you have two arabs and two
blacks (laughing) who are asking an old lady for directions, that's for robbing
her, for sure. (E., 19 years old, male)

It's a cliché, my brother has been checked at the station [in Seine-Saint-Denis]
a dozen times. And yet he did nothing. [...] Once he ran after a bus, he told me
a police woman stopped to search him. Because she had found that suspicious,
didn't understand why he ran. And then that's it. (O., 24 years old, female)

From these stories, it appears that especially the young men who live in
the *banlieues* have to deal with the police and therefore experience a limited sense of mobility.

For the young men it is always worse than for the girls from the banlieue. The
girls from the banlieues can go anywhere, work in Paris, go out in Paris, we go
like anybody. A boy from the banlieues who goes to Paris he is seen like a... like a
delinquent, really. (O., 24 years old, female)

My big brother, he lived in the cité and it is like I told you, everybody treated him
like scum but he succeeded in his life. (D., 16 years old, female)

The ways in which youths navigate public space, and navigate the interactions they have with the police in public space are part of their daily life
in the *banlieue*. From their movements in- and outside their neighborhood, to anticipating on being identity-checked and keeping calm when
being searched, youths deal with their social and spatial position as being
a black and/or arab and/or *banlieue* youngster in the city. Their everyday
interactions produce the social structure of city life and indicate ways in
which youth 'make the city'. Their experience of a good life in the city
largely depends on a sense of community and free mobility. Hence, their
ability to successfully evade or contest identity checks and other confron-
tations with the authorities contributes to the quality of their city lives and
their sense of belonging within the city, indicating what a 'livable' city
might mean for them. Those who lack 'linking social capital', and who do
not have direct access to institutional governance procedures, engage in
informal practices to gain space and respect in the city. In this light, the
evasion of police interactions, but also the direct contestation of the police
in case youth feel unjustly treated, could be seen as 'everyday acts of resistance', or instances of micropolitics, through which young people that are

not well connected to established institutions or governance partnerships may express their engagement, raise their voice and gain empowerment (Kaulingfreks 2015; Rios 2011, pp. 116–117).

With Lefebvre, we can understand the city as a meeting point for building collective life. Not all young inhabitants of the *banlieues* might take part in formal governance arrangements, but they do shape the city in their everyday social interactions. As much as they make the city, the city makes them. It shapes their identity and it is the place where they find shelter in the communities that make them feel at home. The collective life they build on the streets of their neighborhoods suggest new ways in which the city might be used and navigated, other than those intended by architects and city planners. Hence, their everyday practices could be seen as ways to make the city livable according to their particular needs and wishes. These are often the needs and wishes that are overlooked by policy makers and professional city planners.

13.3.3   Bridging a Gap Between 'Governing the City' and 'Making the City': The Role of Associations

We have seen that some youths contribute to 'governing' their cities, while others 'make' their cities in everyday social interactions. Many young people feel that their interests are not sufficiently advocated for within formal governance arrangements, and they find themselves at a distance of governing the city, while they do have clear ideas about how to improve life in their city. In order to reach more inclusive urban decision making processes, the informal ways in which youth participate in making the city deserve more attention. Associations often play a role in connecting youths to institutions and in bridging the gap between those who 'govern' the city through formal institutions and those who 'make' the city through daily practices.

Local associations traditionally play a significant role in French neighborhoods. Also for youths growing up in the *banlieues* there are many associations that aim to provide a variety of services. The people working for these associations range from sport teachers to trained social workers, self-employed youth workers and volunteers. Many of these associations started as grassroots initiatives, initiated bottom up by residents who then became local professionals. Most of them are officially registered and have a core professional team consisting of at least two people. Apart from most of the local social centers and youth centers, the majority of associations is not initiated by the municipality, although the municipality sometimes (structurally or incidentally) financially supports them. At first glance, most associations seem to simply offer fun, leisure time activities for youth, from hiphop dance classes to making music or just hanging out and playing video games. For many of these associations, however, there is a deeper social and pedagogical significance to their work. It is not only about having fun, but even more so about learning about life.

> *My first battle, my first fight is to explain how hiphop is really important finally in the life of... like we say in French la vie quartier, la vie banlieue (neighborhood life, banlieue life). [...] And this is why my fight is to explain that hiphop is not just dance but that it's a culture with some important things. Which is unity, sharing, love, and respect. [...] Values, but not only values. Values and also actions.* (T., head of a youth association)

> *Our work is about prevention. It's to prevent, it's to advice. It's to show the possibility of a different direction to young people, for certain. To choose: if you choose this, you will end up badly, if you choose that, you will move out of it.* (M., head of a youth association)

Associations try to provide the social services and guidance that are often missing in the lives of these youths growing up in the *banlieue*. Many young people grow up in large households with parents working around the clock to make a living, and do not have a trusted relationship with teachers at school. At the associations, they can discuss their everyday hopes, fears and challenges with adults who can serve as accessible role models. The associations also offer safe spaces, free of charge, where young people can socialize in the evenings, instead of spending time out on the streets.

> *Young people do not meet others. The youths are always alone. What is needed is the encounter with others [...] there is a need to develop spaces to talk. We talk about everything and nothing. Soccer, we talk about work, racism, the future, the relationships between boys and girls, the police, we talk about everything.* (M., head of a youth association)

> *What we want to teach them, we do mostly in the camps. [...] What I think our youths lack, unfortunately, is a bit the know-how. I mean really how do I position myself in society. And the codes of that society that they haven't mastered*

really well. The camps is a bit that, that side. We live together, there are rules to respect, there is a schedule. (R., head of a youth association)

The municipality also provides for support and social services, such as the youth employment center, and the youth information point where youths can get legal counselling or information about housing and activities in their neighborhood. However, many people working for the municipality and associations, as well as youths themselves, describe a difficult-to-bridge distance between those institutional services and the everyday lives of youths in the neighborhood.

> *More and more, especially in the [town's] north, there are youths that are completely distant from institutions.* (B., works at one of the municipality's social centers)

> *That is also one of the problems we have. Especially between youths and the institutions. There is some sort of rupture. A rupture between youths and institutions, with a climate of distrust. [...] The youths don't believe in institutions because they say they are discriminating, they don't take me into account, they don't listen, they don't understand us. And also vice versa sometimes the institutions have a cliché attitude and hold prejudices towards the youth.* (M., works at one of the municipality's youth services)

The associations describe themselves as being a bridge between youths and the more formal institutions. These institutions cannot reach youths, and thus cannot teach them vital life lessons. So these associations function as a mediator and a more trusted source of guidance for youngsters. At times they support youth by simply 'being there', spending time with them and listening to their stories, at times they use their established rapport to give them advice on important personal issues, and sometimes they guide them towards formal institutions like the employment service.

> *It's called a street visit. And I do it in a rather informal way, but that's important, yes it's to show that we have a presence in the neighborhood.* (R., head of a youth association)

> *Youths do not always go to the institutions. If they don't go, it is up to us to go and find them, and bring them along with us afterwards. [...] We come to them, and bring them to the institutions. We do mediation.* (M., head of a youth association)

We are not a youth employment center, we are not a youth information point, we are not all that. We are just the link between the youths and the institutions that are already there and that function well. That's it. (R., head of a youth association)

The municipality actively aims to work in 'proximity': to be close to the everyday lives of young citizens. However, it remains difficult for the more formalized institutions, like a youth information point, to have an out-reaching function in the neighborhood. To establish a relationship of trust it helps to be an 'insider' in the community of the neighborhood, which is emphasized both by people working at youth associations and at the municipal services.

It is because I am, like the people here, also from the banlieue. That's maybe the thing that makes that I can say it like it is. (R., head of a youth association)

We discover the problems from inside the neighborhood, bit by bit, by living with the people as neighbors, creating connections in a quite informal and natural way. (L., head of an association)

I have a bit of an atypical life story. So what I can do is tell my story [of how I got where I am now]. So when I tell them [youths] my story they say ok, alright, so it is possible. (S., head of a municipal youth service)

It's a plus [that I am from the banlieue]. People sometimes feel they confide in me a bit more. (I., works at an association)

The relationship between youth and associations is often characterized by the proximity that the municipality aims for, but finds difficult to establish. People who work for associations can reach youths because they are close to them: because of their shared life history or *banlieue* background and their informal, familiar and accessible way of providing guidance and services within the context of fun activities.

The successful role that associations play in reaching youths is crucial in our understanding of how more inclusive partnerships of governance could be build. Where other studies emphasize a bridging role for professionals guiding urban renewal processes, by 'civilizing', 'activating' and 'empowering' citizens (Duyvendak et al. 2009, p. 18), our study adds to that in two ways. First, we argue that not only professionals but even more so volunteers and residents involved in associational life play a crucial role in articulating the ideas and activities of (other) residents to institutional levels. They can thereby contribute to the 'voicing' of the experiences, dreams and concerns which young people have regarding the quality of life in their neighborhood, and engage in informal and semi-formal advocacy in relation to government institutions. This claim is supported by Dutch research indicating how informal parties, such as volunteers, active residents and members of neighborhood initiatives, offer assistance to citizens who do not reach or trust institutions (Welschen 2019). Second, we stress that associations play a key role exactly because they do not aim to 'activate' youths, but because they connect with the already existing agency and activities of youths and acknowledge non-traditional ways of (political) engagement.

Civil youth participation is often understood in formal terms; as voting, starting a petition, participating in a co-creation session, setting up an association, demonstrating, taking a seat in a youth council. These are the best known and acknowledged activities in which citizens may engage to impact and revitalize their city, to make a change. However, youths growing up in the *banlieues* also strive for social change in other ways, outside of the institutional procedures they distrust or experience as alienating. Associations could help youth to take a step from expressing their engagement in everyday practices and social interactions to gaining influence on urban decision making, because they have insight in both processes of governing ánd making the city. Partnerships for urban governance in which youth participate should take into account the historically constructed distrust between youths and formal institutions. They have a better chance at becoming inclusive and successful if urban decision making is not confined to 'the well delimited space of the political' (Dikeç 2007, p. 147). If we wish to overcome existing democratic deficits and wish to pursue truly participatory urban governance, the informal ways in which youth choose to express their citizenship should not be disregarded.

13.4   Conclusion

Livability is not a neutral concept. In this chapter we have explored the livable city as a city that is livable also for youths and also in marginalized urban areas. Zooming in on the case of youths growing up in the French *banlieues*, we have shed light on the ways in which groups that are often underrepresented in partnerships for urban governance make the city livable according to their own terms and interests. We have illustrated how youths often express their civil engagement at a micropolitical level in everyday activities and establish a sense of belonging to the city through informal processes of place-making. For many youths, this is rooted in distrust of authorities, feelings of being unjustly treated by the forces of order, or the experience of institutional governance as inaccessible. For others, because they simply voice their ideas about the city in non-traditional ways. They not only 'govern' their city via formalized partnerships, but also 'make' the city in informal daily practices and social interactions.

To bridge the gap between 'making the city' and 'governing the city', we argue for a shift from 'activating' youths to participate in formal processes or partnerships for urban governance to exploring how youths are already active in making their cities a good place to live, not only for a 'participation-elite' but also for marginalized populations in deprived urban areas. In that regard, we suggest that institutional partners may engage in partnerships with both youth and associations, since associations do not try to 'activate' youths, but build on the activities that youths already engage in, connect to the ways in which youth already navigate their urban lives, and aim to reinforce the community structures that are already in place in the neighborhood. Exploring the activities that youths take to 'make the city', this chapter teaches us not only that youths can be vital actors in partnerships for livable cities, but even more so how these partnerships can be effective and legitimate from the perspective of marginalized urban youths.

References

Body-Gendrot, S. (2010). Police marginality, racial logics and discrimination in the banlieues of France. *Ethnic and Racial Studies, 33*(4), 656–674.

Brandsen, T., Trommel, W., & Verschuere, B. (2017). The state and the reconstruction of civil society. *International Review of Administrative Sciences, 83*(4), 676–693.

Cassiers, T., & Kesteloot, C. (2012). Socio-spatial inequalities and social cohesion in European cities. *Urban Studies, 49*(9), 1909–1924.

Conger, B. (2015). On livability, liveability and the limited utility of quality-of-life rankings. *SPP Research Paper, 7*(4).

Délégation Interministérielle à la ville. (2000). *The French Urban Regeneration Programme, a new objective for towns and cities.* http://www.ville.gouv.fr/IMG/pdf/regeneration_cle7ba1cc.pdf. Accessed 1 Oct 2019.

Dikeç, M. (2007). *Badlands of the republic, space, politics, and urban policy.* Oxford: Blackwell Publishing.

Dikeç, M. (2017). *Urban Rage, the revolt of the excluded.* Yale: Yale University Press.

Duyvendak, J. W., Hendriks, F., & van Niekerk, M. (Eds.). (2009). *City in sight, Dutch dealings with urban change.* Amsterdam: Amsterdam University Press.

Elwood, S. (2004). Partnerships and participation: Reconfiguring urban governance in different state contexts. *Urban Geography, 25*(8), 755–770.

Enright, T. (2013). Illuminating the path to grand pari(s): Architecture and urban transformation in an era of neoliberalization. *Antipode, 46*(2), 382–403.

Farthing, R. (2010). The politics of youthful antipolitics: Representing the 'issue' of youth participation in politics. *Journal of Youth Studies, 3*(2), 181–195.

Florida, R. (2002). *The rise of the creative class and how it's transforming work, leisure, community and everyday life.* New York: Basic Books.

Foo, K., Martin, D., Polsky, C., Wool, C., & Ziemer, M. (2015). Social well-being and environmental governance in urban neighbourhoods in Boston, MA. *The Geographical Journal, 181*(2), 138–146.

Glaeser, E. (2012). *Triumph of the city: How urban spaces make us human.* London: Pan Macmillan.

Global Liveability Index. https://www.eiu.com/topic/liveability. Accessed 1 Oct 2019.

Harvey, D. (2008). The right to the city. *New Left Review, 53*, 23–40.

Huang, S. L. (2010). The impact of public participation on the effectiveness of, and users' attachment to, urban neighbourhood parks. *Landscape Research, 35*(5), 551–562.

INSEE. (2017). *La population de la Seine-Saint-Denis à l'horizon 2050.* https://www.insee.fr/fr/statistiques/3277148. Accessed: 1 Oct 2019.

Kaal, H. (2011). A conceptual history of livability. *City, 15*(5), 532–547.

Kaulingfreks, F. (2015). *Uncivil engagement and unruly politics.* Basingstoke: Palgrave Macmillan.

Kaulingfreks, F. (2016). Senseless violence or unruly politics? The uncivil revolt of young rioters. *Krisis, Journal for Contemporary Philosophy, 2*(1), 4–21.

Koppenjan, F. M., & Enserink, B. (2009). Public-private partnerships in urban infrastructures: Reconciling private sector participation and sustainability. *Public Administration Review, 69*(2), 284–296.

Lefebvre, H. ([1974] 1991). *The production of space* (Nicholson-Smith, Trans.). Malden: Blackwell Publisher.

Lloyd, K., Fullagar, S., & Reid, S. (2016). Where is the 'social' in constructions of 'liveability'? Exploring community, social interaction and social cohesion in changing urban environments. *Urban Policy and Research, 34*(4), 343–355.

Michels, A. (2012). Citizen participation in local policy making: Design and democracy. *International Journal of Public Administration, 5*(4), 285–292.

Musterd, S., Murie, A., & Kesteloot, C. (2006). *Neighbourhoods of poverty: Urban social exclusion and integration in comparison.* London: Macmillan.

Nabielek, K., Hamers, D., & Evers, D. (2016). *Cities in Europe, facts and figures on cities and urban areas.* The Hague: PBL Netherlands Environmental Assessment Agency.

PBL. (2016). *De verdeelde triomf. Verkenning van stedelijk-economische ongelijkheid en opties voor beleid. Ruimtelijke Verkenningen 2016.* Den Haag: Planbureau voor de Leefomgeving.

Rios, V. (2011). *Punished: Policing the lives of black and Latino boys.* New York: New York University Press.

Rodríguez-Pose, A. (2018). The revenge of the places that don't matter (and what to do about it). *Cambridge Journal of Regions, Economy and Society, 11*(1), 189–209.

Ruth, M., & Franklin, R. S. (2014). Livability for all? Conceptual limits and practical implications. *Applied Geography, 1*(49), 18–23.

Schneider, C. L. (2008). Police power and race riots in Paris. *Politics and Society, 36*(1), 133–159.

Sennett, R. (2018). *Building and dwelling, ethics for the city.* London: Penguin Books Ltd..

Slooter, L. (2015). *The making of the banlieue, an ethnography of space, identity and violence.* Doctoral dissertation, Utrecht University, Utrecht.

Slooter, L., & Diphoorn, T. (2016). Introduction: The contested making of the city. *Etnofoor, 28*(2), 7–11.

Swyngedouw, E. (2005). Governance innovation and the citizen: The Janus face of governance-beyond-the-state. *Urban Studies, 42*(11), 1991–2006.

United Nations Human Settlements Programme. (2013). *State of the world's cities 2012/2013, prosperity of cities.* New York: Routledge.

Van de Wetering, S. A. L. (2017). Stigmatization and the social construction of a normal identity in the Parisian banlieue. *Geoforum.* https://doi.org/10.1016/j.geoforum.2017.05.009.

Van Gent, W. P. C., Musterd, S., & Ostendorf, W. (2009). Disentangling neighbourhood problems: Area-based interventions in Western European cities. *Urban Research & Practice, 2*(1), 53–67.

Veenhoven, R. (2000). *Leefbaarheid: Betekenissen en meetmethoden.* Ministerie van VWZ. http://repub.eur.nl/res/pub/8786. Accessed 1 Oct 2019.

Wacquant, L. (2008). *Urban outcasts: A comparative sociology of advanced marginality.* Cambridge: Polity Press.

Website conseils citoyens. https://www.conseilscitoyens.fr/. Accessed 1 Oct 2019.

Welschen, S. (2019). *Informele partijen zijn hulpverleningsgids voor wantrouwende Amsterdammers.* https://www.socialevraagstukken.nl/informele-partijen-zijn-hulpverleningsgids-voor-wantrouwende-amsterdammers/?fbclid=IwAR3xn6E fjLYr31HMdy8fTed1rOoFNX6d3n79d8dYUmnpcjQR2iCdrzk-FzAE. Accessed 1 Oct 2019.

CHAPTER 14

The Effectiveness, Legitimacy and Robustness of Hybrid Livability Governance: The Case of Quartiersmanagement in Berlin

Niels Karsten, Carlo Maria Colombo, and Linze Schaap

14.1   Introduction

The effectiveness, legitimacy and robustness of governance arrangements has been subject to critiques in various professional and scientific debates (Mike 2003; Rhodes 2007). Key points in these discussions are the roles and responsibilities of different actors, in relation to the effectiveness and legitimacy of partnerships and their outcomes. In response to such

N. Karsten (✉)
Tilburg Law School, Tilburg University, Tilburg, The Netherlands
e-mail: n.karsten@uvt.nl

C. M. Colombo (✉)
Faculty of Law, Maastricht University, Maastricht, The Netherlands
e-mail: Carlo.colombo@maastrichtuniversity.nl

L. Schaap
Northern Audit Office, Assen, The Netherlands
e-mail: l.schaap@noordelijkerekenkamer.nl

© The Author(s) 2020
C. van Montfort, A. Michels (eds.), *Partnerships for Livable Cities*,
https://doi.org/10.1007/978-3-030-40060-6_14

critiques, in 1999, the German federal government developed the 'Socially integrative city' program, which is a prime example of a more hybrid form of governance focusing on the collaboration between governments, the private sector, and civil society partners (see also Battilana et al. 2017; Denis et al. 2015). Within the program, the Land Berlin has become one of the most active partners (BMVBS 2008; Eick 2011). The main objective of this ongoing EU-funded program is to stabilize and improve socially, economically and physically disadvantaged urban districts by investing in public infrastructures, spaces and neighborhoods. In particular, it aims at counteracting the growing socio-spatial polarization and fostering integrated stabilization and development in areas with special social integration needs (SSU 2014). One of the core features of the program is a system of *Quartiersmanagement* (QM) where, under supervision of the Land Berlin, private companies develop and implement public policies in conjunction with neighborhood residents and civil society organizations. In particular, through a model of public procurement, the public administration externalizes to private subcontractors the task of developing and implementing local development plans as well as to enable citizens' participation to this purpose. The latter implies that local residents and stakeholders can actively participate in the development of their neighborhoods either by proposing or by selecting projects in local councils. As such, the QM model is an illustrative example of 'hybrid governance' since it combines state, market, and civil society logics in the development and implementation of policies (Battilana et al. 2017; Harrison and Hoyler 2014; Skelcher and Smith 2015), with the aim of fostering the livability of urban neighborhoods.

In this contribution, we evaluate the effectiveness, legitimacy and robustness of the QM governance model, focusing on a specific case: the redevelopment of the inner-city Wiesenburg area. In our analysis, this case provides an illustrative example of some of the challenges that are produced by hybrid governance. It represents a typical combination of seemingly incompatible logics, which may very well weaken the effective governance of livability (see also Battilana et al. 2017; Morrison et al. 2012). Our analysis is based on 15 interviews with representatives from the actors involved, document analysis, non-participatory observation, as well as a two-day interactive workshop with local stakeholders from the Senat, the Bezirk, QM, and neighborhood residents. The ambition of this workshop was to stimulate common reflection on the concrete and contemporary governance challenges that participants were dealing with as regards hybridity on a day-to-day basis. The workshop consisted of various researcher-designed sessions using different discussion techniques, including a field visit and dilemma co-exploration, rich picture, world café, visioning and action list session (see also Blackmore et al. 2016), each of which invited the participants to reflect on the role of QM and the effectiveness, legitimacy and robustness of the governance model as expressed in the Wiesenburg case. Data was collected between 2016 and 2017.

14.2   The Neighborhood Management Model

In the post-war period, German national policies towards the welfare state tried to solve the social question by providing housing to the working class (Reinprecht and Levy-Vroelant 2008). As a consequence of the movements against the establishment in the late 60s, urban regeneration as the mere remaking of the existing city came under pressure (Droste et al. 2008). The previous top-down reconstruction policy was replaced by the provision of social infrastructures focused on popular demand and social needs. After Germany's reunification, the city of Berlin saw a new, social form of separation (URBACT 2008). Because of social problems related to poverty and inflow migration, the Berlin Senate decided in 1999 to start the integrated program called 'Socially integrated City' ('*Stadtteile mit besonderem Entwicklungsbedarf—die soziale Stadt*'), which involved the creation of the neighborhood management. Its main objective is to stabilize and improve socially, economically and physically disadvantaged urban districts by investing in public infrastructure, public space and neighborhoods. In particular, the program aims at counteracting the growing socio-spatial polarization and to foster integrated stabilization and development in areas with special social integration needs (SSU 2014). Therefore, local activities are supported and citizens of the districts are involved in the project management. Also, the policy is temporal by nature: once questions of gentrification and polarization in a specific area are resolved, there is no need to further fund interventions for neighborhood improvement. At the beginning, only fifteen areas, selected based on demographic and economic criteria, were involved. Over time, the scope of the project and the areas has undergone several changes. Most notably, the Federal government ended its co-financing, so the Berlin Senate and the EU (ERDF funds) now fund the program.

From a legal perspective, the model falls within the participatory procedures set up to involve social actors. In particular, this model adds a participatory element to the general principle of representative democracy, which is laid down in most of the Land constitutions and implies that decisions at local level are taken by democratically elected institutions. The Senate of Berlin determines the neighborhood area, in which measures of the QM shall be undertaken, in cooperation with the concerned district and other stakeholders on the basis of a development concept (§ 171e III, IV, 137, *139* Baugesetzbuch, § 29b Gesetz zur Ausführung des Baugesetzbuches). The measures in the so-determined neighborhoods are then financially supported, pursuant to Art. 171e VI, 164a, b Baugesetzbuch. This specific participatory model of the Berlin's QM is thus based upon the commitment by the politics and administration to delegate the decision-making process partly to the citizens. It was a decision of the Senate department of urban development in 2005 to join this method of decision making by empowering and encouraging the residents (bottom up).

One of the characteristic aspects in the *Soziale Stadt* policy is the governance approach followed to take decisions. Under the QM model, citizens and private companies co-decide, together with the Senate, on projects to be financed within the program. To enable this co-decision-making, the QM model uses public procurement procedures to select a QM company. This is a private law company hired by the Senate to run the making and implementation of urban development plans at a neighborhood level of a specific area. To this purpose, each QM company employs a QM team, consisting of professionals specialized in urban development. As such, the QM teams act in the QM model as promoters of new initiatives, as well as mediators with the actors (public and private) in the area.

The model, thus, rests on the logic of market competition for developing policies that are commonly seen as being public. But, there is also a hierarchical logic to the model since private companies decide on public policies as subcontractor of the state. As such, the Berlin's QM may be considered as a model of hybrid governance to the extent that its decision-making combines hierarchical instruments and governmental institutions with non-state actors (civil society and professionals) and typical market mechanisms (Battilana et al. 2017; Denis et al. 2015). One of the main drivers behind hybridity in this case was that it enables metropolitan government authorities, of which the Senate is the most important here, to hire people with an expertise in citizen participation and neighborhood management that it cannot offer itself. Quartiersmanagers are seen to be better equipped to develop urban development plans for the neighborhood bottom up and with the close involvement of neighborhood residents.

Several actors are involved in the QM decision-making, which consists of several phases. The first step involves developing and approving an integrated concept for the area, named 'Integrated action and development plan' (*Entwicklungskonzept* (IHEK)). With the involvement of the main stakeholders in the neighborhood, this strategy is developed by the local Quartiersmanagers and details the main ideas and projects that will be implemented in the area during the following two years. After being approved by the *Quartiersrat,* local development strategy does form the basis upon which all projects can be developed. The second step entails the selection of the projects. These include small-scale local urban development initiatives such as the building of a playground, neighborhood embellishments and events aimed at improving the local social cohesion. Depending on the available funds, one could distinguish between few governance mechanisms to approve and finance projects. Civic involvement in the respective areas mainly happens through the Action Fund Jury (*Aktionsfondsjury*) or through the Neighborhood Council (*Quartiersrat*). The former is composed by neighborhood representatives, who are directly elected by neighborhood residents in informal and open election, that decide (with a three-quarters majority) over grants on small-scale projects (€10.000 budget which can be used for short-term projects up to €1500), whilst the latter consists of people living/working in the area (51%) and of other stakeholders (49%) and selects projects starting from €5.000. The Neighborhood Council decisions are then submitted to the steering committee (*Steuerungsrunde*), a body consisting of representative of the *Senatsverwaltung* and district administration, a team member of the QM and often a member of the *Quartiersrat.* Within the steering committee, the proposals are discussed and the decisions on the grants are taken. The decision is ultimately passed by the *Bezirk* administration—*Bezirksamt* -, which is legally responsible for the project. The Action Fund Jury, Neighborhood Council and Action Fund Jury decision-making processes, thus, represent informal mechanisms (i.e., with no official legal form) of citizens participation in the QM decision-making process that are used to prepare relevant project for the areas. The basic idea, though, is one of co-creation between state, market and civil society actors.

The ambition of the QM model is to also incorporate the strong partners in the area (*Partner der Quartiersentwicklung*), including housing associations, neighbourhood centres, schools and local businesses that operate in the QM area. The development of strong partnerships is an important element of the QM, both in the areas of intervention and prevention. The underpinning logic is that, if the stabilization and improvement processes of the QM are indeed to achieve long-term and lasting effects, the institutions or companies present in the area must be integrated into the neighbourhood development process at an early stage. To this purpose, the system aims to mobilize the available financial and human resources in relation to the development of the neighbourhood, and to jointly develop and implement corresponding measures and projects in close cooperation with strong partners. Although these partners are not directly involved in the decision-making within the Action Fund Juries or Neighborhood Councils, the Quartiersmanagers play an important role in connecting these organizations and coordinating actions between them, also in connection to the integrated action and development plans.

The basic idea, though, is one of co-creation between state, market and civil society actors. In its design, the QM model can, thus, be positioned near the center of triangle of forms of governance that was introduced in the opening chapter of this book. And, since there is an ambition in the governance regime to contract out the making of 'public' urban development plans to private actors, one could argue that, in essence, the model is meant to represent a partnership between civil society and private organizations. Figure 14.1 illustrates this position of the QM model in the triangle.

Fig. 14.1 The position of the QM model in the triangle state-market-civil society

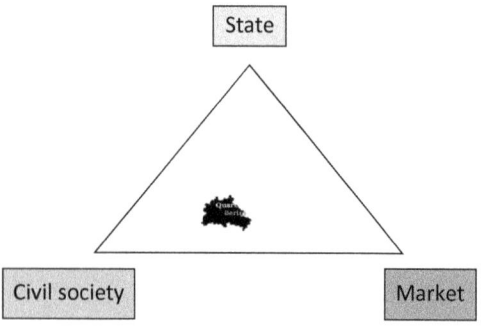

14.3 THE WIESENBURG CASE AS 'AMPLIFIER' OF HYBRID GOVERNANCE'S CHALLENGES

In this chapter, we evaluate the workings of the QM model by evaluating the governance interactions in the specific case of *Wiesenburg*. This case concerns the redevelopment of a historical place, located in the district of *Wedding*, into a residence area. Although this research approach may seem to be quite idiosyncratic since we focus on one particular case one, we are convinced that the role conflicts for Quartiersmanagers that we find in this case are not restricted to the Wiesenburg case as such, but they are indicative of the governance model in general, as they are an outcome of the various and conflicting logics of coordination operating therein.

The Wiesenburg area is situated in the neighborhood of Reinickendorfer Strasse/Pankstrasse in the district of Wedding. This neighborhood has a heterogeneous building structure. Even though there are a few compact sections of Wilhelminian-style buildings, the larger part of the area is characterized by a mixture of old and new buildings, as well as of residential and business premises. The area is cut across by large public highways and the circular S-Bahn, so that it is not possible to properly define where the actual center of the area is located. Many of the residents have a migration background, and social facilities and schools are facing various challenges in their integration efforts. Given the high level of migration and of poor residents, the area has been included among the assisted areas of the program since its very beginning in 1999. The QM Reinickendorfer Strasse/Pankstrasse is run by 'L.i.s.t. Gmbh', a private QM company that at the time ran three assisted areas in the district of Wedding. In addition to the predefined fields of intervention involving integration and participation, the QM is dedicated to improving the living environment and the overall image of the neighborhood (Photo 14.1).

The specific case of Wiesenburg concerns the redevelopment of a historical place into a residence area. At the time of our research, in 2016 and 2017, the condition of the Wiesenburg area was directly connected to its ownership and utilization, which have changed significantly over the years. Since the end of the nineteenth century, private entrepreneurs developed buildings in the area to be used as shelters for homeless. After the Second World War, the family owners converted the Wiesenburg into a place for housing, as well as for culture, art and film production. In particular, the 'Berlin Asylum Association for the Homeless', which was reactivated in 1961, became the legal successor of the original founding association and

Photo 14.1 Wiesenburg

managed the property until 2005. However, after a long judicial litigation over the ownership of the land, the association was recognized as a non-profit organization and could not use the area freely anymore. This is because the conditions for the use of the area were deemed to be changed, since its previous use as shelter for homeless ceased. As a consequence, the district court declared the state of Berlin as the owner of the area.

On 1 November 2014, the area was then transferred by State of Berlin to 'Degewo AG', a private-law housing company that is fully owned by the Berlin Senate, by way of an ownership agreement. This event has altered the equilibrium of the area. Following its mandate, Degewo AG planned to develop a housing complex, a project that is at odds with the interests of the current residents (a group of artists represented by the association 'The Wiesenburg e.V.') to preserve the place as it stands now. To find a balance among these conflicting interests, there have been numerous negotiations between the residents, Degewo AG, and the administration. The residents have specifically asked the QM of Reinickendorfer Strasse/Pankstrasse to assist them in their negotiation with Degewo AG, in order to find a common solution for the redevelopment of the area. In particular, the residents and the QM support the preservation of the current utilization as cultural and artistic place available to the inhabitants of the neighborhood, while limiting the housing complex to a restricted part of the Wiesenburg.

The discussion between the stakeholders has led to a number of workshops organized by the housing company. During these events, architects were requested to develop an urban development concept for the area which was evaluated by a panel of experts (consisting of 5 members of Degewo AG within its own architect, and 6 consultants for the residents and the QM company). In addition, the issue has been repeatedly discussed during the district council (*Bezirksverordnetenversammlungen*, BVV) with political representatives. However, the negotiation process has not yet led to a shared conclusion, an impasse that could prompt Degewo AG to take decisions on its own in the near future.

At the time of our research, we evaluated the workings of the QM model in this case by focusing on the role of the Quartiersmanagers. In particular, in interviews, and throughout our two-day workshop we focused on the role conflict that the Quartiersmanagers experiences as they were in the center of this hybrid governance model. The focus, thus, was not on the decision-making process around the redevelopment of the Wiesenburg area itself or on the overt conflict between stakeholders, which was the result of that. Rather, we focused on the challenges of hybrid governance, as they were experience by the Quartiersmanagers. This is because they found themselves, and their policies, being caught up between the interests of their commissioning body, the Senate, which supported the building of apartments in the Wiesenburg area, on the one hand, and the interests of some the neighborhood residents that they were supposed to support and represent and who opposed the redevelopment initiative on the other. In essence, the Quartiersmanagers were caught between two fires and experienced role conflicts in negotiating the various interests that they represented, which we stakeholders collectively reflected on in the workshop.

One of the main role conflicts was that, for Quartiersmanagers, it was not always clear whom to represent and whose interest to serve, not only in the Wiesenburg case, but also more broadly. This was because, in the hybrid governance regime that they were in, QM has to fulfill multiple and contradictory assignments at the same time: as a subcontractor of the Senate, it served they interest of the state, but it also had the tasks of formulating and representing the interests of the neighborhood residents. 'In essence, Quartiersmanagers belong to no one', one participant observed in a workshop discussion, flagging the fact that the position of Quartiersmanagers in the local hybrid governance constellation is difficult to pin down. This complexity became notoriously difficult to manage when the two interpretations of what the public interest became as different from each other as in the case of Wiesenburg.

Our interviews and the workshop discussions indicate that there are at least two reasons of why these role conflicts emerged in the case of Wiesenburg. First, there is a more institutional dimension to the complexity of Quartiermanagers' position that was the direct result of their 'hybrid' role in the local governance model. As a market party, they had the responsibility of connecting the interests of the state to the interests of neighborhood residents and the civil society. But, where, on paper, the QM model represents a regime of co-creation between state, market and civil society actors, the actual governance practices were much more guided by hierarchy. This is because, in the way it operates, the public procurement model induces conformity on the part of the Quartiersmanagers, who act as subcontractors of the Senate, and allows the Senate to precisely determine and also monitor the activities of the Quartiersmanagers. Our interviews indicate that the latter experience a strong 'shadow of hierarchy' (see also Levelt and Metze 2014), where Quartiersmanagers act as the long arm of the state. In the *Steuerungsrunde*, for example, the public actors were very much dominant since they continued to control the formal decision-making power as well as the finances. The private-market logic of subcontracting may even strengthen this element of hierarchy as compared to the discretion that street-level bureaucrats have in public organizations (Bovens and Zouridis 2002). The creation of discretion for Quartiersmanagers, thus, does not seem to have been one of the main reasons for choosing this particular hybrid governance model in which private companies perform the task of neighborhood management. Instead, one of the more prominent motivations for the use of a public procurement model seems to have been to provide neighborhood management with some welcomed operational flexibility in terms of, e.g., employment contracts, insurance, working outside of office hours and the like. In addition, the expertise of Quartiersmanagers is not always used to its full potential beyond the urban development plans. Interviews indicate, for example, that Quartiersmanagers feel frustrated with the fact that the Senate has developed guidelines for citizen's participation in policy-making without making use of their knowledge and experience. Here, the logic of procurement, where Quartiersmanagers are subcontractors of the Senate, thus, conflicted with the logic of political representation, where Quartiersmanagers acted in the interests of the neighborhood and its citizens.

In practice, rather than representing a case of partnerships between civil society and private organizations in the center of the triangle, the QM model, in the experience of those involved, functioned much more as a state-controlled public-private partnership in which civil society had a limited role to play. The QM model, thus, clearly illustrates that the introduction of hybrid governance in the form of a procurement procedure, which very much resonates the private logic of competition, does not necessarily take away and may even strengthen the logic of hierarchy. In other words, the logic of public hierarchy evidently suppressed the hybrid nature of the governance model. Figure 14.2 illustrates this in-practice position of the QM model in the triangle.

Second, as indicated by our interviews and workshop discussion, the role complexities that the Quartiersmanagers experienced in the Wiesenburg case were also the results of the roles and identities that the

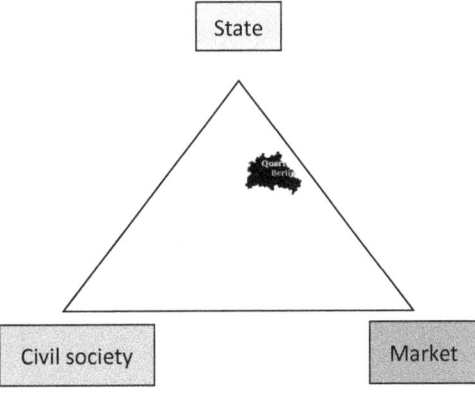

Fig. 14.2 The in-practice position of the QM model in the triangle

Quartiersmanagers took up themselves over the course of the process. These were of a particularly hybrid nature too (see also Denis et al. 2015), which added to the role conflicts that they experienced.

Originally, one of the main aims of QM was to set up and organize an infrastructure for citizen participation in the area. This can be described as a role that is relatively 'neutral', in the sense of being a-political, as it aimed to inform residents about its existence, to identify and mobilize active citizens and to establish channels of communication between citizens, the *Bezirk* and the Senate. Over time, and as the infrastructure for participation became more well-established, QM however took on a more autonomous and more political role in the sense that it developed and advocated its own vision for the area as it was developed in cooperation with local residents.

In the case of Wiesenburg, this evolution is all the more evident. In the analysis of the majority of our respondents, over the course of the process, the Quartiersmanagers involved came to identifying themselves more and more with the perspective of the people who lived on the Wiesenburg estate and took on the role of defending the latter's interests. 'It is our task to activate neighborhood residents and to develop special locations in the area also in cooperation with the residents and also with house- and land-owners' (Quartiersmanager).[1]

Starting out from their role of more neutral 'citizen empowers', in the analysis of our respondents and to the dislike of some of the other partners in the area, Quartiersmanagers in the Wiesenburg case may have sided too strongly with the neighborhood residents. In the experience of others, QM acted as a promotor of particular neighborhood citizens' interests and, consequently, found itself in conflict with the housing ambitions of its commissioning body, that is the Berlin Senate. As a result, it became more and more impossible for Quartiersmanagers at this point to function as a neutral facilitator of the participation process. In part, this situation was the result of how the Quartiersmanagers positioned themselves in the conflict between the housing company and the Senate, on the one hand, and the neighborhood residents, on the other. This is also something that our Quartiersmanagement respondents reflected on explicitly in our workshop discussions; they too recognized that they have become too

---

[1] 'Wir sind halt ein Quartier, wir haben die Aufgabe, die Leute vor Ort zu aktivieren und auch die besonderen Standorte auch zu entwickeln und teils auch die mit den Bewohnern und auch mit den Eigentümern weiter zu entwickeln.'

partisan to fulfil effectively the role that Quartiersmanagers are expected to take. There is, thus, a strong personal dimension to this complexity.

At the same time, these conflicting identifications, in part, seem to have been the result also of the hybrid position Quartiersmanagers are in as a consequence of how the governance model is designed. This is because, whereas Quartiersmanagers are in fact private companies and compete in commercial tender procedures, which indicate to a private organizational form and organizational logic of the governance arrangement, their role is in the governance arrangement is very much public one. This results from the fact that the Senate has tendered out the task of making a public policy of the area to its private subcontractors, which clearly illustrates the hybrid nature of the urban development plans. As a result, the public identity of Quartiersmanagers often clashes with their role as private subcontractors of the Senate, causing perceived role conflicts and frustration.

14.4 Effectiveness, Legitimacy and Robustness

In full recognition of the limitations of our study, in the current paragraph, we evaluate the effectiveness, legitimacy and robustness of the Berlin QM model, with a particular focus on the Wiesenburg case.

14.4.1 Effectiveness

In fact, effectiveness remains one of the main points debated in relation to Berlin's QM model. On the one hand, some authors observe that the neighborhood management has been able to outcompete the state and the commercial sphere by policy-making 'below the state' in the labor market (re)integration (Eick 2011). In addition, by concentrating on qualitative problems, the system has led housing companies to support it as a long-term investment (Ewert and Evers 2013), and the same approach has been supported by planners attempting to change the patterns of urban revitalization (OECD 2003; Penta 2007). On the other hand, the major criticism is against both the scope of activity and the criteria upon which the project is built. In particular, one of QM's core challenges is its strict territorially-bound organization. Although there are possibilities to develop, through the network fund, projects in adjoining neighborhoods, QM is not allowed to act beyond the geographical borders of its neighborhoods. Some of the problems that QM aims to address, however, do transgress these boarders. Inhabitants of a QM area can easily move and relocate in other urban areas, especially in the case—as is currently the case in the metropolitan area of Berlin—raising housing and living costs force underprivileged citizens to move to the suburbs. This type of inner city migration, which crosses the boundaries of the QM, may lead to gentrification effects, which makes it difficult for QM to address individual people's problems in the longer term (see also Gualini and Fricke 2019). While improved indicators lead certain QM areas to be dismissed, corresponding surging deficits in other areas of the city seems to suggest that improvements sometimes descend from inner-city dynamics and citizens' displacement rather than by the QM activity itself (AEIDL 2012; Expert Groups on Urban Development Planning and City Planning 2013). As an instrument of urban development, QM, thus, may be very effective in achieving much-needed urban regeneration effects, but it will not be able to address many of the social problems that are typical for deprived areas as well. In addition, QM initiatives are relatively small-scaled and are seldom integrated in larger programs. Consequently, the system has shown limited impacts on the permanent services of Berlin (URBACT 2008). The Wiesenburg case, too, indicates how difficult it is to integrate local QM initiatives in broader Bezirk and Senate policies.

14.4.2   *Legitimacy*

In comparison to other forms of hybrid governance in the context of metropolitan governance, the democratic legitimacy of the Berlin QM model, or rather its decisions, seems to be relatively well-developed (Schaap et al. 2019). This is because, notwithstanding its limitations, the model starts from the idea of direct involvement of neighborhood residents in the Neighborhood Councils and the Action Fund Juries. In addition, these are supported by direct and open, yet informal, elections. Even though, as described above, there is a strong shadow of hierarchy on project level, the QM model relies strongly on co-creation between state, market and civil society actors. This situation, however, creates its own governance challenges.

One of these is the difficulty of striking a balance between the participatory democracy instruments at the neighborhood level and representative democracy on the Bezirk and Land levels. Since it is based on participation in (formal) planning procedures, the socially integrative project represents one of the many instances of participatory democratic. Because of providing citizens with the role of 'expert citizens' with an advisory vote to their committees, the program is praised for satisfying the calls for greater transparency of planning and decision processes, as well as to put emphasis on society's potential for self-regulation (Ülker 2016). However, whether this model of the citizens' community is viable in practice is an open question of a number of reasons. First, the limited participation of immigrants and segregated population to the elections continues to pose considerable hurdles to the functioning of the QM (AEIDL 2012; Expert Groups on Urban Development Planning and City Planning 2013). Experience shows that people with a lower socio-economic status and other vulnerable groups such as migrants, elderly and youngsters with no previous knowledge of the subject tend to be under-represented at public participation events. Among others, burdensome legal procedures and red tape are seen as great disincentives for wide involvement. This limited participation, however, has resulted in inadequate representativeness of the outcomes of participation processes (Franke 2003). Second, to arrive at legitimated decisions, QM still depends on the legitimated political and administrative structures. The dilemma of 'double legitimation' for planning decisions by democratically legitimated bodies and by the citizens themselves may lead to disappointment and a lack of mutual acceptance. Critics argue also that the QM serves the sole purpose to promote voluntary engagement to relieve the pressure on public budgets, justify privatization of public interest services, or seek public understanding for cuts in services (Franke et al. 2000). Public participation in systems as QM can nevertheless be a considerable enrichment for representative democracy, in that it enables people to experience democracy in practice. This gives them a new competency in process management and process control.

On a more abstract level, one could say that the QM governance model amounts to the co-existence of a grassroots democracy, as it is developed and supported by the Quartiersmanagers, and the more traditional top-down representative democracy, as represented by the Berlin Senate and the Bezirk, or district council. This 'double mandate' is not necessarily a bad thing, since clashes between the two can trigger discussions about what the public interest is and who represent it (Hendriks 2010). However, in the case of QM, Quartiersmanagers, as private subcontractors, are caught up between the various interests, resulting in role conflicts. In addition, as the Wiesenburg case shows, the promise of citizen participation in decision-making can create false expectations in the case of direct conflict between lower and higher level policies: 'As a consequence of the whole neighborhood management program, neighborhood residents may have become a bit spoiled. They readily assume that they will invited to participate and to bring forward their ideas and request, and they expect these to be implemented at short notice' (Quartiersmanager).[2]

14.4.3   Robustness

Finally, also stability and robustness are possible challenges to the Berlin's QM. The program is based on an amendable legal basis (the Federal Planning Act and the Senate Standing Order) and pursues short-term and provisional objectives. Further, not only does the funding depend on the annual resources made available by the Senate, but also the institutions created are not protected by the German Constitution, which accords precedence and primacy to the principle of representative democracy (art. 28, German Basic Law) (Wollmann 2002). These are all factors that may raise doubts on the robustness of the program, which are also expressed by our respondents in the Wiesenburg case.

> Since the funding will expire it should be used as quickly as possible. [...] We don't have the time to wait until 2018 because the Quartiersmanagement is commissioned until 2020 only. Before we leave the neighborhood, we would like to... It wouldn't make sense to leave before we were able to establish something. It wouldn't make sense to leave the neighborhood before there is a self-supporting structure in place. That's why we want to spend the time that is still available for neighborhood management on working with strong partners, and with the people that we've activated and who are ready to take on responsibility, on building that structure. Only then, we as neighborhood managers can say: "Okay, we have fulfilled our mission. We have not only discovered unique places and activated the inhabitants, but we have also transferred responsibility to them in a way that they can go forward for the next 10/20/30 years." (Quartiersmanager)[3]

---

[2] 'Unsere Bewohner sind vielleicht durch das ganze Quartiersmanagement-Verfahren auch bisschen verwöhnt. Sie werden halt gefragt, sie werden beteiligt und auch die Wünsche und die auch Visionen, die werden auch in kurzer Zeit auch umgesetzt.'

[3] 'Und bis jetzt, weil auch die Fördermittel befristet sind und die möglichst schnell auch eingesetzt werden sollen, weil die ja sonst verfallen. [...] Wir haben halt keine Geduld bis 2018 zu warten, weil das Quartiersmanagement ist bis 20 / 2020 beauftragt: Wir würden gerne, bevor das Quartier verstetigt wird, ohne etwas aufzubauen, ohne eine Struktur ins Quartier zu hinterlassen, wäre natürlich jetzt nicht sinnvoll. Deswegen möchten wir diese restliche Zeit, die uns übrig bleibt als Quartiersmanagement, dafür nutzen, gemeinsam mit unseren starken Partnern und mit den Menschen die wir aktiviert haben, die auch bereit sind,

However, recent success and appreciation for the program may lead the Senate to reconsider the prolongation after 2020 and, possibly, the stabilization of the QM model is each area of the city.

14.5 Discussion and Conclusions

One of our main conclusions is that, because of the hybridity of the Berlin governance model, it is not easy to define the role and tasks of QM. This is because Quartiersmanagers combine various responsibilities, which can sometimes be contradictory. The Wiesenburg case gives a clear illustration of the complexity of QM's tasks. In this particular case, QM acts as a protagonist of particular neighborhood citizens' interests, but at the same time finds that its ambitions conflict with some of the ambitions of the Senate, of which QM is a subcontractor. The complexity of QM's tasks is amplified by the fact that, while it is expected to be a politically neutral facilitator of the participation processes in neighborhoods, it is required, at the same time, to develop and strive for the realization a particular vision for the area, which may not be uncontroversial. Consequently, QM is seen both as a neutral facilitator as well as an involved agent in the same area. This combination sometimes produces role conflicts, for which the Wiesenburg case is exemplary. We believe, however, that these role conflicts are not restricted to the Wiesenburg case as such, but that they are indicative of the governance model as such. Both elements make QM an intermediary organization that aims to establish and nurture the relationship between citizens and government institutions but also positions Quartiersmanagers as defenders of particular interests.

Second, the QM case shows how hybrid governance arrangements can produce strong tensions between the public ('state'), private ('market') and civil society (community) modes of coordination. The basic organizational structure of the governance arrangement is that of a procurement model, which rests on the market logic of competition between private companies. At the same time, the QM model uses this organization model to privatize the task of public policy-making, which involves the formulation of a policy vision. In our study, we found that the resulting visions can

Verantwortung zu übernehmen, Strukturen für sie aufzubauen, wo wir dann als Quartiersmanagement sagen können: „Okay, wir haben unseren Auftrag erfüllt. Wir haben nicht nur die Orte entdeckt und die Bewohner aktiviert, sondern wir haben denen auch Verantwortung in die Hand gegeben und dann auch in den nächsten 10/20/30 Jahren auch weitergetragen und weitergegeben.'

and do sometimes conflict with the political preferences of the state and that a shadow of hierarchy than emerges that demands conformity on the part of the Quartiersmanagers. Such conflicts between the logic of procurement and the logic of political representation are seen to produce strong role conflicts and operational complexities in the ever-day operations of the QM governance arrangement. In practice, these tensions are increased by the way the Quartiersmanagers perceive their identity and sometimes take up their role in the governance arrangement. They strongly identify with the role of public policy-makers and position themselves as representatives of the neighborhood residents advocating a partisan vision for the neighborhood. Particularly when there are high stakes involved, this identification of Quartiersmanagers is to the dismay of the Senate that expects them to act as docile subcontractors, or politically neutral facilitators of citizen participation at best. In addition, we find that, mirroring a private logic, one of the main motivations on the part of the Senate for using a procurement model is the desire to create operational flexibility and not always the aspiration of benefitting from the substantive expertise of Quartiersmanagers. This attitude, in turn, has caused frustration on the part of some of the people involved. Hence, in the QM case, we see a series of clear frictions between the organizational aspects of hybridity on the one hand, and some of its manifestations in actual decision-making processes and the roles and identities of those involved, on the other. This complex situation is illustrative for some of the challenges that are produced by hybrid governance, since it sometimes presents a combination of seemingly incompatible logics, which may very well weaken the governance of metropolitan areas (see also Battilana et al. 2017; Morrison et al. 2012).

These results indicate that hybrid governance is not a solution for all seasons as regards the governance of livability since it can produce tensions between the logics of the state, the market, and the civil society that are present in a partnership. At the same time, our analysis shows that some of these tensions are not necessarily the result of institutional aspects of the cooperation but also relate to how the people involved perceive and take up their roles in such governance arrangements. As indicated by our workshop discussion, this finding suggests that some of the complexities of hybrid governance can be negotiated by explicit and collective reflection on the roles and responsibilities that state, market and civil society have in local governance arrangements.

REFERENCES

AEIDL. (2012). *Reinventing Europe through local initiative*. Brussels: European Association for Information on Local Development.

Battilana, J., Besharov, M., & Mitzinneck, B. (2017). On hybrids and hybrid organizing: A review and roadmap for future research. In R. Greenwood, C. Oliver, T. B. Lawrence, & R. E. Meye (Eds.), *The SAGE handbook of organizational institutionalism* (pp. 133–169). London: SAGE.

Blackmore, C., van Bommel, S., de Bruin, A., de Vries, J., Westberg, L., Powell, N., et al. (2016). Learning for transformation of water governance: Reflections on design from the climate change adaptation and water governance (CADWAGO) Project. *Water, 8*(11), 510.

BMVBS. (2008). *Status report: The programme "Social City" (Soziale Stadt)*. Berlin: Bundesministerium für Verkehr, Bau und Stadtentwicklung.

Bovens, M., & Zouridis, S. (2002). From street-level to system-level bureaucracies: How information and communication technology is transforming administrative discretion and constitutional control. *Public Administration Review, 62*(2), 174–184.

Denis, J.-L., Ferlie, E., & Van Gestel, N. (2015). Understanding hybridity in public organizations. *Public Administration, 93*(2), 273–289.

Droste, C., Lelevrier, C., & Wassenberg, F. (2008). Urban regeneration in European social housing areas. In K. Scanlon & C. M. E. Whitehead (Eds.), *Social Housing in Europe II. A review of policies and outcomes* (pp. 163–196). London: LSE London.

Eick, V. (2011). Policing 'below the state' in Germany: Neocommunitarian soberness and punitive paternalism. *Contemporary Justice Review, 14*(1), 21–41.

Ewert, B., & Evers, A. (2013). *How to approach social innovations: Lessons from Berlin*. Paper presented at the 1st International Conference on Public Policy, Grenoble.

Expert Groups on Urban Development Planning and City Planning. (2013). *Culture of participation in integrated urban development*. Berlin: The German Association of Cities.

Franke, T. (2003). Activation and participation in Germany. *Soziale Stadt—Archiv für Kommunalwissenschaften II* (pp. 243–268). Berlin: Halbjahresband.

Franke, T., Löhr, R. P., & Sander, R. (2000). *Soziale Stadt—Stadterneuerungspolitik als Stadtpolitikerneuerung*. In Stuttgart: Halbjahresband.

Gualini, E., & Fricke, C. (2019). 'Who governs' Berlin's metropolitan region? The strategic-relational construction of metropolitan scale in Berlin–Brandenburg's economic development policies. *Environment and Planning C: Politics and Space, 37*(1), 59–80.

Harrison, J., & Hoyler, M. (2014). Governing the new metropolis. *Urban Studies, 51*(11), 2249–2266.

Hendriks, F. (2010). *Vital democracy: A theory of democracy in action*. Oxford: Oxford University Press.

Levelt, M., & Metze, T. (2014). The legitimacy of regional governance networks: Gaining credibility in the shadow of hierarchy. *Urban Studies, 51*(11), 2371–2386.

Mike, M. (2003). Governing beyond the centre: A critique of the Anglo-governance school. *Political Studies, 51*(3), 592–608. https://doi.org/10.1111/1467-9248.00443.

Morrison, T. H., Wilson, C., & Bell, M. (2012). The role of private corporations in regional planning and development: Opportunities and challenges for the governance of housing and land use. *Journal of Rural Studies, 28*(4), 478–489.

OECD. (2003). *Urban renaissance Berlin: Towards an integrated strategy for social cohesion and economic development*. Paris: OECD Publishing.

Penta, L. (2007). *Community Organizing: Menschen verändern ihre Stad*. Hamburg: Körber Stiftung.

Reinprecht, C., & Levy-Vroelant, C. (2008). Housing the poor in Paris and Vienna: The changing understanding of 'social'. In K. Scanlon & C. Whitehead (Eds.), *Social Housing in Europe II. A review of policies and outcomes* (pp. 297–313). London: LSE London.

Rhodes, R. A. W. (2007). Understanding governance: Ten years on. *Organization Studies, 28*(8), 1243–1264.

Schaap, L., Colombo, C., Damen, M., & Karsten, N. (2019). Shedding light on hybrid city-region governance: Effectiveness and legitimacy in four metropolitan areas. In J. Koppenjan, P. M. Karré, & K. Termeer (Eds.), *Smart hybridity: Potentials and challenges of new governance arrangements* (pp. 69–81). The Hague: Eleven.

Skelcher, C., & Smith, S. R. (2015). Theorizing hybridity: Institutional logics, complex organizations, and actor identities: The case of nonprofits. *Public Administration, 93*(2), 433–448.

SSU. (2014). *Verwaltungsvorschrift über die Gewährung von Fördermitteln im Programm Soziale Stadt (VV SozStadt 2014)*. Berlin: Senatsverwaltung für Stadtentwicklung und Umwelt.

Ülker, B. (2016). *Enterprising migrants in Berlin*. Bielefeld: transcript Verlag.

URBACT. (2008). *Social cohesion in neighbourhoods across Europe baseline study*. URBACT – European Programme for Urban Sustainable Development.

Wollmann, H. (2002). The civic community ('Bürgergemeinde') in Germany: Its double nature as political and as (civil) societal community. *German Journal of Urban Studies, 41*(2), 1–14.

PART V

Partnerships and Urban Living Labs

The Governance Challenge of Urban Living Laboratories: Using Liminal 'In-Between' Space to Create Livable Cities

Lieke Oldenhof, Sabrina Rahmawan-Huizenga,
Hester van de Bovenkamp, and Roland Bal

15.1 INTRODUCTION

In order to address urban challenges, such as the creation of livable and healthy cities, Urban Living Laboratories (ULL's) are set up as new forms of partnership. ULL's are different from other forms of public-private partnerships due to their focus on co-creation through experimentation, their explicit geographical embeddedness in a particular area (as a 'protected' experimental space), and the ambition to experimentally explore, evaluate and incrementally learn from new interventions in order to go beyond business as usual and shape alternative futures for cities (Bulkeley et al. 2016; Voytenko et al. 2016). The primary focus of studies into

L. Oldenhof (✉) • S. Rahmawan-Huizenga • H. van de Bovenkamp • R. Bal
Erasmus School of Health Policy & Management, Erasmus University Rotterdam, Rotterdam, The Netherlands
e-mail: oldenhof@eshpm.eur.nl; huizenga@eshpm.eur.nl; vandebovenkamp@eshpm.eur.nl; r.bal@eshpm.eur.nl

© The Author(s) 2020
C. van Montfort, A. Michels (eds.), *Partnerships for Livable Cities*,
https://doi.org/10.1007/978-3-030-40060-6_15

ULL's is an evaluative one: i.e. whether ULL's deliver their intended promises of innovation and learning. In this chapter we take a different approach by responding to the recent call of Bulkeley et al. (2016) to adopt a more critical approach to studying ULL's as a particular form of governance and wider politics of experimentation that shapes the urban milieu:

> *The practices commonly associated with ULL—of partnership, participation, learning, data mining—are not neutral mechanisms but central ways in which governing is achieved and in shaping the possibilities for transformative processes.* (Ibid., p. 16)

By considering ULL's as a form of governance with political effects we are able to explore how value trade-offs are made in urban development in an experimental setting. Examples of potential value-conflicts vary from inclusion/exclusion of stakeholders to inclusive housing versus gentrification and accountability and learning versus rule-free experimentation. Interestingly, these value trade-offs in urban governance are increasingly 're-placed' from traditional political fora, such as municipal councils, to ULL's (Bovens 2005; Hajer 2003). It is therefore important to research how these trade-offs are made in these new spaces of governing.

Due to their relatively early stages of development and their experimental set-up, ULL's lack clear rules and norms for making and agreeing upon such value-trade-offs. As a consequence, ULL's are not yet considered 'governance proper' and seem to operate 'betwixt and between' what is normally expected. Moreover, being positioned *in-between* bottom-up and top-down approaches to policymaking, ULL's may generate certain benefits (crossing institutional boundaries; co-production of knowledge; experimental learning), yet may also generate new risks (lack of legitimate decision-making and accountability).

To further conceptualize the *in-between* nature of ULL's as an experimental space for governing and making value-trade-offs, we draw on the concept of liminality. This concept describes 'a condition where the usual practice and order are suspended and replaced by new rites and rituals' (Czarniawska and Mazza 2003, p. 267). Our research question is: *Which key value trade-offs are made in the liminal space of ULL's and which new institutional rules emerge in order to deal with these trade-offs?*

We zoom in on a Dutch case of ULL's in the Randstad. After the financial crisis in 2008, this area experienced an institutional void in urban development due to a double retreat of market developers and the local government. In this institutional void, new urban initiatives popped up to improve the livability of derelict areas and address social issues, such as health, in non-institutionalized ways. By temporarily dispensing 'common' practices and methods of urban development and introducing experimental modes of intervention, these initiatives gained attention of the local government and were subsequently labeled and funded as 'urban labs'.

On the basis of qualitative interviews with initiators of these labs and municipal policymakers and observations of meetings, we describe recurring value trade-offs of ULL's and discuss the emergence of new institutional rules to solidify this new *liminal space* for decision-making. Before doing so, we will first conceptualize the 'in-between' space of ULL's by using insights from liminality literature.

15.2 Conceptualizing the *In-between*: ULL's as a Liminal Space for Urban Governance

The concept of liminality was originally developed by French anthropologist Van Gennep (1960 [1909]) to analyse rituals of transition and the *in-between* time/space during an individual rite of passage (Short 2015). During the liminal period, usual norms and practices are suspended which may create feelings of uncertainty and anxiety. Van Gennep's work was further developed by Turner (1974, 1982) who argued that liminality can also be a positive space of liberation to do things differently and be creative. When being 'betwixt and between' social positions, a person can be free of obligations and therefore 'anything can happen' (Turner 1974, p. 13).

Although Turner and Van Gennep both used the concept of liminality in a temporal sense referring to rites of passage, in science and technology studies (STS) and organizational studies liminality has been widely applied in a spatial sense too, focusing on place and space (Rahmawan-Huizenga and Ivanova submitted; Ivanova et al. 2019; Short 2015; Iedema et al. 2012; Ellis and Ybema 2010). Examples of liminal places range from border-zones, disputed 'no-man's land' and hospital corridors (Iedema et al. 2012) to transitory dwelling places at work (Short 2015) and 'non-places' like airports and hotels (Augé 1995).

In contrast to liminal places that are physical locations invested with ambiguous meaning (Gieryn 2000), liminal space is a more abstract product of social relations, values and meanings (Lefebvre 1991). Spatial categories such as boundaries and scale offer actors a means to demarcate space in certain ways for particular purposes. In case of liminal space, these spatial categories are particularly contested and perceived differently.

For the purpose of this chapter, we specifically focus on Urban Living Labs (ULL's) as a liminal space for governing cities in alternative ways. We argue that this conceptualization generates new insights into how experimental governance of urban development is done in many cities today. Due to the specific characteristics that are mentioned in the literature, ULL's can be viewed as liminal space in at least three respects.

First, ULL's claim to bring together stakeholders from different sectors—science, policy, society and market—in a so called 'quadruple helix mode' (Bulkeley et al. 2016). Liminality in this sense consists of ULL's being positioned in-between different organizational boundaries and different stakeholders that adhere to particular values, norms and rituals. This liminal space can be used to join-up efforts, bridge organizational boundaries and bring together 'top-down' and 'bottom-up' approaches of policymaking.

Second, ULL's can be conceived as liminal space as they are geographically 'emplaced' into specific urban contexts and areas while at the same time 'placeless' as insights from experiments in laboratories are claimed to be generalizable to 'anywhere' (Gieryn 2006; Gopakumar 2014; Karvonen and Van Heur 2014). By mediating between spatial uniqueness and placeless generalization, ULL's claim to address local issues, while also contributing to the development of universal strategies for global problems.

Third, thanks to their experimental status, ULL's are temporarily exempted from normal rules and regulations, which arguably enables them to experiment with new methods, (financing) models and concepts. This third sense of liminality closely aligns with Turner's conception of liminality as a free space to innovate (Turner 1974).

Common to all three aspects of liminal space is that value-trade-offs are part and parcel of daily decision-making. The implicit assumption in much of the literature is that ULL's—as a new experimental governance form—can contribute to more effectively dealing with tricky trade-offs that benefit the future of the city. For example, by bridging organizational boundaries, it becomes possible to co-produce knowledge and innovate on a system level. However, liminal space may also generate certain risks in terms of legitimate decision-making and accountability. Because ULL's often lack generally accepted rules and norms about decision-making and the inclusion of stakeholders in participation processes, they can lead to an institutional void (Hajer 2003; Leong 2017). In this institutional void, powerful stakeholders can potentially tweak decision-making their own way by prioritizing certain values over others. The institutional void is not all bad news though. In fact, it can be used to 'deliberate new institutional rules, develop new norms of appropriate behavior and devise new conceptions of legitimate political interventions' (Hajer 2003, p. 176). Hence, liminal space offers opportunities for new contemporary forms of legitimate decision-making in addition to classical political fora.

By zooming in on the empirical case of ULL's in a large Dutch city in the Randstad area, we ask how different stakeholders attribute specific meanings to the *in-between* position of ULL's, deal with value trade-offs in urban development and in the process of dealing with these trade-offs develop new institutional rules for decision-making.

15.3 Brief Introduction into ULL's and Methods

Our case study city hosts about 20 ULL's (Boonstra et al. 2018). Although some ULL's were initiated by residents/citizens of a neighborhood, most ULL's are led by entrepreneurial professionals (in architecture, design, urban development) as local residents, that present themselves as engaged 'city makers'. The local government and housing associations are often partners in ULL's. Interestingly, big corporate companies do not play a key role in most ULL's in our case study.

Thematically, ULL's often focus on issues such as sustainability, energy transitions (e, g. making houses energy efficient), livability (e.g. of derelict areas), re-use of vacant buildings/areas, air pollution, and green public spaces. Remarkably, less attention is paid in ULL's to social issues such as debts, health and well-being. In addition, ULL's often aim to change the policy agenda, for example by introducing new criteria for public tendering or by creating awareness of issues of concern. With regard to finance, most ULL's make use of national and local subsidies provided by the Stimulation Fund for Creative Industry, the Architecture Institute (an organization that is partially funded by the local government) and the local government (Table 15.1).

The aim of the research was exploratory in nature: to describe the key issues and dilemmas in the governance of ULL's. As researchers, we did

Table 15.1 Overview of the different characteristics of the labs in this study

Urban lab	Area of contribution	Stakeholders	Categorization (see typology Fig. 1.1, Chap. 1)
I	Urban and social development, social cohesion, Resilience, social safety index	Cooperation with municipality, citizens, healthcare institutes, a bank, research institutes, students	H. Partnerships in which civil society, market and state are involved
II	Urban renewal, public space	Architects in cooperation with municipality, entrepreneurs, students	E. Partnership between civil society and public organizations
III	Redevelopment public (green) space, mobility challenges	Architects in cooperation with municipality, local entrepreneurs, citizens	H. Partnerships in which civil society, market and state are involved
IV	Social urban development Social cohesion	Artists in cooperation with citizens, local healthcare institutes, entrepreneurs, farmers market	F. Partnership between civil society and private organizations
V	Urban redevelopment, built environment	Designers in cooperation with municipality, housing association, local entrepreneurs	H. Partnerships in which civil society, market and state are involved
VI	Health, wellbeing Social cohesion	Cooperation with municipality, local healthcare institutes, citizens, housing association	E. Partnership between civil society and public organizations
VII	Urban health, public health	Designer, architects, cooperation with municipality (temporary support) and (national and local) environment and health institute, citizens to a lesser extent, students	E. Partnership between civil society and public organizations
VIII	Redevelopment urban wasteland	Cooperation with municipality, entrepreneurs, citizens	H. Partnerships in which civil society, market and state are involved

(continued)

Table 15.1 (continued)

Urban lab	Area of contribution	Stakeholders	Categorization (see typology Fig. 1.1, Chap. 1)
IX	(social) resilience, urban environment, energy	Initiated by municipality, cooperation with urban research institute, citizens (attempt), energy supplier, students	E. Partnership between civil society and public organizations
X	Urban redevelopment Public space	Architects in cooperation with municipality, local entrepreneurs, citizens, different local healthcare institutes, primary schools, housing association, real estate project development	H. Partnerships in which civil society, market and state are involved
XI	Social resilience, urban development	Formal cooperation municipality, students, citizens, research institutes, universities	E. Partnership between civil society and public organizations

not play a part in the design and/or evaluation of interventions developed in the ULL's. The second author conducted various semi-structured interviews (N=16) and informal interviews (N=8) with organizers of ULL's and policymakers.[1] In addition, observations (N=12) were conducted of workshops, meetings of ULL's and conferences and semi-formal get-togethers. This enabled the second author to observe social interactions and discursive framing of ULL's *in situ*. Last, we analyzed documents produced by urban lab initiatives such as pamphlets, essays and manifests.

For data-analysis, all observations were processed into field notes and the interviews were transcribed by the second author as part of her PhD research about 'the experimental city'. The first, second and third author coded and extensively discussed the data for recurring themes. Since many respondents explicitly described labs as an 'in-between space' that connected the lifeworld of citizens with the system, this inductive theme was subsequently analyzed in theoretical terms of liminality and different value trade-offs that were made in the in-between space of the ULL.

---

[1] We would like to thank Wouter Berkhof, former intern at the municipality, who conducted part of the interviews together with Sabrina Rahmawan-Huizenga.

15.4   LIMINAL SPACE: ULL's DISCURSIVELY POSITIONED *IN-BETWEEN* SYSTEM AND LIFEWORLD

Many 'city makers' and policymakers framed the ULL as a space 'in-between' the 'bottom-up' lifeworld of citizens and the 'top-down' system of institutions. By invoking this dichotomy, they discursively created a liminal space for labs to span boundaries between disconnected worlds, as becomes evident from the following statement from two well-known urban opinion makers in the city (one of which also participated in an ULL):

> *City making can best be described as an innovative way to connect lifeworld and system world on a local level. The lifeworld stands for the daily reality of inhabitants, working people and or (small) entrepreneurs. The system world stands for the government, supplemented with specialists and experts, institutions and powerful corporate companies. So the focus in urban labs is on the practice of connecting those worlds (…). An urban lab challenges the bi-polar model of government versus citizens: executives, civil servants and experts on the stage and angry citizens in the room. In an urban lab, everyone is sitting on the stage. Everyone listens to everyone.* (Westerhout and Bongers 2017)

In the above quote, the liminal position is associated with the possibility of equal conversation between stakeholders even though they hold different power positions and have different interests. ULL's in this sense create a space for Habermassian *Herschaftsfreie Diskussion*. This positive reading of liminality was reiterated by other respondents active in ULL's and officials from the Architecture Institute (fieldnotes citymaking conference). Moreover, the experimental nature of ULL's was used as a justification for temporarily 'putting aside' individual interests to be able to alternatively envision the future of the city (e.g. as more resilient, livable, inclusive etc.). Some ULL's experimented with role plays to switch stakeholder positions (i.e. of corporate developers, small entrepreneurs, individual renters) and create more equal and shared relationships. This was viewed as a necessary step to be able to move beyond fixed interests:

> *We started playing games, like the prisoner dilemma: why don't you stand in our shoes? We will stand in your shoes and what does that mean? (…) We started thinking along with them and we said: your problem is our problem. You need to get rid of the buildings, which means for us an end to our rental*

space. So we both have an interest and how are we going to solve this together? (Initiator ULL with a focus on the built environment, September 2018)

In addition to (more) equal relationships between different stakeholders, other positive readings of liminality encompassed the possibility to 'cross over', 'join-up' and 'connect' different sectors. In this regard, the ULL was positioned as a place where the 'social' (healthcare, well-being, education) and the 'material' (mobility, energy, buildings) could happily meet and re-connect. Rhetorically, the metaphor of the system/lifeworld was a particularly useful resource as respondents argued that in the lifeworld of inhabitants these domains were not separate but part of a whole. This holistic view of citizens' daily life was contrasted with the 'siloed' departments of the municipality that worked according to different methods, financial systems and regulations. The *in-between* space of the ULL was thus framed as a possibility to connect the material and social in concrete local experiments: not by endlessly talking about it, but by means of design and visualizing new futures through well designed maps, video's and prototypes.

Finally, liminality of ULL's was framed in terms of space to 'freely' experiment with new forms of collaboration/interventions without having to comply with standard accountability criteria and output targets that are common in local government. By temporarily dispensing 'business as usual', it would become possible to experimentally learn, i.e. 'learning by doing' (Rahmawan-Huizenga and Ivanova submitted).

The term *lab* however was used only in specific policy contexts. In communication with neighborhood residents the term was rarely used and even actively avoided. As an organizer from the municipality remarks, using the term urban (living) lab would potentially alienate residents from participation:

> *The question is how residents will interpret the term urban lab. Well, with the term urban living lab, I know for sure they will say: "just give my plate to Vicky (the dog)."* (Initiator ULL with a focus on resilience, September 2018)

In a similar vein, the director of the local urban knowledge institute that promotes urban labs as a promising form of partnership remarked that he altogether avoided using the term in direct communications with citizens:

It sounds a bit denigrating: you live in a lab. (director of the local urban knowledge institute, December 2018)

The experimental and liminal status of the ULL—that is seen to be productive in the sense that it creates a space for experimentation outside 'normal' administrative routines and at least partially leveling power imbalances—is regarded as to potentially backfire as inhabitants generally do not like to be guinea pigs or subjects of experiments. This raises the question how value-trade-offs are made within these liminal spaces.

15.5   Value Trade-Offs in the Governance of ULL's

Below, five prominent value trade-offs are discussed that are pervasive in the liminal governance of ULL's. They respectively focus on the positioning of ULL's in terms of its relation to the institutional environment (collaborative or activist), key participants (professional or lay), focus (social or material), strategy for experimental learning (place-bound experimentation or placeless learning) and outcome of experiments (capital or societal value).

1. *Institutional collaboration versus autonomous activism*

In policy discourse, urban labs are portrayed as a neutral place: because of their 'in-between' status they could ideally 'connect' different worlds without necessarily choosing sides. Yet, in the daily management of ULL's, organizers often felt the need to take position: i.e. by working closely together with policy makers or taking an autonomous activist position.

Given the fact that the majority of ULL's were partially financed by the municipality and national funds (such as the Stimulation Fund for Creative Industry), they already had to comply with institutional criteria regarding work methods and focus to be able to attract funding in the first place. Most city makers also stressed the need for financial support as ULL's lacked business models to generate their own income. Moreover, collaboration with the local government was deemed necessary to get things done:

We think it is convenient to collaborate with the local government on all kinds of matters. We have asked someone from the local government (...) whether he wants to be involved in this project. And of course, you need the local govern-

ment with all kinds of little things. For example, in case you want less parking spots and you can convince people to give up their parking spot in exchange for extra greenery, then you need to coordinate with local government to ensure that they don't give off new licenses. (Initiator ULL with a focus on public space, March 2018)

Strategic positioning sometimes had to be done publically. During the yearly city-making conference (well attended by civil servants), initiators of ULL's had to position themselves on a line with two extremes: 'the local government sets the tone' and 'local initiative is leading'. Most initiators opted for an 'in-between' position, but stressed simultaneously the need to connect to local policy:

You need the local government, otherwise you stay a hobby club. (field notes city making conference, November 9th 2018)

To further solidify the connection with local governments which was considered crucial for the sustainability of urban labs, the Stimulation Fund for Creative Industries decided to change the funding criteria in 2018. Instead of providing financial support to independent local initiatives, municipalities can apply for guidance in setting up or improving their ULL. After selection, municipalities receive the help of a designer and expert in the field of ULL's.

Despite the fact that most labs considered collaboration with institutional partners as a matter of fact, some labs took an activist stance. An illustration is the ULL *air quality* that was successful in putting the topic of air pollution on the political agenda. By inventing playful interventions, such as tableware that was made out of polluted particles from the air, they visualized the 'invisible' problem of air pollution. Other city makers stressed the risks of working too closely together with local government as they could 'swallow up' the lab or use it 'instrumentally' to implement government policies. Examples of instrumental use of labs that were mentioned were solving failing participation policy of the local government (field notes city making conference 2018) and implementing housing policies that would benefit gentrified neighborhoods ('cargo bike neighbourhoods', symbol of YUPPIES). In the view of these respondents, the liminal status of ULL's was a vulnerability which could lead to co-optation in the institutional world or—to put it in Habermassian terms—'colonization' by the system.

Other city makers adopted a more pragmatist stance towards the urban lab's positioning. Depending on the particular problem at hand, the ULL could switch its position from collaborator to activist. For example, when local government was unwilling to collaborate, an activist position could be adopted to put pressure on the government:

> *That indeterminate status is actually convenient because you can never be pushed into one particular corner.* (Organizer several ULL's with multiple foci, April 2018)

The liminal status of labs thus creates strategic maneuvering room, as becomes evident in the above quote of a city-maker.

2. Professional versus lay participation and values

Despite the inclusive rhetoric of urban labs to include lay citizens from different backgrounds (SES/minorities), it was difficult to actually accomplish inclusive participation in practice. Especially after the financial crisis of 2008, ULL's were primarily initiated by highly educated professionals that often had a background in urban design and architecture. This creative professional group, sometimes dubbed 'the city making caste/bubble' (Boonstra 2018), was keen to fill the institutional void in urban development that had emerged as a consequence of the retreating local government and market. The crisis thus presented an opportunity for professionals to do something good for the city (e.g. by developing derelict areas), while simultaneously upgrading their CV in a difficult job market by doing voluntary work. Because of their professional background in urban development and their ability to speak the right language and 'morph to the institutional world' (Interview city-maker, April 2018), they could effectively collaborate with civil servants and access financial funds to support their local initiatives:

> *Certain well informed groups in the (local) society know how to find the instruments for city making easily. Often they are groups from neighbourhoods with an established city-making tradition or they are (local citizens) with a professional background related to city making (architect, designer, city planner, entrepreneur). Residents that want to do something in their neighbourhood but don't have this background have a hard time accessing the right channels.* (Boonstra 2018)

As a consequence of this difference in access, and the fact that the creative caste tends to live in central areas or in gentrified pockets, many neighborhoods in the periphery did not have local initiatives that were labeled as ULL's. The ULL's that were located in more peripheral areas were based on policy initiatives of the local government and commercial developers, such as a mega renovation project of a public transport hub or a local government lead energy transition project.

The professional background of many city-makers and their sensibility to 'hot' policy issues had consequences for the values and types of interventions that were promoted in ULL's. Examples of dominant values were sustainability, circular economy, green living, work and healthy lifestyles. These values were operationalized in concrete interventions in various ULL's, varying from public campaigns to persuade residents to give up their parking spot in exchange for green space, the agenda-setting of air pollution by art projects, and energy transition projects for households (cooking on induction rather than gas), to community gardens and waterside regeneration projects. These projects enthused city-makers and policymakers and were viewed as an important step towards more livable and resilient cities. Yet, the values underlying these interventions clashed in various projects with views of lay citizens and residents:

> For many people cooking with electricity is a real issue. People find it silly to cook on induction. Then you can't cook, a lady explained to me. She said: "I don't eat dinner at someone's place when they cook on induction". (Organizer ULL with a focus on energy transition, September 2018)

This same city-maker explained a recurring tension in her work between working demand driven versus tempting residents to get enthused about new ideas:

> Neighbourhood based working is based on the idea that residents determine what is important (…). Uh, but residents do not ask "could I get a resilient schoolyard? A water cooling tank? Or what do you think of creating a circular sewer system and what if we add shells to it?" (Ibid.).

City-makers dealt with this tension in different ways. Some argued that it was sufficient to 'inform' residents about activities without necessarily requiring their input from the start; others argued that ULL's did not have to do 'representative participation' because this would lead to bland compromises rather than radical interventions that changed the future. In this regard, the framing of ULL's as space in between the lifeworld and system, enabled the justification that labs were something quite different than bottom-up participation or top-down policy. Working from a middle position, creative professionals and policymakers in civil service argued, it is possible to potentially bridge the gap between bottom-up and top-down initiatives, framing it as a 'middle-up-down' approach. Yet the results indicate that the bridging of worlds and ideas is more difficult than initially thought.

3. *The social versus the material*

Ideally, ULL's were viewed as a means to jointly tackle social issues (well-being, health, debt, work) and material challenges in urban development (energy sustainability, redevelopment projects). Both respondents in local government as well as ULL's mentioned that this was necessary given the highly fragmentized work methods of local government and the compartmentalization of social and material issues into different departments. Despite the ideal of joining up the socio-material, trade-offs between the social and material were part and parcel of ULL's. In fact, material challenges were often prioritized in many ULL's as key themes for interventions. With many city-makers having a background in architecture, design and urban development, for them, it made sense to primarily link urban interventions to buildings, physical locations and areas. Although city-makers mentioned dealing with social issues 'in the wake' of material interventions, social issues came less to the fore than the physical re-ordering of places. This was also noted by city-makers themselves:

> Urban labs often emerge in spatially defined environments: neighbourhoods, urban redevelopment locations (...). (Here) we explore whether urban labs can also be of value for non-spatial processes, such as problems of debt. (Document analysis: Pamphlet for city making, November 2018)

While it could be argued that debt problems also have spatial dimensions (i.e. some neighborhoods experience a higher concentration of households with debts than others), this quote shows that social issues received less priority in most ULL's. Notable exceptions are two ULL's that focus on getting unemployed neighbourhood residents back to work. According to an interviewed city-maker, the relative lack of attention for social issues in most labs can also be explained because of the particular funding criteria for urban labs that required a design method:

Well, our claim was that in a city such as (this) there are many young people who should be coached in an informal learning route. To make sure that they will become a good artist. That was the idea behind that urban lab. And this idea was already turned down in the pre-selection phase. Sorry, we like it very much, but it lacks a design element. (City-maker and opinion-maker, May 2018)

Most ULL initiators, however, did have a background in design and architecture, which explains why many initiatives were primarily focused on the built environment. Additionally, the fact that ULL's could also receive national funding from Stimulation Fund for Creative Industries explained why creative design was so prominent in many of them.

4. *Place bound experimentation versus placeless learning and accountability*

The label of 'urban lab' guaranteed a certain level of freedom *in situ*: i.e. experimentation with and learning from new ideas and interventions without having to comply with generic accountability criteria, such as key performance indicators, that can be applied anywhere. City-makers argued that a New Public Management free bubble was a necessary condition for experimental learning from new forms of local partnership and system innovation that could not be pre-defined in targets. By demarcating and embedding experimental ventures in a particular geographical area (e.g. a couple of streets or whole neighbourhood), experiments (and possible failures) were locally contained and granted a pilot status.

Despite the so-called benefits of experimentation, the relatively free conditions of the urban labs and their experimental status simultaneously raised concerns about the limited possibilities to upscale learning experiences and transfer lessons to other places (as best-practices). The Stimulation Fund for Creative Industries raised this concern in a recent manifest:

Experimenting in urban labs requires special conditions: a creative free place outside of regular practice that explores and tries out new matters, confined to a specific area, with a couple of enthusiastic frontrunners. The more these condi-

tions are in place, the more space there is for the experiment. Yet, those exact same conditions simultaneously ensure a limited spread and upscaling of learning effects. In fact, upscaling asks for embedding into an organization, representation, connection to frameworks, policy and regular budgets. Paradoxically, the free conditions of the experiment hamper the further upscaling of it: the pilot paradox! (Stimuleringsfonds Creatieve Industrie 2018)

In addition, local knowledge institutes that supported urban labs urged initiators to monitor progress to enable exchange of learning experiences and to account for results. Especially labs that were closely affiliated with these local knowledge institutes were keen to do so by coupling their experiments to performance indicators of the local government, such as the social safety index. They thereby seemed to adopt the 'system' logic of the local government. Yet, other labs which took a more autonomous stance, resisted monitoring of their own activities, because they feared to be held accountable for (lacking) results, thereby being limited in their freedom to experiment:

Normally speaking, they (local government) work with a long-term planning and public tenders. But in this area, they want to give themselves the space to not do that (...). They do not really want to make a planning. X says: "if I make a planning, then they will hold me to account". (Director local urban knowledge institute, December 2018)

As a result of this different approach, policymakers from local knowledge institutes questioned the fact whether this was a 'real' urban lab, since a 'real' lab would engage in monitoring of evidence and exchange of learning experiences.

Generally speaking though, most initiators of urban labs engaged in alternative forms of monitoring and reporting of learning experiences. This often took a narrative (written reports/stories) or visual form (pictures, small scale models of interventions, social maps):

You have to learn from experiments, so yes, you need to write that down somewhere. That's why we wrote down our "principles" (new principles for public tenders based on citizen participation)." (initiator ULL, with a focus on the built environment, September 2018)

The narrative and visual form of accountability seemed to be able to convey the place-boundedness of experimentation (showing the particularities of places), yet also lend itself for translating at least some lessons to other places, such as how to collaborate with different stakeholders or to connect various green initiatives in one network. The exchange of lessons was done during a yearly well-attended conference about city making. Additionally, some labs exchanged learning experiences with each other on a more ad-hoc basis by sending each other updates or informally meeting up for a coffee to catch up. By engaging in local knowledge exchange and alternative forms of accountability (visual/narrative), urban labs partially seemed to 'work around' the trade-off between place bound experimentation and placeless learning.

5. *Capital value versus societal value*

Despite the turn to alternative forms of accountability, many urban labs struggled to convey the societal value of their experiments in such a way that it would convince institutional stakeholders, such as local government and housing associations, to financially invest in successful experiments on a long-term basis. This issue was taken up by the Architecture Institute that commissioned a researcher to write an essay about the recent challenges of urban labs:

> *The local government still works with project-based performance norms and less so with societal added value that is generated by (civil servants') efforts. As long as that doesn't change, regular professional work will be more important than city making of which the value is difficult to express in outcome targets or monetary value.* (Boonstra 2018)

Due to difficulty of capitalizing the 'soft' societal value of experiments, urban labs did not have a strong position towards powerful stakeholders, such as (commercial and public) developers. Despite good collaborations, being at the mercy of these powerful stakeholders generated feelings of dependence and fear. This was for example seen in the urban lab that focused on the built environment, where a group of local entrepreneurs had revitalized a derelict area after the financial crisis, thereby contributing to the livability for local entrepreneurs who were located in the area and the broader gentrification of this area. Although the local entrepreneurs were successful in setting up good working relations with the commercial developers in order to develop new criteria for quality-based tendering of the area, they feared that in the end commercial developers would prioritize 'hard' monetary value over 'soft' societal value, such as livability:

> With this initiative, everything is very soft. And that's problematic, because how are you going to develop an area based on soft values? How can you measure those values? (...). Now it's an exciting time and I am also fearful (...). What if the management of the housing association says: we just want to go for the money? (...). Then we are nowhere with our quality. (initiator ULL with a focus on the built environment, September 2018)

This trade-off between capital and societal value was not only experienced in this specific lab. In their national manifest for urban labs, the national Stimulation Fund for Creative Industry, signaled this as a broader tension:

> Urban labs try to revitalize derelict, unused areas with concrete societal initiatives. By doing so, they add value to the area which in turn enables large-scale redevelopment. The added value however is going to the developers and governments, whereas the pioneers are left behind empty-handed. (Stimuleringsfonds Creatieve Industrie 2018)

To change this situation, several initiators of labs as well as the Architecture Institute pleaded for a cultural transition:

> We need a new way of thinking about investments, accountability, value development and measurement and a cultural transition in the long run. (Boonstra 2018)

In line with this plea, initiators of ULL's discussed the possibility of developing societal business models to be able to operationalize the monetary value of societal interventions. As of yet, these discussions have not resulted in a different financial infrastructure for the urban labs in the municipality.

15.6   Dealing with Trade-Offs Differently: A New Social Contract for ULL's?

Urban lab initiators as well as policymakers feel a lingering unease about how trade-offs are currently being dealt with. Although the liminal space of ULL's offers possibilities of doing things differently, it simultaneously creates vulnerabilities for the legitimacy of decision-making and the future position of urban labs. Precisely because liminal spaces lack clear boundaries and are fluid, they can be pushed back by institutional players, like the local government or real estate developers, that can mobilize formal mandates and rules.

In our case study we see that the liminal space of urban labs is currently at risk of being curbed and reigned in. Market developers and local government have started to regain the lead in urban development after the recovery of the crisis, whereas professionals that initiated the urban labs have less time for city-making now that the job market has recovered. With the new large-scale municipal mission to build 18.000 houses in the next four years, it remains to be seen whether the liminal space of the urban lab will be used in the future to incrementally learn from experiments and local forms of collaboration. Urban lab makers seem to be acutely aware of their vulnerable status. Not only in terms of the future use of labs in urban development, but also in terms of how value trade-offs currently are made in an institutional void.

As a response to deal with the vulnerabilities of decision-making in liminal space, various opinion-making lab makers as well as local policy makers, have plead for institutionalization of urban labs by developing a new 'social contract'. In a presentation by the Architecture Institute on the yearly city making conference, this social contract was presented as follows:

> *A city making contract will ensure that the rules of the game, developed by urban city-makers and urban labs, will be coupled to smart and transparent tender procedures, to ensure that the future production of public housing and other major challenges will be dealt with in manner worthy of city-makers.*
> (Document analysis: Pamphlet for city making, November 2018)

Key principles of this social contract include: 'equality of participants of urban labs' (in terms of determining activities, vision documents, etc.), 'publicity of data that are used in decision-making', 'transparency of process' (start and end date), 'manoeuvring room for civil servants to creatively think about the options that stakeholders put on the table'. This proposal for a social contract was subsequently taken up by the political party Green Left in the local council. In 2018, this political party filed a motion for establishing city making rules based on the experiences with the urban labs, including the introduction of new public tender criteria.

Although the motion was accepted in the council, as of yet, no concrete actions have been taken to implement city making rules in practice. On a national level, the Stimulation Fund for Creative Industries has plead for a new legal status and financial arrangements to better support urban labs.

These local and national pleas can be understood as attempts to deliberate new institutional rules and norms in urban development. Supposedly, these rules would potentially enable stakeholders to make different decisions, e.g. prioritizing 'soft' societal value over 'hard' capital value instead of the other way around. The potential success of these emerging institutional rules in terms of more legitimate decision-making about value trade-offs depends on the incorporation and acceptance of these rules by traditional political fora (such as the local council) and institutional players, such as housing developers and local government.

15.7   CONCLUSION

In this chapter we argued that the primary governance challenge of is to effectively use their liminal *in-between* position to create livable cities. We conceptualized this liminal position in at least three respects: (1) ULL's are positioned in-between different organizational boundaries, stakeholders and domains (market, society, science, policy), (2) ULL's are geographically 'emplaced' in particular areas while at the same time being 'placeless' by generalizing knowledge to elsewhere (3) ULL's are considered a free space to innovate due to the temporary exemption from normal rules and regulations. Due to these liminal positions, ULL's are expected to more effectively deal with trade-offs in the creation of livable cities. For example, by bridging boundaries between market and society, it would become possible to co-produce knowledge and innovate on a system level. However, liminal space at the same time is claimed to generate certain risks in terms of legitimate decision-making and accountability. Because ULL's often lack generally accepted rules and norms about decision-making and the inclusion of stakeholders in participation processes, they can potentially lead to an institutional void (Hajer 2003; Leong 2017).

As our analysis demonstrates, the liminal space of ULL's offers both advantages and disadvantages for the creation of livable cities. Liminal space, for instance enabled the regeneration of derelict areas by joining-up efforts between local entrepreneurs, designers, housing associations and local government. In addition, the temporary exemption from normal rules and regulations was used to experimentally learn from new interventions outside the dominant NPM culture of local government. Yet, liminal space also created vulnerabilities. Despite the attention for inclusive participation and decision-making, initiators of ULL's (who often had a professional background in architecture or urban design) implicitly favoured design-led approaches to urban development and prioritized developments of physical buildings/areas over social issues that were less tangible, such as debt. Due to the dominance of this 'creative professional caste', inclusive participation by 'lay' residents, and their perceptions of what a livable city should constitute, was less of a priority. Another vulnerability in ULL's was the prioritization of 'hard' capital value over 'soft' societal value due to a lack of societal business models and the renewed dominance of developers and local government once they had recuperated from the credit crisis. These results show that the creation of livable cities is not merely a technical or neutral matter. Initiators of ULL's dealt with many value trade-offs in terms of its relation to the institutional environment (collaborative or activist), key participants (professional or lay), focus (social or material), strategy for experimental learning (place-bound experimentation or placeless learning and accountability) and outcome of experiments (capital or societal value).

In the making of these value trade-offs, ULL's can make an important contribution to the livability of cities, yet their potential is not entirely met. As van Montfort and Michels state in the opening chapter of this book, both management factors (legitimacy, responsiveness, stable funding, leadership) and contextual factors (path dependency, political environment, demographics, good governance), play an important role in how effective the contribution of partnerships is to the creation of livable cities. With regards to both sets of factors, our case study reveals that the ideal conditions are not yet in place. Lack of stable funding, leadership by a professional designer caste, and little participation by lay residents potentially diminishes the responsiveness and legitimacy of ULL's. Moreover, the path dependency of a historically strong local civil service in urban planning and the large-scale nature of public tenders may limit the room of ULL's to maneuver and make their own decisions.

Because currently many ULL organizers feel uneasy about the vulnerability of the liminal status of ULL's, they argue for the development of new institutional rules for city making, such as transparent tendering criteria and transparency about conflicting values. Whether these attempts to institutionalize the liminal space of urban labs will result in a more powerful position of labs in the future will remain to be seen. However, an implication of institutionalization on request can be that liminal space of urban labs becomes less liminal. This can potentially address the lack of legitimacy in decision-making in which difficult value trade-offs are made, yet may also hamper the open-ended nature of experimentation by introducing bureaucratic procedures and co-opting labs into implementing formal policy. For future city-makers it thus remains a careful balancing act between cherishing the fluid nature of the in-between space for experimentation while at the same time being politically savvy enough to deal with institutional stakeholders that may instrumentally use this fluidity for their own purposes.

REFERENCES

Augé, M. (1995). *Non-places: Introduction to an anthropology of supermodernity.* London: Verso.

Boonstra, B. (2018). *De volgende stap voor het Rotterdamse stadsmaken.* English title: *The next step for Rotterdam city making.* Commissioned essay by the Architecture Institute of Rotterdam.

Boonstra, B., De Vrieze, R., & Bongers, H. (2018). *Beknopte analyse stadslabs legacy.* Rotterdam: SMC 18.

Bovens, M. (2005). De verspreiding van de democratie. *Beleid en Maatschappij, 32*(3), 119–127.

Bulkeley, H., et al. (2016). Urban living labs: Governing urban sustainability transitions. *Current Opinion in Environmental Sustainability, 22,* 13–17.

Czarniawska, B., & Mazza, C. (2003). Consulting as a liminal space. *Human Relations, 56*(3), 267–290.

Ellis, N., & Ybema, S. (2010). Marketing identities: Shifting circles of identification in inter-organizational relationships. *Organization Studies, 31*(3), 279–305.

Gieryn, T. F. (2000). A space for place in sociology. *Annual Review of Sociology, 26*(2000), 463–496.

Gieryn, T. F. (2006). City as truth-spot: laboratories and field-sites in urban studies. *Social Studies of Science, 36*(1), 5–38.

Gopakumar, G. (2014). Experiments and counter-experiments in the urban laboratory of water-supply partnerships in India. *International Journal of Urban and Regional Research, 38*(2), 393–412.

Hajer, M. (2003). Policy without polity? Policy analysis and the institutional void. *Policy Sciences, 36*(2), 175–195.

Iedema, R., Long, D., & Carroll, K. (2012). Corridor communication, spatial design and patient safety: Enacting and managing complexities. In A. van

Marrewijk & D. Yanow (Eds.), *Organizational spaces: Rematerializing the workaday world* (pp. 41–57). Cheltenham: Edward Elgar.

Ivanova, D., Wallenburg, I., & Bal, R. (2019). Place-by-proxy: Care infrastructures in a foundling room. *Sociological Review, 68*, 144. https://doi.org/10.1177/0038026119868642.

Karvonen, A., & Van Heur, B. (2014). Urban laboratories: Experiments in reworking cities. *International Journal of Urban and Regional Research, 38*(2), 379–392.

Lefebvre, H. (1991). *The production of space.* Oxford: Blackwell Publishing.

Leong, C. (2017). Hajer's institutional void and legitimacy without polity. *Policy Sciences, 50*(4), 573–583.

Rahmawan-Huizenga, S., & Ivanova, D. (submitted). The Urban Lab as interpretative grid: Unraveling dominant urban imaginaries, Science as Culture.

Short, H. (2015). Liminality, space and the importance of 'transitory dwelling places' at work. *Human Relations, 68*(4), 633–658.

Stimuleringsfonds Creatieve Industrie. (2018). *Manifest stadslabs. Pionieren aan de grote maatschappelijke opgaven.* English title: *Manifest Urban Labs. Pioneering big societal challenges.*

Turner, V. (1974). *Dramas, fields and metaphors.* Ithaca: Cornell University Press.

Turner, V. (1982). *From ritual to theatre: The human seriousness of play.* New York: Performing Arts Journal Publications.

Van Gennep, A. (1960 [1909]). *The rites of passage.* Chicago: University of Chicago Press.

Voytenko, Y., McCormick, K., Evans, J., & Schliwa, G. (2016). Urban living labs for sustainability and low carbon cities in Europe: Towards a research agenda. *Journal of Cleaner Production, 123*, 45–54.

Westerhout, A., & Bongers, H. (2017). *Stadsmaken in stadslabs. Een nieuwe aanpak van stedelijke ontwikkeling.* English title. *City making in urban labs. A new approach for urban development.* https://www.puntkomma.org/voytenkog-opakumarartikelen/stadmaken-in-stadslabs. Assessed 28 Mar 2019.

CHAPTER 16

Partnerships for Innovation: The Case of Urban Living Lab in Turin

Giorgia Nesti

16.1   Introduction

Cities matter. They are the core of territories and the place where citizens live their social, cultural, and political lives. But cities are also experiencing new challenges. International organizations like the UN or the European Union as well expressed their concerns about the process of demographic growth due to migrations that is affecting cities all around the world. This phenomenon has direct impacts on urban contexts such as rapid urbanization, ageing, and increased social inequalities but it also affects the environment and raises problems such as pollution and climate change. Local policymakers are called to handle those challenges with limited resources, increased economic constraints but also without the appropriate policy tools. Thus, in order to solve new and complex policy problems, politicians and public managers are pushed 'to think outside the box' and to look at novel instruments for novel answers. Among those policy tools, the Urban Living Labs (ULL) have recently become very popular. An

G. Nesti (✉)
Department of Political Science, Law, and International Studies,
University of Padova, Padova, Italy
e-mail: giorgia.nesti@unipd.it

© The Author(s) 2020
C. van Montfort, A. Michels (eds.), *Partnerships for Livable Cities*,
https://doi.org/10.1007/978-3-030-40060-6_16

317

Urban Living Lab can be defined as 'a forum for innovation that integrates residents and other stakeholders to develop and test new ideas, systems, and solutions in complex and real contexts' (Juujärvi and Lund 2016). They are considered a useful strategy to deal with multidimensional problems, since they involve various stakeholders, including citizens, in a process of experimentation of possible new solutions. More precisely, ULL are characterized by an open approach to innovation, aimed at eliciting knowledge from local actors about potential new policy solutions for local problems (Nesti 2018). This experience takes place in a real-life setting though their engagement in a collaborative process of design, production and evaluation of innovative products or services for local communities.

Furthermore, a number of studies have recently investigated ULL's potential in promoting the diffusion of new policies, programs and governance models to mitigate climate change (Evans and Karvonen 2014; Bulkeley et al. 2016; Evans 2016; Frantzeskaki et al. 2018; Bulkeley et al. 2018; Kronsell and Mukhtar-Landgren 2018; Von Wirth et al. 2019; Voytenko et al. 2016). These scholars quite unanimously consider ULL a valuable governance approach to support the definition and implementation of environmental policies for sustainable development at the local level. ULL, in fact, can address complex issues such as the fight against climate change, transition to low carbon economy, or the management of new technological solutions like Beacons,[1] Internet of Things[2] (IoT), Internet of Data[3] (IoD), autonomous vehicle technologies at least at a

---

[1] Beacons are small transmitters that can be used to identify and track smartphones. They work by sending and receiving signals across small physical areas so they can be used in stores for mobile marketing to offer customized special deals, or they can distribute messages at a bus stop, or in a cultural site. (See also https://www.independent.co.uk/life-style/gadgets-and-tech/news/ibeacon-what-is-it-and-why-should-i-care-9311014.html—Accessed September 24, 2019).

[2] IBM defines the Internet of Things (IoT) as 'the concept of connecting any device (so long as it has an on/off switch) to the Internet and to other connected devices'. The IoT is a giant network of connected things and people—all of which collect and share data about the way they are used and about the environment around them. Devices and objects with built in sensors are connected to an Internet of Things platform, which integrates data from the different devices and applies analytics to share the most valuable information with applications built to address specific needs' (from: https://www.ibm.com/blogs/internet-of-things/what-is-the-iot/ for more details—Accessed September 24, 2019).

[3] According to Fan et al., 'the Internet of data represents the extension of the IoT in the digital world [...]. Within the system of the IoD, people can monitor all the data entities, which can interconnect with one another with the help of virtual tags and data vitalization

twofold level. One the one side, they promote multi-stakeholder partnerships that can foster mutual learning and the study of joint solutions for urban problems. On the other side, ULL provide a physical space where those solutions can be directly tested by users and recalibrated by producers. Collaboration and experimentation are, therefore, two major characteristics of the ULL approach.

Despite the strong emphasis on these two aspects, nevertheless, there has been little discussion about how partnerships for ULL are created and managed at the local level, and for the benefit of whom. On this basis, the main purpose of the present chapter is to analyze all these aspects by looking at an interesting case-study, the Turin Living Lab created by the Municipality of Turin in 2016 and now operating under the label Turin City Lab.

The chapter proceeds as follows. After a brief introduction of the concept of ULL and its main characteristics (Sect. 16.2). Section 16.3 first describes when and why the Turin Living Lab and Turin City Lab were created, and then describes the initiatives promoted by the Labs from 2016 onward. Section 16.4 analyses the structure of partnerships put in place for the Turin Living Lab by identifying the type of actors involved in the experimentations, their roles and the characteristics of the model of partnership adopted. Finally, the conclusion summarizes the main findings and assesses main strengths and weaknesses of the approach adopted in Turin, with a special focus on the impact Turin Living Lab had and Turin City Lab is having on the livability of the city.

16.2   The Urban Living Lab Approach

The first use of the concept of the 'Living Laboratory'—or Living Lab—is traced back to the article by Bajgier et al. published in 1991 where authors describe an innovative learning methodology to engage university students in 'real-world projects' of public management in a neighborhood of Philadelphia (Bajgier et al. 1991, p. 701). The concept was then applied by William J. Mitchell from the MIT Media Lab and School of Architecture in 1995 to examine routine activities in real-life contexts (Ballon and Schuurman 2015). But Living Lab initiatives, indeed, flourished in the early 2000s when the European Commission financed their creation under

could be applied [...]. All the data entities in the IoD are connected with the support of the Internet' (2012, pp. 661–662).

the Seventh Framework Programme for Research and Development (European Commission 2009). Over recent years they gained popularity among academics and practitioners due to their approach based on open innovation, experimentation and citizen participation (Nesti 2018). Living Labs, in fact, are environments where stakeholders collaborate to co-design, co-create, prototype and testing innovative products or services. Living Labs usually involve firms, public agencies, research centers, users, and non-profit organisations in real-life settings under the supervision of an expert or a practitioner to design and test new products (Westerlund and Leminen 2011; Karvonen and van Heur 2014; Ballon et al. 2018). The Living Lab methodology is usually based on four stages: context analysis, observation of everyday users' behavior, collaborative innovation (co-designing, prototyping, and testing of products and services), and participants' evaluation of prototypes (Nesti 2018).

Urban Living Labs (ULL) fall within the family of Living Lab. They can be defined as 'a local place for innovative solutions that aims to solve urban challenges and contribute to long-term sustainability by actively and openly co-constructing solutions with citizens and other stakeholders' (Chronéer et al. 2019, p. 60). Thus, through the adoption of ULL, local authorities involve citizens and other relevant stakeholders on small-scale experiments aimed at creating and testing innovative modes of governance, policies, products, and services. ULL's methodology is based on several steps such as: (a) analysis of urban context (starting conditions, strengths and challenges, possible previous experience in the same policy domain) and definition of the problem to be solved; (b) selection of residents and stakeholders to be involved in the ULL, and analysis of their needs; (c) definition of common goals and of a shared vision for ULL actions; (d) identification of roles, procedures, management tasks, and documentation to be collected; (e) definition of the time plan and of communication strategies; (f) implementation of the experimental approach through prototyping; (g) collection of users' feedbacks and evaluation of the best solution (Friedrich et al. 2013; Nesti 2017). Different methodologies from user-centered design, participatory design and citizen participation are usually applied in each stage of the experimental process—understanding of problems, generating ideas, presenting and evaluating solutions. The most used are interviews, questionnaires, brainstorming, storytelling, focus groups, idea competition, scenarios, and mock-ups (Friedrich et al. 2013).

Beside experimentation, open innovation and an extensive use of ICTs, a peculiar characteristic of ULL is their approach based on PPPP, or public-private-people partnerships (Nesti 2018). Like Living Labs, in fact, ULL adopt a Quadruple Helix approach that gather public and private actors, knowledge centers, firms and citizens in a process of collaborative experimentation (Leminen et al. 2012; Schuurman and Tõnurist 2017; Westerlund et al. 2018). According to the categorization presented in Fig. 1.1 (Chap. 1), ULL are a type H partnership, based on the collaboration of civil society, market, and state. Namely, in ULL city representatives define the vision, allocate the budget, exert leadership, create and coordinate the partnership, while research centers usually provide knowledge and methodology, private firms produce the prototype of the product or the service to be tested, and citizens-users contribute to define residents' needs, to find new possible solutions to local problems and to evaluate potential policy impacts (Juujärvi and Lund 2016). Due to their active involvement in the process of experimentation, indeed, citizens are often viewed as co-producers of the innovation (Nesti 2018).

Even though partnerships supporting the creation of ULL are an interesting aspect, literature on this topic is not thoroughly developed. More precisely, there's little empirical evidence about the way through which partnerships are created and possibly formalized, the type of actors involved, with what roles, and the benefit they are supposed to offer to residents. The purpose of this paper is to try to fill this gap in literature by analyzing a case study of ULL developed in Italy, the Turin Living Lab set up in 2016 and then renamed Turin City Lab in 2018. This Lab has been selected as a typical case study of ULL since it encapsulates most of the characteristics of an ULL (Yin 2009). The empirical research has been conducted following a qualitative approach and fieldwork. Information related to the Lab was collected from the website[4] and integrated with two face-to-face open interviews with key informants carried out in July 2017.

16.3   DESCRIPTION OF THE CASE: TURIN LIVING LAB (2016–18) AND TURIN CITY LAB (2018–19)

In 2013 the former Executive Councilor for the Environment and the Chief Officer for Innovation and Economic Development of the Municipality of Turin ideated, in the context of the Smart City Strategy, the initiative 'Turin Living Lab', an urban laboratory located in the

---

[4] See https://www.torinocitylab.com/en/ for more details (Accessed September 24, 2019).

neighborhood Campidoglio.[5] The lab was aimed at promoting the collaboration between the City administration and local enterprises, associations, research centers, and residents to experiment, develop, and testing innovative technological solutions in a specific area of the city. The ULL approach was specifically chosen because it would help decision makers to understand potential impacts of innovations both on public administration and citizens on a small scale, before upscaling it to the whole city.

The initiative Turin Living Lab was officially launched by the Municipality in January 2016 with the public call 'Living Lab Campidoglio' that specifically searched for profit and non-profit partners interested in testing innovative solutions for Turin Smart City—a project aimed at promoting a social, economic, and environmental sustainable development in the urban area of Turin. The Smart City was initially implemented through the Master Plan SMILE made of 45 projects focused on Mobility, Inclusion, Life and Health, and Energy. Thirty-six organizations answered to the call 'Living Lab Campidoglio' and 31 proposals were selected to be implemented in the District. Projects lasted two years and covered several policy domains such as environment, mobility, and tourism—testing concerned, among the others, a street vacuum cleaner, recycled paper for food, apps to monitor children, to use public transport, to incentivize sustainable mobility and tourism, control units to monitor pollution, portable sensors, car-pooling to go to work, neighborhood watching, evaluation of tangible and intangible public assets, participatory security.

The Municipality issued another call at the end of 2016 to find partners interested in developing and testing mobile payment services for the Registry Office. Three companies submitted their proposals and one was selected ('CityPay Anagrafe'). The experimentation tested citizens' payments through an app and a dedicated website.

On April 2017, the call Living Lab IoT was launched to test Internet of Things and Internet of Data solutions for Turin Smart City. Fourteen enterprises participated in the call and seven projects have been implemented in the fields of cyber security, flood monitoring and alerting, retrofitting and smart buildings, seismic monitoring for public assets, sensors to monitor the environmental quality, rainfall monitoring and analysis, and Beacons for tourism.

---

[5] Campidoglio is a residential area, with a population of 14.889 inhabitants located in a semi-central position in the north-western quadrant of the City of Turin (District 4).

In spring 2018 the Lab Sharing&Circular on the circular and collaborative economy was created as part of the Program AXTO (Actions for Turin Peripheries), a project of regeneration of urban peripheries promoted by the City of Turin and funded by the Italian Presidency of Ministers with EUR 18 million. AXTO is targeted to improve the livability of public spaces, to secure public housing, to revitalize the local economy, to implement socio-cultural programs, and to enhance citizens' participation. The Lab Sharing&Circular funded the eight best organizations that would implement projects aimed at responding to social challenges and at improving the quality of life in the target areas of the AXTO program. The eight projects concerned the collaborative economy and the creation of Solidarity Purchasing Groups (GAS); plastic recycling and transformation into design objects; the preparation of meals for homeless and the collection of food surpluses; the application of the concept of reuse and recycling in the construction industry; the creation of an e-commerce portal for the recovery, recycling and enhancement of goods; transformation of inert material into recycled soil; reuse and recycling of textiles; collaborative system for the production and consumption of vegetable products based on hydroponic cultivation techniques.

In 2018 the Municipality started implementing also the project Too(L) Smart in collaboration with the University of Messina and the Italian cities of Padua, Lecce, and Syracuse. The experimentation is aimed at testing a network of sensors that collect data on the urban physical environment. The leading partner is the Municipality of Turin and the project has been financed by European Structural Funds Program.

Finally, during the same year, the Municipality of Turin launched the project Smart Road to test smart grids, optic fiber, and cameras on a 35 km circuit, in order to create city road infrastructures for autonomous car testing. The specific aim of the City of Turin was to enhance the collaboration with firms and research centers in order to develop digital solutions, monitoring platforms, new services of data elaboration for road infrastructure and to test autonomous cars. The project involved 11 partners—big players of the automotive sector and research centers—and was part of the experimentation of APW technologies launched by the Italian Ministry for Transport.

The last initiative of Turin Living Lab was the Campidoglio Laboratory, an initiative linked to the European project Life—Living Streets coordinate by the Municipality, aimed at controlling traffic, and at promoting a sustainable mobility in the area Borgo Vecchio of the District. The project started in June 2016, when the Municipality, with the support of external experts, organized four meetings with residents and made 34 interviews with local associations, artisans, and dealers. The first meeting was organized using the 'World Café' technique and involved 34 persons—citizens, representatives of associations, architects, and artisans—who collected 68 ideas for the events. A second meeting was organized in July with 23 participants—the same group that participated in the 'World Café'—to co-design the events, to plan the related activities, and to enhance networking among residents. Two two-day events were organized between September and October 2017 by citizens, local associations, schools, artisans and artists of the neighborhood, where 370 persons participated. As part of the experimentation, also a public consultation was held, and 158 persons answered to it. In the consultation residents were asked to express their opinions about the hypothesis to expand the pedestrian area and cycling tracks, and to lower speed limits in the neighborhood. At the end of the participatory process, the pedestrian area in Borgo Vecchio was expanded.

On July 2018, Turin Living Lab was transformed into Turin City Lab. Drawing on past experiences, the Municipality decided, in fact, to redefine its approach to innovation and to transform all the city of Turin in a 'open-air' laboratory where firms could test the quality and technical validity of their product or services at the pre-commercial stage. Thus, Turin City Lab, represents the 'scaling up' of the experience made with Turin Living Lab, with which it shares the approach focused on quick experimentation. But through Turin City Lab the Municipality also fosters simplification, deregulation, and the creation of multi-stakeholder partnerships with big players and SMEs, public utilities, research centers, civil society organizations, and other local stakeholders. Namely, Turin City Lab is a platform aimed at reducing red-tapes and at promoting collaboration with companies interested in testing innovative solutions for urban living in a real-life context. Turin City Lab is now coordinated by the Executive Councilor for Innovation and by the Chief Officer for the area Innovation, European Funds and Information Systems and its mission is to provide 'simplified access to public spaces and assets, including intangible assets (processes, services and data)'.[6] Turin City Lab is currently completing the projects financed under Turing Living Lab and it is imple-

---

[6] Source: https://www.torinocitylab.com/en/welcome-to/about-torino-city-lab (Accessed September 24, 2019).

menting new ones in the areas of drones and autonomous cars. The following paragraph analyses how partnerships have been created and managed in order to implement the projects related to Turing Living Lab.

16.4 ANALYZING PARTNERSHIPS

The initiative Turin Living Lab was started in 2016 by the Municipality with the specific aim to find partners to co-produce innovative solutions for Turin Smart City. More precisely, the Municipality launched six public calls (one for each project) in 2016 and 49 activities were undertaken. Experimentations covered different topics, but environmental sustainability was the most addressed issue. The map of actors reveals that collaboration promoted in the context of Turin Living Lab had a very broad nature since it encompassed the Municipality, one research centers and two universities, 33 firms, 7 non-profit organizations (associations, foundations, cooperatives, social enterprises), schools, Neighborhood Committees, and citizens (see Table 16.1).

Within this collaborative environment, nevertheless, participants performed different roles. More precisely, it is possible to identify five roles that participants can accomplish in the ULL: promoter, leader, designer, producer, and user. The first role is performed by the actor who sponsors the Lab, who defines how the partnership should take place, who makes available structures and funds. The leading actor coordinates and manages the whole process of experimentation. Designers and producers are actors responsible for designing and producing the product or service—usually in the form of prototype—that should be tested in the Lab. Users, finally, are those who are called to test or use the prototype in order to give feedbacks to designers and producers for improvements.

Table 16.2 summarizes the role performed by each type of actor, based the Lab's documents and its website.

As clearly emerges from the data, the role of promoter is monopolized by the Municipality of Turin. This finding is consistent with the literature on ULL already highlighting the centrality of local governments in this form of experimentation (Bulkeley et al. 2016; Kronsell and Mukhtar-Landgren 2018; Chronéer et al. 2019). The City administration represents the engine of Turin Living Lab—but of Turin City Lab as well: It ideates the experimentation, defines aims and contents of partnerships and signs the Agreements with the partners. More specifically, in their study Kronsell and Mukhtar-Landgren (2018) identified three roles performed

Table 16.1 Types of actors involved in Turing Living Lab

Name of the project	No. of activities	Topics	Type of partners
Living Lab Campidoglio	31	Environment and territory Data integration Data security Integration and life-style Culture and tourism Commerce Mobility Health and wellness Energy	Municipality Private firms Shops Polytechnic of Turin University of Turin Cooperatives Associations Foundations Citizens
Mobile payment	1	Mobile tax payments	Municipality Private firms Citizens
Living Lab IoT	7	Cyber security Rain & flood monitoring Retrofitting of public buildings Seismic monitoring Waste and noise monitoring Tourism	Municipality Private firms
Sharing&Circular	8	Collaborative economy Recycling of plastic Sustainable food consumption Circular construction E-commerce portal Recycling of soil Horticulture	Municipality Cooperatives Associations Social enterprises Private firms Foundations Consultancies University spin-off Neighborhood committees Citizens
Too(L)Smart	1	Sensors for environmental monitoring	Municipalities University
Smart roads	1	Smart infrastructure for autonomous car testing	Municipality Private firms University Foundations Associations
Campidoglio Laboratory	1	Sustainable mobility	Municipality Citizens Schools Associations

Table 16.2 Actors' roles in Turin Living Lab

	Promoter	Leader	Designer	Producer	User
Municipality	X	X	X	X	X
Research centers and universities		X	X	X	X
Private firms		X	X	X	X
Non-profit organizations		X	X	X	X
Citizens			X	X	X

by Municipalities in ULL according to their degree of collaboration with the other actors: promoter, enabler, and partner. In Turin, the Municipality clearly performs the role of 'enabler', that is of facilitator of the experimentation process. The City, in fact, supports projects by offering places, structures, and/or administrative support; by enabling collaboration with partner, and by providing economic incentives. But, on the other hand, the Municipality generally does not have an explicit leading role and leaves it to the other partners, in particularly firms. The only exception to this trend is the project Campidoglio Laboratory: Here the Municipality assumed the role of promoter since it not only allowed for the creation of the partnership, but also leaded the collaborative process. Moreover, it also participated in designing and producing the events in collaboration with residents. Finally, the City administration collaborated in the project Mobile Payment by testing with citizens the ICT services for its offices.

Private firms were key actors of Turin Living Lab: they were the recipients of the initiative, but they also leaded experimentations, provided the knowledge and expertise to define and to carry out the process of experimentation, they designed and produced the artifacts or the services that were tested. Albeit to a less extent, in several projects they also performed the role of users of products or service, since they directly conducted the trials. Research centers and non-profit organizations were mainly leaders, designers, and producers as well. Like private firms, they were the principal target of the initiative Turin Living Lab and they are the target now of the new program Turin City Lab.

Citizens can have an active role, a passive role or no role in the experimental process (Menny et al. 2018). In the Turin Living Lab they were not promoters or leaders of the activities and they had a very limited role as designers or producers of innovative products and services. More precisely, only in the Campidoglio Laboratory citizens performed a relevant role of co-creator with the Municipality, due to their involvement in designing and delivering the events for the project Living Streets. In the projects Living Lab Campidoglio, Mobile Payments, and Sharing&Circular, citizens had principally the role of users of innovations since they tested prototypes and provided information and opinions about trials, but they did not participate directly in designing or producing them. Finally, in the projects Living Lab IoT, Too(L)Smart and Smart Roads, citizens did not take part into the experimentations, and tests were directly carried out by firms using infrastructures and places made available by the Municipality.

All in all, partnerships promoted through the ULL by the administration were mainly with private firms and/or with civil society organizations and/or with other public partners such as Universities. The fourth 'P' referred to people—or individual citizens—was present but not in central position. These partnerships, therefore, were based on the collaboration among various stakeholders to experiment innovative solutions for urban problems, but this collaboration did not imply the coproduction of the innovation. Apart from the Campidoglio Laboratory, each actor was involved in a specific stage of the experimentation and he or she did not share its 'duties' with other partners.

The whole process of innovation was meta-governed by the City administration that organized it almost in a similar way for each project. First, the Office Employment, development, European Funds and Smart City of the Municipality of Turin launched a public call opened to private firms, associations, non-profit organizations, and research centers. Projects were examined by a technical commission made of representatives belonging to the Municipality. The selected organizations signed a Partnership Agreement with the Municipality, where they accepted to implement their projects without charges and without purchase obligations for the Municipality. The Partnership Agreement also specified the characteristics of the experimentation, the duration, the number and type of partners involved in the project. Property rights, costs and responsibilities related to the project are attributed to the organization. The Municipality, on the other side provided its expertise to organizations, and strove to reduce administrative burdens and to simplify red tapes.

In the project Living Lab IoT the partnerships between the Municipality and the firms selected with the public call were created using a slightly different approach. In the first phase the Municipality of Turin and each firm cooperated to analyze threats, obligations, and all the elements characterizing the experimentation that should be taken into consideration to frame the Implementation Agreement. In the second phase, the Implementation

Agreement came into force and the project started. As stated in a City Deliberation,[7] the Municipality decided to adopt this two-steps approach because of the novelty of the call's topic. The preliminary dialogue between the City administration and the selected firms was meant as necessary in order to define the proper business model to be adopted, since public and private partnerships for the application of IoT and IoD to municipal services are not thoroughly developed in Italy. Thus, the joint definition of the Implementation Agreement would be also relevant to the City administration to evaluate whether to directly invest in the creation of the technological infrastructure, like for instance the narrow band, necessary to apply IoT and IoD or to leave this investment to the private market.

In the Project Sharing&Circular the call included a non-repayable grant of maximum 15.000 Euros. Projects were selected on the basis of their technical feasibility, their coherence with the purposes of the call, their novelty, their capacity to involve local stakeholders, and the economic and financial sustainability of the proposed business model. The Municipality also supported the selected organization with a service of project management, mentoring, business coaching, project evaluation, communication and networking with citizens and local stakeholders.

Finally, in the project Smart Roads, a Memorandum of Understanding among the Municipality and several local partners and big players, such as FCA Group, Polytechnic and University of Turin, Foundation Torino Wireless, Italdesign Giugiaro, Industrial Association, and Telecom Italy was signed.

In general, all the forms of partnerships have been formalized through Partnership Agreements, Implementation Agreements or Memorandum of Understandings where reciprocal duties are specified. This degree of formalization helped the City administration to manage effectively the collaboration since it clarified roles and responsibilities and bound all partners to achieve the expected results. Moreover, in the case of the Living Lab IoT the choice to implement a two-steps procedure for the definition of the agreements was due to a cautious approach adopted by the Municipality, since established rules and business models for the application of IoT to local territories are not present in Italy.

---

[7] Città di Torino, *Deliberazione della Giunta Comunale del 21 marzo 2017*, n. 2017 01018/027.

16.5   Conclusions

The experience of Turin City Lab draws on the legacy of Turin Living Lab and follows the pattern of collaboration previously traced with that project. The initiatives Turin Living Lab and Turin City Lab were created by the Municipality—the Executive Councilor for Innovation and by the Chief Officer for the area Innovation, European Funds and Information Systems—with the purpose of exploring new forms of cooperation with local stakeholders to create a local ecosystem favorable to innovation, to scout new trends in environmental and technological policy, and to identify the necessary skills to develop them. The specific aim of the two Labs was to dedicate a specific area of the City to quick experimentation of innovative products or services in order to test their quality, feasibility, and transferability in other neighborhoods or in other cities as well.

The approach followed by the Municipality through the creation of partnerships is twofold. On the one side, the City administration aspired to drive the transition to a new sustainable and knowledge economy through the creation of an 'enabling bureaucracy'. According to this approach, the Turin administration defines the regulatory framework where innovation can take place, it supports experimentations by offering places, structures and infrastructures to test them, and it guarantees the whole coordination of the process. On the other side, through the Urban Living Lab (ULL) the Municipality assigns to market and to civil society the tasks to produce innovation and it also transfers the costs and risks for its production to external partners.

Main strengths of this approach are, for the Municipality, the adoption of an incremental strategy that reduces costs and risk aversion; for firms and civil society the advantage is to share the burden of research & development activities with the City. The experience of Turin Living Lab and Turin City Lab represents a successful experience of multi-stakeholder partnerships since it created a safe, reliable, and trusty environment for participants, namely the Municipality, civil society organizations and private firms. Partnerships are, therefore, appealing for private actors because they can test innovative products in a pre-commercial environment. On the other side, through Turin Living Lab and Turin City Lab the Municipality of Turin can improve its administrative capacity to boost and manage strategic partnerships with external actors and can create an attractive economic environment for enterprises. Certainly, this success stems from a favorable socio-economic context (Nesti 2018). Turin has, in fact, a long-standing tradition of innovation due to presence of famous enterprises in the automotive and in the telecommunication sector, such as FCA or the headquarters of Vodafone Italy. In Turin are also present several research centers such as the University, the Polytechnic, and Nexa. Moreover, in the city several experimentations in the field of social innovation and smart city already took place in the previous years so that the City won the prize for the European Capital of Innovation in 2016.

Yet, the main limit of Turin's Labs concerns the lack of citizens' participation. Even though residents are involved as users in the experimentation, they do not participate in other stages of the process of innovation nor are they called to formally adhere to partnership agreements. Apart from the project Campidoglio Laboratory that was specifically designed to engage citizens in planning and delivering events and that adopted a participatory approach to urban need assessment, in the majority of projects citizens are passive users and not fully co-producers of innovation. As a result, the opportunity to really engage citizens through mechanism of co-production is not fully exploited and the Lab results weighted too heavily toward firms and organized civil society. This result is quite in line with Turin Living Lab and Turin City Lab's explicit goals to create a favorable environment for firms. Even if citizens are only marginally involved in the innovation process this exclusion did not raise concerns from the population. Rather—and quite paradoxically—the Turin approach to innovation is praised by the Five Star Movement, a political group that usually supports grassroot engagement and of which the Mayor of Turin Chiara Appendino is a member.

The second critical point of Turin's experience concerns the contribution of partnerships developed for the Labs to the livability of the city. Turin Living Lab's experimentations relate to the areas of environmental sustainability and to ICT, data management and security. All projects are ideally targeted to improve the quality of life of people living in Turin but, in the end, experimentations are not solving problems explicitly addressed by the local population. Moreover, the partnerships developed for the program Turin Living Lab proved to be effective just for short-term projects and their impacts have not been assessed yet. To date, therefore, it is still unclear who will benefit from their implementation.

The approach followed by Turin Living Lab and now by Turin City Lab is consistent with the 'mission' of ULL that is quick experimentation, as highlighted above. But one of the main limits of such an approach is that it's missing the opportunity to transform ULL pilot projects into continuous policy programs (Nesti 2018). For this reason, partnerships developed for Turin Living Lab and Turin City Lab have the potential to improve the quality life of residents but only if those experiences will be scaled up for the benefit of all city residents.

REFERENCES

Bajgier, S. M., Maragah, H. D., Saccucci, M. S., Verzilli, A., & Prybutok, V. R. (1991). Introducing students to community operations research by using a city neighborhood as a living laboratory. *Operations Research, 39*, 701–709.

Ballon, P., & Schuurman, D. (2015). Living labs: Concepts, tools and cases. *Info, 17*(4), 1–11.

Ballon, P., Van Hoed, M., & Schuurman, D. (2018). The effectiveness of involving users in digital innovation: Measuring the impact of living labs. *Telematics and Informatics, 35*(5), 1201–1214.

Bulkeley, H., Coenen, L., Frantzeskaki, N., Hartmann, C., Kronsell, A., Mai, L., Marvin, S., McCormick, K., van Steenbergen, F., & Voytenko Palgan, Y. (2016). Urban living labs: Governing urban sustainability transitions. *Current Opinion in Environmental Sustainability, 22*, 13–17.

Bulkeley, H., Marvin, S., Voytenko Palgan, Y., McCormick, K., Breitfuss-Loidl, M., Lindsay, M., von Wirth, T., & Frantzeskaki, N. (2018). Urban living laboratories: Conducting the experimental city? *European Urban and Regional Studies, 26*(4), 317–335.

Chronéer, D., Stahlbrost, A., & Habibipour, A. (2019). Urban living labs: Towards an integrated understanding of their key components. *Technology Innovation Management Review, 9*(3), 50–62.

European Commission. (2009). *Living labs for user-driven open innovation, directorate-general for the information society and media.* Luxembourg: Office for Official Publications of the European Communities.

Evans, J. (2016). Trials and tribulations: Problematizing the city through/as urban experimentation. *Geography Compass, 10*(10), 429–443.

Evans, J., & Karvonen, A. (2014). 'Give me a laboratory and I will lower your carbon footprint!'—Urban laboratories and the governance of low-carbon futures. *International Journal of Urban and Regional Research, 38*(2), 413–430.

Fan, W., Chen, Z., Xiong, Z., & Chen, H. (2012). The internet of data: A new idea to extend the IOT in the digital world. *Frontiers of Computer Science, 6*(6), 660–667.

Frantzeskaki, N., van Steenbergen, F., & Stedman, R. C. (2018). Sense of place and experimentation in urban sustainability transitions: The resilience lab in Carnisse, Rotterdam, the Netherlands. *Sustainability Science, 13*(4), 1045–1059.

Friedrich, P., Karlsson, A., & Federley, M. (2013). *Report 2.1. Boundary conditions for successful urban living labs.* The Hague: SubUrbanLab.

Juujärvi, S., & Lund, V. (2016). Enhancing early innovation in an urban living lab: Lessons from Espoo, Finland. *Technology Innovation Management Review, 6*(1), 17–26.

Karvonen, A., & van Heur, B. (2014). Urban laboratories: Experiments in reworking cities. *International Journal of Urban and Regional Research, 38*(2), 379–392.

Kronsell, A., & Mukhtar-Landgren, D. (2018). Experimental governance: The role of municipalities in urban living labs. *European Planning Studies, 26*(5), 988–1007.

Leminen, S., Westerlund, M., & Nyström, A. G. (2012). Living labs as open-innovation networks. *Technology Innovation Management Review, 2*(9), 6–11.

Menny, M., Voytenko, P. Y., & McCormick, K. (2018). Urban living labs and the role of users in co-creation. *GAIA—Ecological Perspectives on Science and Society, 27*(1), 68–77.

Nesti, G. (2017). Living labs: A new tool for co-production? In A. Bisello, D. Vettorato, R. Stephens, & P. Elisei (Eds.), *Smart and sustainable planning for cities and regions. Green energy and technology* (pp. 267–281). Cham: Springer International Publishing.

Nesti, G. (2018). Co-production for innovation: The urban living lab experience. *Policy & Society, 37*(3), 310–325.

Schuurman, D., & Tõnurist, P. (2017). Innovation in the public sector: Exploring the characteristics and potential of living labs and innovation labs. *Technology Innovation Management Review, 7*(1), 7–14.

Von Wirth, T., Fuenfschilling, L., Frantzeskaki, N., & Coenen, L. (2019). Impacts of urban living labs on sustainability transitions: Mechanisms and strategies for systemic change through experimentation. *European Planning Studies, 27*(2), 229–257.

Voytenko, Y., McCormick, K., Evans, J., & Schliwa, G. (2016). Urban living labs for sustainability and low carbon cities in Europe: Towards a research agenda. *Journal of Cleaner Production, 123*, 45–54.

Westerlund, M., & Leminen, S. (2011). Managing the challenges of becoming an open innovation company: Experiences from living labs. *Technology Innovation Management Review, 15*, 223–231.

Westerlund, M., Leminen, S., & Habib, C. (2018). Key constructs and a definition of living labs as innovation platforms. *Technology Innovation Management Review, 8*(12), 51–62.

Yin, R. K. (2009). *Case study research design and methods.* London: Sage Publications.

CHAPTER 17

Conclusions: The Dynamic and Fluid World of Partnerships

Ank Michels and Cor van Montfort

17.1 INTRODUCTION

The introductory chapter outlined the context of the central question of this book: how do partnerships between public and private actors contribute to the livability of cities? The conclusions in this chapter summarize the main patterns that we have distilled from the various chapters of the book. We start with a number of observations about the variation in partnerships. Second, the role of context and the characteristics of partnerships with respect to livability are analyzed. Third, we focus on the question of who benefits in terms of livability and who is excluded. Fourth, we discuss the different roles that the government may play in

A. Michels
Utrecht University School of Governance, Utrecht, The Netherlands
e-mail: a.m.b.michels@uu.nl

C. van Montfort (✉)
Tilburg Center for Regional Law and Governance (TiREG), Tilburg University, Tilburg, The Netherlands

Vrije Universiteit Amsterdam, Amsterdam, The Netherlands
e-mail: c.j.vanmontfort@tilburguniversity.edu

© The Author(s) 2020
C. van Montfort, A. Michels (eds.), *Partnerships for Livable Cities*,
https://doi.org/10.1007/978-3-030-40060-6_17

developing and sustaining partnerships that contribute to livability. And, fifth, we draw several general conclusions and return to the central question of this book.

17.2   Partnerships

In the introductory chapter, we developed a broad understanding of the concept of partnerships, taking the relationship between state, market, and civil society as a starting point for exploring different types of formal and informal partnerships between public and private actors. The types presented in the chapters of this book range from formal partnerships between government and companies (see the chapter by Pill, Chap. 12) to informal partnerships between city government and civil society associations (see Van de Wetering and Kaulingfreks, Chap. 13), partnerships as 'liminal spaces' in between system and society (see Oldenhof et al., Chap. 15), partnerships as 'multidisciplinary teaming' (Groenleer et al., Chap. 11) and partnerships that started as bottom-up initiatives by citizens (see de Abreu et al., Chap. 3 or Berti Suman, Chap. 10).

A first observation relating to the variation in partnerships is that is not always easy to define what is public and what is private in a public-private partnership. For example, Lu, Sun and de Jong (Chap. 5) point out that, because the government in China retains a controlling interest in state-owned enterprises, private enterprises of the type found in Western countries do not exist in China. Hence, it may be more appropriate to refer to public semi-public partnerships in the context of China. A more general observation is that the concept of partnerships may differ in post-industrial western countries from authoritarian states. As van der Heijden and Hong (Chap. 2) argue: 'the development strategy that drives state-guided economies such as South Korea, but also Japan and Singapore, has an inherently different understanding of the relationship between government, civil society and the business sector from that in, for example, liberal capitalist economies.' Where their analysis of cases in Seoul shows a far-reaching partnership between citizens and the state with a strong commitment from the Seoul government, from a Western point of view, this hardly constitutes a partnership but at best a form of 'tokenist' citizen participation (Arnstein 1969).

A second observation regarding the variation in type of partnership is that partnerships as such are not static but dynamic; they are fluid and often continue to develop and shapeshift over time. Numerous chapters provide examples of bottom-up initiatives that were taken forward in a later phase by other parties such as professional organizations, civil society organizations, and municipal governments. Examples are the case descriptions of neighborhood initiatives in Paris (Van de Wetering and Kaulingfreks, Chap. 13), the green initiatives in Tilburg (van Montfort and Michels, Chap. 4), and the citizen sensing initiatives in Fukushima and Eindhoven (Berti Suman, Chap. 10). The fluid nature of partnerships and their capacity to morph from one type into another is also shown in the cases of Seoul (van der Heijden and Hong, Chap. 2) and in the examples of urban labs (Oldenhof et al., Chap. 15). Partnerships seem to adapt their form according to what is needed given the tasks they are performing and the challenges they are facing.

A final observation is that sometimes, partnerships begin in one particular area but then show scaling-up effects to other areas as well. Interesting examples are provided by de Abreu et al. (Chap. 3) who demonstrate how micro-scale forms of urban agriculture started off as small projects focusing on food production, but gained a much broader spin-off in education, health provision, and in environmental and food practices.

17.3   LIVABILITY

In the introductory chapter, we assumed that there were two sets of factors that influence how partnerships contribute to livability: on the one hand, the characteristics and the management of the partnership and on the other, the role of context.

As regards the characteristics and the management of partnerships, we see that a strong commitment to the partnership and its goal is essential for a partnership to be effective. This commitment can be based on a common interest or on the self-interest of the partners in a partnership. When different parties collaborate, as is common in type H of our typology, it is important that, participant diversity notwithstanding, all participants be committed to a shared goal, as Berti Suman (Chap. 10) and Groenleer et al. (Chap. 11) point out in their contributions. Also, an early open attitude towards each other stimulates engagement and mutual trust (Berti Suman, Chap. 10). This should always be accompanied by good governance. As Mwangi (Chap. 6) shows in her chapter, corruption is a major threat to the effective functioning of any partnership and its contribution to livability.

Another aspect that is mentioned is the role of stable funding and stable (political) leadership. For example, as Lima demonstrates in her chapter (Chap. 7), if the funding provided for new social housing is inadequate, other partners, such as the not-for-profit housing providers, will not be capable of contributing to affordable housing supply. Another observation is that a change of political leadership (e.g. the appointment of a new mayor) might also imply a change in the regulations and (informal) agreements between the partners in the partnership (see e.g. van der Heijden and Hong, Chap. 2).

At the same time, partnerships must remain responsive to the (changing) needs and wishes of the public and private partners. This requires a constant balancing act between on the one hand strong commitment, shared goals, stable leadership and funding and, on the other hand, a constant willingness to be responsive to the outside world and a capability to adapt agreements according to changing needs and challenges. Many examples in this book show the capability of partnerships to adapt to changing circumstances and to develop over time.

In order to understand the relationship between partnerships and livability, the role of context must also be taken into account. Context, first of all, defines the type and urgency of livability problems that cities are facing. For example, an immediate crisis, such as the 2011 earthquake and subsequent 15-metre tsunami which destroyed the Fukushima Daiichi nuclear plant caused public discontent. People were upset about the lack of—and often contradictory—information on the actual radiation levels and livability in the region, and this gave rise to a sense of urgency among citizens to do something about this (Berti Suman, Chap. 10). Another context factor concerns the political constellation. For example, the mayor of Seoul played a significant role in promoting the energy conservation efforts of Seoul residents (van der Heijden and Hong, Chap. 2). And in Tilburg and Melbourne, too, the political climate played a major role. In Melbourne, the neo-liberal governance regime at the beginning of the century thwarted efforts to green the city, while in Tilburg, the coalition of mostly center and left-wing parties that took office in 2014 made the implementation of a green policy one of its top priorities (van Montfort and Michels, Chap. 4). Other relevant context factors are population growth or decline, economic decline, and climate change. In San José, explosive population growth resulted in a city that expanded outward in a non-structured way (urban sprawl). This forced the city to reconsider its urban planning and to focus on improving the quality of the existing space (van Montfort and Michels, Chap. 4). In Nairobi, the growth of the economy and the population, in particular, the middle-income groups, put pressure on creating affordable housing for many people (Mwangi, Chap. 6). And in Baltimore, it was population decline and the governance imperative to increase the City of Baltimore's population and thus alleviate its 'fiscal squeeze' that pushed the issue of the livability of this 'shrinking city' to the fore. Baltimore's city government has a long history of seeking partnerships with private (corporate and non-profit) actors to develop and deliver a policy agenda to stabilize and grow the city (Pill, Chap. 12). Also, the need to adapt the city to changing (climate) conditions can create a sense of urgency, for example in response to severe bouts of draught in Melbourne or extreme rainfall in Tilburg (van Montfort and Michels, Chap. 4).

In addition to this, context also sets the social and institutional framework within which partnerships operate and livability problems are faced. For example, strongly increased housing prices and a general decline of affordable housing are now common phenomena in many countries of the world. However, the hukou-system, the system of household registration in China which is used to control access to social services, is typical for China and contributes to a lack of access by migrant workers (people who migrate from rural areas to urban areas for work) to affordable housing in the larger cities (Liu and Chew, Chap. 8). Also, as previously noted, in authoritarian and state-controlled economies the far-reaching participation of citizens and the private sector is considered to be inconsistent with their institutional and governance structure.

17.4   LIVABLE FOR WHOM

In the introduction, we argued that the question is not so much whether a city is livable, but rather for whom it is livable. While the degree of livability of the city may increase for some, others may be mainly confronted with negative effects. We also suggested that there may be a trade-off between green, safe, and affordable housing; a greener and safe city could lead to higher housing prices and thus to less affordable housing for lower-income groups.

Some of the chapters in this book present examples of uneven developments in livability in cities, forms of exclusion, and other negative impacts which partnerships can have on livability. In Baltimore, for example, the policy to increase livability through partnerships with private parties by predominantly attracting a young and rich population, reinforced the existing power differences between rich white neighborhoods and poor neighborhoods with predominantly African American residents (Pill, Chap. 12). In Berlin, too, inner-city migration led both to a flow of inhabitants from improved neighborhoods to more deprived areas, possibly due to gentrification, but also the other way around (Karsten, Colombo and Schaap, Chap. 14). The authors suggest that the policy of collaborating in the form of partnerships to improve and increase the livability of particular neighborhoods may have played a role in this, but that we should not rule out the possibility that the reported economic and social improvements in formerly deprived neighborhoods are due to inner-city dynamics and citizens' displacement.

Exclusion and other negative consequences of partnerships in relation to livability are prominent in the cases presented on urban living labs. Urban living labs develop multi-stakeholder partnerships to address complex urban issues. However, Nesti describes how in the case of Turin, these partnerships were dominated by the local authorities and the private sector, instead of highly engaged citizens; they were passive users and not full-fledged co-producers of innovation (Nesti, Chap. 16). Likewise, although the urban living labs in Rotterdam tried to include lay citizens, they were unsuccessful in attaining inclusive participation. In practice, 'urban living labs were primarily initiated by highly educated professionals that often had a background in urban design and architecture' (Oldenhof et al., Chap. 15). As a result of this, urban living labs did not emerge outside the central areas of Rotterdam and values upheld by the more left-wing liberal residents, such as sustainability, circular economy, and healthy lifestyles, dominated the interventions of the urban living labs.

Partnerships between citizens and the government might also lead to polarization and conflicts among the residents who, while not part of the partnership, must deal with its impact. For example, many cities now have community safety initiatives. Van Eijk shows that these community safety initiatives in cities in the Netherlands and Belgium sometimes lead to increasing tensions between residents and members of the neighborhood watch teams (van Eijk, Chap. 9).

Partnerships in a corrupt society benefit only a few people, as Mwangi demonstrates in the case of Nairobi (Mwangi, Chap. 6). There, the informal collaboration between urban planners and private developers led to non-compliance with laws and building regulations and, as a consequence, poor quality dwellings were built, leading to collapsing buildings, and the loss of lives.

Despite these—at times—negative aspects of the contributions of partnerships to livability, there are also examples of partnerships that achieve more than was expected. De Abreu et al. show how initiatives for urban agriculture can sometimes start as very small local initiatives, but subsequently turn into larger public initiatives that even scale up to larger initiatives in agriculture, as well as in other areas such as the environment and health care (de Abreu et al., Chap. 3).

17.5   The Role of Government

Many chapters show that governments play a strong, albeit not always the same, role in developing and sustaining partnerships. These different roles can be characterized as: (1) facilitating, (2) regulatory, (3) financial, and (4) investing. Sometimes the different roles are combined, depending on the phase of the project.

17.5.1   *Facilitating*

An example of a facilitating role for government is shown in the chapter on the Turin Urban Living Lab, in which Nesti (Chap. 16) illustrates how the municipality of Turin is both the promotor and the facilitator of the Turin Living Lab: it develops the ideas for the experimentation, defines the aims and contents of the partnerships and signs the agreements with the partners. Other examples are the green projects in Tilburg, Melbourne, and San José (van Montfort and Michels, Chap. 4). In all projects, the municipal government had an important role in initiating and supporting the policy towards the greening of the city. However, the way municipal governments interact with citizens, the community, and business organizations differs across the cases, leading to differences in the available opportunities for these parties to initiate, develop, and implement plans for more green in the city.

17.5.2   *Regulatory*

Governments may also take up a more formal, regulatory role. Clear examples can be found in China where public-semi-public partnerships prevail in the eco-city projects because of the dominant role of state-owned enterprises (Lu, Sun and de Jong, Chap. 5). As the government retains a controlling share in the state-owned enterprises, this form of partnership will probably be dominant for a long time. Also, current policies and practices of public-private partnerships with respect to affordable housing in Chinese cities show a dominant regulatory role for the government (Liu and Chew, Chap. 8).

Another example comes from the experiences with regenerating disadvantaged urban neighborhoods in Berlin. Karsten, Colombo and Schaap (Chap. 14) show that the German federal government developed the 'Socially integrative city' program, aimed at counteracting the growing socio-spatial polarization and fostering integrated stabilization and development in areas with special social integration needs. The state of Berlin became one of the most active partners. Under the supervision of the state, private companies collaborate with neighborhood residents and civil society organizations in developing and implementing public policies.

17.5.3   Financial

Governments also play a financial role by funding projects. The chapter by Lima (Chap. 7) about affordable housing in Dublin suggests that it is almost impossible for not-for-profit housing providers to continue adding to the affordable housing supply at the required scale, unless the government commits itself to providing an adequate level of public finance for new social housing. She concludes that 'the prospect of improving the finance of affordable housing and having a more enabling role in land and incentives still lays lies with the government'. Also, green projects in Tilburg (the Netherlands), Melbourne, and San José (USA) (van Montfort and Michels, Chap. 4) and urban agriculture projects in Orizânia (Brazil) and Montreal (de Abreu et al., Chap. 3) could never have existed without government funding.

17.5.4   Investing

Finally, governments can also engage in the development of projects. An example is the case of Baltimore as presented by Pill in her chapter (Chap. 12). In Baltimore, city government collaborated with private (corporate and non-profit) actors in developing and implementing a policy of neighborhood revitalization. Another example is the city of Melbourne, which is still responsible for most of the projects which help sustain its transformation into an even greener city (van Montfort and Michels, Chap. 4).

17.6   Conclusions

17.6.1   Form Follows Function

A number of contributions in this book show that partnerships develop over time: sometimes becoming deeper but essentially remaining the same type of partnership and sometimes by transforming from one type into another (see the typologies in Chap. 1). In order to be resilient, partnerships need to adapt and be responsive to changing circumstances and needs. It is important for form to follow function in this transformation process. Both the inability to change as well as an autonomous transformation (for instance, into a more formal partnership) can lead to a decreasing legitimacy of the partnership. Participants in a partnership should therefore continuously ask themselves: does the way we are organized or financed contribute to our goal or should the form and organization of the partnership be changed. From a governance perspective, this changing nature of partnerships is challenging. If, for example, a partnership evolves from an informal to a formal or from an open to a closed partnership, the governance structure that defines who is responsible and accountable for what must also evolve.

17.6.2   Government Matters

Government matters. In the first place, because a partnership always operates within a political context. Sometimes governments and partnerships can complement each other, for example, if the activities of the partnerships fit into local policy agendas. But, just as often, the relationship is stressful (see, for instance, the chapters in this book about citizen sensing and urban living labs). Local governments are influential actors that cannot be ignored, which means that a partnership must relate in some way or another to the world of politics.

In the second place, government matters because it often plays a role in enabling the partnership or making a partnership work. In most of the case studies in this book, the government plays an active role in creating or facilitating partnership. This does not automatically mean that this role should always be an interventionist one. On the contrary, enabling a partnership sometimes requires that the state does not intervene and has the courage to just let things happen. Government does matter, but can do so only with the help of a broad repertoire of (non-)interventionist measures.

17.6.3   Success as a Contingent Variable

The case studies in this book show that many, often interrelated, variables play a role in making a partnership successful or not. This multiplicity of interdependent determining variables does not make it easy to answer the central question in this book: *how do partnerships between public and private actors contribute to the livability of cities?* However, taking an overall perspective on the different chapters offers a means to do so. It then becomes clear that partnerships can contribute to the livability of cities if (1) goal, (2) type of partnership, (3) internal factors and (4) external factors fit together (see Fig. 17.1).

This multiplicity of determining variables makes it difficult to predict what will work, for whom and under what conditions (see the new rules of realistic evaluation, Pawson and Tilley 1997). But it can be helpful to re-arrange the above mentioned determining variables into four building blocks. Together they form a design (ex ante) or evaluation (ex post or ex durante) framework of partnerships.

This 'toolbox', shown in Fig. 17.1, can help practitioners and academics to systematically pose the relevant design- or evaluation questions. Re-arranging the multiplicity of determining variables into four building blocks can help to stimulate what we call *realistic learning*. In realistic learning, good practices are not copied as a whole; instead, only those elements that will work in the specific context are adopted. Every partnership requires a specific set of optimal conditions to make it work. Hence, readers can learn from the case studies described in this book, without copying the practices in full. The Figure above shows four building blocks to design or evaluate partnerships. These building blocks are:

1. *Goal of the partnership*

It all starts with the goal of the partnership: are the goals of the partnership clear for all the participants and is there a shared vision (see also Kenis and Provan 2009, p. 451)? Such goals may include, for example, putting a livability issue on the political agenda (such as 'the lack of affordable

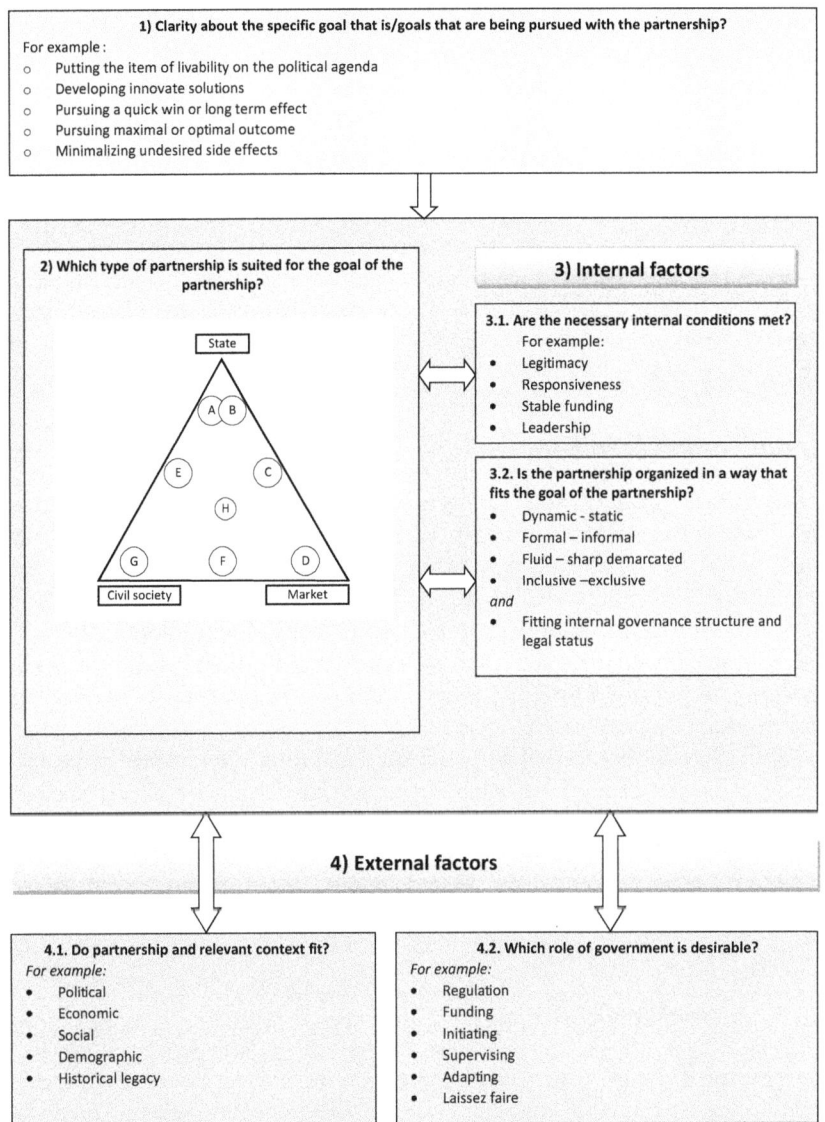

1) Clarity about the specific goal that is/goals that are being pursued with the partnership?

For example :
- o   Putting the item of livability on the political agenda
- o   Developing innovate solutions
- o   Pursuing a quick win or long term effect
- o   Pursuing maximal or optimal outcome
- o   Minimalizing undesired side effects

2) Which type of partnership is suited for the goal of the partnership?

State

A B
E
C
H
G   F   D

Civil society   Market

3) Internal factors

3.1. Are the necessary internal conditions met?
For example:
- Legitimacy
- Responsiveness
- Stable funding
- Leadership

3.2. Is the partnership organized in a way that fits the goal of the partnership?
- Dynamic - static
- Formal – informal
- Fluid – sharp demarcated
- Inclusive –exclusive

and
- Fitting internal governance structure and legal status

4) External factors

4.1. Do partnership and relevant context fit?
For example:
- Political
- Economic
- Social
- Demographic
- Historical legacy

4.2. Which role of government is desirable?
For example:
- Regulation
- Funding
- Initiating
- Supervising
- Adapting
- Laissez faire

Fig. 17.1   Building blocks for successful partnerships

housing in the city'), creating innovative solutions (such as 'developing technological solutions to improve neighborhood safety') or pursuing short term effects (such as quick wins by expanding the amount of greenery in the city). Depending on the goal, some types of partnerships, specific cultural and organizational characteristics of these partnerships, contexts and roles of government may offer a better -or worse- fit.

If the goals or vision behind the project are not clear or if the participants pursue different goals, the risk of a suboptimal outcome for one or more partners increases. Clarity about the purpose of the partnership and the vision behind it is also important for step 2: who are the relevant partners with whom to pursue this goal, or in other words: who should be in the partnership?

2. Type of partnership

In Chap. 1, we introduced eight types of partnerships (A—H) occurring within the triangle formed by the state, civil society and private parties. To be successful, the type of partnership should fit the goals of the partnership. Complex challenges, such as the development of technical tools to improve the safety in specific urban areas, often require active collaboration between the state, citizens and local business, while for other goals—like putting a livability issue on the political agenda—fewer actors are needed in a partnership.

Sometimes a partnership will be shaped as a *layered partnership* (see also Chap. 12). An example of such a partnership would be if one specific group of public and private partners worked together for the funding of the project while other parties were involved in the project's financial exploitation and day-to-day management. The Millennium Park in Chicago is an example of such a layered partnership (Millennium Park 2009).

3. Internal conditions

The third design or evaluation question is: 'are the necessary internal conditions met and does the organizational structure fit the goal of the project?'. A number of important requirements for successful partnerships, including legitimacy, responsiveness, stable funding and leadership, were identified in Chap. 1 and briefly reviewed in the above, in Sect. 17.3. In addition to these internal requirements, a partnership should be organized such that it fits the goal of the partnership. For example, the approach to wicked problems will require a more open and adaptive form of collaboration than the approach to a clear and well-defined problem. Moreover, as shown in the previous chapters, successful partnerships may also be dynamic, fluid (not exclusive) and can take on a different form over time, rather than remaining static and fixed.

Next to these organizational characteristics, two more elements—not extensively discussed in the chapters in this book—are important, namely legal status and the governance structure. Every form of partnership has a legal status. This may vary from 'informal' covenants or declarations of content to a 'formal' foundation or (private) limited company. This legal status should fit the goal and the above mentioned organizational characteristics. For example, the status of a limited company does not suit an informal, fluid partnership. The legal status determines to a large extent the governance structure in which roles and responsibilities, as well as requirements for accountability, are defined by law or by the participants in the partnership.

4. *External conditions*

The fourth building block refers to the external conditions for a successful partnership: the context and the role of government. Government is part of this external context but, in many cases, is also a partner in the partnership.

The role of context has been discussed in almost every chapter in this book: a partnership will not succeed if its ambitions do not fit the political, economic or historical context. The chapters in this book show that the context, in some cases, offers a 'window of opportunity' for new and innovative initiatives but also can set limits.

The second external factor concerns the role of the government. As discussed in the previous section, government matters, although its role can vary from a financial and regulatory one, to one of adaption and 'laissez-faire'. Government can make or break a partnership. Too much (financial) interference can make the partnership too dependent on the government, and too many rules and regulations can smother innovation completely. But on the other hand, the government can be a game-changer in stimulating active or passive innovative bottom-up initiatives, for example, by providing seed money or paving the way for experimental new initiatives. A successful partnership, therefore, requires a delicate balance between laissez-faire and intervention by the government.

To conclude, partnerships between public and private actors can contribute to the livability of cities if form follows function, if we accept that government matters and we take into account the contingent nature of success.

REFERENCES

Arnstein, S. (1969). A ladder of citizen participation. *Journal of the American Planning Association, 35*(4), 216–224.

Kenis, P., & Provan, K. (2009). Towards an exogenous theory of public network performance. *Public Administration, 87*(3), 440–456.

Millennium Park. (2009). *Rudy Bruner Award: Silver medal winner*. Chicago: Millennium Park.

Pawson, R., & Tilley, N. (1997, 2003). *Realistic evaluation*. London: Sage.

Index[1]

[1] Note: Page numbers followed by 'n' refer to notes.

Lightning Source UK Ltd.
Milton Keynes UK
UKHW040711171220
375372UK00001B/22